THE FILMS OF HARRISON FORD

THIRD EDITION

Lee Pfeiffer and Michael Lewis

CITADEL PRESS
Kensington Publishing Corp.
www.kensingtonbooks.com

CITADEL PRESS BOOKS are published by

Kensington Publishing Corp.
850 Third Avenue
New York, NY 10022

All Kensington titles, imprints, and distributed lines are available at
special quantity discounts for bulk purchases for sales promotions,
premiums, fund-raising, educational, or institutional use. Special book
excerpts or customized printings can also be created to fit specific
needs. For details, write or phone the office of the Kensington special
sales manager: Kensington Publishing Corp., 850 Third Avenue,
New York, NY 10022, attn: Special Sales Department,
phone 1-800-221-2647.

Designed by Andrew B. Gardner

First printing: July 2002

10 9 8 7 6 5 4 3 2 1

Printed in the United States of America

Library of Congress Control Number: 2002100675

ISBN: 0-8065-2364-6

To Bev, Ed, and Richard Plaza—
who bring to mind three other great intellects of the Western World—
Moe, Larry, and Curley
—L.P.

To my wife, Amy: everything I do,
I do it for you.
—M.L.

Contents

Acknowledgments

The authors gratefully acknowledge the following companies and individuals: Mike Boldt for his superb artwork; Columbia Pictures; DreamWorks, LLC; Paramount Pictures; 20th Century Fox; LucasFilm; Universal Pictures; Ripon College photo archives; NBC TV; Jerry Ohlinger's Movie Memorabilia Store; Bill Duelly for his expertise on *Witness* and *Star Wars*; The Arts and Entertainment Network; Patricia and Chris Cellary; Rita Eisentstein of *Starlog* Magazine; Loren J. Boone, Director of College Relations at Ripon College; David Miller of M&M Enterprises, 706 Springbrook, Allen, Texas, 75002, which offers fans videos of rare TV episodes; Kevin Clement of Chiller Theatre; Tom Rogers; Hiroki Takeda; Al Marill; Bob Klepeis; Robert Hannaford, professor of philosophy at Ripon College; Ron Plesniarski of www.spyguise.com memorabilia site; from Citadel Press, Bruce Bender, Margaret Wolf, and Steve Brower; and a very special "thank you" to Eileen Bolender, whose website at www.harrisonfordweb.com is the ultimate tribute to "The Man." We also thank our patient and long-suffering family members, Janet and Nicole Pfeiffer and Amy, Samantha, and Sydney Lewis for having to learn more than they ever cared to about the films of Harrison Ford!

We are particularly grateful to Pat McQueeney, Harrison Ford's longtime manager and friend, for her kind participation in and encouragement for this project. Without her help, this book would not have been nearly as comprehensive. Most of all, we extend our heartfelt thanks to Harrison Ford for his support and for giving this book his "blessing." Harrison, we hope you find more than a few good memories within these pages. (Excluding, of course, your lost "art masterpieces" from the Ripon College newspaper, which we hope you forgive us for resurrecting!)

Introduction to the Third Edition

Despite the fact that Harrison Ford is currently at the top of his game in terms of his reputation as an actor and his popularity with the film-going public, he is not immune to the types of personal crises that afflict more ordinary individuals. In recent years, there were indications that his marriage to Melissa Mathison was going through rocky times. Ford, always reluctant to discuss his personal life, spoke little about the rumors. However, he finally had to confirm the obvious: despite unprecedented success in his professional endeavors, his second marriage was coming to an end. Following the failure of his first marriage, Ford publicly stated that he would be a more devoted father and husband the second time around. By all accounts he took his responsibilities seriously and his aversion to the Hollywood party scene reaffirmed his reputation as a devoted family man. Typically, Ford has refused to be interviewed about the causes of the breakup, but one can assume it has been a painful decision for both partners. Ford is well aware of the fact that his celebrity status does not protect him from personal crises. He said "There's the adolescent belief that fame solves all problems, and people old enough to know better still have this obsession with celebrity and success. And in this culture, what counts for success and celebrity is a pretty grim study."

Ford has found a distraction from the pressures of his personal life through his love of flying, a hobby he has devoted an increasing amount of time to in recent years.

He owns a number of small planes as well as a helicopter, all of which he enjoys personally piloting. One of his passions is to travel across America in the company of a small group of fellow pilots who have become close friends, stopping to refuel at obscure airfields in rural sections of the country. More than one patron at a roadside diner has been startled to see the world's most bankable movie star casually walk in and order breakfast while his copter is being serviced. He said "Everybody thinks I'm flying aimlessly across the country, but I'm not. I'm going somewhere usually. I take the helicopter and the other planes out to Wyoming for the summer and then back to New York for the winter. . . . People are inevitably surprised to see me descend on them from out of the sky. They make a fuss or sometimes are unprepared to make a fuss. Sometimes I'm there for fifteen minutes; other times I'll stick around until the weather clears and have more interaction with the people I meet. It's always fun, though. They have no choice but to relate to you first of all as a pilot, since that's how you've obviously arrived there. It takes a little bit of the strain off." Discussing Ford's competence at performing a particularly frightening training maneuver which involves landing a helicopter after turning off the power to the engine, Toby Wilson—his flight instructor—said, "It's a black-and-white issue. Either you live or you die. And I think Harrison likes the clarity of that." Ford's "hobby" has paid off in practical ways—he has personally rescued stranded hikers who were lost in potentially deadly conditions in high mountain ranges. As per the norm, Ford has downplayed his involvement. However, he has earned the respect and gratitude of rescue workers who don't hesitate to call upon his services in times of crisis.

In between flying sessions and making high-profile films, Ford also devotes a good deal of time to issues relating to human rights and conservation. Like a number of other celebrities, he has used his status in Hollywood to ensure greater public awareness of the Dalai Lama's attempts to improve conditions for the people of Tibet, who have long suffered under the dictatorial rule of Communist China. He also serves as a board member of Conservation International, a Washington, D.C.–based environmental group. Far from limiting his involvement to "window dressing," Ford has impressed fellow board members by traveling the world and participating in in-depth studies of ecological problems. "The Earth we live on is facing a threat unlike anything it has ever encountered," Ford told *Good Housekeeping*. "There are more of us packed into the same amount of space, and we are using up resources that can never be replaced. The way we are living is causing an animal extinction rate second only to the loss of the dinosaurs."

Curiously, one area that does not ignite a passion in Ford is motion pictures. He enjoys the art of filmmaking as a participant, but admits his knowledge of cinema history is seriously lacking. He said, "I'm not a filmgoer . . . I didn't grow up loving movies, which is not to say that I don't like movies, but I don't have a great store of knowledge about them. I still haven't seen *Casablanca*, and despite everyone's great amazement and confusion about that, I haven't gone out and rented it. It's just not something that interests me. What interests me is taking a form of written screenplay and taking that through a process." Ford admits that this irony is "Very odd. Bizarre. I'm totally ignorant of it, from that point of view. . . . I'm not audience, I work here—you see the distinction that I make? And the fact that I work there makes me a poor audience, many times. At the same time I am occasionally swept away. I can sit there and watch part of a movie on television and enjoy it very much and get up and walk away. If the phone rings and I get involved in something else, I won't go back and bother with it. That's a terrible admission to make, and it seems to indicate that I have not an appropriate respect for other people's talents, ambition, and hard work. It's not that. It's not that at all. I do admire them; I just don't find that it's helpful to me."

Although Ford continues to maintain that winning an Oscar is not a priority for him ("I've made a very nice living, you know, doing this without it"), he has graciously accepted those awards that have been bestowed on him. In 1998, he was named by *People* magazine to be The Sexiest Man Alive and in 1999 he was named by the People's Choice Awards as Favorite All-Time Movie Star. The year 2000 found Ford the recipient of the American Film Institute's Lifetime Achievement Award—an honor previously bestowed on such legends as John Ford, James Cagney, and Henry Fonda. The star-studded ceremony drew a "Who's Who" of the Hollywood elite, including George Lucas who "roasted" Ford by saying that the role he gave the actor in *American Graffiti* "accomplished a great deal in Harrison's career—it took him right back to being a carpenter." Ford confessed to being a nervous wreck over having to speak at the ceremony, saying "I was scared for weeks before this appearance." Nevertheless, he characteristically deferred much of the credit for his success, saying "The work you saw tonight was shaped by many hands, animated by many hearts."

In 2002, he received the coveted Cecil B. DeMille Lifetime Achievement Award at the Golden Globes ceremony. The negative reviews and disappointing box-office results of his 1999 romantic drama *Random Hearts* did not seem to negate Ford's status in the film community, though—unlike some other top stars—he doesn't pretend to have a blasé, "take-the-money-and-run" attitude toward the fate of his films. "I want to make films that people go to see," he said. "I think it's an effort at communication, so you don't want to make a movie that no one's going to be interested in seeing. I don't expect every film to have the same degree of success, but I always think about the commercial viability because this is my business, this is a job for me. And I want our efforts to be successful, not just for myself but for the other couple hundred people involved. So you don't set out to do something that takes so much time and money and not have an ambition for it to be seen."

During the filming of *Random Hearts*, Ford suffered a terrible personal blow when his father passed away at age 92. The actor recalled his father fondly, saying "When I was growing up my father, Christopher Ford, was in advertising, but he had been a radio actor and writer in his early years. . . . He toured in 'Gangbusters,' which used to broadcast from vaudeville stages, and toured the country with a group of five or six actors dressed in tuxedos who'd stand around two microphones on a stage. They would feed it live to the radio network. After my father's career in advertising, he spent quite a few years doing voiceovers in commercials. He was very successful at that." Appropriately, *Random Hearts* bears a dedication to Christopher Ford during the credits.

What Lies Beneath, Ford's year 2000 film release,

A sight seldom seen: a publicity campaign for a Harrison Ford film not utilizing Ford's familiar face. (Courtesy of DreamWorks/20th Century Fox)

He was

the perfect husband

until his one mistake

followed them home.

A ROBERT ZEMECKIS FILM

WHAT LIES BENEATH

Coauthor Lee Pfeiffer with Harrison Ford at the Film Society of Lincoln Center's reception for Sean Connery, New York, 1997. (Lee Pfeiffer's personal collection)

was a daring departure from his typical role as stalwart hero and leading man. His character turns out to be a murderous heavy in the Robert Zemeckis–directed supernatural thriller. The movie was a substantial hit with both critics and the public and quickly overrode any negative response attached to *Random Hearts*. The 2002 release of *K-19*, which pairs Ford with co-star Liam Neeson, promises to cement his status as the screen's most enduring leading man in the action film genre. As of this writing, it appears that Ford and Steven Spielberg have finally approved a script for a fourth Indiana Jones film, which Spielberg will direct. Spielberg's wife, actress Kate Capshaw, who co-starred in *Indiana Jones and the Temple of Doom* will also appear in the latest sequel. As of this writing, no other specifics have been announced. Responding to an inquiry as to whether he would still be able to meet the physical demands of the role, Ford quipped, "I have not yet seen the action film where the

protagonist wields a cane or his crutches to win the day, but as long as I'm fit enough to play tennis or run faster than Sean Connery, I think I can manage."

Like every other American, Ford was deeply affected by the terrorist attacks of September 11, 2001. The actor was in downtown New York at the time, not far from the site of the devastation at the World Trade Center. "I heard it all," he told columnist Liz Smith. "I was asleep in my bed at the Mercer Hotel, which is downtown. I heard the noises of a plane and sensed something was off because the engine sounds were too loud and too low. I then did exactly what other old guys would do. I got up, took a pee, and turned on the television." The incredible violence of that terrible day only reinforced Ford's convictions to avoid gratuitous brutality in his films. "I don't do violent films," he told Smith. "I would not be unhappy to see a mood change in what Hollywood turns out and what the public likes to see." He continued, "I'd like scripts with a more positive message. Story lines that give people something to hope for in place of the current diet of repetitive violence and retribution. I think we need to focus on stories that raise the barrier to a higher level of emotion." Ford helped support charitable contributions to funds of the 9/11 disaster by making a rare live appearance at the Concert for New York City, an extraordinary event which was telecast nationwide on numerous TV networks. A host of major stars including Paul McCartney, Clint Eastwood, and Bruce Springsteen joined the lineup in a successful appeal which raised tens of millions of dollars.

In an age in which most actors so adore the spotlight that they strike a pose each time they open the refrigerator door, Ford's low-key nature and self-deprecating humor have endeared him to the film-going public. Although his heart remains in his rural retreat of Jackson Hole, Wyoming, he spends most of the year in New York City— one of the few urban areas where the public remains unimpressed by the presence of celebrities. He said recently, "I walk across town every morning when I play tennis, then walk back. People nod, say hello; sometimes they'll ask for an autograph or something. It's New York. They see people who they recognize all the time. It's really not much of a bother." Despite his own modest assessment of his legacy, this, a statement issued by the American Film Institute when it chose to honor him with its Lifetime Achievement Award, seems more appropriate: "It is fitting that the AFI begin the new millennium by honoring Harrison Ford—the most popularly acclaimed actor of our day. To movie audiences around the world, Harrison represents the quintessential American film hero, and when the history of the twentieth-century art form is written, Harrison will play a leading role."

Harrison Ford: Reluctant Superstar

"My occupation is assistant storyteller. It is not Icon"

—Harrison Ford

With this characteristically modest self-appraisal, the world's most successful movie star dismisses his status in the international film community. For thirty years, Harrison Ford has been honing his craft, and since 1977, he has emerged not only as a respected actor but—whether he likes it or not—as a genuine icon within the motion picture industry. Because Ford does not seek publicity or engage in self-promotion, the extent of his accomplishments and durability at the box office do not often receive deserved recognition. Consider for a moment just a few of the legendary films in which he has had a leading role: the Star Wars trilogy, the Indiana Jones trilogy, *Witness, The Fugitive, Blade Runner,* and the Jack Ryan films *Patriot Games* and *Clear and Present Danger.* Ford's body of work has been one of the great Hollywood success stories, and—unlike most of his contemporaries—the public has embraced virtually every film he has appeared in and every different persona he has brought to the screen.

Yet Ford is not the type of actor who elicits discussions around the office or provides fodder for gossip magazines and talk show hosts. If one interprets this as an indication that he leads a rather pedestrian and unremarkable life offscreen, that is just fine with Ford. He is an anomaly in today's publicity-hungry world: a man who exhausts himself to give his audience his best effort, but who insists upon the public respecting his desire for complete and total privacy when not working. He has stated his beliefs bluntly, telling an interviewer, "Our culture's interest in actors' personal lives and opinions is just mythicalization and bullshit."

Harrison Ford is the very personification of the American dream. His nondescript background led him to comment, "I don't think anyone who had known me as a child would have predicted that I would follow the path I have." Ford was born on July 13, 1942, to an Irish Catholic father (Christopher) and a Russian Jewish mother (Dorothy). His father was an advertising executive and a modestly successful pioneer in the field of television commercials. (It was his idea to use a see-through washing machine to show a detergent's effectiveness in cleaning clothes, and he was also the first person to employ stop-action photography in TV ads.) At the time, Chicago was regarded as one of the premier centers of the radio industry, and the elder Ford wrote and performed in that medium. The family's other link to show business was the man Harrison Ford was named after—his maternal grandfather, Harrison Needleman, a vaudevillian who worked in blackface before finding steadier if less glamorous work, on a streetcar line in Brooklyn.

Despite the influence of the stage and radio in his family, Harrison Ford did not exhibit any particular interest in the arts during his formative years. He confessed, "I didn't spend much time at the movies. I'm not a scholar of Bogart's mannerisms, so I miss a lot of the film references that people like Spielberg and Lucas toss around." He described his childhood as "nothing too remarkable....

Just the usual. Baseball, fooling around with cars. I was the loner type. Not very active in sports. I didn't know what I wanted to do when I was a kid." Movies did provide a modest distraction for Ford and his younger (by three years) brother Terence. The first film he saw was *Bambi*, and as he grew older, his interest in the movies was due less to his regard for the medium as an art form than as a place to take dates. He said that theaters merely provided a "cheap, dark place you could go with a girl."

A portrait of a hero as a young boy and toddler: Harrison in his formative years.
(*Hollywood Reporter*)

As a boy, Ford was not inspired by the prospect of becoming a businessman. In fact, his greatest admiration seemed to be for the man who delivered coal to the houses in the neighborhood. Ford recalled, "My dad got all dressed up, went to work, came home, sat at the dinner table, and bitched like crazy about those bastards at work. The coalman, you know, he didn't go home at night and tell his wife how uncooperative the coal was."

If Ford wasn't enamored of his limited vision of the working world, he at least excelled in his schoolwork. Growing up in the Chicago suburbs of Park Ridge and Morton Grove, he attended Graham Stuart Elementary School (graduating in 1954) and East Maine Township

Junior High in Des Plaines (class of 1956). However, his academic achievements were overshadowed by the adversity he encountered when he entered Main East Township High in Des Plaines. He would later lament, "I was kind of a runty thing. And I liked to hang out with the girls. That annoyed the boys. So every day after school, they would throw me over the edge of the parking lot and roll me into the weeds. Eventually, my beatings were so inevitable that I'd just go to the lot and wait." On another occasion, he elaborated on the rather unfriendly atmosphere the future Indiana Jones had to confront on a daily basis: "The entire school would gather to watch this display. I don't know why they did it. Maybe because I wouldn't fight the way they wanted me to. They wanted a fight they could win. And my way of winning was to just hang in there." If one parallel emerges between Ford's personal background and his cinematic personas, it is that stubborn ability to not surrender.

Eventually, Ford, who was emboldened by the support of twin girls with whom he was friendly, struck back by knocking a bully down the stairs. Suddenly, the self-described "class wimp" was no longer the object of cruelty and jokes.

Not all of Harrison Ford's high school years were occupied with confronting sadistic classmates. During a summer vacation, Ford got a job as a nature counselor at a Boy Scout camp, and he indulged in a hobby of catching and collecting snakes. (Ironically, the character of Indiana Jones would be petrified by the creatures!) At home, Ford continued his interest in animals, albeit the type which might cause others to be somewhat squeamish. He raised rats in his garden and found the hobby preferable to indulging in sports and physical activities. When not tending to rats, Ford's hobbies and interests were so unremarkable that today he cannot recall how he spent most of his time. He said in a 1981 interview, "I really can't remember what I did instead [of sports]. I probably just read and cleaned up my room." Like much of Ford's self-analysis, this statement seems to be somewhat understated. Indeed, his high school yearbook shows he was actively involved with the Model Radio Club, served as president of the Social Science Club and as representative of the

Boys Club, and belonged to the Model Train Club. Despite his aversion to sports, he also showed a talent for gymnastics.

Still, as recently as 1986, the pain of Ford's high school years remained evident. He professed, "I never had a focused goal or ambition. I never set out to be held in esteem. I just wanted to be able to hold my head up in private. I couldn't even find a niche in high school. My classmates considered me an oddball, and they were probably right. Not that I cared much for what my classmates thought. I didn't know my classmates then. I don't know them now. I've never been to a reunion."

Ford continued his life as a loner when he attended Ripon College, a small liberal arts school in central Wisconsin. Ion Harris, the secretary to the dean at the college, recalled Ford as being an unremarkable but fairly dedicated student. "I wouldn't call him a scholarly person, but he wasn't a problem by any means. He was no genius, but he did well in the subjects that interested him." Like so many young people in the midsixties, Ford was adrift in a rapidly changing world. "I did not fit in, and I did not want to fit in," he said recently of those days. He considered joining the R.O.T.C. but changed his mind when they insisted that he cut his hair. He told *Vanity Fair* in a 1993 interview, "When I look back, I suspect I was in a clinical depression. I would sleep four or five days at a time. There was one class I never went to. I remember once when I slept for several days and finally roused myself, got myself out of bed, managed to get dressed—this seemed to be taking an intense effort—and actually made it to class. All of this seemed to be happening in slow motion. I even put my hand on the door of the classroom, but I seemed unable to turn the doorknob. So I let it go and went back to sleep. . . . The kindest word to describe my performance was *sloth*."

Despite these personality quirks, Ford realized he had to work to maintain even the modest lifestyle he was leading. Like most students, he took on a variety of odd jobs during summer vacation. Finding work was never a problem when Ford opted to put on the charm. He summed up the attributes which helped him excel in the work world: "I'm real polite. I know how to sit straight and keep my head up. People think I'm not going to steal from them. Getting jobs is like acting." Among Ford's short-lived "careers" during his college years was that of a chef on a yacht on Lake Michigan. The job had one obstacle: Harrison Ford did not know how to cook! His mom bought him a copy of *The Joy of Cooking*, and Ford religiously read culinary columns in the *Chicago Tribune*. He recalled the numerous times the paper received calls for advice from the hapless "chef": "This is Harrison again. I know you told me yesterday, but how long do you

Ford's high school yearbook photo appeared in a 1994 issue of *The Star*.

have to bake a potato? What temperature?" He sarcastically told *Playboy* in 1988 how he had succeeded in bluffing his employers: "All they ever wanted was dead cow anyway. They were very easy to fool. Unfortunately, we were out on the water frequently, and Lake Michigan can get very choppy. I was deeply seasick most of the time. In retrospect, managing to cook under those circumstances was probably the most heroic thing I've ever done."

At college, Ford studied English and philosophy. However, he was frustrated by his own shyness. Surprisingly, he opted to attend a drama class, despite the fact that it would necessitate his performing in front of audiences. He confessed that his initial reason for taking the class was "trying to get my grade average up and meet some girls." When it came time to perform on-stage, however, he found he lacked confidence to face an audience. "I was really, literally, pushed up there on-stage," he recalled. "It scared me. It scared me something fierce." However, he found that acting was an effective therapy for curing his shyness. "When I first started acting, the main satisfaction came from conquering the fear of actually getting up and doing it. I began to experience the fun of it," he would later say.

In addition to making him more of a social animal, acting was a pragmatic way for Ford to plan his life after college. The thought of taking a tedious office job frightened him. In 1995, he would recall his mindset during

Harrison Ford at Ripon College, circa 1964. (Courtesy Ripon College)

es. Once we had a fire, and I remember Harrison running from the building, carrying out this man's books and records. Tears were running down his cheeks. He was very, very upset that this was happening."

Although Ford continued to excel at acting, his grades in other classes deteriorated drastically in his senior year. While his social life was improving due to his camaraderie with his fellow thespians, he found little time or energy for scholastic studies. He became associated with the campus newspaper and contributed stories and artwork. Such devotion was a rarity, however. He admits, "I slept pretty well all through my last year, just waking up from time to time to eat pizza. . . . [it was] a total academic breakdown." Nevertheless, the now-outgoing Harrison Ford began dating Mary Louise Marquardt, an honors student. During the spring of 1963, the couple married. Being a newlywed with a wife devoted to her studies did not improve Ford's performance in class, however. When he failed to complete a thesis on playwright Edward Albee, he was told he would not be allowed to graduate, despite the fact that the ceremony was only three days away and his parents were already in town, planning to attend. Ford left college and would later remember, "I really didn't know what the hell to do with myself. . . . I couldn't figure out what I wanted to be when I grew up. I think the difficulty was with the idea of growing up. I'm a late bloomer."

Without the benefit of a college degree, Ford decided the mainstream work world was more unsuitable than ever. He would pursue acting as a full-time career, and if he failed, he reasoned philosophically, "working in a chic ladies dress shop wouldn't be entirely without its rewards." In June 1964, he joined the Williams Bay Repertory Theater, which performed stage productions in Lake Geneva, Wisconsin. Mary Ford served as the company's secretary. The young couple lived among fellow actors in a dormlike mansion adjacent to the Belfry Theater. Ford made his formal stage debut on June 26, 1964, in a production of *Take Her, She's Mine*. The road to learning his craft was not without its potholes, however. During a performance of Tennessee Williams's *Night of the Iguana*, Ford suffered the ultimate horror of all stage performers—he forgot his lines. Years later, he chalked up the experience as a valuable lesson: "I learned in public, and I made a lot of mistakes along the way—they're on television late at night!—but I'm the kind of person who learns from experience; I don't learn from books."

Ford often felt uncomfortable with the fact that he frequently found himself playing parts he felt "totally unsuitable for." Yet audiences and critics disagreed and found him charming in his wide diversity of roles. These

those college years: "All I knew about acting was what I had imagined. My decision to go into acting was mostly a reaction to my friends and college classmates who knew what they were going to do with their entire lives. They were all going off to work in the same office year after year, in the same job—maybe until they got a gold watch. That would be the limit of their life experience. Maybe they'd be doing fantastic things and would be very successful, but I just couldn't imagine doing that—the same thing year after year. I thought acting would give me the opportunity to confront new and interesting challenges, to work with certain people on a finite problem within a finite period of time and then do it again with another set of problems, different people. You would travel to interesting places and meet interesting people. All of it turned out to be essentially what I've gotten."

Ford continued to polish his craft as an actor, and his enthusiasm for the profession increased significantly after playing the role of Mr. Antrobus in a college production of Thornton Wilder's *Skin of Our Teeth*. He remembers, "I wore a fake mustache and a half a pound of talcum powder in my hair. That's when I caught the illness [the love of acting]." Ford was influenced by his drama class instructor, Richard Bergstrum, who was responsible for Ford pursuing an acting career full-time after college. Ion Harris recalled Ford's devotion to his mentor: "He was very close to the professor who taught drama class-

4

included supporting parts in *Sunday in New York*, *Dark of the Moon*, and even musicals such as *Little Mary Sunshine* (a spoof of the Nelson Eddy–Jeanette MacDonald screen operettas, in which he played "Eddy"). The program for the last named noted that Ford possessed "a beautiful singing voice," but he felt this was not an example of truth in advertising, saying, "I *can* sing—very, very badly!" (a truth eventually proven by Ford's warbling in 1973's *American Graffiti*). Nonetheless, he proved popular with audiences while playing a lead in a production of *Damn Yankees*.

Despite his modest success in summer stock, Ford felt as though his calling would be in a different medium—perhaps that of motion pictures. His expertise in this area

Indiana Jones meets "Mack the Knife": Ford participates in a 1964 Ripon College production of *Threepenny Opera*. (Courtesy Ripon College)

hardly qualified him as a "star of tomorrow." Yet with the support of Mary, he made the decision to head west to see if confidence and talent alone would allow him to succeed where so many others had failed: "I went to Los Angeles. I didn't know the names of the motion picture studios. I didn't know any actors. And of course I'm not an Angeleno by birth or by heart—it's just the place where I find myself today. But Los Angeles is where you have to be if you want to be an actor. You have no choice. You go there or New York. I flipped a coin about it. It came up New York, so I flipped again. When you're starting out to be an actor, who wants to go where it's cold and miserable and be poor there? Better to be poor in the sunshine than in the snow. That was my idea, anyway. So we loaded all our stuff into the Volkswagen, drove off, and didn't stop until we saw the Pacific. As far as I was concerned, that ocean must mean California—fine! Let's stop here. Laguna Beach. About sixty miles south of L.A. I did a play, *John Brown's Body*, at the playhouse there, but the thought of doing it over and over again just stopped me."

The theater's artistic director Doug Rowe recalled being impressed with Ford's work in the play: "He had just moved into town, and he came down for an audition. I cast him as Clay Wingate, the Southern soldier. . . . I played the Northern soldier opposite him. It was the only play he did for us. It was a remarkable piece. The play sold out every night for three weeks. And there was never any question that Harrison Ford had the potential to be

an outstanding actor. There's an honesty to his work—an ability to get right into the heart of the line. He's a very subtle actor, and he never overplays."

During the run of *John Brown's Body*, two other future celebrities were practicing the profession of acting in other productions at the playhouse: Mike Farrell (*M*A*S*H*) and Toni Tenille (later to find fame as one half of the Captain and Tenille in the seventies.) Doug Rowe recalls, "All three of them appeared at the same time. It was an incredible season."

Like most aspiring actors, Ford had to support himself with a variety of odd jobs. He toiled as a pizza chef, a yacht broker, a paint store employee, and "an assistant buyer of knickknacks" at Bullock's department store. During this period, Ford was involved in a near-fatal car crash. On the way from one acting gig to another, he was driving his Volvo on a treacherous, winding mountain road through Laguna Canyon. He leaned over—ironically to fasten his seatbelt, which he always wore except for this one occasion—when the car hit a curb, went up on two wheels and hit a telephone pole at 35 MPH. Although battered, he was not rendered unconscious. Managing to crawl from the wreck of his car, he was shocked to find every motorist passing him by. As late as 1990, he admitted the incident still haunts him: "I remember very vividly that although my car was in the middle of the road, no one would stop. They would just creep around me at five miles an hour and keep on going. I was just standing in the road, bleeding quite profusely. It pissed me off so

Taking a break during rehearsals of a college stage production.
(Courtesy Ripon College)

chemistry, to put it mildly. He would later refer to the executive as "a little, bald-headed guy" who looked at him "as if he'd discovered a snake in his soup." Gordon's assistant asked the stock questions given to young actors. What was his weight and height? Could he speak any foreign languages? Could he ride a horse? The meeting ended with Ford receiving the standard answer as he was escorted out: "Okay, kid, thanks a lot. If we find anything, we'll let you know." In a weird twist of fate, Ford backtracked past Gordon's office while trying to find the men's room. Suddenly, Gordon called him in and said, "Look. You're not the type we're really interested in, but how'd ya like to be under contract?" Ford would recall twenty years later the irony of the situation: "I knew right from the beginning that if I had gone down to the elevator instead of going to take a pee, it wouldn't have been worth chasing me down the street." Nevertheless, he jumped at the job offer: "Sure I was thrilled. Columbia wanted me. It was my first big break." Or so he thought.

A few months after this meeting, Ford was signed to a "short-term," seven-year contract. The traditional studio system of building box-office stars by placing them under contract was rapidly coming to an end. Actors were becoming fiercely independent, and the power of the studios in controlling them was declining. Still, Ford was content bringing home a steady paycheck that totaled an impressive $150 per week. He was enrolled in Columbia's short-lived "New Talent" program, but soon learned that the studio was more interested in maintaining control over his life rather than in developing his acting talents. He would later lament, "They gave me enough money to pay the rent, but the attitude that they could manufacture a star from raw material was silly. Styling your hair, dressing you—it was all so deadly wrong, calculated to remove all those particularities which made you interesting in the first place. . . . I was sure that the most important thing for an actor was to hold on to what was individual about himself."

The shy Ford's distaste for being treated like a commodity by Columbia reached almost unbearable levels when forced to endure endless and intrusive photo shoots. "Nobody even knew your name at the studio, or cared a damn about you," he complained years later. "I went nuts." His hairstyle was changed to that of a pompadour. He was advised to change his name (Harrison was "too pretentious"). In his first act of rebellion, he cynically suggested calling himself "Kurt Affair." He grudgingly endured daily acting classes that were valueless to him. They were unrealistic settings and merely taught the students how to act in an acting class. Ford longed for the real world experience which would help him develop his skills.

much that no one would stop that I refused to gesture to them. So I stood there until somebody finally stopped and took me to the hospital." The accident left Ford with the now-familiar scar on his chin. He jokingly explained that the resident who treated the wound did "a terrible job" and probably used paper clips instead of stitches. "I'm sure the guy did the best he could at the time. It was probably something that should have been done by a plastic surgeon rather than a resident."

His first brush with his own mortality aside, Ford's fortunes were about to dramatically change. During a performance of *John Brown's Body*, composer Ian Bernard was impressed by the young man's acting abilities. He sent Ford to his colleague Billy Gordon, who was the head of casting at Columbia Pictures. The meeting was notable, but not for the right reason. From their first encounter, Ford and Gordon displayed a certain lack of

Ultimately, Ford landed a minuscule role for his big-screen debut. The film was *Dead Heat on a Merry-Go-Round*, a 1966 tongue-in-cheek crime caper which starred James Coburn, who had only recently graduated from supporting roles to leads. He was forced to bill himself as Harrison J. Ford, so as not to confuse him with a deceased silent screen star named Harrison Ford, and his "performance" consisted of playing a bellhop who hands Coburn a telegram. The part took less than a day to shoot. Although Ford had virtually no role to play and almost no dialogue, a studio executive cautioned him that the brass was not happy with his screen presence. Years later, however, Walter Beakel, who was the head of Columbia's New Talent program confessed, "Everybody could tell very early that the kid had potential. But he did not have enough confidence and enough technique to cut it, because he was very young. He hadn't matured enough to go into creative, emotional leading-man roles."

Ford continued to toil in unremarkable films like the 1967 Glenn Ford Western *A Time for Killing* and the screen adaptation of the Broadway hit *Luv* the same year. The former turned out to be an interesting but rather standard horse opera in which Ford (Harrison—not Glenn) was unceremoniously killed after having spoken only a few lines of dialogue. The latter film, in which Ford appears for only about forty-eight seconds, was a dreadful misfire despite a cast that included Jack Lemmon, Peter Falk, and Elaine May. Ford was not living up to the expectations of the brass at Columbia—but how could he generate interest when his roles could be measured in seconds? Eventually, the studio decided to exercise an option to cancel his contract after eighteen months. Ford still remembers with some bitterness the insensitive way he was informed of this decision: "The head of the studio, Mike Frankovitch, was in Europe, so this other guy had to make the determination whether or not they should take up the option on my contract. . . . 'Kid,' he said. 'When Frankovitch is back, I'm going to tell him we ought to get rid of you. I don't think you're worth a thing to us. But I know your wife is pregnant, you need the money, so I'll give you another couple of weeks. Just sign the piece of paper my secretary has. Okay, boy? Now, get out of here.'" Ford let it be known that he was choosing not to sign the paper. He told the executive so in less than flat-

A rare photo of Ford singing in public, via the Ripon College version of *Threepenny Opera*. Ford would later joke, "I can sing—very badly!" (Courtesy Ripon College)

Although a lackadaisical student, Ford did serve as art director for the Ripon Campus newspaper, *The Mug*. These cartoons show his penchant for offbeat humor. (Fortunately, he had no delusions of a career as an artist!) (Courtesy Ripon College)

tering terms and was summarily "terminated."

With his incipient career on the rocks, a wife to support, and a baby on the way, Ford reluctantly turned to learning a more practical craft—of carpentry. He began to study how-to books from the library and instantly showed a talent in this area. Simultaneously, his acting career enjoyed a sudden boost when he was placed under contract with Universal. The atmosphere at this studio was less restrictive than at Columbia, and Ford was put to work in such television series as *The Virginian*, *Ironside*, and *The F.B.I.* He landed his largest role to date in Universal's 1968 Western *Journey to Shiloh*, made as a TV movie but ending up instead in theaters as the bottom half of a double bill. By 1969, he was still playing in TV "classics" like *Love American Style*, where he was humiliated into being cast as a middle-aged executive's idea of a genuine hippie, complete with an ascot-like scarf! Ford griped to the producer that the fashion statement was absurd, only to later discover the gentleman had an identical wardrobe!

In 1970, frustrated by his inability to get Universal to provide him with more meaningful parts, Ford made a decision that would benefit him for the rest of his career. He chose to get a manager and picked Patricia McQueeney to represent him. The relationship between these two would become a Hollywood success story. Remarkably, in an industry in which loyalty is almost frowned upon, their business partnership still thrives today. McQueeney would guide Ford through his most challenging years, instilling in him the confidence and business savvy required to emerge as a genuine star. In 1993, McQueeney, who now solely represents Harrison Ford, recalled her first impression of the aspiring actor: "He sat on the couch in my office—his head down, his hands between his knees—and kind of [frowned] at me, looking up at me underneath his brows, extremely uncomfortable and slightly embarrassed. At that time, he was working as a carpenter and had done some parts around town, and I can remember looking at him and thinking, 'What in the world am I going to do with him?' Harrison always had enormous dignity and was extremely smart. If he didn't like a role that I gave him, he would just turn it down. And sometimes they were good jobs, very lucrative. But they were television jobs, and he wouldn't tie himself up with a series. . . . He'd say 'No, I'm not going to do it. I'll go build a cabinet instead.' "

Producer Fred Roos, whom Ford had met while doing some carpentry work and who would later help him land supporting roles in major films, saw the actor's potential. He, too, was impressed by Ford's determination and refusal to conform—despite the fact that he had yet to establish any clout with the studios. "He was not a leading man in the way they thought of leading men at the time—not pretty enough," recalls Roos. "The strongest quality I saw was his great sense of masculinity. There was kind of a dangerous intensity that he had, and combined with that was this droll sense of humor. He had extreme confidence but nothing braggadocio. And he was so tasteful and caring about the way he did carpentry; he wouldn't accept anything that wasn't perfect. If I would suggest [building] something I wanted that he thought was in bad taste, he would refuse to do it. And he was always right."

Ford continued to be frustrated by the fact that virtually all of his acting assignments were in television. His enthusiasm rose when Universal loaned him to MGM for *Zabriskie Point*, director Michelangelo Antonioni's offbeat counterculture misfire. Antonioni made a splash in the international cinema world with *Blow-Up*, his bizarre but fascinating 1966 murder mystery set among the "mod" atmosphere of London. Anticipation within the industry was high for *Zabriskie Point*, a film which would—on the surface at least—appear to be a coherent crime story. Ford played a minor but visible role, in a subplot that was eventually edited out entirely. Ultimately, this proved to be an act of mercy for Ford. *Zabriskie Point* was a pretentious, confusing, pseudo-intellectual "statement" on the negative influence sex and wealth had on society. The film, released in 1970, was one of the major bombs of the decade.

Ford did get a more visible role in one of the best-reviewed films of 1970, the counterculture campus satire *Getting Straight*. Elliott Gould and Candice Bergen were the stars, and Ford appears only fleetingly, but he did receive screen credit and had a bit of dialogue. More television work followed, generally with Ford in distinctly supporting roles. He did episodes of *Dan August* (with Burt Reynolds) and *Gunsmoke*, wherein he had to play virtually the same character in two episodes which aired within three months of each other. (During the shooting of "The Sodbusters" episode of *Gunsmoke*, a mishap involving a gun resulted in Ford's front teeth being knocked out. The future star had to suffer the frustration of buying his own set of crowns after the ones provided by the studio dentist fell out, thus lowering the low salary he was drawing.)

Disillusioned, Harrison Ford decided to place his still burgeoning acting career on hold—barring a significant role—and turn to carpentry as a full-time profession. He was concerned that his frequent television appearances were making him overexposed, while not significantly helping his big-screen ambitions in any dramatic way. "I decided to stop taking small TV parts and become a carpenter," he recalled. "I'd no training in car-

Table of Contents

The staff tips its MUG to the Garter, humor magazine of San Francisco State College who's model greatly helped us.

Contents page for a 1962 issue of *The Mug* (Note Ford's cartoon at left, and his listing in the credits as "Harry Ford.") (Courtesy Ripon College)

pentry, any more than I'd had in acting. But I set my mind to it. My first assignment was a $100,000 recording studio for musician Sergio Mendes." Today, Ford can afford to look back on his precarious position with levity. "[Mendes] didn't ask me if it was my first job and I never told him. . . . I'd be standing on Mendes's roof with a textbook in one hand and a hammer in the other."

Mendes recently recalled his first meeting with Harrison Ford: "A friend of mine had recommended him for the job. He seemed to know what he was talking about, even though he had no papers or anything that indicated he was a carpenter. He seemed to take a lot of care in what he was doing, and I like that. I hate to use the word 'perfectionist,' but he was very careful and neat and did a great job. During his break time, he would read books about carpentry, as well as film scripts. He told me that he wanted to be in the movie business. He worked here for more than six months. The studio came out gorgeous, with stained glass we got from a mausoleum in Tennessee, and handcrafted hardwood floors. It was a fantastic job—we still use the studio today. Ford was a very quiet fellow, who didn't socialize much. His wife used to come over and bring him food on his lunch break. . . . [He was] a guy who knew what he was doing, and took care of business." Today, Ford insists, "I didn't know what the hell I was doing. . . . I guess [Mendes] wouldn't have had much faith in me if he'd seen me up there checking out the next step in a book."

Nevertheless, unlike his acting career, Ford found immediate success in carpentry. Before long he could command sizable fees, based largely on his reputation as a perfectionist who would do the job right in spite of any and all obstacles. "When I started carpentry," he reflected, "I liked it so much because it was such a relief from what I'd been doing before. For about eight years in the late sixties and early seventies, I did cabinets, furniture,

remodeling. It was great! I could see my accomplishments. So I decided not to do any more acting unless the job had a clear career advantage. . . . I didn't worry about money. I had an understanding wife. I was playing pretty fast and loose with life."

Ford's success in carpentry allowed him to move with his wife Mary and young son Ben into an $18,500 home in the hills above the Hollywood Bowl. The investment meant lean times for the family. A blanket served as the bathroom door (ironic in the house of a carpenter!), and a tarp covered the exposed living room wall. Actress Cindy Williams, who would appear with Ford in *The Conversation* and *American Graffiti*, recalled, "Sometimes his wife Mary would call me and say, 'Harrison is depressed. Would you talk to him?' They were poor as church mice, and it broke your heart that he wasn't working all the time. And that's when I'd say, 'Someday, Harrison, you'll see! You'll be like Cary Grant.' And lo and

Ford (*second from left in back row*) with his Sigma Nu fraternity brothers at Ripon College in 1961. (Courtesy Ripon College)

behold, from my mouth to God's ear!"

Ultimately, Ford's reputation as a carpenter allowed him to gain lucrative contracts from major names in the film industry. He jokingly referred to himself as the "Carpenter to the Stars," and he developed a list of clients which included James Caan, Richard Dreyfuss, Sally Kellerman, Talia Shire, director Richard Fleischer, and former *Dead Heat on a Merry-Go-Round* costar James Coburn. "I worked mostly for people who were well-off and who could afford to indulge me," he admitted.

Ford's success with carpentry allowed him to gain a great deal of confidence as well as self-discipline. "What I learned from carpentry, above all, was a work ethic. I used to be very lazy, but now I find I can't enjoy myself when I'm not working. . . . It saved my life to have another way of making a living. Carpentry gave me the possibility of choice, the ability to turn down roles. . . . I didn't want to do episodic TV anymore, because I was afraid I'd burn myself out before I got a chance to do any decent feature films. Besides, I was too young. I was twenty-four and looked nineteen." Yet he persisted in his desire to become a successful actor. He would often attend auditions wearing his carpenter's clothes to illustrate to the studio and himself that he had an alternate career. "If they know you are dependent on them, they value you less," he rationalized.

Just when Ford was about ready to concentrate solely on his carpentry business, Fred Roos, who was doing the casting for *American Graffiti*, recommended him to the film's director—a young maverick named George Lucas. The movie would center on the adventures (and misadventures) of a group of high school friends on the last evening before the end of summer vacation in 1962. When Lucas offered Ford a small but visible part as an arrogant drag racer, Ford was less than enthusiastic. The role would pay him less than half of what he could have earned as a carpenter, and Lucas's credentials were less than spectacular at the time: he was primarily known for the cult science fiction film *THX 1138* and for working as a cameraman on the classic Rolling Stones documentary *Gimme Shelter*. (Curiously, Ford had also tried contributing to the documentary genre, having worked for one week on a concert film about the Doors. Ford admitted, "I couldn't keep up with those guys. It was too much. I was part of the camera crew—second camera. I don't think any of it was in focus, not a bit of it.")

Despite the low pay, Ford's instincts told him to accept the role in *American Graffiti*, which would team him with other up-and-coming actors like Ron Howard, Richard Dreyfuss, Cindy Williams, and Suzanne Sommers. Ford's rebellious nature was apparent on the set. Years later, George Lucas recalled his antics: "He was a little

The original Harrison Ford, a silent film actor with no relation to the younger Ford. Because of the similarity of names, however, the future Han Solo originally had to bill himself as "Harrison J. Ford"—even though his predecessor had died in 1957.

bit on the wild side. We shot all night—it was pretty boring—and he had a tendency to drink a few beers and get in that Chevy, which was incredibly hot, and sort of race up and down the streets. The police . . . kept threatening to impound the car and take him downtown. . . . There was an incident where [Ford] and Paul Le Mat threw Richard Dreyfuss into a swimming pool right before Rick was going to do a lot of close-ups. [Dreyfuss] whacked his head [and] got cut across his forehead."

Minor filming incidents aside, *American Graffiti* was the "sleeper" hit of 1973 and one of the most acclaimed films of the decade. Ultimately, most of its cast would find varying degrees of stardom in the years which followed. Yet the big roles continued to elude Harrison Ford in the

This early publicity photo of Ford was airbrushed to eliminate the scar on his chin, the result of an automobile accident.

James A. Michener's "*Dynasty*," a big-budget miniseries which toplined Sarah Miles, Stacy Keach, and Amy Irving.

It had now been eight years since Ford had given up his status as a contract player at Universal. He reflected many years later on his studio work during that period of time, saying of his acting jobs, "three of them were good ones: *American Graffiti*, *The Conversation*, and *The Court Martial of Lt. Calley*. After eight years, nobody thought of me as a person who had been in anything but three good films."

Nevertheless, Ford faced a financial dilemma. By 1976, his wife had given birth to their second son, Willard, and Ford found that his SAG (Screen Actors Guild) health insurance had elapsed because he had not earned $1,200 from acting in the previous year—a necessity for keeping the policy active. Word was out that George Lucas had begun the casting process for his upcoming science fiction epic *Star Wars*. However, the fact that Ford had worked for the director previously was proving to be a detriment in this case. He explained, "George had let it be known that he wasn't going to use anybody from *American Graffiti*. Not because we'd disappointed him, but he was writing a whole new thing and needed new faces. But old Fred Roos did it again. He prevailed on George to see me after he'd seen everyone else."

Initially, Ford—who was "coincidentally" doing carpentry work in Lucas's office during the casting calls—was asked by the director to act out the role of Han Solo in various screen tests with other actors. It was apparent, however, that casting Ford in the role of Solo was not foremost in Lucas's mind. The actor's aggravation at this situation caused him to act in an edgy, sarcastic manner which impressed Lucas. Ultimately, Ford won the part when Lucas saw a great deal of chemistry between him and two other prospective costars, Mark Hamill and Carrie Fisher.

Lucas depended heavily on improvisations and cre-

months immediately following *Graffiti*'s release. He had a small but pivotal role as a mysterious executive who covers up a murder in Francis Ford Coppola's 1974 thriller *The Conversation*. The film was not a box-office hit but received unanimously enthusiastic reviews. However, Gene Hackman received the lion's share of the notices, and few critics could realize the improvisations which Ford brought to his otherwise nondescript role (i.e., playing him as a homosexual). After *The Conversation*, Ford resumed his carpentry work on a steady basis, pausing only for some work in television movies, such as *Judgment: The Court Martial of Lt. William Calley* ("I played the witness who cries," notes Ford); *The Possessed*, an *Exorcist*-like horror flick for NBC; and

ative advice from his cast and crew. He allowed Ford to more fully develop the character of Han Solo, the likable but rebellious smuggler who becomes a reluctant hero in the battle to save the universe from the evil forces of the Empire. Ford recalled, "George Lucas gave me a lot of freedom to change little parts of the dialogue which weren't comfortable. . . . We worked on it together. I really liked working with him. . . . This was the first time I had a character big enough to take space instead of just filling in spaces, as I did at Columbia and Universal."

Upon its release in the summer of 1977, *Star Wars* established itself as a box-office phenomenon and ultimately became the highest-grossing motion picture ever up to that time. Of all the principal actors, Ford was the one most embraced by the public—perhaps his character of Han Solo was the most dynamic. Overnight, he had gone from a largely unknown screen presence to being the idol of millions of movie fans. His agent Pat McQueeney recently reflected on Ford's reaction to the stardom he had worked so hard to achieve: "When the movie came out, there was no doubt in my mind where Harrison was headed. And no question in his mind, either. Harrison came into my place and sat down and looked up to me and said, 'Patricia, this is a miracle.' Because it had been very, very tough for him."

George Lucas noticed that *Star Wars* had benefited Harrison Ford in ways which exceeded financial security. "The experience of the *Star Wars* films—especially—the first one—and of working with a lot of British actors like Alec Guinness mellowed him out a lot as an actor. He began to see how it was a real profession—in terms of how to act professionally on the set—by being around a lot of actors who did their job and didn't cause a lot of difficulties and didn't take a lot of time and did their homework before they came on the set. All the kinds of professional things you expect caught him at the right moment and made him realize how important the job of an actor is and how everybody depends on everybody to do their job well and not be self-indulgent. He became a very good professional actor from that point on. He disciplined his talent in a much different way, which makes it a dream to work with him."

Following *Star Wars*, most actors would have been content to capitalize on their newfound action hero image. Not so with Harrison Ford. To the surprise of many, he intentionally sought roles which were the antithesis of Han Solo. He ended up taking a supporting role in *Heroes*, an episodic comedy-drama of the road, which teamed Henry Winkler and Sally Field. The 1977 release brought him back to Universal, albeit with the benefit of not having to work under contract. *Heroes* was primarily a vehicle to allow Winkler to diversify from his image as Fonzie

on the hit ABC sitcom *Happy Days*, which ironically owed its very existence to *American Graffiti*. Ford was paid relatively well for his supporting stint in it, but his main motivation was to portray a midwestern redneck. The film was not a major hit with audiences or critics, but most of the positive reviews centered on Ford's low-key method of stealing scenes.

Henry Winkler was impressed with Ford's abilities even in those early years. He recently said, "Harrison doesn't do anything halfway. You had to be on your toes, because he acts with the same passion and intensity that he lives. And he's only gotten better; the way he has matured is incredible. The naturalness with which he acts, the comfort level, is enviable. It is very difficult to get so simple, to just be. It takes a tremendous amount of self-confidence and courage not to push."

Ford chose his next role—that of an army officer in *Force 10 From Navarone*—for a variety of reasons. The first was that it would offer him "above the title" billing beside Robert Shaw—an actor he was enthusiastic about working with. The large cast also included Franco Nero, Edward Fox, Barbara Bach, Richard Kiel, and Carl Weathers in a belated sequel to the 1961 film *The Guns of Navarone*. Whereas the earlier film is one of the best of its kind, *Force 10* was a misfire from minute one. Logistically, it was a challenge to make, due to adverse conditions and locations in Yugoslavia. The movie proved to be astonishingly inept, despite the high level of talent both in front of and behind the cameras. It also started tongues wagging about Ford's sense of judgment in choosing parts. The industry expected great things of him after *Star Wars*, but on the basis of *Heroes* and *Force 10*, many were wondering if he would prove to be a mere "flash in the pan."

Ford's troubles extended to his personal life. Like so many other actors, the rigors of filmmaking and location shooting distanced him from his wife and family. Despite the couple's extraordinary attempts to remain close while Ford toiled in films, the two realized that a divorce was all but inevitable. Ford placed much of the blame on the process of moviemaking, saying, "The cinema separated us and I will never forgive it for that." The marriage ended in 1978, but Ford took the lion's share of the blame for its dissolution, telling an interviewer, "I was definitely not Mr. Sweetness and Light. And frankly, I was an inadequate husband and father. . . ." In a more recent interview, he confessed, "I wasn't prepared, either by experience, maturity, or disposition, to be a good husband or good father the first time around. I wasn't easy to live with. I was bitter and cynical." Nonetheless, Ford continued to maintain an amicable relationship with Mary, stating publicly, "I owe everything to Mary. Without her, I wouldn't be in the cinema today, because I wouldn't have accepted the role of Han Solo. When Lucas made me the offer, I hadn't been in front of the camera for three years. Mary wasn't only beautiful and kind, she gave me the confidence to accept. She pushed me back into the cinema."

Ford was disillusioned by the breakup of his marriage. He had always taken the vows seriously and felt that married couples should remain together forever—the way his parents had. He began to lose himself in his work and did a small role in Francis Ford Coppola's Vietnam War epic *Apocalypse Now*. He next accepted the lead role in *Hanover Street*, after Kris Kristofferson bowed out. The World War II romantic soap opera cum adventure film was roundly scorned by critics, who took a perverse pleasure in predicting that Ford's career was becoming derailed. In his quest to experience as many diverse roles as possible, Ford next costarred with Gene Wilder in *The Frisco Kid*. Director Robert Aldrich's 1979 comedy Western was only modestly successful but proved that Ford could play a light role with great skill.

Ford's romantic life took an upturn when he began to become seriously involved with screenwriter Melissa Mathison. The two had first met on the set of *Apocalypse Now*, where she had worked as an assistant to Francis Ford Coppola. They continued to keep in touch after filming, and a relationship eventually developed. Ultimately, the couple moved in together, and Mathison pursued her career as a successful screenwriter. (She wrote the screenplay for Steven Spielberg's *E.T.: The Extra-terrestrial*.)

Harrison Ford and his new love shared many common interests and opinions, notably their mutual disdain for "the Hollywood scene." They decided to live away from central L.A., choosing an Alpine chalet in the hills of Benedict Canyon, only a few minutes from where his ex-wife Mary and their children resided. Being geographically close to his kids was important to Ford, probably because he was cognizant of his frequent absences in previous years due to the trials of filmmaking. Ben and Willard Ford were now able to visit their dad frequently, and he could not have been happier. In an 1982 interview, he said, "We're best friends. I like to think I'm a fun dad. My boys come first for me. I try and include them in every part of my life." On any typical night, Ford and his boys would simply stay home and enjoy videos together, causing Ford to jokingly gripe, "We saw *Star Wars* repeatedly, until even I could speak the other characters' lines!"

Melissa Mathison enjoyed the presence of Ben and Willard, and was so inspired by their interplay that she modeled dialogue and situations in *E.T.* after the boys. She commented, "I get all the pleasure of Harrison's kids, without having to discipline them or lay down the law."

Ford and Mathison made for the most creative household imaginable, and rumors inevitably flew that they would collaborate on a film project. Ford politely disagreed, saying, "We're helpful to each other's careers, but we don't have any intention of working together. We keep our own track." Years later, he did concede, "We have a couple of things that we are noodling around with. But there is no great ambition to work together. Part of the pleasure of our lives is that we both have this independent thing that we do and we go away and work with other people and we bring that experience back into our marriage."

Ford's next cinematic undertaking (following a cameo appearance in the ill-conceived *More American Graffiti*) was the much anticipated sequel to *Star Wars*. Under Irvin Kershner's direction, *The Empire Strikes Back* was shot in Norway and England in 1979. (George Lucas was so frustrated by the troubles encountered in directing the original film that he vowed to limit his contributions in future projects to writing and producing.) To be able to keep a sense of spontaneity in his performance, Ford read only the portions of the script in which he appeared. "I asked Irvin if I had to read this section or that," he recalled. "He said there was no need to. So, when I finally saw the finished movie, I learned for the first time all the things that happened to Luke [Skywalker]. It was great."

What *wasn't* so great were the technical problems which dwarfed those encountered in the original film. *Empire* came in far behind schedule and considerably above its already sizable budget. Yet Ford was happy that he was again allowed to improvise in his depiction of Han Solo, and he worked well with Irvin Kershner, who had an appreciation for Ford's creative suggestions. "He was wonderful," Ford said of Kershner. "He's a different kind of director. But we also had a very close relationship on the level of freedom to contribute."

When *Empire* opened in 1980, many critics and fans felt the film exceeded its predecessor in overall plot and character development. The movie broke the rule that most sequels were but pale imitations of the original. *Empire* was a blockbuster hit, and suddenly the considerable press which had been given to its production difficulties faded away. Ford, the perfectionist, admitted even he was pleased with his own performance: "It's the first time I've ever seen anything I've done that I'm happy with."

By now, Ford's contribution to the success of the two *Star Wars* films was beyond dispute. By all accounts, he had dominated both movies, despite the presence of a tal-

Ford's distaste for studio publicity seems to be illustrated in this somber promotional photo taken while the aspiring actor was under contract with Universal in the late sixties.

A 1967 television appearance with Victor Jory in NBC's *Ironside*.

ented cast. However, nagging doubts remained in the industry about his ability to carry a non–*Star Wars* film to the level of a box-office blockbuster. At precisely this time, George Lucas and Steven Spielberg were finalizing plans for their collaborative project *Raiders of the Lost Ark*. The big-budget homage to the old-time serials would introduce the character of Indiana Jones, with the hope that this could be the beginning of a successful franchise for Paramount Pictures the way the James Bond films had been for United Artists. With Lucas producing and Spielberg directing, only one obstacle stood in their way: with just weeks to go before principal photography was to begin, they still did not have a leading actor. Tom Selleck had been their first choice, but his contractual obligation to his television show *Magnum P.I.* prevented him from accepting. As if struck by a bolt from the blue, both men suddenly decided on Harrison Ford. Spielberg declared that "Harrison can be villainous and romantic all at once"—perfect qualifications for the character of

the mild-mannered archaeologist who leads a double life as a superheroic ladies' man.

Ford, aware that he was second choice for the role, did not instantly leap at the opportunity to play Indy. He was concerned that the character would simply resemble Han Solo in a Guyana hat. Spielberg and Lucas assured him that any such resemblance would be purely coincidental, and Ford signed on for what would become one of the most lucrative roles ever given an actor. Despite the trials and tribulations of shooting in the inhospitable Tunisian climate and other grueling locales, Ford enjoyed an instant chemistry with Spielberg, who encouraged Ford's practice of making creative suggestions. Spielberg praised his leading man's instincts: "Harrison Ford was more than just an actor playing a role in *Raiders of the Lost Ark*. He was involved in a lot of decision making about the movie as we went along. And this wasn't by contract; it was because I sensed an exceptionally strong mind and a very smart person, and called on him time and time again." Indeed, Spielberg was also impressed with the creativity of Melissa Mathison, who spent a good deal of time visiting her husband on the set. Mathison had been disillusioned with her own recent work and had decided to stop writing. However, Spielberg, who had admired Mathison's highly praised screenplay for *The Black Stallion*, persuaded her to pen the forthcoming *E.T.*, and the rest is history. (Mathison went on to write the hit 1995 Disney film *The Indian in the Cupboard*.)

Raiders was the box-office smash of 1981 and exceeded everyone's expectations, proving that audiences wanted to see Harrison Ford the actor, not just Harrison Ford impersonating Han Solo. On the eve of the film's release, Ford was told by an interviewer that the "buzz" was that the movie was a winner. Asked if he felt he might be responsible for its succeeding at the box office, he again downplayed his own contribution, saying, "Besides the full frontal nudity, the sex with a camel, the free place setting we're giving away in the theaters, and the opportunity to win the presidential yacht? Folks will see it I guess because it's going to be a hell of a lot of fun. If not, I'd ask for my money back!"

Now an international superstar, Ford found that one of the negative aspects to his fame was the inability to move about unrecognized—a frustrating problem for a man treasuring privacy. He acknowledged that his strategy for avoiding recognition was to avoid the habits of many publicity-hungry movie stars: "It's the 'look at me' attitude that gets you into trouble. The secret is not to catch anyone's eyes. Keep your head down and count the cracks in the sidewalk—along with walking fast and forcefully so that by the time someone realizes who they have seen, it's too late." However, Ford has always been appreciative of his public. He remembers his roots as a starving actor and is grateful that the fickle public has embraced him for so many years. If approached, he will smile and sign autographs "if I'm not having sex at the time or doing something important."

Ford also tries to respect the privacy of others—a trait which sometimes causes him some embarrassment. "I have this funny thing that happens to me," he said. "When I see famous people on the street, I turn away so as not to embarrass them by staring. But sometimes it's someone I know, only I've forgotten I know them—I think I'm only imagining I know them, because they're famous. Jack Nicholson has been a friend of mine for years, but every time I see him, my instinct is to turn away, to preserve his privacy. I have to remind myself that I can't do that. I do know Jack, and I've got to say 'Hi.' "

While finishing the filming of *Empire*, Ford had been approached to star in *Blade Runner*, a big-budget science fiction epic to be directed by Ridley Scott, whose 1979 film *Alien* was regarded as one of the most original and dynamic entries in the genre in decades. Ford was intrigued by the script, which is set in twenty-first-century Los Angeles and centers on a man named Deckard, who is a "blade runner"—a futuristic euphemism for paid assassin. However, blade runners do not kill actual *people*, but rather, replicants—robotic

Even after achieving stardom, Ford has continued to hone his skills as a carpenter. He personally helped construct his house in Wyoming.

slave workers who are virtually indistinguishable from human beings. The replicants have predetermined life spans and are programmed to self-destruct. When several of them rebel and go on a murderous mission to prolong their lifespans, Deckard is reluctantly dragged into the case to "terminate" them.

Ford initially was reluctant to sign for the project, citing the fact that it would be filmed in England. He had

shot five of his last eight movies there and had no desire to have another prolonged work assignment outside of the U.S. However, when production relocated to the Warners backlot in L.A., Ford consented. Ridley Scott and Ford almost immediately found themselves at odds as to what direction the film should take—a portent of things to come. Scott envisioned the tale as sort of a futuristic Philip Marlowe story, with the accent on film noir. His

With his second wife, Melissa Mathison, the prolific screenwriter of *E.T.* and others.

original perception of the role of Deckard was too close to that of Han Solo and Indiana Jones for Ford. The actor did all he could to distance his characterization from those other roles. He chose to accentuate Deckard's seediness and play him as a mysterious, ambiguous man with close-cropped hair, indicative of someone who had long ago given up on his personal appearance.

Ford and Scott's styles of filmmaking conflicted more than complimented each other. Ford believes a director's first priority should be to work closely with actors and discuss their characterizations. Scott was far too preoccupied by the magnificent set designs and the technical aspects of the film. The director's penchant for perfectionism resulted in endless takes of the same scene. Adding to the problem was the fact that the film was shot entirely at night, thus disrupting everyone's natural cycles and making the cast and crew somewhat testy.

When audiences failed to respond favorably to the original ending of the film, which leaves the fate of Deckard and his replicant lover unresolved (and hints that Deckard himself may be a replicant), the studio convinced Scott to shoot an alternate ending in which the couple literally fly off into the sunset. Added to this was the inclusion of a pointless narration throughout the entire film. Ford objected to this but was contractually bound to do the voice-over. He confessed, "I went kicking and screaming to the studio to record it." In hopes that the narration would be cut, Ford delivered his dialogue in a monotonous, boring tone. Unfortunately, the strategy failed to work, and Ford received some of the worst reviews of his career largely on the basis of the absurd narration he was forced to deliver in *Blade Runner*.

Ironically, the film became a cult favorite from the beginning and in recent years has become a popular staple on video. In 1991, Ridley Scott's original director's cut of the film was rereleased theatrically (sans narration) to widespread praise. Although this is an infinitely superior film compared to the original release, Harrison Ford still detests *Blade Runner* and cannot be persuaded to watch it again. Making the movie was an unpleasant experience, and he apparently cannot view the film objectively without incurring unhappy memories.

Following *Blade Runner*, Ford was to begin production on the third *Star Wars* film, *Return of the Jedi*. However, the pressures of working seemingly nonstop were taking their toll on him physically and emotionally. On the physical level, the big-budget productions with which he had been associated required grueling work schedules, often on location in remote areas. Ford's insistence on doing most of his own stunt work added considerably to the realism of his films but were leading him to exhaustion. On the emotional side, he recognized that his frequent absences from home due to work had been placing a strain on his relationship with Melissa and his children. Ultimately, he vowed to take six months off to concentrate on his personal life, telling the press, "It would take an act of Congress to get me to work before *Jedi*. I haven't had six months with the kids for a long time."

Ford was not initially enthused about returning to the role of Han Solo for the third time. However, he felt a personal obligation to George Lucas and realized the importance of his character to completing the first trilogy in what Lucas envisioned to be an ever evolving series of *Star Wars* films. In the previous entry, *The Empire Strikes Back*, the fate of Han Solo had been left intentionally ambiguous. George Lucas could have explained that Solo died, had Ford refused to appear in *Jedi*. To everyone's relief, this option did not have to be utilized. Ford would star once again with Mark Hamill and Carrie Fisher, this time under the direction of Richard Marquand, in the biggest budgeted of the *Star Wars* films.

What *Jedi* possessed in grandeur, it lacked in plot and pacing. The movie falls into the age-old trap that many big-budgeted films fall victim to (notably the later Bond movies): the technology, though impressive, overwhelms the human aspects of the story. In *Jedi*, the character of Han Solo is distinctly secondary to that of Luke Skywalker, and Ford had little to do but make wisecracks and point laser guns. Critics pointed out that, for the first time, Ford had too little to work with, and as a result, *Jedi* is very much a film dominated by Mark Hamill. Despite its flaws, however, *Jedi* was a marvel of high-tech entertainment and the box-office smash of

1983. While most fans seem to feel it was the least of the *Star Wars* films, it was still light years ahead of other movies in the sci-fi genre. No one complains they do not get their money's worth when George Lucas oversees a project as personal as this.

During the filming of *Jedi*, Ford commented on his

Ford was finally an established superstar when he appeared on the cover of *People* magazine in 1980 to promote *The Empire Strikes Back*, along with Billy Dee Williams, Carrie Fisher, and Mark Hamill. (*People Magazine*)

relationship with Melissa Mathison, telling the *London Daily Mail*, "We've been together for four years. But I won't even be quoted on saying that I don't know whether we'll get married or not." Indeed, six months later—on March 14, 1983—the couple were wed. Mathison cited the desire to begin a family as the primary motivation for the marriage, saying "Harry's old-fashioned that way." The ceremony was very much in line with Ford's personality—low-key and unpretentious. The fifteen-minute wedding was conducted by a judge in his chambers. The couple presented each other with white roses, kissed, then sped away in Ford's black Porsche.

While Ford and Mathison never collaborated on a film project, he explained, "We respect each other considerably, both as professionals and as people." Ford valued his wife's opinions of prospective projects, and her success as a screenwriter allowed her to give him insightful advice. "If she doesn't like me in something, she's usually got a damn good reason. And usually she's right," he said. Certainly, the couple's instincts about Ford's films were "on the money." A 1983 survey showed that Ford ranked third in popularity among the American public, behind Eddie Murphy and Alan Alda. (How times have changed!) The couple almost appeared in cameo roles in the Mathison-scripted blockbuster *E.T.* Mathison was set to play a school nurse in a scene in which Elliot is drunk and disorderly in class; Ford was to walk on as the principal. The sequence was scrapped when Melissa's nervousness in front of the camera would not abate, and her "acting debut" ended up on the cutting-room floor. Perhaps it's just as well, considering Ford's assessment of the "lovable" E.T.—he told *Time Out* magazine at the time, "Two weekends ago I called him an ugly little fuck. And Steven [Spielberg] went apeshit!"

Ford's next cinematic undertaking was the sequel to *Raiders of the Lost Ark*, to be directed by Steven Spielberg (who evidently forgave Ford for his less-than-kind assessment of lovable old E.T.). *Indiana Jones and the Temple of Doom*, filmed primarily in Sri Lanka, would be as ambitious and as arduous to make as its predecessor. Ford claimed his agreement to do the movie was motivated by his desire to have fun with Spielberg and Lucas. Yet the result was regarded as a disappointment by those who made it, as well as many critics. Unlike *Raiders*, *Temple* was a dark, depressing adventure that dealt with ritualistic murders, deadly cults, and child abuse, and included the stomach-turning use of bugs, monkey brains, and reptiles. While Ford and Spielberg circled the wagons in a staunch defense of attacks on the movie's violent content, they would later confess that the movie is not the pleasant ride *Raiders* was. Despite the colossal box-office success of *Temple*, both men harbored dreams of doing another Indy film to put the series back in balance.

"I don't want to bemoan any films of the past, but I think this is the most complicated role I've played in quite awhile. And this time, it's one with adult appeal." So said Harrison Ford as he embarked upon filming what would become his most highly acclaimed performance to date—that of John Book, a honest detective assigned to protect a young Amish boy who is the sole witness to a murder. In the process, he learns the murder was ordered by a corrupt corps of police officers, including his own superiors. Wounded and fleeing for his life, Book seeks refuge in the boy's home, where he is cared for by the lad's mother (Kelly McGillis), a traditional Amish woman with whom he falls in love. The film was *Witness*, Australian director Peter Weir's thinly veiled remake of the 1947 John Wayne–Gail Russell Western *Angel and the Badman*. A lyrical, lovely, touching, and thrilling film, it represented the most ambitious acting assignment Harrison Ford had yet undertaken. He was grateful for the opportunity and felt confident in the project, even though the script had many other actors' fingerprints on it by the time it reached him (including those of the "Man Who Would be Indy," Tom Selleck). Ford told an interviewer, "*Witness* is really acting. It's great to get a chance to play a real person."

Witness was critically acclaimed, despite the absence of advance publicity and the fact that the project was deemed "box-office poison" by many industry "know-it-alls." Ford's fans and the general public finally got to see the actor away from the distractions of high technology and special effects. The success of the film, both financially and artistically, proved to be an important development in Ford's career: no longer would skeptics be able to say that he couldn't carry a movie without Spielberg or Lucas. *Witness* depended on the charisma and skill of its lead actor, who is in virtually every scene. Ford's work was impressive enough to earn him an Oscar nomination. Of that development, he said, "When I got the nomination, my friends told me I should feel vindicated for all the critics who said I walked through the Spielberg/Lucas movies. Well, I don't feel vindication. It's just not in my repertoire. Besides, no one could criticize me as harshly as I do myself." Of the Oscar itself, he said, "It's a high honor. I don't disdain it. It's just not the most important thing in my general scheme."

Always an actor determined to place his craft above purely financial considerations, Harrison Ford ignored all advice—including that of his longtime manager Pat McQueeney—to do *The Mosquito Coast*, an ambitious film which would reteam him with director Peter Weir. The totally uncommercial project cast Ford as Allie Fox, a sometimes-lovable, more-often-than-not obnoxious eccentric and inventor whose tirades against the evils of modern society lead him to relocate his family to the "paradise" of a remote jungle in South America. Here he hopes they can bring about the start of a new civilization, uncontaminated by the corrupting influences of urban life. Although the script, based on Paul Theroux's novel, toned down the more sordid characteristics of Fox's personality

A rare photo of Ford with Ben and Willard, his two sons by his first wife, Mary.

as depicted in the source material, this would clearly be a role unlike any Ford had played before. Allie Fox is more self-centered than generous, more nervous than heroic, and although well-intentioned, his dictatorial manner brings tragedy to his family and himself.

Ford said of the role, "I don't have any trouble representing something that I understand, and this is a character that I've never felt any difficulty understanding. So I don't think of it as a more difficult job than what I'd done before. On the other hand, I was aware that there was opportunity here for more complicated characterization, and because the character is so verbal and effusive, it goes against the kind of characters for which I'm best known. That was the attraction the part held for me: to do something different."

Although Pat McQueeney's dire prediction that *The Mosquito Coast* would be rejected by the public came true, Ford was justifiably proud of the film and felt it was his most personal performance to date. Had the movie

been more mainstream, it might have earned Ford a richly deserved second Oscar nomination. Perhaps his performance was so intense because he shares a few philosophies with Allie Fox. He told reporters, "I guess I worry about society almost neurotically, though I don't do anything practical like stocking my basement with emergency provisions. Civilization is at a point where our concerns seem to be how less to harm people than how to make them any better, and I find that fairly depressing. It wouldn't help for me to become some kind of martyr, pleading to a crowd to avoid this or embrace that, and fans who expect it are really misinterpreting a performer's job. We're in another branch of public service— we're assistant storytellers, not role models or pontiffs of morality and logic." Ford's philosophy is at odds with the many celebrities who think their talents entitle them to be self-professed experts on every social issue imaginable. Ford is not a political animal, at least not in the public arena, and follows a sensible belief that beyond his mis-

21

Relaxing on the set of *Raiders of the Lost Ark* in 1981.

ties had to be brought in especially for Ford's rustic house, notable for its lack of pretension. (The only exceptions being a Mercedes in the driveway and a satellite dish on the roof.) The tranquility of his and Melissa's ranch provided a perfect haven for escape. Ford did not want to intimate that he had a disdain for people in the movie industry, despite his pains to distance himself from the "party scene" in L.A. In 1993, he said, "A great deal has been made out of me not living in Hollywood and my revulsion at the Hollywood system. It's not true. I very much admire a lot of people who work here. I think a lot of people work very hard and with a good motive. I just don't like cities. I don't like to live there. I don't like the smog. I don't like the congestion. I don't like the feeling, the energy of the place. I simply prefer to live in the country. It is not, as is often said, a result of moral judgment about Hollywood. I live in Wyoming because I love the nature there and I'm left alone."

The residents of Jackson Hole respect Ford's desire for privacy even when he shops in the tiny town (population: 4,500). He jokes, "I think they'd prefer it if I did behave like a film star because then I'd represent something exciting. As it is I'm ordinary, totally comprehensible to them." He has also proven to be a good neighbor. He and Melissa have donated 132 acres of their land to the Western Wyoming Jackson Hole Land Trust, thereby insuring that the land can never be developed. He explained his motivation: "I really want to preserve it for my kids, to let them know this is what's dear to me rather than a big pile of money in the middle of the floor. I can't think of a better legacy than to do what you can to protect a small piece of wilderness."

Ford's lifestyle in Wyoming is the antithesis of what one might expect of a major movie star. "When I finish doing a movie, I can't wait to get back home where I can go grocery shopping or go to the hardware store. When I'm working, I miss driving my own car and cooking my

sion to give audiences two hours of entertainment, he is not obligated to vent his personal views in public.

In March 1987, Ford's wife Melissa gave birth to their son Malcolm—Ford's third child and Mathison's first. In an indication that she shared her husband's old-fashioned family values, Mathison retired from screenwriting for a two-year period to devote her full attention to raising the baby. By this time, she and Ford were living on a ranch in Jackson Hole, Wyoming—far from the maddening crowd of Los Angeles. The couple felt it was vitally important to shield themselves and their family from Hollywood. In 1985, Ford and some helpers began the construction of the ranch, which is located in a remote area near the Snake River. The setting was so rural, a road had to be built leading up to the property, and utili-

own eggs. . . . Being normal is kind of a victory. What I really like is peace and quiet." Ironically, Ford's favorite pastimes do not include going to movies—much to the consternation of his wife: "I'm really very embarrassed by my lack of knowledge about film," he confessed. "My wife would like to see a lot more movies than we do, but she finds it hard to drag me out of the house. I'm a real bore." Yet even "boring" Harrison Ford has hobbies, including hiking, skiing, horseback riding, tennis, and fishing. "I particularly like to fish alone," he admits. "I just walk out the door, walk five or ten minutes and I am at the stream where I know the fish by name." He also finds time to practice his former livelihood: "I still do a lot of carpentry. It's something I've always done, always enjoyed doing. I wouldn't actually call it therapy, but it is a valuable part of my private life."

Upon the birth of Malcolm, Ford responded to a question about his goals for the future: "Raise more kids, look forward to life on the ranch. I'm slowly trying to transfer stock to my personal life and make sure I still have some years left for that." Commenting on the Ford's "new arrival," he joked, "He's remarkably self-possessed. And I mean from the time he was born. After the birth, he just rested on Melissa's chest for about seven hours, while she and I talked to him. And he kept looking back and forth at us. It was strange—not how you expect a newborn to act. . . . Malcolm has taught me a lot. He taught me about giggling and laughing and patience and . . . poop!"

Due to work demands, Ford maintains homes in Brentwood, California, and New York City. Since accepting the fact that a part-time urban lifestyle is inevitable, he admits, "I rather enjoy New York now. It's a great contrast to Wyoming. My little boy [Malcolm], strangely enough, loves it. It's very exciting for him."

Ford's other sons, Benjamin and Willard, were described by their father as "not fan types. They're not impressed by what I do at all. They see it as just the job that I happen to have. They don't display much enthusiasm for my work. I'm just another dad—somebody's dad who's got this odd job!" When the boys were younger, Ford was still a struggling actor who could not afford to take his family with him on most locations. Aware that such prolonged separations paved the way to his divorce from Mary, Ford tried hard to ensure that this would not be the case with Melissa and Malcolm. They were inevitably with him when he was on location, and Ford used his substantial clout to say, "If I can't bring them with me, there's no deal." Reflecting on his first marriage, he candidly admitted that his frequent absences caused him to "miss some very important times in Ben and Willard's lives . . . I've learned a lot since then—not just about being a father, but about being a human being."

Pat McQueeney, Ford's longtime manager-agent-friend, has played an instrumental role in his success right from the beginning. (McQueeney Management)

While Harrison Ford still shies away from the press and publicity, those who know him agree that the actor has become more outgoing since his marriage to Melissa. Several years ago, in an unusually introspective mood, Ford told an interviewer he had changed considerably—and for the better—since his early days in show business: "I'm much more mature. I still have the same moral values as before, the same few friends and I basically think the same old thoughts. I'm a bit older and wiser. Nothing more." Among "the same few friends" Ford has remained loyal to is George Lucas. Cognizant that the prolific filmmaker made him one of the highest-paid actors in the world, Ford has publicly acknowledged his gratitude on many occasions. In 1987—the tenth anniversary of the release of *Star Wars*—Ford gave this personal salute to Lucas in *Starlog* magazine: "George Lucas. Maker of Myths. Champion of the Innocent. Defender of the faith—or Force, if you will. My colleague. My friend. Let's face it—my mentor. Best wishes on the 10th anniversary of *Star Wars*. Love, Harrison."

Following *The Mosquito Coast*, Ford's next cinematic sojourn was *Frantic*, the 1988 thriller directed by Roman Polanski. Ford referred to Polanski as "one of the best directors I've ever worked with, one of the best in the world." The Hitchcock-like thriller was set entirely in Paris, a city Ford never could warm to: "The way life is conducted there doesn't interest me much." Ford could take consolation from the presence of Melissa and

Malcolm, both of whom would join him in screening the dailies. "[Malcolm] used to come all the time," he noted. "But now that he's older he wants to talk back to the screen, so we don't bring him as much. So far, he hasn't made any critical comments about my work."

Frantic, an eerie, underrated thriller, was too off-beat and "European" for American audiences. The film was a rarity in the Ford canon: a box-office failure. Sensing that audiences might want to see him in a less somber role, Ford accepted the male lead in director Mike Nichols's contemporary urban comedy *Working Girl*. He did not have a wealth of confidence about his ability to play in this type of lightweight film: "I've seen myself and deduced that when I go for laughs I come across as kind of wooden." Yet he felt confident that a strong director like Nichols could help him develop an audience beyond the action film genre. (Previously, Ford had considered starring in Nichols's *Silkwood*, but a scheduling conflict made that collaboration impossible.)

Working Girl was unique in that it presented Ford in what was very much a secondary role, despite his being given first billing. The movie belonged to Melanie Griffith and Sigourney Weaver, both of whom earned Oscar nominations as rival love interests for Ford. The bitchy satire on the oppression of everyday workers in the nerve-wracking environment of Wall Street struck a chord with the general public, and *Working Girl* became *the* date movie of 1988. A more egotistical actor would have demanded that the script be rewritten to allow him more screen time, but Ford claimed he was content to take it easy this go-round and let his costars handle most of the pressure. He joked that he was happy to play "the girl's part—the love interest." In comparison to the arduous conditions under which most of his films had been made, the urban jungle of Manhattan seemed downright serene. Best of all, Ford's witty, low-key performance won him respectable and even enthusiastic reviews. Clearly, he had succeeded in his stated goal of proving he could play "Cary Grant–type roles . . . screwball comedies."

Despite the fulfillment of having found success out-

With director Robert Aldrich and costar Gene Wilder on the set of *The Frisco Kid* in 1979.

Enjoying a laugh with Kelly McGillis and Jan Rubes while between takes on *Witness* in Lancaster, Pa., 1985.

side his traditional genre, Ford was lured by Spielberg and Lucas to play the role of Indiana Jones for a third time. The three men agreed that the dark and disturbing *Indiana Jones and the Temple of Doom* should not be the hero's cinematic swan song. It was their intention that the final Indy film would bring back the levity of the original *Raiders of the Lost Ark*. It would be titled *Indiana Jones and the Last Crusade*. Did Ford have concerns about resuming the role after five years, especially since his scope as an actor had broadened considerably since then? "Well, I'll tell you," he said in a 1988 interview, "it's the same process whether it's a so-called serious movie or a not-serious movie. The job of acting is the same. What I really enjoy is the kind of problem-solving aspect of getting stuff off the page and onto its feet, and for that there's no one better than Steven [Spielberg]. He's got one of the most facile minds you're ever going to meet in moviemaking. And besides, playing Indiana is fun. It's every boy's dream."

This time around, Ford's body was not only five years older but had suffered considerably in the ensuing time due to his insistence upon doing many difficult stunts

himself. He trained extensively to get back into shape for the inevitably grueling demands of this epic production. In an ingenious casting coup, the character of Indy's father was to be portrayed by Sean Connery. Despite the inevitable box-office dollars this collaboration would bring, many wondered if the two private, publicity-shy actors would find working together to be an obstacle. Both were among the few genuine superstars of the cinema, and there was concern that their egos might clash. However, Ford and Connery exhibited a wonderful chemistry on and off screen. Connery praised Ford with rare enthusiasm, and Ford returned the favor by saying, "Sean is, of course, such a terribly experienced actor, and that made it interesting to work with him. He's an awfully nice guy, too. I've enjoyed knowing him as well as working with him."

The two men shared a common "Bond": both had initially feared being typecast in the roles that helped cement them as superstars: Ford as Han Solo and Indiana Jones, and Connery as Agent 007. Significantly, both men eventually established themselves as fine enough actors, in a diversity of roles, that they felt comfortable returning

Harrison Ford—always the solitary man.

to the screen in the personas they initially feared would pigeonhole them. Ford would return as Han Solo and Indiana Jones twice (and is now preparing to do one more Indy film), while Connery—despite his early disdain for Bondmania—played the character in two well-received comeback performances in 1971 and 1983.

Last Crusade is arguably the best of the Indy films, largely because it emphasizes the fun aspect of the series as opposed to blood and guts. The rapport between Connery and Ford earned almost unanimously enthusiastic reviews and helped catapult the movie to blockbuster status at the international box office. Ford's affection for Connery was such that he made a rare appearance at a Hollywood party—a surprise bash to celebrate Connery's sixtieth birthday. The event was a Who's Who of world cinema, and by all accounts, Ford had fun joking all night with the likes of Steve Martin and Clint Eastwood. To paraphrase an old showbiz joke, if a bomb had gone off in that restaurant, Pia Zadora would have become the reigning box-office attraction in the world.

Ford received the ultimate compliment when the Smithsonian Institution, which displays the artifacts most reflective of American culture, requested the original whip and fedora he utilized as Indiana Jones. Ford personally made the donation in the Washington museum, saying, "I'm flattered to be here and have these artifacts on display here." He did confess, however, that he kept a "spare" whip at home: "It's on the top shelf of my hall closet, handy in case I need it." (On another occasion, he donated another whip for auction at Christies in London. The prop raised $24,300, with the proceeds appropriately donated to the London Institute of Archaeology.)

By 1989, Harrison Ford was a mellow man who had seemingly found solace in life through his work and family. Of his wife, he said, "Melissa probably wouldn't say that I was easy to live with. But I think she'd say that I'm easier to live with now than when she first met me. And I certainly give her some of the credit for my change. She sets a good example. She's a happy person. I don't express happiness perhaps as much as I should. There was a time when I was worried about losing my anger, worried that losing that edge would hurt my work. But when I married Melissa, I found that it was such a pleasure not to be angry and not to have that bitterness running around in my system. . . . I don't get crazy anymore."

Ford continued to expand into different on-screen roles. His performance in director Alan J. Pakula's 1990 screen adaptation of Scott Turow's best-selling book *Presumed Innocent* proved that Ford could shed his 'nice guy' image enough to convince audiences he just might be a cold-blooded murderer. The film was a major critical and box-office success, and he impressed the cast and crew with his understated ability to ease tensions on the set. Much of the filming was done in the ninety-year-old home of Chris and Patricia Cellary, an Allendale, N.J., couple who one day discovered that Harrison Ford and the movie crew would be at their house every day for four weeks. The Cellarys were impressed by Ford's down-to-earth attitude and his willingness to chat with anyone at any time. By all accounts, Ford does not come across as a movie star but rather "the guy next door"—a factor which explains why international audiences have embraced his work so enthusiastically. People relate to him.

While promoting *Presumed Innocent*, Ford became a father for the fourth time when Melissa gave birth to their daughter Georgia. The nervous father-to-be made sure that he carried a beeper to every press interview, so he could rush to his wife's side when the big moment came.

The 1991 film *Regarding Henry* allowed Ford to team again with Mike Nichols, who had helped him expand into comedy with *Working Girl*. For Ford, *Henry* would also be a daring departure. The story finds him as a successful, power-obsessed lawyer who is ruthless and unscrupulous in his desire to win high-profile cases. When he is shot in a bungled robbery attempt, he suffers brain damage, resulting in amnesia. The film chronicles his virtual rebirth as a totally new person, devoid of the obnoxious, unsympathetic characteristics he used to display. For the first time, he becomes a loving and caring husband and father and willingly sacrifices wealth for personal happiness. Ford worked hard to capture the essence of his character and lived among handicapped patients who were actually suffering from Henry's on-screen affliction. It was a daring and mesmerizing performance but not "showy" or gimmicky enough to gain widespread acclaim. The film was not a hit at the box office and proved to be a disappointment for Ford, who vowed to give his audience what they obviously desired—Harrison Ford in a big-budget action film.

When Alec Baldwin bowed out of Paramount's *Patriot Games* due to a variety of disputes, Ford was approached to play the role of Tom Clancy's Central Intelligence Agency hero Jack Ryan. Baldwin had established the character on-screen in the hit 1990 thriller *The Hunt for Red October*, although Ford had originally been offered the Ryan role in that film. Ford was now in the awkward position of taking over an established persona. The second film also proved to be controversial and troubled on a number of fronts. Clancy, who wrote the best-selling source novel, launched a highly publicized campaign to protest the changes made in his story. There was also criticism from the Irish communi-

By 1990, Ford's box-office record had earned him the title of "The Billion Dollar Man." (*Orbit Video* magazine)

ty about the film's depiction of the Irish Republican Army as something other than a bunch of avuncular old salts who meet in a Moose Hall–type environment for drinking and darts. While the film doesn't vilify the organization, the politically correct times resulted in a scathing review of the movie in *Variety* by a writer who critiqued the politics of the screenplay as opposed to its merits as an action film.

Patriot Games also proved to be cursed on a technical level as well, with some disturbing publicity surrounding the necessity to reshoot the ending when test audiences reacted unfavorably. Yet under the competent direction of Philip Noyce and with Harrison Ford's forceful star power on the screen, *Patriot Games* was a sizable hit, albeit not a blockbuster by Fordian standards. Its success was enough to encourage Paramount to launch a series of Ryan films in the hopes that the studio could create a Bond-like franchise. Ford enthused about continuing to play the character, saying, "I think Jack Ryan will be continually interesting, that the dilemmas he finds himself in will be rich stuff for myself or any other actor. The characters that are out are ones like Han Solo, who

Promoting *Regarding Henry* on *Good Morning, America* with show cohost Charles Gibson, 1991. (ABC-TV)

don't have a lot to say. They have attitude but not much more than that."

Ford continues to be selective about the parts he chooses and is candid about taking on action roles while he still can. He often cites the fact that he is already middle-aged and his opportunities to play men of adventure are dwindling. The concern seems somewhat overstated—stars like Connery and Eastwood continue to thrive in action films even though they are in their midsixties. By all accounts, Ford has a way to go in this genre—assuming the physical demands of the films and his penchant for doing his own stunts don't provide insurmountable obstacles. He professes not to fear growing old, saying, "I never think about age. I liked being young, even though I had no success. When I was thirty I could walk down any street and not be recognized. That was wealth of a sort. Then being forty held no fears, because I felt some of my best work lay ahead. Now I have no plans to fall apart."

Ironically, it was Alec Baldwin who once again inadvertently provided Harrison Ford with another super role. Ford had originally been approached to star in the big-

screen version of *The Fugitive*, based on the television series which starred David Jannsen as Dr. Richard Kimble. (Kimble, as the world—except for one obsessed lawman—knows, was an innocent man wrongfully convicted of his wife's murder. A train wreck enroute to the death house allows him to escape and to pursue a one-armed man whom he knows committed the crime.) Ford was not interested in the project at the time, and the producers then went after Alec Baldwin. When negotiations with Baldwin fell through, Ford was asked to reconsider. This time, he approved of the changes made to the script and accepted the role of Kimble. Ironically, he confessed he was about the only person over thirty-five years old in the U.S. who had never seen the television show. He was intrigued by the project for several reasons, not the least of which was a desire to work throughout 1992 so he could spend the following year relaxing with his family in Wyoming. He also felt the screenplay would make a top-notch thriller.

The physically demanding film found Ford punishing himself more than ever to attain the realism he felt was essential to the final cut. Under Andrew Davis's skillful direction, Ford gave a poignant and gritty performance that should have lead to his second nomination for Best Actor. Costar Tommy Lee Jones walked off with the award for Supporting Actor, courtesy of his entertaining scenery-chewing turn as Lieutenant Gerard, the lawman obsessed with hunting down Richard Kimble. *The Fugitive* was the hit of summer 1993.

The star's "gift" to the film industry for the summer of 1994 was his second screen appearance as Jack Ryan, in an adaptation of Tom Clancy's *Clear and Present Danger*. A complicated, highly intelligent espionage thriller which pits Ryan against a corrupt White House, the movie eclipsed its predecessor *Patriot Games* at the box office by over $40 million in North America alone. Like *Patriot Games*, however, *Clear and Present Danger* would prove to be a nightmare for the filmmakers in terms of logistical problems and the perennially grouchy Tom Clancy, who once again threw brickbats (until rewarded with another fat paycheck for screen rights to create original Jack Ryan stories for the screen). The character of Ryan is everything audiences want to see in a Harrison Ford film: the honest, brave loner combating evil at all levels.

With the arrival of the new millennium, Harrison Ford is busier than ever. Regarding the huge paychecks he is now commanding, Ford told an interviewer, "You know, milk and eggs have gone up, too. Everything has gone up. It's a reflection of the spiraling costs of doing business in any endeavor. Having said that, it is, of course, absurd the prices that are being paid these days." His 1995 comedy

Sabrina performed only mildly at the box-office, but the actor received excellent reviews. In 1996, with Melissa working with Martin Scorsese on *Kundun* and Ford about to embark on his second Big Apple location shoot in a row, the Fords decided to move their family to their New York City apartment. In an online interview, Ford said, "We brought the kids to New York and found that the schools there were very satisfying for them. For that reason, mostly, we still live there . . . but it frustrates me that I can't do repairs around the apartment."

In early 1997, Ford's box-office standing received yet another boost via the long-anticipated rerelease of the *Star Wars* trilogy. Marketed as "special editions," the films allowed a new generation to see these groundbreaking films on the big screen. The rereleases benefited from the inclusion of additional sequences (including Han Solo's meeting with Jabba the Hutt in the original *Star Wars*) and enhanced special effects, although many purists railed at what they considered to be unnecessary distractions. Twentieth Century–Fox and George Lucas anticipated significant interest in a theatrical revival of the movies, but no one expected their ultimate success. The reissues grossed more than most new films and contributed to a resurgence in the sales of *Star Wars* merchandise. Ford took the attention in stride: "I just think it's curious that there's twenty-year-old acting out there that people are going to. I'm not really interested in seeing it myself. I'm glad it still has appeal, though." Lucas is currently at work on the first trilogy of the three-trilogy *Star Wars* saga and, although he has stated that he will not be employing any of the human stars from the initial *Star Wars* films (R2D2 and C-3PO notwithstanding), don't be surprised if Ford turns up in an unbilled cameo when the first film is released in 1999.

"I still like making running, jumping, and falling down movies. When you do them well, I think it's worth your time and energy." Having said that, Ford ventured on to the 1997 drama-thriller *The Devil's Own,* a troubled production beset by rumors of tension between Ford and costar Brad Pitt. The stars denied the stories, but the production limped to completion as the budget ballooned well over the original estimate. Too dark and somber for action audiences, the movie proved to be a financial and critical disappointment. Reviewers seemed unduly influenced by the cost of the film as well as the negative word-of-mouth about the "feuding" costars. In fact, *The Devil's Own* had many merits and remains one of Ford's most underrated films.

By summer 1997, Ford was clearly back on track in terms of exercising his box-office clout. *Air Force One* was a blockbuster hit with audiences and won over critics as well. Directed by Wolfgang Petersen, whose *In the Line of Fire* provided a similarly intelligent thriller for Clint Eastwood, the film cast Ford as a charismatic president of the United States, a role he handled so convincingly that more than one writer jokingly suggested he try the role on for real. Even Pat McQueeney told *George* magazine, "I can't think of anyone in the industry who would make a better real president than Harrison. He's very stern."

By all accounts, the making of *Air Force One* was a rewarding experience all around. Coproducer Jon Shestack said, "Harrison knows how making a movie works, inside and out. He knows how to block a fight scene. He gets down alongside the cinematographer and discusses camera angles. And when the day is over, he is the first one to pop a beer and kick back with the rest of the crew." The film quickly became one of the top grossing films of the decade, proving accurate Pat McQueeney's comment that "audiences love to see Harrison as the consummate all-American hero. When they don't see him in those roles, they have a tendency not to support the film."

Following his stint as President Marshall, Ford was set to star in *The Age of Aquarius* with Kristin Scott Thomas. However, Universal canceled the project, which was to have been directed by Phil Alden Robinson, in 1997 amid concerns about the high budget and the logistics of shooting in Bosnia. Ford wisely turned down offers to appear in a sequel to *The Fugitive*, but that didn't stop a watered-down attempt to cash in on the film from materializing. *U.S. Marshals* starred Tommy Lee Jones, reprising his Oscar-winning role from *The Fugitive*, but sans Ford, the movie did only mediocre business at the box-office.

Ford's 1998 endeavor would be the romantic adventure-comedy *Six Days, Seven Nights*. For his role as the somewhat offbeat cargo pilot Quinn, Ford spiked his hair and even got an earring. "It's just something I always meant to get around to do and never did till a few months ago. I was with a couple of friends, [singer] Jimmy Buffett and [*60 Minutes* correspondent] Ed Bradley, having lunch, and I realized they both had earrings. So, I just said, 'That's it, c'mon, let's go and get the ear pierced.' " One wonders what Indiana Jones would think; yes, there is an Indiana Jones IV project being bandied about. Ford told the New York *Daily News* in 1997: "I'd love to play Indiana Jones again. It'll take a while for a script to develop, and then George and Steven and I have to get together on a time. But we certainly all have the ambition to do it. . . . We've strung this thing out so many years that signs of Indiana's age are apparent. I'd like to see us sneak up into the fifties, perhaps. That's got some potential." Rumor has it that the next Indy film revolves around Jones stumbling upon the lost continent of Atlantis.

Ford continues to make public appearances but only occasionally. Aside from publicizing his latest films on the talk-show circuit, he did participate in a documentary profile about his life on the E! cable network in 1998. The previous year, he made a rare public appearance at Lincoln Center in New York City for a tribute to his old friend Sean Connery. The notoriously shy Ford was said to be reluctant to speak in front of the audience, but when he did, his low-key approach proved to be refreshing. He cited the fact that neither he nor Connery overstated the importance of acting, saying that they simply learned their lines, did their best, and went home every evening. Of his chosen profession, he said, "Hey, it ain't brain surgery!" as the audience roared.

On the personal front, Ford admits to devoting time to flying his plane and playing tennis. "I never did any physical exercise till I was forty-five and then I realized I was getting kind of creaky. So I started skiing and playing tennis. I really love tennis and I play it all over the world with different pros. I never play socially because it seems like a waste of time. I like to get out there and work on skills and run around and sweat." Today, sneaking up on the age of sixty, and sporting the bumps, bruises, and scars of more than twenty years in the action film business, Ford is in better shape than many men half his age. However, Ford reveals he's an amateur photographer and likes to ride motorcycles, but regrettably is no longer doing his therapeutic carpentry. "I have to pay for it like everybody else now. I've lost all my tool skills. . . . I don't have time to work with wood anymore, and I've lost my chops. It's like a skill that you lose. Like a musician loses his skill if he doesn't practice every day."

With Sean Connery on the set of *Indiana Jones and the Last Crusade* in 1989. (LucasFilm)

Pat McQueeney described Ford's values when it comes to choosing his projects: "When Harrison does a movie, it's like a big honeymoon. Everybody has a good time. But he's extremely careful about whom he gets on the set. If he has heard that a director is mean or is mean to women, for example, he won't work with that person—no matter how good the project is. He doesn't want to spend his time in a hostile or contentious environment. His attitude is: It's just too hard to spend all those months of your life working that intimately with someone you are not totally in sync with."

Ford's faith in McQueeney's judgment speaks volumes about his personal values. He knows she believed in him when no one else did and has remained loyal to her as well. Both he and McQueeney admit to some friendly but spirited debating over specific projects, but Ford maintains he prefers that to having someone "try to coddle me or kiss my ass or misdirect me." In an 1993 interview, he said, "[Pat] is no longer just my manager. Pat has been my agent for the last five years. I was with a monster agency once. I rode up on the elevator with three guys who were supposed to be my agents. By the time we got to the top floor of the building, they still hadn't figured out who I was. So I never got off the elevator. I just went right back down. . . . Without minimizing the importance of anybody else, I've always made my own decisions. Sometimes Pat agreed with them, and sometimes she didn't. She didn't see my attraction to *The Fugitive*, didn't get it. We argue about stuff all the time. I don't need a rubber stamp or someone to continually check against."

Despite being a major star for three decades, Ford is still growing as an actor and as a person. He is still hungry and looks forward to new challenges. In a 1994 interview with *GQ*, he admitted, "I have had scientifically provable luck from time to time. Being in the right place at the right time and then *doing the right thing*. You cannot get where I got without luck. Bags of it. . . . You can be as good as I am or better. You can be incredibly more attractive and charming and capable and still be shit out of luck. The only thing I have done that is not mitigated by luck, diminished by good fortune, is that I *persisted*. And other people gave up."

He told *Playboy* in 1988: "I don't have any rules. I just try not to be in films with a point of view with which I'm not sympathetic. I'm not interested in films that have nothing to say. I can't say I wouldn't, for instance, play a Nazi war criminal. I would do anything if it made a good point, had significance. I haven't ruled out musicals, either. Maybe I could be a musical Nazi war criminal. . . . It's a thought."

Ford sees some parallels between his real-life persona and the characters he's portrayed on-screen: "Han Solo is a cynical kind of guy with a heart of gold, if you will. There's a little of that in me. The character in *Hanover Street*, I played a real romantic, there's a touch of that in me. *The Frisco Kid* was basically a person that couldn't turn somebody down. A guy who just wasn't too smart, but was generous of heart. One thing that I think

Han and Jabba, in the restored scene from the *Star Wars* rerelease (Lucasfilm Ltd)

was most prominent in Indiana Jones was his tenaciousness, his unwillingness to give up, and I am tenacious. *Witness*: he's again a sentimental person who wants very much to be a part of life, a part of community, but he's an outsider, a loner."

Ford is clearly established as one of today's action/adventure icons—despite the fact that he downplays being described as such. Certainly, few other contemporary actors have had so many certifiable hits. His few box-office failures (*The Mosquito Coast*, *Frantic*, *Regarding Henry*) were still artistic successes, and by the mid-1990s, Harrison Ford seems to be a man who has succeeded in achieving the goals he set for himself as a young actor. By all accounts, he is the craftsman he

describes himself as. In terms of his legacy, he favors the simplistic, basic principles he has tried to adhere to throughout his life: "I want my colleagues and fans to say of me: 'He understands the true value of life, the importance of traditional values. He didn't lose touch with reality, like most people who head off to seek fame and fortune in Hollywood.' "

In terms of regrets, he does confess to one goal he has yet to accomplish: "I always wanted to look older than I am, and I always wanted to be bald. I love what it looks like. It's the coolest thing. You don't have to fuck with hair!"

So says Indiana Jones.

1

Dead Heat on a Merry-Go-Round (1966)

"You ain't got it, kid!"

—Studio executive assessing Harrison Ford's potential as a movie star

CAST:

Eli Kotch: James Coburn; *Inger Knudson*: Camilla Sparv; *Eddie Hart*: Aldo Ray; *Frieda*: Nina Wayne; *Milo Stewart*: Robert Webber; *Margaret Kirby*: Rose Marie; *Alfred Morgan*: Todd Armstrong; *Dr. Marian Hague*: Marian Moses; *Paul Feng*: Michael Strong; *Miles Fisher*: Severn Darden; *Jack Balter*: James Westerfield; *Bellboy*: Harrison Ford.

CREDITS:

Director and Writer: Bernard Girard; *Producer*: Carter De Haven; *Director of Photography*: Lionel Lindon; *Editor*: William Lyon; *Art Director*: Walter M. Simonds; *Set Decorator*: Frank Tuttle; *Music*: Stu Phillips. *Running time*: 107 minutes. Released by Columbia Pictures.

Harrison Ford's screen debut was an inconspicuous one for the future box-office king. Unlike today, when heretofore unknown actors are prepackaged and marketed as instant superstars (e.g., Steven Seagal), Ford entered the industry in the traditional way—by playing a bit part as a contract player, albeit in a major theatrical release for Columbia Pictures. *Dead Heat on a Merry-Go-Round* was a starring vehicle for James Coburn, who only recently had graduated to the (then) relatively exclusive group of actors who could command their names above the title. Coburn had also struggled for success the traditional way, scoring with memorable supporting roles in *The Magnificent Seven* (1960), *Charade* (1963), and *The Great Escape* (1963). He reached star status in 1966, playing the title role in *Our Man Flint*. Eager to capitalize on Coburn's popularity, Columbia made the actor's charisma the central theme of the marketing campaign for *Dead Heat on a Merry-Go-Round*.

Coburn was cast as a charming but ruthless con man named Eli Kotch, who seduces a female psychiatrist pivotal in getting him paroled. He immediately plans his most ambitious caper ever: using the confusion of the Soviet premier's visit to pull a bank robbery at Los Angeles International Airport. Along the way, Kotch beds numerous pliable beauties, adopting various guises in his elaborate plan to commit the perfect crime. The key to his scheme is Inger Knudson (Camilla Sparv), a loyal maid to

Original pressbook advertisement. (Columbia Pictures)

a rich heiress. When Kotch goes so far as to marry Inger to insure the success of his scheme, he finds his new bride as gullible and naive as his former conquests. Enlisting a small group of professional criminals, Kotch narrowly pulls off the ingenious play. The film ends with an amusing and ironic twist that indicates Kotch may not have had the last laugh after all.

Dead Heat on a Merry-Go-Round is a lightweight but generally engrossing crime thriller that avoids any hint of violence or brutality by concentrating on affable James Coburn. He is constantly engaging, and one can only wonder why Hollywood failed to utilize his considerable talents in any significant ways in the years that followed. Bernard Girard's script has more than a few holes and some occasional padding, but his direction is impressive, particularly in the climatic getaway sequence. The movie has a distinctive midsixties look about it: a jazzy musical score that would be equally at home in an episode of *Family Affair*, a patronizing attitude toward beautiful women (they are all brainless sexpots who instantly succumb to Coburn's needlessly complicated seduction attempts), and a casual attitude about sex that recalls those days when fornicating did not mandate that both partners wear scuba suits for protection. You know you're going back quite some time when Rose Marie (of *The Dick Van Dyke Show*) was a hot enough property to merit

"Brando-like" special billing for a cameo appearance. (Coburn even beds *her*; luckily, this is merely alluded to, and the viewer is spared the carnage.)

Midway through the film, Harrison Ford appears for less than one minute as a bellboy who inadvertently assists one of Coburn's schemes. Looking a bit nervous, Ford adds a bumbling quality to the role—making it a bit more noticeable than it deserved to be. Still, it would have taken Nostradamus to foresee a blockbuster career in film based on Ford's few lines of dialogue. He did not impress the Columbia brass with his one day's work on the film. Ford is fond of recalling how he was chastised by a studio executive who said, "Sit down, kid. I want to tell you a story. The first time Tony Curtis was in a movie, he delivered a bag of groceries. We took one look at him and knew he was a movie star. But you ain't got it, kid." Ford pondered the criticism and responded with courageous cynicism about the Tony Curtis analogy: "Gee, I thought you were supposed to look at him and say, '*There* is a grocery boy!'" Ford later explained, "It didn't occur to me until years later that what they wanted me to do was act like a movie star." He says that his screen debut "made absolutely no impression at all. Not a particularly uplifting experience." This incident early in his career seems to have had a profound influence on Ford and the way he works. He shuns stardom and most of its trappings,

Although he was on-screen only briefly in *Dead Heat*, Ford's film debut did result in the studio including this publicity shot in press kits. (Columbia Pictures)

"Just fills the space between a frisky title and a tricky TV-comedy ending, but doesn't fill it with any revels that require a viewer's complete attention."

TIME

"A briskly convoluted and easily spinning crime jape that comes off nearly all the way. Personally to the fore is James Coburn, already launched in the James Bond school of daredeviltry in Our Man Flint. *He has himself here a clever writer-director, Bernard Girard, who breezily spins out a colorfully persuasive trail of incident and characters—but forget story credibility."*

—NEW YORK TIMES GUIDE TO MOVIES ON TV

choosing instead to devote himself entirely to the role he is playing, not his celebrity status.

Dead Heat on a Merry-Go-Round (the intriguing but meaningless title refers to a play written by Coburn's character) cost $2 million to make and was not particularly successful. Critics were also lukewarm, although—astonishingly—Ford was cited in one notice which mentioned he "came from a show business family and is making his way to screen fame." In 1994 during a Ford appearance on *The Tonight Show*, host Jay Leno jokingly announced that "my favorite Harrison Ford film is *Dead Heat on a Merry-Go-Round*." He then proceeded to screen Ford's scene as the bellboy. The audience roared with laughter as a visibly embarrassed Ford good-naturedly all but disowned the film. He need not have. *Dead Heat* is not a work of art, but neither is it a film to be ashamed of.

Aldo Ray (*left*) and Coburn pose as lawman and con man in their elaborate escape plan from L.A. airport. (Columbia Pictures)

©CPC-LUV-126

2

LUV (1967)

"I never could understand why I was getting the break until I learned enough to see that I was useful to them. I was doing the work."

CAST:
Harry Berlin: Jack Lemmon; *Milt Manville*: Peter Falk; *Ellen Manville*: Elaine May; *Linda*: Nina Wayne; *Attorney Goodhart*: Eddie Mayehoff; *Doyle*: Paul Hartman; *Vandergrist*: Severn Darden; *Motorist*: Harrison Ford.

CREDITS:
Director: Clive Donner; *Producer*: Martin Manulis; *Screenplay*: Elliott Baker; *Based on the play by* Murray Schisgal; *Director of Photography*: Ernest Laszlo; *Production Designer*: Albert Brenner; *Set Decorator*: Frank Tuttle; *Editor*: Harold F. Kress; *Music*: Gerry Mulligan. *Running time*: 95 minutes. Released by Columbia Pictures.

A "madcap" moment from the frantically unfunny *Luv*. Falk is obviously heading for the border, while Lemmon appears to have just read the film's reviews. (Columbia Pictures)

A few notable exceptions notwithstanding, the decade of the sixties presented a multitude of cultural irritants. Aside from the obvious examples (Tiny Tim, Nehru jackets, *My Mother the Car*, Mrs. Miller, and George Lincoln Rockwell), there is the film adaptation of the Broadway play *Luv*. If a Hall of Fame existed for the most obnoxious comedies of that decade, *Luv* would hold a special place of honor. Murray Schisgal's hip play, which examined the intermingled sexual frustrations of two very bizarre couples, was a success when it premiered on Broadway in 1964 and ultimately was translated into nineteen different languages and presented in twenty-six different countries. Additionally, a virtual cottage industry of stock company performances performed it in the U.S. Whatever charm the comedy may have had is not apparent in the disastrous film version, released in 1967. While the American public was preoccupied with the war in Vietnam, the biggest bombs could be found in theaters showing prints of *Luv*. The pretentious title is explained in the studio pressbook: "The film's title *Luv* is used by the play's author as a protest against today's misuse and commercialization of the real world 'love,' to the point where it is now less of an emotion than it is a commodity." (True, perhaps, but wanna bet author Schisgal "luv'd" the fat paycheck he received for the very commercial film version of his play?)

The nonstory finds a despondent Jack Lemmon about

to commit suicide, due to his disillusionment with women and his inability to find true romance. Before he can jump from the Manhattan Bridge, he is saved by his old college buddy, Peter Falk, a milquetoasty business executive who moonlights as a junk (he calls it "bric-a-brack") dealer. Falk brings Lemmon home to meet his wife Elaine May, an intellectual who is the antithesis of Falk. Their marriage has deteriorated, and May constantly complains about their lack of sex, to the extent that she has diagrammed their decreasing rate of frequency on a chart worthy of an I.B.M. boardroom. Falk schemes to get a divorce by making May fall in love with Lemmon, so he can then marry his sexy girlfriend (Nina Wayne). The bizarre plan works all too well. Lemmon and May fall in love atop a ferris wheel (a yawn-inspiring cliche even in 1967) and marry. Falk weds Wayne, but the problems are just beginning. May finds Lemmon to be—well, a lemon, a chronic hypochondriac who has even less of a sex drive than her previous husband. Meanwhile, Falk finds that beyond her stunning looks, his new bride is a lazy airhead. In the film's "ironic" climax, Falk and May realize they're still crazy over each other and scheme to get divorced from their new spouses—by causing them to fall in love with other people. That they succeed is hardly a surprise, especially when the script allows enough unbelievable twists of fate and coincidences to rival a science fiction epic.

Given the talented cast, it is hard to believe there is nothing of merit to emerge from this promising project. Yet this is precisely the notable achievement to which director Clive Donner and screenwriter Elliott Baker can lay claim. Donner had been hired to helm *Luv* on the basis of his 1965 counterculture comedy *What's New, Pussycat?* In that film, he was blessed with an eclectic cast—including Peter Sellers, Peter O'Toole, and Woody Allen, to name a few—as engagingly nutty as the script

itself. With *Luv*, Donner attempts to recreate the *Pussycat* zaniness, but the end result is ludicrous, because here his lead actors are generally associated with "the Establishment." Watching Lemmon and Falk banter about like overage hippies is a painful experience. Equally uninspiring is the casting of Elaine May as Falk's frustrated wife. May became a sensation in the early sixties with partner Mike Nichols, creating some of the best comedic set pieces of the era. When the act broke up, Nichols stayed in the public eye and prospered, while May dropped out of sight for several years to concentrate on writing. She ended her self-imposed seclusion in 1966 to make her big-screen debut in Carl Reiner's *Enter Laughing*. Her second feature film would be *Luv*, and although she performs gamely, she is completely miscast, as are her costars.

WHAT IS LUV?
LUV IS WHEN YOUR HEART GOES PITTER-PATTER, PITTER-PATTER
LUV IS A NEW MOVIE ♥ WHO'S IN LUV? JACK LEMMON'S IN LUV
WHO'S IN LUV WITH JACK LEMMON? PETER FALK & ELAINE MAY
LUV IS SUGGESTED FOR THE MATURE AUDIENCE
WHERE IS LUV? LUV IS WHERE YOU FIND IT ♥ LUV IS JUST
AROUND THE CORNER ♥ ANYONE FOR LUV?
LUV IS A FUNNY THING ♥ LUV ♥ TRY AND MAKE IT

COLUMBIA PICTURES Presents
JACK LEMMON
IN A MARTIN MANULIS PRODUCTION
LUV
Co-starring
PETER FALK | ELAINE MAY

From the hilarious success that cracked up Broadway!

NINA WAYNE and EDDIE MAYEHOFF   Screenplay by ELLIOTT BAKER | Based on the play by MURRAY SCHISGAL | Produced on the stage by CLAIRE NICHTERN | Music by GERRY MULLIGAN | GORDON CONNELL
Produced by MARTIN MANULIS | Directed by CLIVE DONNER | PANAVISION® | EASTMAN COLOR | Suggested For Mature Audiences | C

Original pressbook advertisement. (Columbia Pictures)

The role of Harry Berlin must certainly go down as the most irritating and obnoxious screen character Jack Lemmon has ever portrayed. He meanders through the entire film in a shabby state of attire, screaming epithets about the senselessness of life and undergoing psychosomatic illnesses which leave him unable to see, speak, or hear for extended periods of time. (Not coincidentally, these are the only moments in which the character is tolerable.) The following year, Lemmon would play Felix Unger in *The Odd Couple* and somehow make *that* potentially nauseating character hilarious. However, the script for *Luv* does not provide him with a single funny line or situation. The story requires that Lemmon overact, and he does so to wild abandon. Within minutes, we begin to regret that his old friend has talked him out of suicide. (If only he knew Dr. Kevorkian.) Lemmon does not have a monopoly on hammy acting, however. Peter Falk overdoes the sleazy side of his character, making him a mere caricature who is impossible to relate to (Lemmon and

Falk had previously yelled at each other again throughout *The Great Race*.) Nina Wayne, who in those less than politically correct times would have been labeled "a blond bombshell," manages to come across the best, if only because her mousy voice and stunning looks come naturally and don't require the manic, overdone, scene-stealing techniques of her fellow cast members. She merely has to strip down to her bathing suit, which she does in the finale—thereby providing literally the only reason to struggle through to the irritating and unbelievable climax.

For all of its sixties-era hip dialogue (including dated references to lesbianism and gay sex), *Luv* is never believable enough to make us care about its characters (who are slightly less lovable than *The Dirty Dozen*) or outrageous enough to allow us to just suspend belief and sit back and wallow in its eccentricities. One almost wishes for the relative pleasures of *What's New, Pussycat?* and *Casino Royale* (also released in 1967). With those epics of the "mod" era, the filmmakers realized the scripts were beyond any hope of making sense, so they dispensed with any hint of reality and concentrated on the bizarre comedic talents of the actors, turning them loose to improvise. With *Luv*, it's as though Columbia Pictures wanted to make a counterculture film for Wall Street executives.

Harrison Ford appears in an ever-so-brief sequence about one-third of the way through, in which his car is struck by Elaine May's in a fender-bender. Sporting a beret and a furry vest and made up to look like a hippie (or at least a middle-aged movie executive's idea of a hippie), Ford emerges from his car, walks over to May's vehicle, says "Hi," and takes out his frustration by punching passenger Jack Lemmon in the nose before driving away. This leaves the viewer jealous, wishing *he* was the one busting this annoying character in the snoot. Ford was under contract with Columbia, and this role followed his equally unimpressive part in *Dead Heat on a Merry-Go-Round*. While he acknowledged he was not yet leading-man material, this was not quite the career he had envisioned upon becoming a contract player. He had even less to do in *Luv* than in *Dead Heat*. Not coincidentally, *Luv* reunited him with two other cast members from the latter film: Severn Darden and Nina Wayne, who were probably also under Columbia contract. As in the first film, however, he never appears on-screen with either.

The advance word of mouth on *Luv* was that it was a

dud. To spark public interest, the Columbia marketing department came up with a number of proposals for publicity gimmicks to help theater owners promote the film. One such "brainstorm" suggested working with a local ice cream parlor to create "The Luv Sundae"—"it's too much for any one person, but perfect for two!" Another gimmick

Ford's appearance as a hippie in *Luv* was mercifully brief. (Columbia Pictures)

entailed getting a theater employee to dress like Jack Lemmon and walk around the neighborhood with a sandwich sign promoting the film. (Just how one "dresses like Jack Lemmon" is never explained.) Other tips highlighted sexpot Nina Wayne's performance. Since Ms. Wayne's ample cleavage is displayed in several sequences, including one in which she stands on her head, theater owners were advised to "offer guest admissions to all girls coming into the theater who will stand on their heads on a pillow in the lobby for three or four minutes." (We're not making this up, folks).

Luv was not released, as the old joke goes—it escaped. The film was immediately denounced by critics and rejected by audiences, despite Lemmon's generally loyal following at the box office. In a noble attempt to promote the movie, Lemmon said, "I've never done anything *remotely* like it in the past!" The reason he remains a respected and honored actor today is that he had the good sense not to do anything remotely like it again. He also described the movie (in the jargon of the times) as "a

wild, way-out gas!" Today, much like the era in which it was released, the film still bears a resemblance to gas—because *Luv* stinks.

Reviews

"Luv . . . has no heart. . . . Jack Lemmon wasn't meant to be Harry. He may look like a loser— Bowery thin with rheumy eyes. But looking isn't enough, and trying so hard to be funny in the part is too much."

—KATHLEEN CARROLL, *NEW YORK DAILY NEWS*

"It has Jack Lemmon staggering dumbly through the surrealistic role of a consistently frustrated loser who is kept from jumping off the Manhattan Bridge by the chance intervention of an old schoolmate, played moronically by Peter Falk. And it has Elaine May prissing haughtily as the latter's know-it-all wife, who is fobbed off on Lemmon to clear the way for Falk to another "luv." The three of them clomp and clown broadly . . . [and] tend to become monotonous, especially the blowsy Mr. Lemmon and the starchily dead-panned Miss May."

—BOSLEY CROWTHER, *NEW YORK TIMES*

"Of the three principals, only Elaine May as the wife is well cast, but she is pitching in a game with no catchers. Peter Falk is too simian and heavy for the popinjay part of her wayward husband, and as a Jewish urban type, Jack Lemmon is frantic without being funny. Luv is too good a comedy to die this way: people who have never seen it will do better to find a road company of the play."

—TIME

Jack Lemmon (*here with Peter Falk*) climbs a lamppost to escape the heartaches of love. Audiences wanted to climb a tree to escape the heartache of *Luv*. (Columbia Pictures)

3

A Time for Killing (1967)

(a.k.a. *The Long Ride Home*)

"I needed a lot more experience before I was worthy of better parts, but you still have to work over your head a little bit."

CAST:

Maj. Charles Wolcott: Glenn Ford; *Emily Biddle*: Inger Stevens; *Captain Bentley*: George Hamilton; *Blue Lake*: Paul Petersen; *Luther*: Max Baer Jr; *Billy Cat*: Timothy Carey; *Lieutenant Prudessing*: Todd Armstrong; *Sergeant Cleehan*: Kenneth Tobey; *Corporal Darling*: Richard X. Slattery; *Sgt. Dan Way*: [Harry] Dean Stanton; *Lieutenant Shaffer*: Harrison Ford.

CREDITS:

Director: Phil Karlson; *Producer:* Harry Joe Brown; *Screenplay:* Halsted Welles; *Director of Photography:* Kenneth Peach; *Editor:* Roy Livingston; *Music:* Van Alexander and Mundell Lowe. *Running Time:* 88 minutes. Released by Columbia Pictures.

Harrison Ford continued to pay his dues as a working actor, slowly increasing his visibility in feature films. In *A Time for Killing* (originally released as *The Long Ride Home*), Ford had to use facial expressions to compensate for lack of character development, not to mention a scarcity of lines. He plays a young Union officer ordered by a sadistic commander to execute a Confederate prisoner. The resulting action causes the other prisoners to riot and escape. Lead by a sadist of their own (George Hamilton), the Rebs succeed in kidnapping Inger Stevens, fiancée of the Yankee major (Glenn Ford) who is pursuing the renegades. Fanatical to the Southern cause, Hamilton doesn't tell his men when he learns the war is over. He also rapes Inger as a way of humiliating Glenn Ford. However, the stalwart major reacts upon learning of his betrothed's violation with about as much urgency as if she had stubbed her big toe on a cactus. Ultimately, she humiliates the major into leading his men into Mexico to avenge her abuse. (Like Hamilton, she neglects to mention the minor detail that the Civil War is officially over.) The resulting battle leaves most of the combatants dead. Party pooper that he is, Hamilton uses his dying words to tell the major that Stevens has caused the senseless deaths of his men to get personal revenge. The downbeat ending finds a dejected Glenn Ford abandoning the disgraced Stevens.

If Sigmund Freud had written a Western, the result would be something like *A Time for Killing*. Admittedly a B Western, the film has the distinction of at least attempt-

41

ing to be something more. However, the script suffers from making the only interesting characters the least important. It is never clearly defined just what Glenn Ford and Inger Stevens see in each other, since they bicker like pioneer versions of Ralph and Alice Kramden, not to mention the fact that he could pass himself off as her father-in-law. Equally mysterious is George Hamilton's obsessive hatred for Glenn Ford, whose character, in turn, is given absolutely no motivation or background, thereby making the central hero of the film little more than a cliché. Save for a few lighthearted moments, the film is unremittingly grim and made even grimmer by the efficient but downbeat performances of the cast. Bad guy Hamilton tries to breathe some life into his on-screen persona, but his character's mood changes are as inconsistent as his Southern accent.

Curiously, the liveliest performance of the film comes from Max Baer Jr, on hiatus from his role as Jethro Bodeen on *The Beverly Hillbillies*. While he always professed to hate that character, Baer inexplicably plays the role of a psychopathic Confederate soldier with many of the same mannerisms, reminding one of a cross between Jethro and Charles Manson. He looks as though he's hankerin' for a slice of Granny's possum pie. However, when Baer is on-screen, things *do* liven up. In what might be described as a perverse Old West version of *Battle of the Network Stars*, the film presents the dubious coup of showing one TV sitcom idol assassinate another, in the sequence in which Baer murders Paul Petersen of *The Donna Reed Show*!

Original pressbook advertisement. (Columbia Pictures)

Still billed as "Harrison J. Ford," here in the role of the ill-fated Lieutenant Shaffer. (Columbia Pictures)

As in his previous screen appearances, Harrison Ford (billed here as "Harrison J. Ford") was given little to work with in his quest to make an impression. He does get to emote a bit in the film's best sequence, wherein he plays the nerve-racked officer forced to preside over a firing squad (giving Ford the challenge of making his one line—"FIRE!"—sound memorable). His character is later killed in an ambush, and the script does not even provide him with the opportunity for an interesting death scene. Probably just as well, as he is "offed" by ol' Jethro Bodeen himself, albeit out of camera range. Nevertheless, this was Harrison Ford's largest big-screen appearance to date. While *A Time for Killing* will not rank among his best-remembered movies, it was not a film to be ashamed of. Resourceful director Phil Karlson manages to occasionally rise above the clichés, which often threaten to pile higher than the majestic mountain ranges. The script is never laughable or dull, as were so many other modestly budgeted Westerns of the era, and the cast performs gamely. The movie was released as the second feature on double bills and therefore never got an opportunity to make an impression at the box office. However, for Harrison Ford, it was another precious opportunity to hone his craft as an actor.

The film was shot on location in Kanab, Utah (a popular locale for Westerns), in an expeditious and efficient manner. The main obstacle encountered was

Inger Stevens informs fiancé Glenn Ford of her molestation at the hands of escaped prisoner George Hamilton. (Columbia Pictures)

a recent drought, which posed a problem when filming a key sequence along a riverbed. The stream had gone dry, forcing the filmmakers to import thousands of gallons of water in tanker trucks from Tuscon. Director Karlson had one opportunity to get the shot right, as the mini–tidal wave was unleashed to simulate a flowing brook. He succeeded, but the same cannot be said for Columbia's marketing department. Its hokey campaign to promote *A Time for Killing* rested largely on the perceived uncontrolled hysteria to see Glenn Ford in his 100th motion picture! The film's pressbook suggests such innovative promotional schemes as a contest in which participants would submit essays titled "Why I Want to See Glenn Ford's 100th Starring Film, *A Time for Killing*." As if this were not enough, a "one-two" punch would maximize the movie's appeal to female audiences by stressing

Lieutenant Shaffer (*Ford*) reluctantly follows orders to execute a prisoner. (Columbia Pictures)

Inger Stevens's role as a nurse from Massachusetts. Exhibitors were advised of the following plan to insure long lines at the box office: "New England theatres may not find it feasible, but women from Massachusetts may prove rare in some areas, and therefore worth special attention. Especially so, if a local ex-Massachusetts girl is active in the community."

Anemic publicity campaigns aside, however, one could do worse than give this offbeat Western a chance. It doesn't always achieve its noble goals, but at least it makes an earnest attempt to strive for them.

Reviews

"Fairly savage western with something to say about the corruption of war."
　—Halliwell's Film Guide

"Director Karlson has done some good minor films in the past; this isn't one of them."
　—Leonard Maltin's Movie and Video Guide

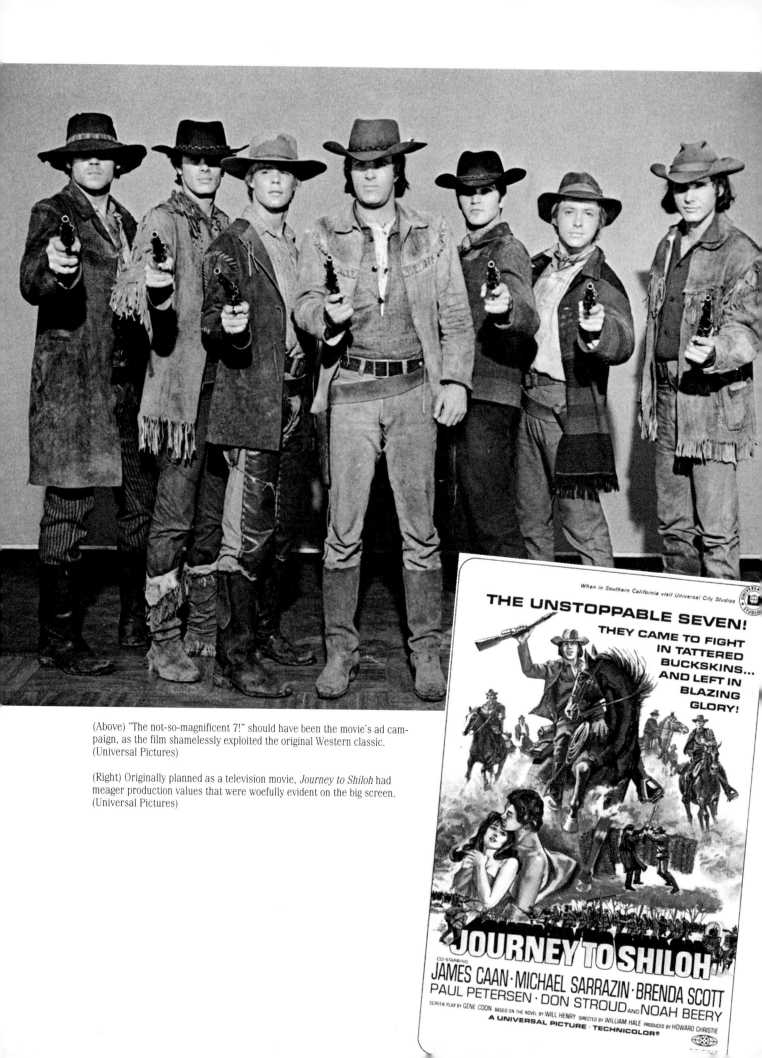

(Above) "The not-so-magnificent 7!" should have been the movie's ad campaign, as the film shamelessly exploited the original Western classic. (Universal Pictures)

(Right) Originally planned as a television movie, *Journey to Shiloh* had meager production values that were woefully evident on the big screen. (Universal Pictures)

When in Southern California visit Universal City Studios

THE UNSTOPPABLE SEVEN!

THEY CAME TO FIGHT IN TATTERED BUCKSKINS... AND LEFT IN BLAZING GLORY!

JOURNEY TO SHILOH

CO-STARRING

JAMES CAAN · MICHAEL SARRAZIN · BRENDA SCOTT
PAUL PETERSEN · DON STROUD AND **NOAH BEERY**

SCREEN PLAY BY GENE COON BASED ON THE NOVEL BY WILL HENRY DIRECTED BY WILLIAM HALE PRODUCED BY HOWARD CHRISTIE

A UNIVERSAL PICTURE · TECHNICOLOR®

4

Journey to Shiloh (1968)

While under contract to Universal, Harrison Ford landed a role in the studio's 1968 Civil War "epic" *Journey to Shiloh*. The film might have been more appropriately titled *The Magnificent Seven Go to K-mart*, as this low-budget horse opera attempts to emulate the 1960 western classic—right down to referring to the heroes in the advertisements as "The Unstoppable Seven!" The movie teamed Ford with a number of other up-and-coming young actors in an often pretentious "message" film whose noble intentions are consistently undercut by its low production values. (It was originally slated to be a TV movie.) The plot traces a group of idealistic young men from the South who anticipate the glories of battle, only to find disillusionment and tragedy when they are subjected to the slaughter at the infamous battle of Shiloh—one of the bloodiest engagements in the Civil War.

Universal obviously was inspired by the success of the original *Magnificent Seven* (and its tepid sequels), so for no other apparent reason, they chose seven actors to round out the group of would-be Confederate heroes. "They came to fight in buckskins—and left in blazing glory!" screamed the one-sheet poster for the film. Unfortunately, the actors' real fate was somewhat less glorious. The only substantial roles were given to James Caan as the group's de facto leader and to Michael Sarrazin as his right-hand man. Paul Petersen (yes, of *The Donna Reed Show*!) plays a more tarnished version of the Horst Bucholz role from *The Magnificent Seven*.

Harrison Ford is buried among the rest of the cast members, playing second fiddle to Jan Michael Vincent (billed here as Michael Vincent) and Don Stroud.

Unlike his costars, however, Ford isn't given the slightest opportunity to develop his character and has virtually no lines. He is used as the cinematic equivalent of ballast and serves only to flesh out the group to that "magnificent" number of seven. The script doesn't even allow him the dignity of a memorable death scene. (Although that may have been a blessing, considering Jan Michael Vincent's drawn out "speechifying" during his grand exit.) Ford and several other minor stars are simply explained away by saying they died tragically in battle. Naturally, the real reason for Ford's offscreen death was that the studio did not want to incur the cost of an additional action sequence—a rip-off unequaled until the 1977 pseudoepic *MacArthur*, in which the entire battle of Inchon is represented by having flashing lights reflect on Gregory Peck's face.

Ford's character was anything but memorable, although it did afford him his most extensive screen time to date. (Universal Pictures)

Clearly Universal was using low budget vehicles like *Journey to Shiloh* as a training ground to develop talent it had under contract. Occasionally the strategy worked. Don Stroud and Tisha Sterling, who both appear in the film, would both score with fine performances later that year in the Clint Eastwood thriller *Coogan's Bluff*. However, the studio's attempts to groom Paul Petersen into a method actor did not pay off. Petersen, who appeared briefly along with Harrison Ford in 1967's *A Time for Killing*, is given a meaty role here, but his sitcom background makes for negligible training for the required dramatics. Had Ford been given the same role, he undoubtedly would have brought a brooding intensity to the part. However, the studio continued to waste his talents in meaningless roles that made it impossible for the frustrated young actor to prove his talent.

Journey to Shiloh is notable for providing James Caan with one of his first starring roles. But even Caan's charisma and larger-than-life personality are all but buried under a bizarre and distracting "hippie"-style jet-

In one of the film's more poignant moments, Caan and his men are repulsed by the hanging of a runaway slave (a sequence often cut from TV broadcasts). (Universal Pictures)

James Caan tries to keep Brenda Scott from seeing that he is wearing the worst toupee in the history of film. (Universal Pictures)

black hairpiece. Indeed, the hirsute chapeau that adorns his cranium makes Caan resemble a cross between a frontier Elvis impersonator and Peter Sellers in *What's New, Pussycat*? Until he actually removes his ten-gallon hat, one might presume that the "rug" was simply sewn into it.

The film at least attempts to explore a few social issues, such as the inhumanity of slavery. In the most poignant scene in the picture, Caan and his naive group are conned into returning a runaway slave to the "safety" of his former owner. Later, they find the man has been murdered as an example to other runaways. As well intentioned as this particular scene may have been, the film suffers from treating blacks in the typical "white man's burden" style beloved by the Hollywood of old. In one particularly patronizing sequence, an elderly slave drones on about how happy he is on the plantation, thanks to the kindness of his good ol' "massa." The character makes Step 'N Fetchit look like Ice-T.

Journey to Shiloh was filmed entirely on the Universal backlot, which explains why the film has all the sweep and grandeur of an episode of *F Troop*. Because of budget constraints, there is a conspicuous lack of battle scenes. Those which do appear are lifted in their entirety from Universal's own Civil War film *Shenandoah*, which was released a scant three years earlier. Even this unimaginative practice is poorly accomplished, as we swear we counted the same soldier firing the same cannon at least five times. Aside from the clips from *Shenandoah*, the entire battle of Shiloh is reduced to a few stray bombs exploding among the principals.

To compensate for the lack of grandeur, the story centers on the trials and tribulations of the individual soldiers in the aftermath of the battle. In one presumably moving sequence, the Confederates ask a wounded Yankee to lead them in prayer. Although the man is gutshot and dying, once he gets behind the pulpit, he starts to preach with enough vim and vigor to put Jimmy Swaggart to shame. Such miraculous recoveries were not possible for the film itself, however, and *Journey to Shiloh* remains mostly notable for its unintentional laughs. (Pay special attention to the folksy title song—the most embarrassing western recording since Ben Cartwright and his boys were forced to sing the lyrics to "Bonanza" in the show's premiere episode.)

Coincidentally or not, the cast of *Journey to Shiloh* did emulate the cast of *The Magnificent Seven* in one respect: several of the actors went on to varying degrees of stardom. The earlier film helped catapult Steve McQueen, Charles Bronson, Robert Vaughn, and James Coburn to leading-man status. Among the *Shiloh* cast, Caan would gain fame and fortune in 1972 with his role as Sonny in *The Godfather*, Jan Michael Vincent would become a heartthrob in the 1970s, Don Stroud would emerge as a well-known character actor. It is doubtful that appearing in *Shiloh* played a significant role in these success stories, however. Harrison Ford would continue to suffer the frustration of seeing his peers gain increasingly better roles while he watched from the sidelines.

Reviews

"Limp Civil War programmer about young Texans anxious to engage in battle. Veterans Rex Ingram, John Doucette, and Noah Beery are lost in the jumble."

—Leonard Maltin, TV Movies And Video Guide

47

5

Getting Straight (1970)

"I was given tiny spaces to fill. Nothing where you could take space. Maybe they were right. I probably wasn't ready."

CAST:
Harry Bailey: Elliott Gould; *Jan*: Candice Bergen; *Nick*: Robert F. Lyons; *Dr. Wilhunt*: Jeff Corey; *Ellis*: Max Julien; *Dr. Kasper*: Cecil Kellaway; *Vandenburg*: Jon Lormer; *Lysander*: Leonard Stone; *Wade*: William Bramley; *Judy Kramer*: Jeannie Berlin; *Jake*: Harrison Ford.

CREDITS:
Director and Producer: Richard Rush; *Screenplay*: Robert Kaufman; *Based on the novel by* Ken Kolb; *Director of Photography*: Laszlo Kovacs; *Art Director*: Sydney Z. Litwack; *Editor*: Maury Winetrobe; *Music*: Ronald Stein. *Running time*: 123 minutes. Released by Columbia Pictures.

At the height of the counterculture revolution, Columbia Pictures released *Getting Straight*, an offbeat comedy starring the seventies' cinematically omnipresent cynic, Elliott Gould. The razor-thin plot finds Harry Bailey (Gould), a thirtyish former student activist who returns to his old university, hoping to take the responsible road in life by obtaining his master's degree and settling down to a middle-class life as a teacher.

Given the nature of the times, however, Harry inevitably finds himself at odds with his radical past, as well as with friends who berate him for "selling out" to the Establishment. Harry constantly fights his urges to rejoin the protest movement and rebel against the very system he is seeking to perpetuate. The decision to conform costs him his libertarian girlfriend Jan (a frighteningly young Candice Bergen—twenty years prior to *Murphy Brown* and those irritating Sprint commercials), who is a campus activist. As the anti–Vietnam War movement gains momentum at the university, Harry succumbs to his inner desires and deliberately flunks his oral exam. He then participates in the destruction of his school, thereby regaining his self-respect and the respect of his peers and lover.

The anarchic *Getting Straight* was a rather daring film for its time, and in retrospect, it might seem shocking that it was funded by a major studio. Columbia, however, had been emboldened by the surprise success of *Easy*

Ford as Jake, the rumpled party animal. (Columbia Pictures)

Ford (*background*) observes Gould debating Candice Bergen about allegations that he is becoming too Establishment. (Columbia Pictures)

Rider the previous year. Studio executives recognized there was box-office gold among the great unwashed masses of youths who patronized such revolutionary films. The irony, of course, is that such motion pictures were financed by rich, middle-age executives who represented the very culture their films denounced, a situation mirrored by the rap music industry today.

Filming took place at Lane Community College in Eugene, Oregon. In a fit of inspired casting, over four-hundred students were cast as—well, students. Others eagerly agreed to portray the "fascist" National Guard troops who besiege the campus in the film's climax—providing an ironic juxtaposition to the movie's "message" of not forsaking one's principles for monetary gain. Proving that the Establishment was no less entranced by the lure of a fleeting moment of fame and a studio-provided box lunch, the university faculty served as willing extras—despite the fact that the screenplay vilifies their entire lifestyle. In return for this extraordinary cooperation, Columbia Pictures established a new class on campus dedicated to film theory and cinematic history. The cast and crew of *Getting Straight* inaugurated the program by serving as the first guest lecturers.

The movie itself is not without merit, and Elliott Gould's performance is the glue which keeps the rambling screenplay in some semblance of order (at least until the ridiculously "over the top" climax). Gould, then on a career roll, was riding high from his previous successes in *Bob and Carol and Ted and Alice* and *M*A*S*H*, and in *Getting Straight*, he gives a deft performance that today

makes one wince at how Hollywood—and Gould himself—would allow his talents to be trashed in the years to come. Indeed, one of the film's main ad campaigns entirely rested on promoting critics' quotes which called Gould one of the foremost and influential leading men of the era. Within a couple of years, those accolades would be passé, as Gould labored through a series of nothing movies which would ultimately see him reduced to a character actor on sitcoms. Conversely, Candice Bergen received scorn at the time for being an actress whose range was somewhat less than that of her father Edgar Bergen's dummy. Ironically, Bergen would gain respect and popular acceptance at the very time Gould's star was waning. Her performance in *Getting Straight* is not overwhelming, but she certainly displays a charm and radiance that makes one wonder why she was singled out for such vicious criticism during the early years of her career. The talented supporting cast included Harrison Ford as Jake, the burned-out host of a wild campus party which Gould reluctantly attends. It's a throwaway role which provides Ford with only a few lines of forgettable dialogue. However, he did gain screen credit, and the role allowed him to figure in a few publicity stills. (Curiously, Ford is seen in the sames clothes throughout, although his sequences take place days apart. Apparently, the producers cut costs to afford Gould's salary.)

Getting Straight was both a critical and box-office hit in 1970. Watching the film today, however, one is distracted by how dated it seems, as well as the naiveté of its politics. Taken in the context of the time, with an unpopular war raging thousands of miles away, the film's endorsement of violence as a means of protest probably seemed justified. Viewed in the 1990s, the climactic trashing of the campus wherein the students destroy a citadel of learning and tolerance seems hopelessly misguided at best and inexcusably dumb at worst. Anarchy as a political tool has long since been discredited by all but those who still think the 1992 L.A. riots really had something to do with making a statement about racial injustice. Yet the film does reflect the frustrations of a generation that was at least motivated by passion and convictions. As a straightforward comedy, the film has its moments, but clocking in at over two hours running time, it needs almost as much trimming as Elliott Gould's facial hair. The story wanders lazily to its bizarre and rather pretentious conclusion.

For younger viewers, *Getting Straight* must seem as timely as *The Birth of a Nation*. But for those of us who were there, it is an accurate—though imperfect—depiction of the mood of a nation torn between its convictions.

Reviews

"A brilliant, mercurial performance by Elliott Gould steadies and vivifies but cannot save Getting Straight. *The extraordinary magnetism and supple skill of this strapping hirsute young man, with his probing eyes and bristly walrus mustache, fires this misguided picture with a fervor and wonderful comic sense of reality. Sadly, for this is a truly promising project, these two qualities sail right out of the movie toward the home stretch. A serious, freewheeling comedy, pivoting on student unrest and rebellion on the contemporary campus scene, succumbs to theatrics and, structurally, the very convention it deplores. . . . Candice Bergen, for the first time, comes to life for the camera . . . the picture ends as a cop-out of its own professed principles and initial honesty."*
—HOWARD THOMPSON, *NEW YORK TIMES*

Gould returns to his radical roots and trashes the campus in the film's over-the-top finale. (Columbia Pictures)

Gould "grooves" with Ford at a wild party on campus. (Columbia Pictures)

"An outstanding film. It is a comprehensive, cynical, sympathetic, flip, touching, and hilarious story of the middle generation—those millions a bit too old for protest, a bit too young for repression. . . . The episodic story covers a lot of ground as it permits the very large and extremely competent supporting cast to limn the attitudes of an entire population. While the film is a parade of accurately-hewn postures, the root story never strays too far."
—VARIETY

"It is just possible that Elliott Gould is the number one offbeat actor in this country. Candice Bergen, like almost everything about the film, is a pleasure. Getting Straight *is among the finest."*
—DAVID GOLDMAN, CBS RADIO

"FOUR STARS–HIGHEST RATING. Whopping good!"
—WANDA HALE, *NEW YORK DAILY NEWS*

"Directed with great skill by Richard Rush . . . Elliott Gould is a most ingratiating screen personality."
—CHARLES CHAMPLIN, *LOS ANGELES TIMES*

51

6

American Graffiti (1973)

"It was fun. It was like a party, but not a Hollywood party. It was a real low-budget movie, even for those days. I only got a couple of hundred dollars a week. There were no dressing rooms. The actors sat in the same trailer as the costumes."

CAST:

Curt Henderson: Richard Dreyfuss; *Steve Bolander*: Ronny Howard; *Big John Milner*: Paul LeMat; *Terry "The Toad" Fields*: Charlie Martin Smith; *Laurie Henderson*: Cindy Williams; *Debbie*: Candy Clark; *Carol Morrison*: Mackenzie Phillips; *Disc Jockey*: Wolfman Jack; *Joe*: Bo Hopkins; *Bob Falfa*: Harrison Ford; *Peg*: Kathy Quinlan; *Falfa's Girl*: Debralee Scott; *Badass #1*: Johnny Weissmuller Jr; *Judy*: Susan Richardson; *Blonde in the T-Bird*: Suzanne Somers; *Jane*: Kay Lenz.

CREDITS:

Director: George Lucas; *Producer*: Francis Ford Coppola; *Screenplay*: George Lucas, Gloria Katz, and Willard Huyck; *Directors of Photography*: Ron Eveslage and Jan D'Alquen; *Visual Consultant*: Haskell Wexler; *Art Director*: Dennis Clark; *Editors*: Verna Fields and Marcia Lucas. *Running time*: 110 minutes (1973 release); 112 minutes (1978 rerelease). A LucasFilm Ltd./Coppola Company Production; Released by Universal Pictures.

Studio publicity photo of Harrison Ford and one of his on-screen babes, Linda Christensen. (Universal Pictures)

In the two-year period following the release of *Getting Straight*, Harrison Ford continued to labor in nondescript roles on television. He would reflect much later about the bland types of characters he was being cast as: either "as the guy who didn't do it, or if there were two bad brothers, I was the sensitive one." Frustratingly, no other big-screen roles came his way. Ford confessed to being envious of other actors—most younger than himself—who seemed to be getting their big break: "I was wondering if it would ever be my turn." He later told *You* magazine: "That's when I began to realize that if I didn't take control of my own career and my own life, I'd always be at the mercy of others, and I'd soon be a worn-out case." Ford took control by buying some power tools, reading books about woodworking, and literally tearing down his house and rebuilding it so he could master the craft of carpentry. With a family to support and bills to pay, Ford was tired of placing his fate in the hands of unresponsive and seemingly uncaring producers and studios. Regarding his newfound profession of carpentry, he said, "I taught myself. It's the only way I can do anything." As with other goals Ford has put his mind to, he did it well. Before long, his carpentry business was booming. Although he did not intend to give up acting completely ("I still wanted to be an actor when I grew up," he quipped) carpentry afforded him the luxury of auditioning for roles without feeling desperate. "I behaved less like a victim," he said. "I wasn't the bleeding sore that is the out-of-work actor."

Falfa (*Ford*) and Laurie (*Cindy Williams*) narrowly escape death in the fiery climax to the drag race. (Universal Pictures)

At the same time, a young filmmaker named George Lucas was also trying to achieve the ambitions he had set for himself. Lucas had won praise for his imaginative 1970 science fiction film *THX 1138*, although it was not a box-office success. Lucas intended his follow-up film to be a humorous and sentimental tribute to his high school days in Modesto, California. Lucas approached Warners, the distributor of *THX 1138*, with the proposed project, which he titled *American Graffiti*. The studio was unimpressed and declined to advance any funding. Undaunted, Lucas asked two of his high school classmates, Gloria Katz and Willard Huyck, to help him write a treatment (i.e., an outline) of the script. It was presented to United Artists, which agreed to finance a final script. At this point, however, Lucas's plans went awry when Katz and Huyck left for England to direct a B horror film called *Messiah of Evil*, so he hired another former schoolmate, Richard Walters, to help write the script. Unfortunately, Lucas was dissatisfied with Walters's vision of the film, which was considerably different from his own. To make matters worse, all of the up-front money had been spent for Walters's fee. United Artists dropped the project, leaving Lucas in creative limbo.

Good luck finally smiled on George Lucas when Gloria Katz and Willard Huyck returned from England, after having not set the world on fire with their own film. Determined to return to doing what they did best—writing screenplays—the two joined Lucas to work on finalizing the *American Graffiti* script. Ultimately, Universal Pictures agreed to finance the film, as long as the budget was limited to $750,000. Even this meager sum came with a caveat: Lucas had to secure the services of his old friend and mentor Francis Ford Coppola as producer of the film. Presumably, if Lucas proved incapable of finishing the movie, Coppola would be able to step in and take over the direction as well. This was a tall order. Coppola was riding high as the director of *The Godfather* and could pretty much name his price in Hollywood. Yet in a gesture of loyalty and faith that is all too rare in the movie business, Coppola agreed to Universal's conditions so that Lucas could get his film made.

George Lucas hired former Columbia Pictures executive Fred Roos to begin aggressively seeking out suitable "no-name" actors for the wide range of roles in *American Graffiti*. The script would follow the relationships of a diverse group of high schoolers on the last night of summer vacation following their graduation. Set in a small California town (meant to resemble Lucas's hometown of

Modesto in 1962), the film had the teens learning about love, romance, jealousy, courage, and personal convictions—all within the course of the hours between dusk and dawn. When the new day comes, the group will be separated as some of the kids will be leaving the fold to attend college in the "outside world." The script traces the teens' trauma as they await the dawn with a mixture of excitement, anticipation, fear, and sadness. Lucas felt that by casting unknown actors in the roles, the audience would not be distracted by images of characters they may have played previously. Additionally, there was a more practical reason: the budget could hardly afford anyone making much more than "scale." Only one exception was made: the casting of Ron Howard. Howard had been featured in films since the age of five and was popular in the role of Opie on the long-running *Andy Griffith Show*. His name would lend some credibility to an otherwise undistinguished project. Ironically, Howard's actor-father and mentor Rance Howard advised him against doing the film, dismissing it as fare for drive-ins. However, Ron Howard wanted to escape the Opie image and prove he could play more mature roles. In one of the most astute decisions of his career, he accepted the part of Steve Bolander, a high school graduate whose eagerness to leave for college reverses itself completely in the course of a fateful evening.

Fred Roos was having great success in securing the services of a group of enormously talented young actors: Richard Dreyfuss, who would portray Curt, the cynical graduate whose dread of leaving for college is the antithesis of Steve Bolander's initial enthusiasm; Charles Martin Smith as Terry the Toad, the archetypical "nerd" who finds love in a most unexpected way; Candy Clark as Debbie, the air-headed but sweet-natured bimbo who pairs with Terry to make one of the cinema's most memorable odd couples; Cindy Williams as Laurie, the frustrated girlfriend of Steve Bolander; Paul LeMat as John Milner, the tough-guy, drag racing legend of this otherwise unremarkable small town; Mackenzie Phillips as Carol, the preteen would-be nymph who forces Milner to be her "date" for the evening; and Suzanne Somers in the wordless but unforgettable role as the mysterious blonde in the T-Bird whom Curt pursues—with only limited success—throughout the film. One supporting role remained to be cast: Bob Falfa, an egotistical drag racer who has come to town to take John Milner's "crown" away. Roos, who had continued to champion Harrison Ford and recommend him for parts whenever possible, immediately did so again for the part of Falfa. (Ford was doing carpentry work for him at the time.)

It was a far less desperate Harrison Ford who auditioned for *American Graffiti*, compared to his economic

The 1978 reissue poster heavily promoted its all-star cast, most of whom were unknowns when the film was originally released. (Universal Pictures)

status in the past. He recalled, "When I went for the interview, I wasn't there as a person who needed a job to put bread on the table. I had, for once, a real life behind me. When you're an out-of-work actor and you walk into an audition, you're an empty vessel. So this was a significant change in my personality. I had got my pride back." Roos was impressed with Ford's screen test, which, like those of the other cast members, had been shot on videotape (a unique procedure in 1972). Roos reflected in an interview with *Premiere* magazine about the qualities which helped Ford land the role of Bob Falfa: "Harrison was not conventionally good-looking. He was also tight-lipped, standoffish, and most people thought he had an attitude. . . . But I thought he was going to be a star. And we got along famously." Ironically, when Ford was formally offered the role, he declined as it only paid $485 per

55

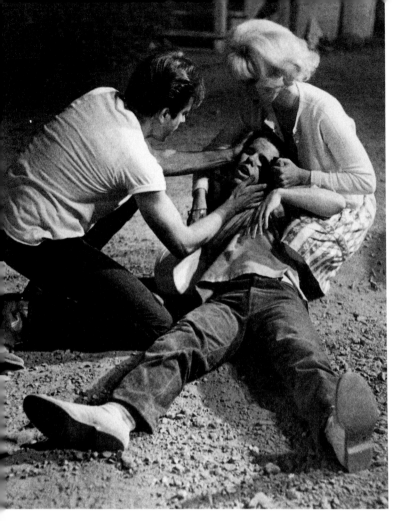

Milner (*Paul LeMat*) and Debbie (*Candy Clark*) rescue Terry the Toad (*Charlie Martin Smith*) from teenage hoods. (Universal Pictures)

improvise. Ford said, "It was the first time I had a part big enough for me to do the work the way I do it. I had other acting jobs before that, where I would ask the director a question and he would say, 'Don't bother me, please, I'm trying to make a movie here. Go away, kid.' " Lucas wanted the character of Bob Falfa to have a distinguishing feature, so he suggested a short haircut. Ford suggested he wear a straw cowboy hat instead, describing his character as "a sort of shit-kicker-cowboy-truck driver-type." For once, Ford's suggestions were met with enthusiasm. Lucas concurred with him, saying, "I knew guys like that in high school—guys who always wore those hats. Yeah, that's a good idea. Let's try it."

George Lucas's hometown had changed too drastically since 1962 for filming to take place there. He settled on the small community of Petaluma, California (now known as San Rafael), where time had seemed to stand still. His first obstacle was to find about three hundred early-sixties automobiles and hot rods for the lengthy sequences in which cars of teenagers "cruise the main" in search of dates and drag racing partners. Ultimately, the cars were secured at the "extravagant" rate of $25 per day. Filming, which was budgeted for only twenty-eight days, took place after nine at night and didn't wrap until dawn. For the cast and crew, this required an immediate adjustment of their sleeping and eating habits—a fact which virtually everyone found difficult to deal with. Lucas succeeded in getting the local merchants to keep

week—about half of what he was earning as a carpenter. "Come on, guys!" he protested, "I've got a wife and two kids to support!" Roos ultimately won Ford over—with an additional $15 per week! Ford was not motivated by the money but by his enthusiasm about the project itself—especially the opportunity to gain more than a minute of screen time.

Meeting George Lucas on the set for the first time, Ford could not believe that this quiet, understated man was the director. "He was so shy, I thought he was an assistant casting person," he recalled to *Vanity Fair.* In fact, Ford and Lucas shared many similarities in their backgrounds: both were about the same age (Ford is two years older); both of their fathers were self-made businessmen (Lucas's dad owned a successful stationery business); both were from middle-class suburbia; both men avoided publicity and the press whenever possible; both led undistinguished academic lives, both loved cars, with each man having cheated death in a serious accident; and both loathed "the Hollywood scene." Ford soon found that he respected Lucas's unpretentious style of direction, as well as his willingness to allow actors to

Debbie (*Clark*) and Terry (*Smith*) inform Steve (*Ron Howard*) that his car was stolen while they were "necking" on lover's lane. (Universal Pictures)

Curt (*Richard Dreyfuss*), the reluctant recruit for the Pharaohs, cruises the local pinball emporium with his new friends. (Universal Pictures)

their store lights on all night so he could complete filming. (They did this at their own expense, as the budget would not allow for the excess electric bills.) The budget was so tight that a production assistant chastised Harrison Ford for taking two doughnuts from a breakfast tray without permission! Many of the extras were not paid in cash but with tickets with which they might win prizes.

Harrison Ford enjoyed the camaraderie on the set and often participated in—or even initiated—the endless practical jokes which took place nightly. When filming would begin, Ford tried to make the most of his small but pivotal role, using improvisation to make his character more interesting. In one sequence, he is seen "cruising" with Cindy Williams in his hot rod. To impress her, he puts his arm around her and begins to sing "Some Enchanted Evening" off-key and with the wrong lyrics. The scene was improvised by Ford, who had earlier tried warbling an Everly Brothers song to less-than-desirable results. Some crew members did not know Ford wanted the scene to be funny and complained that he didn't even know the words. Lucas got the joke, however, and kept the shot. Ironically, prior to the film's release, the precious bit of screen time for Ford was edited from the final cut. This was due to the refusal of composer Richard Rodgers and the estate of his late partner Oscar Hammerstein II to give permission to use the song in such a way. Apparently, they thought Ford was demeaning it.

While Harrison Ford couldn't carry a tune if it had handles, music plays an integral part in creating the atmosphere of *American Graffiti*. Until this time, rock 'n' roll–oriented films generally used a sprinkling of songs written expressly for the movie and interspersed them with the dramatic sequences, usually to mixed results. Universal urged George Lucas to use just a handful of classic rock songs as the background to his film. Lucas protested that he envisioned utilizing a virtual nonstop soundtrack of songs from the era, with no original music recorded for his movie. When the studio balked at this plan, Lucas purchased the rights to forty-two songs for a grand total of $80,000. Artistically, Lucas's vision worked extraordinarily well. The omnipresent rock 'n' roll soundtrack—seamlessly mixed by Walter Murch—complements the action but never overwhelms it. The music adds inestimably to the atmosphere of *American Graffiti*. When the feuding Steve and Laurie reluctantly dance together for appearance's sake at the freshman "hop," the sentimental strains of the Platters' "Smoke Gets in Your Eyes" ultimately brings them together in a scene which illustrates the power of the musical score. Likewise, when the Beach Boys' bouncy "All Summer Long" rolls over the end credits, it is in shocking contrast to the emotionally shattering events which have immediately preceded it.

American Graffiti was the sleeper hit of 1973, but its

As Bob Falfa, the self-professed king of the drag strip. (Universal Pictures)

success took studio executives by surprise. When Lucas screened the film for the "suits," the mood was grim. The studio felt that the film was too offbeat to be a commercial success. They demanded that Lucas recut the movie and make it a more traditional story of teenagers coming of age. At this point, producer Francis Coppola stepped in to use his clout. He warned Universal that the film had to be realized exactly as Lucas envisioned it or he would personally buy the director's final cut from the studio and release it himself. Universal reconsidered, then rejected Coppola's offer. However, the film sat on a shelf until a workable marketing plan could be decided upon. *Graffiti* was shown to influential people in the industry, and word of mouth began to build. By the time it was released to the general public, the buzz on *American Graffiti* was that Universal had a potential blockbuster on its hands. The studio hired noted comic artist Mort Drucker (of *Mad* magazine fame) to create the memorable one-sheet poster which featured a collage of caricatures of the cast. Ads played up the almost uniformly positive reviews. Within weeks, *Graffiti* was the toast of the industry and the type of hit every studio executive dreams of—made on a shoestring budget but ultimately grossing over $100 million. Even the soundtrack was a colossal hit, as the double-platter set sold over 100,000 copies in its first two weeks.

American Graffiti is certainly one of the defining American films of the seventies. Flawlessly directed and brilliantly written and enacted, it comes as close to perfec-

tion as a motion picture can. This is a cinematic yearbook of unforgettable moments, which—like the high school years themselves—range from teenage hijinks to poignant reflections on life. Never before or since has the experience of growing up been captured with such grace and accuracy. Consider just a few of the moments which linger in the mind from this chaotic but mesmerizing film: John Milner's melancholy tour of the drag racers "graveyard"; Curt Henderson's visit to the legendary and mysterious local disk jockey (beautifully played by Wolfman Jack); the hilarious attempts of Terry the Toad to "get some brew" to impress his sexpot girlfriend Debbie; Curt's reluctant participation in an initiation ceremony for the Pharaohs street gang; the climatic drag racing sequence (wonderfully photographed by Haskell Wexler) as dawn rises over the remote highway; tiny Carol Morrison threatening Milner with what would have been the first recorded case of date rape if he doesn't satisfy her by repeating nasty statements about himself; the endless cruising up and down the main street "strip" in a time when juvenile violence was basically restricted to shaving-cream fights between the inhabitants of the hot rods. Perhaps the film's most jarring sequence occurs when we watch Curt on board the plane which is taking him off to the uncertainties of a big-city college education. In a haunting scene, we see the fears, pride, loneliness, and great expectations reflected in his eyes as he catches one last fleeting glimpse of the ever-elusive blonde in the white T-Bird. As the scene fades, we see updates on the lives of several of the key characters. Some are relatively innocuous: Curt Henderson is a writer living in Canada; Steve Bolander sells insurance in California. However, the audience is stunned by the news that John Milner was killed by a drunk driver in 1964 and lovable Terry Fields was reported missing-in-action in Vietnam in 1965. Coming immediately after getting to know and care about these characters makes this a shattering way to illustrate the fact that no generation can remain immune to the tragedies that ultimately invade people's lives. It is a daring and unforgettable ending to a daring and unforgettable film.

The effect of *American Graffiti* on the careers of those involved with it cannot be overstated. For George Lucas, the film allowed him to be Hollywood's newest boy wonder and would give him the opportunity to become one of the most influential filmmakers of the decade. Richard Dreyfuss would become a successful leading man. Ron Howard would parlay his acclaimed work in the film into the long-running, *Graffiti*-inspired sitcom *Happy Days*. This would pave his way for more serious acting jobs in feature films and eventually his status as a film director. Cindy Williams would also become a *Happy Days* cast member and then have her own phenomenally suc-

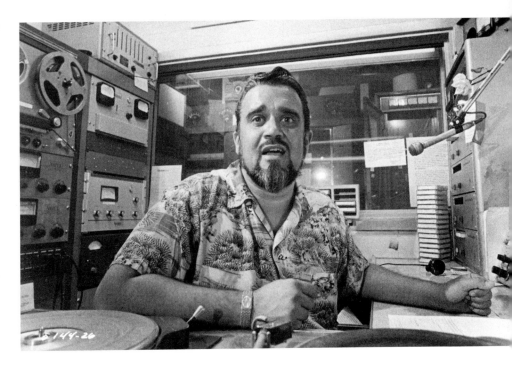

Wolfman Jack in a memorable performance as the mysterious and legendary small-town disc jockey. (Universal Pictures)

cessful comedy series, *Laverne and Shirley*. Candy Clark would win an Oscar nomination for *Graffiti* (but then fade away), and Charles Martin Smith (inexplicably denied the same honor) would become a successful character actor and director. Suzanne Somers would leap to fame in the *Three's Company* sitcom, and Mackenzie Phillips would also find fleeting fame on television's *One Day at a Time*. Curiously, only Paul LeMat, who is so engaging as the overage drag racer John Milner, seems to have been denied the good roles he so richly deserved.

For Harrison Ford, the film did not mean immediate offers for bigger and better roles. Yet he had established himself in the minds of some of the most influential people in the industry. He told an interviewer in 1988, "I didn't really feel comfortable acting until *American Graffiti*. That's when I realized I had requirements just as a director had requirements. I'd always been too different, too nervous to ask the questions necessary to do my job."

American Graffiti enjoyed a major theatrical reissue in 1978, complete with enhanced and rerecorded Dolby stereo soundtrack. By this time, most of the cast members were stars, and the revised advertisements played up their presence. Three scenes were added to this cut by George Lucas: Steve Bolander's "Marble-head" wisecrack aimed at his principal (which according to Lucas "does a lot for his character. He's a stronger person, and I think that makes a difference"); a sequence in which Terry the Toad falls captive to an obnoxious car salesman's relentless "pitch"; and the scene in which Bob Falfa "serenades" Laurie with "Some Enchanted Evening." Apparently, even Richard Rodgers and the estate of Oscar Hammerstein II had become fans of *American Graffiti* in the ensuing years. (Although they may well have insisted that Ford's dubious recording of the song not be added to the original soundtrack album!) *American Graffiti* also spawned a 1979 sequel that is not fondly remembered. This is because the first is a masterpiece. And masterpieces do not require sequels.

Reviews

"One of those rare films which can be advanced in any discussion of the superiority of film over live performance. The latter can vary from show to show, but if you get it right on film, you've got it forever. . . . A most vivid recall of teenage attitudes and mores, told with outstanding empathy and compassion through an exceptionally talented cast."
—VARIETY

"The film has a lot to say [but] it's gloriously free of pretensions."
—HOLLYWOOD REPORTER

"Masterfully executed and profoundly affecting."
—LOS ANGELES TIMES

"It is a very good movie, funny, tough, unsentimental. It is full of marvelous performances from actors hardly known for previous screen credits. But for me its excitement comes at least partly from its indication of what may be a major new career [that of George Lucas.]"
—ROGER GREENSPUN, *NEW YORK TIMES*

"The most important American movie since Five Easy Pieces*—maybe since* Bonnie and Clyde*. The nostalgia boom has finally produced a lasting work of art. Lucas has brought the past alive, with sympathy, affection, and thorough understanding."*
—STEPHEN FARBER, *NEW YORK TIMES*

7

The Conversation (1974)

"I still did the odd carpentry job after American Graffiti. But before long there was Coppola's film The Conversation, *which I did with Hackman. I turned up playing an evil young henchman. There was no role there until I decided to make him a homosexual."*

CAST:
Harry Caul: Gene Hackman; *Stan*: John Cazale; *Bernie Moran*: Allen Garfield; *Mark*: Frederic Forrest; *Ann*: Cindy Williams; *Paul*: Michael Higgins; *Meredith*: Elizabeth MacRae; *Amy*: Teri Garr; *Martin Stett*: Harrison Ford; *Receptionist*: Mark Wheeler; *The Director*: Robert Duvall (uncredited).

CREDITS:
Director and Writer: Francis Ford Coppola; *Producers*: Francis Ford Coppola and Fred Roos; *Director of Photography*: Bill Butler; *Editor*: Richard Chew; *Production Designer*: Dean Tavoularis; *Music*: David Shire; *Art Director*: Dean Tavoularis. *Running time*: 113 minutes. An American Zoetrope Film; Released by Paramount Pictures.

Ford arranges for a payout to Hackman, who has been employed to eavesdrop on an executive's wife and her lover. (Paramount Pictures)

In the early 1970s, Francis Ford Coppola was *the* wunderkind of the international filmmaking community, having gained nearly universal praise for *The Godfather* as well as *American Graffiti*, which he produced. His other area of expertise—screenwriting—made him Hollywood's most promising triple-threat talent since Orson Welles. Prior to starting his much anticipated *Godfather* sequel (which was due for release in December 1974), Coppola wanted to concentrate on directing a "small" film, based on his own original screenplay, written six years previously. *The Conversation*, described by Coppola as "a psychological horror film," was a low budget movie featuring big star Gene Hackman in what would be a prophetic condemnation of the loss of privacy in modern society—and its potentially tragic consequences. Uncommercial in nature, it is doubtful that the film would have found studio backing had it not been for Coppola's leverage. Not coincidentally, Paramount agreed to finance and distribute *The Conversation*, possibly as a lure to get Coppola to work on *The Godfather, Part II*. Many times, studios which grudgingly back such films, in order to get a more commercial vehicle from its star or director, simply regard these vehicles as vanity projects and unceremoniously dump them onto the marketplace. (Witness *The Offence*, released the previous year by United Artists in order to get Sean Connery to return as James Bond in *Diamonds Are Forever*. *The Offence* played one week in a few art houses and vanished, despite boasting one of the

Hackman as Harry Caul, a man obsessed with his profession and oblivious to its immorality. (Paramount Pictures)

specifics of the case or the morality of his services. Caul does not even have an interest in what the case is about. He only cares about the challenge of getting the best audio recording possible under the most adverse conditions. Caul is hired to record the outdoor conversations of a young couple (Cindy Williams—also from *American Graffiti*—and Frederic Forrest), who are apparently having an affair. The audio is "hit or miss," and the conversation between these two obviously tortured souls piques a bit of interest even in Harry. When he tries to turn the tapes in to his client, a mysterious executive simply known as "the Director" (Robert Duvall), he is intercepted by the man's assistant, Martin Stett (Harrison Ford), who becomes irate when Caul refuses to entrust him with the recordings. Caul wins the struggle to retain the tapes but is warned by Stett not to become involved with the case—for his own sake. Caul now becomes obsessed with the specifics of the case but cannot piece together the details. Ultimately, he is conned out of the tapes by a woman he beds who has been hired by Stett. Caul witnesses the devastating impact the tapes have on the Director as he learns of his wife's infidelity.

John Cazale confronts ex-boss Gene Hackman at a trade show for bugging devices. (Paramount Pictures)

best performances of Connery's career.) Amazingly, no such fate awaited *The Conversation*, which went on to become one of the most praised films of the decade.

Harrison Ford had a working relationship with Coppola, due to having appeared in *American Graffiti*. He tested for a small but pivotal role in *The Conversation*, but Coppola decided to go with Frederic Forrest. However, there would be some consolation, as Coppola's coproducer Fred Roos— long a Ford believer—arranged for the actor to land another abbreviated role, albeit one which is essential to the plot.

The film centers on Harry Caul (Gene Hackman), a wiretapping expert. Caul is a lonely, emotionless man who prides himself on carrying out his eavesdropping art on behalf of his clients without getting personally involved in the

Ford assigns Gene Hackman to what appears to be a routine eavesdropping assignment. (Paramount Pictures)

Convinced the man will murder his spouse, Caul is wracked with guilt and attempts to prevent the crime. The events which follow lead to a surprising if somewhat vague and confusing conclusion, in which Caul learns that his actions have indeed lead to tragedy—but in a most unexpected way. In the final ironic twist, Caul becomes another victim of the technology he used to inadvertently destroy others.

Coppola described the making of the film and its origins in a seminar on the cinema: "The process of writing the finished screenplay for *The Conversation* was tricky. I was writing it over a long period of time and I had the concepts in my head way before I was able to make it happen. I did many rewrites. I knew what the ending was and kept cutting in this conversation Harry [Caul] had recorded. When you have a three-minute scene which you are going to repeat eight times in the course of a movie, hopefully each time it will take on different meanings. The film constructs itself sort of like a composition of music in that it uses repetition, repeating the exact same footage several times. The scene hits you differently each time you look at it but you know it's exactly the same footage, so it can't be different. Yet, you notice different things. You suddenly realize it's not what she was saying, it's where she was looking. By my repeating the footage, and sometimes just repeating the conversation without showing the footage, I'm in a way asking the audience to put it together in different ways. There must be a cumulative effect, because as the movie goes on, the audience and the audience's memory becomes a very essential part. I'm interested in films where the audience visits its own emotions and really becomes a participant in the film. *The Conversation* is an experiment in that."

The Conversation is an intriguing but slow-moving film whose parallels to Antonioni's *Blow-Up* are impossible to ignore. In that classic, offbeat thriller, a photographer is obsessed with solving a murder—although we begin to suspect that perhaps there was no murder at all. Similarly, *The Conversation* tells us that first impressions are not necessarily accurate ones, and we are never sure whether what we are observing through Caul's eyes is real or part of his imagination. The surrealistic techniques which worked so well in *Blow-Up* seem like unnecessary distractions here, however. Coppola has fashioned a story and characters which are interesting enough on their own merits without resorting to pretentious hocus-pocus camera shots. (Curiously, the generally innovative director actually resorts to using fog machines to simulate dream sequences!) The plot is somewhat secondary to the other qualities of the film. The central attribute is the well-defined character of Caul. His opaqueness only makes him more interesting. Superbly played by Gene Hackman, Caul is a nerd in every sense of the word. When morality and compassion finally catch up with him, he is incapable of responding to them in a practical way. Even the bare-bones, urban-exile existence he lives is ultimately destroyed by his shallowness.

The Conversation has aged fairly well, although all

Hackman in a tense exchange with Ford, who is attempting to change the ground rules of their deal. (Paramount Pictures)

the warnings about what space-age technology will do to society ring fairly hollow in the 1990s. Because the film was released at the height of the Watergate scandal, it was originally seen as an insightful metaphor for the loss of privacy which will inevitably occur through misuse of technology. Today, for better or worse, society has willingly embraced these technical advances—even at the cost of our privacy.

Still, *The Conversation* has many memorable sequences that linger in the mind. It also benefits from some solid supporting performances from the always reliable John Cazale (who died not long afterward), as well as Allen Garfield and Teri Garr. Robert Duvall appears very briefly in some key scenes but has virtually no dialogue. The film is an impressive but ultimately depressing experience. Its subject matter—technology vs. individual rights—was covered in a less somber way in *The Anderson Tapes*, director Sidney Lumet's 1971 thriller. *The Conversation* is probably the better film, but Lumet's is the one you get the urge to see again.

To return to the comparisons between *Blow-Up* and *The Conversation*, both films involve cold, unfeeling men

who are inadvertently drawn into life-and-death situations that cause them to question their morality as well as their sanity. In *Blow-Up*, a photographer who believes he may have accidentally photographed a murder becomes obsessed with finding the truth. The ending of that film was thought-provoking and controversial, with the message reiterated that what we see may not reflect the reality of what has happened. In *Blow-Up*, there is increasing evidence that the murder was all in the mind of the photographer. In Coppola's film, we know the murder has indeed occurred—albeit in an unexpected way. Still, there are similarities in the haunting final frames of both movies. In Antonioni's film, the protagonist is unable to reconcile his obsession in any satisfactory way. He will presumably be forever obsessed with this one incident. In *The Conversation*, the story ends with Harry Caul obsessed with a paranoid fear that his own devices are being used to destroy him. Of the two films, however, *Blow-Up* remains the more stylish and entertaining.

The Conversation provided Harrison Ford with a brief but pivotal role, and allowed him to turn what could have been a colorless supporting character into something much more. While on-screen for only a few fleeting minutes throughout the film, Ford shows the charisma which would eventually make him a screen idol. His character had been fairly undeveloped in the script, and he took it upon himself to flesh out the character of Stett by implying the man had gay traits. Coppola thought this was an intriguing approach but balked when Ford spent $900 on a billiard-table-green flannel suit which his character would wear. "Jesus Christ," screamed the director upon seeing the flamboyantly attired actor. "What the hell are you?" Ford explained his approach to the role and received enthusiastic support from production designer Dean Tavoularis, who created an office for Stett to match the sensibilities of Ford's character.

Although *The Conversation* won the Grand Prize at the 1974 Cannes Film Festival and received three Oscar nominations (including Best Picture), the film did little to advance Harrison Ford's career. Indeed, he could not even get a break from the Paramount publicity department—the pressbook for the film shows several still photos of Ford from the movie, each of which mistakenly identifies him as actor Mark Wheeler. Harrison Ford would not appear in another feature film until a 1977 picture called *Star Wars*.

Reviews

"An extremely grim movie . . . an impressive portrayal by Gene Hackman. It's a brilliant idea for a movie and much of it works. But some of the action drags—perhaps because the style is so muted, so deliberately dry and cool, that suspense is partially muffled. . . . Mr. Coppola has certainly succeeded in making surveillance repulsive. While that's hardly a new notion, we can thank him for withering the last tendrils of romance."

—NORA SAYRE, *NEW YORK TIMES*

"Absorbing, but extremely difficult to follow in detail, this personal, timely (in view of Watergate), Kafkaesque suspense story centers almost entirely on director and leading actor, who have a field day."

—HALLIWELL'S *FILM GUIDE*

"Haunting and bothersome . . . the film is haunting because its suggestion that technology has gotten out of hand, though not exactly new, is so convincingly and fastidiously detailed. It's bothersome because Mr. Coppola, the writer as well as the director, has nearly succeeded in making a great film, but has, instead, made one that is merely very good. Among its virtues is a superb performance by Gene Hackman in a role that comes very close to being the uptight Watergate era's equivalent of the mad doctors in old-fashioned Vincent Price films."

—VINCENT CANBY, *NEW YORK TIMES*

"Brilliant. . . . One of the best films of the 1970s."
—LEONARD MALTIN'S *MOVIE AND VIDEO GUIDE*

"A major artistic asset to the film—besides script, direction, and top performances—is supervising editor Walter Murch's sound collage and re-recording. Voices come in and out of aural focus in a superb tease."

—VARIETY

"It's not so much a movie about bugging as the man who does it, and Gene Hackman's performance is a great one. . . . The ways in which he interprets the tape, and the different nuances of meaning it seems to contain at different moments, reminds us of Antonioni's Blow-Up. Both movies are about the unreality of what seems real. . . . The Conversation is about paranoia, invasion of privacy, bugging—and also about the bothersome problem of conscience. The Watergate crew seems, for the most part, to have had no notion that what they [were] doing was objectively wrong. Harry wants to have no notion. But he does, and it destroys him."

—ROGER EBERT'S *VIDEO COMPANION*

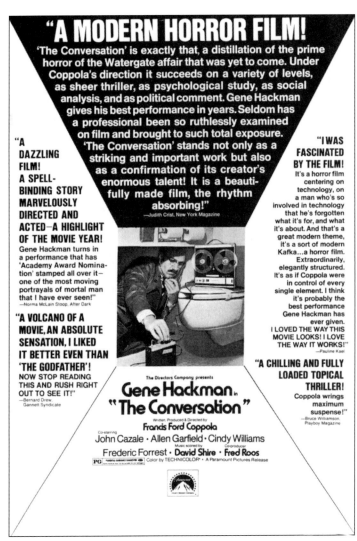

Coppola's film was internationally acclaimed as a warning about the infringement of technology on an individual's privacy. (Paramount Pictures)

8

Star Wars **(1977)**

"I was one of the few people who thought it was going to work . . ."

CAST:

Luke Skywalker: Mark Hamill; *Han Solo*: Harrison Ford; *Princess Leia Organa*: Carrie Fisher; *Grand Moff Tarkin*: Peter Cushing; *Ben (Obi Wan) Kenobi*: Alec Guinness; *C-3PO*: Anthony Daniels; *R2D2*: Kenny Baker; *Chewbacca*: Peter Mayhew; *Darth Vader*: David Prowse (*Voice*: James Earl Jones).

CREDITS:

Director and Writer: George Lucas; *Producer*: Gary Kurtz; *Photography*: Gilbert Taylor; *Visual Effects*: John Dykstra, John Stears, Richard Edlund, Grant McCune, and Robert Blalack; *Production Designer*: John Barry, Norman Reynolds, and Leslie Dilley; *Set Decoration*: Roger Christian; *Editors*: Paul Hirsch, Marcia Lucas, and Richard Chew; *Sound Effects*: Benjamin Burtt Jr.; *Music*: John Williams; *Sound*: Don MacDougall, Ray West, Bob Minkler, and Derek Ball. *Costumes*: John Mollo; *Running time*: 121 minutes. A LucasFilm Ltd. Production; Released by 20th Century Fox.

Publicity photo issued to "LucasFilm Fan Club" members: Ford with Hamill, Fisher, and Mayhew. (20th Century Fox)

It is difficult to imagine what the science fiction film genre would be like today had *Star Wars* not emerged as the landmark film of the 1970s. Like the James Bond films of the sixties, the *Star Wars* movies would transcend commercial success and evolve into cultural phenomena. For Harrison Ford and so many others, this seemingly unpromising updating of the classic sci-fi adventure serials of the 1930s would prove to be a Horatio Alger story of unparalleled proportions. Like many other Hollywood sleeper hits, *Star Wars* was the subject of industry scoffing from the moment George Lucas tried to "pitch" the idea to major studios. Lucas's interest in a science fiction tale which would pay homage to the *Flash Gordon* serials of decades before emerged as early as 1973, when he began writing a draft of an original screenplay. He had been unsuccessful in optioning the rights to the *Flash Gordon* character, due to cost factors and the lack of creative control, which Lucas felt was paramount. At the time, Lucas was preoccupied with preparing *American Graffiti* for release. His second feature film (following the modestly successful *THX 1138*), *Graffiti* would gain Lucas an Oscar nomination for Best Director. Although he suddenly found himself the industry's hot young filmmaker, he had not yet gained enough clout with the studios to interest them in a large budget science fiction epic, let alone convince them to turn over creative control to him. Lucas was reminded at every turn that the last blockbuster sci-fi hit had been *Planet of the Apes* in 1968. Even Kubrick's *2001: A Space Odyssey*, also from 1968, took several rereleases before it earned back its cost.

With Fisher and David Prowse. (20th Century Fox)

Lucas turned virtually all of his attention to completing the script for *Star Wars*. By March 1976, he felt the idea was ready to be aggressively lobbied for once again at the major studios. Universal, which had released *American Graffiti*, had first option on the film. In 1973, the studio felt the project did not even warrant the $25,000 Lucas had requested to develop the screenplay further. Three years hence, the top brass was still convinced the film would not play in Peoria. Lucas was free to present his project elsewhere and submitted the script to Alan Ladd Jr., then head of development at 20th Century Fox. Ladd was saddled with the string of high-profile flops the studio had recently released, among them "The Duchess and the Dirtwater Fox," "The Last Hard Men," and "Lucky Lady," but showed immediate enthusiasm for Lucas's bold attempts to revive the genre long thought to be dead within the industry. Encouraged, Lucas swallowed hard and proposed raising the film's estimated $4 million budget to $8.5 million to allow for state-of-the-art special effects. Ladd recalled his trials trying to get the Fox brass "to commit $8.5 million to a picture without a presold book, without stars—a picture that had nothing conventional about it, that would probably be one of the most unconventional pictures ever made. But I believed in Lucas. I told them that the picture would be very important and that we should make it." Grateful for the studio support, Lucas backed off demanding a great deal of up-front money, and instead emphasized creative control, a large share of the profits, and control of any sequels. Still unconvinced the film would be a hit, the studio brass nevertheless acceded to his requests.

For the handful of hermits who may not have experienced *Star Wars*, it is a modern twist on ancient morality tales, with clearly defined good guys battling the forces of evil. It centers on Luke Skywalker, a nondescript young man who—in the tradition of all great cinematic heroes—is unexpectedly forced to find his inner strength when fate catapults him into a life-and-death struggle over the fate of the galaxy. Skywalker's family is slaughtered by the sinister forces of "the Empire," and he pursues vengeance by joining forces with rebels who are waging a David and Goliath battle against the Empire's merciless military commander, Darth Vader. Skywalker forms a close but sometimes uneasy alliance with the rebel Princess Leia and a renegade space outlaw named Han Solo. Skywalker also shares a spiritual link with Ben Kenobi, a Jedi knight. The Jedi are semimystical guardians of the universe who are dedicated to the triumph of good over evil. Kenobi, a sort of elder statesman of the Jedi, acts as an adviser to Luke and his friends in their seemingly hopeless battle against Darth Vader. With the aid of Ben, coupled with some high-tech weaponry and the wittiest robots since *Forbidden Planet*, the trio gain at least a temporary victory over their foes.

With most of the film's budget reserved for special effects, George Lucas now faced the challenge of finding charismatic and talented actors who would work for modest salaries. It should be noted that in his original drafts of the screenplay, the characters who would later become so beloved were envisioned in an entirely different light. The film's central hero, Luke Skywalker, was originally known as Luke Starkiller and was in fact an elderly general. In yet another version, the hero was transformed into a heroine. The pivotal role of Han Solo, which would bring Harrison Ford fame and fortune, was first scripted as a green-skinned, monsterlike being who had many qualities of the Ben Kenobi character. Lucas tightened the script and finally settled on three main heroes: Luke Skywalker, the young man tossed into the center of an incredible intergalactic adventure; Han Solo, the charismatic scoundrel whose mercenary ways ironically make him a reluctant hero; and Princess Leia, the brave leader of a rebel movement against an evil empire. Lucas began a much publicized series of casting calls, working simultaneously with his friend, director Brian De Palma, who was in the process of hiring actors for his forthcoming adaptation of Stephen King's *Carrie*. Since virtually every young actor in town wanted to be a part of either film, Lucas and De Palma simply set up shop in the offices of colleague Francis Ford Coppola and began a cattle call of hundreds of actors and actresses. Lucas was looking for three individuals who generated a unique chemistry together. He was considering the aspiring actors as trios and was routinely disqualifying all three people if even one individual did not meet his expectations.

At this time, Harrison Ford was so disappointed with the lack of opportunity afforded him in Hollywood that he returned to carpentry work simply to put food on the table for his family. He was desperate to remain on the Screen

Clowning on the set with Mark Hamill and Carrie Fisher. (20th Century Fox)

Actor's Guild health care plan, but unless he could earn a minimum of $1,200 per year from acting jobs, he stood to have his family dropped from the insurance rolls. Because he had worked for Coppola previously, Ford was able to capitalize on the relationship in a most unusual way—he succeeded in getting Coppola to hire him to do carpentry work in his office at the time the casting calls were going on. He recalled, "I knew they were casting, and I thought it would be a bit coy to be around Francis's office being a carpenter during the day. So I did the work at night." Ford fell behind schedule, however, and was forced to continue his work during the daytime hours, precisely when Lucas and De Palma were auditioning actors. Ford felt uncomfortable working in front of such luminaries, and later recalled a particularly humiliating experience when *American Graffiti* costar Richard Dreyfuss paid a visit to the office and saw him frantically trying to complete his woodworking chores. He would later say, "That made me feel just great. I felt about the size of a pea after they walked through."

It was producer–casting-agent Fred Roos, a close associate of Coppola's, who first suggested to Lucas that he consider Ford for the role of Han Solo. Lucas was not enthused—he had made it known that he would not be considering anyone from *American Graffiti*—but with the final decision on casting only weeks away, he consented to have Ford do some script readings. The actor auditioned with fifty prospective Princess Leias, becoming

increasingly despondent and irritable. He was convinced that he was not in the running for the Solo role and was merely wasting time paving the way for other actors. Ironically, it was the crankiness that Ford was beginning to show which increased Lucas's conviction that he *was* Han Solo! Ford was doing carpentry work at the home of actress Sally Kellerman when he received the call that would change his life: he had won the role of Han Solo. Ford dashed from the house with such enthusiasm that he left behind his stepladder, some cans of paint, and a bag of tools. (Kellerman kept the relics and eventually posted a humorous sign over them in her garage: "Harrison Ford Left These!")

Ford's costars would be Mark Hamill, who had landed the key role of Luke Skywalker over such competition as Christopher Walken, and Carrie Fisher, who beat out Amy Irving, a young Jodie Foster, Ford's *American Graffiti* costar Cindy Williams, and four hundred other actresses for the role of Princess Leia. (For the record, those considered for the Han Solo part included William Katt, Sylvester Stallone, and Nick Nolte.) The legendary Alec Guinness would portray the equally legendary (at least in the script) Ben Kenobi, the mystical Jedi knight who comes out of retirement to fight the forces of evil under the command of Grand Moff Tarkin, played by the inimitable Peter Cushing. With major casting finally completed, Lucas could concentrate on the next challenge: ensuring that the special effects would be unlike any seen to date in the cinema. Lucas allocated over $2.5 million to the effects and engaged John Dykstra and John Stears to create them. Dykstra and Stears in turn hired seventy-five enthusiastic technicians and rented an empty warehouse in an unfashionable section of Van Nuys. Despite the emphasis on hardware and gadgetry, Lucas remained committed to the human elements of the story. He stated, "Special effects are just a tool, a means of telling the story. People have a tendency to confuse them as an end to themselves. A special effect without a story is a pretty boring thing."

Eventually, the *Star Wars* company embarked on their journey to begin location shooting in the Tunisian desert. No sooner had the crew arrived than the heavens opened and unleashed the first period of sustained torrential rainstorms in more than fifty years. When the rains stopped, furious sandstorms ensued. The crew was forced to clean virtually every piece of equipment prior to using it. During periods of "normal" weather, the temperature would be sweltering hot in the daytime and freezing cold at night. Many of the crew developed severe dysentery and pneumonia. Yet these problems paled next to the technical difficulties. Most of the robots, who play such a pivotal role in the story line, refused to function properly due to interference on their remote-control devices. Instead of walking normally, many would wander unsteadily around the desert, reminiscent of a Dean Martin version of *Lawrence of Arabia*.

Following the trials and tribulations of the desert shoot, Lucas and company welcomed their arrival at England's Elstree Studios, where interiors would be shot over the coming months. Although far from having state-of-the-art capabilities, the studio did boast nine sound-stages on which Lucas could work simultaneously. Unfortunately, while weather was not a factor in the U.K., heated tempers were. Lucas and his American crew clashed almost immediately with their British counterparts. The Brits considered the Americans to be crass and immature, partly due to Lucas's penchant for keeping morale up by playing practical jokes. (Ford would gripe later, "The only damper on the pure fun was the almost unanimous attitude of the English crew that we were totally out of our minds!") For his part, Lucas was outraged by the British work ethic, which saw the union technicians quitting promptly each afternoon at five-thirty regardless of how close the unit was to completing important scenes. Ford tried to stay neutral but did form a close bond with Lucas, Hamill, and Fisher. Some of the other cast members were not as socially inclined. Alec Guinness threatened to quit the film when Lucas reduced his screen time. (Ironically, Guinness would become familiar to an entire new generation as well as gain an Oscar nomination for his abbreviated role in *Star Wars*). Lucas feuded with cinematographer Gil Taylor on a daily basis and watched in frustration as a litany of problems besieged the special effects work. On *American Graffiti*, Lucas presided over a crew of eighteen. On *Star Wars*, he was responsible for a crew of nine hundred. Additionally, he had to reassure nervous studio brass who kept reminding him that he was behind schedule and overbudget. They openly discussed pulling the plug on Lucas's dream project. Even the gentle Peter Cushing added to Lucas's woes by complaining that he wanted to minimize his long shots due to the fact that his boots were uncomfortable. Lucas complied and Cushing played the role of the terrifying villain Tarkin in his slippers!

While Lucas suffered from severe headaches and stomach

Disguised as stormtroopers, Luke explains to Han the financial rewards of rescuing Princess Leia from the Death Star. (20th Century Fox)

Original British quad poster. (20th Century Fox)

HILDEBRANDT

Starring
MARK HAMILL HARRISON FORD CARRIE FISHER
PETER CUSHING and ALEC GUINNESS
Written and Directed by   Produced by   Music by

pains due to the pressure, his cast and crew had their own problems. Carrie Fisher was not thrilled with Lucas's edict that she tape her breasts to minimize any distracting "jiggling." David Prowse, the actor inside the costume of the notorious villian Darth Vader, griped that he received virtually no direction from Lucas, whom he accused of being distracted by the technical elements of the film. (Prowse would scream even louder when Lucas later decided to dub his voice with that of James Earl Jones.) The film's cast of beloved robots and alien creatures were inhabited by some none-too-happy earthbound thespians. The robot C-3PO was enacted by Anthony Daniels, who bore the inconvenience of emoting while inside the confines of a virtual suit of armor. Diminutive Kenny Baker huddled inside the chrome body of the mini-robot R2D2 in certain scenes, while in others the character was completely operated by remote control. Peter Mayhew, the six-foot-seven actor who played the ominous-looking but heroic Wookie, Chewbacca, had to emphasize the creature's height even more by wearing elevated size-sixteen boots. As with the other members of the cast who played the intriguing aliens of Lucas's fertile imagination, these actors suffered from the interminable heat caused by wearing various costumes and masks for extended periods of time.

For Harrison Ford, the tensions on the set were a small price to pay for being a part of a film he felt would be an unqualified success, although it appeared as though he was alone in that opinion. He told *Rolling Stone* in 1981: "The movie sounded a little nuts, but I didn't give a

shit whether it'd be successful or not. I always thought it was an accessible, human story. . . . I mean, I didn't have to *act* science fiction." Ford believed that the "common mythology" of the story would work for audiences. Ford stated his opinion that "it worked for Grimm in his fairy tales. It worked for Disney, it was going to work for us." Ford was appreciative that Lucas allowed him creative input in developing the character of Han Solo. He recalled, "George Lucas gave me a lot of freedom to change little parts of the dialogue which weren't comfortable. He knew the movie was based so strongly on the relationship between the three of us, that he encouraged our contributions." Ford even ad-libbed some key lines of dialogue, such as his famous line: "Great, kid, don't get cocky!" to Mark Hamill in the midst of a ferocious space battle.

Ford intentionally kept his interpretation of Solo simple. His greatest challenge was playing scenes laden with technicalities. He admitted, "I had a difficult time with lines like 'It'll take a megasecond for the nava computer to calculate the coordinates!' You feel silly, shooting guns that make no sound and destroying battleships that you're unable to see because the special effects won't be done for months." These complaints were more than offset by his chemistry with his costars, including Alec Guinness. Ford confessed to being intoxicated by playing opposite the legendary star: "Me in a movie with Alec Guinness! I thought if he laughed at me just once, I'd pack my bags and go home." Fortunately, if Sir Alec did laugh at Ford's emoting, it was in the right places.

Portrait of a rogue star pilot. (LucasFilm Ltd.)

As the production fell further behind schedule, Lucas found himself facing a crisis in having the film ready for its Memorial Day weekend 1977 premiere. The budget had grown to $10.5 million. At the studio's insistence, a rough work print, minus some key special effects sequences, was screened for Fox executives. Their reaction, to put it charitably, was nonenthusiastic. Film composer John Williams was hired to create a suitable score for the movie, and it became immediately apparent that his work would play an important role in the final cut. (Williams's soundtrack so perfectly suited the action that it would seem inconceivable today to experience *Star Wars* without this superbly stylized score.) Lucas continued to work on the film until one week before its actual premiere. Even Ford began to have second thoughts about the movie's reception by the public: "I really wasn't sure how that first film would do. I thought it would either reach a wide audience who would recognize it as a fun, space-age Western, or it would be so silly that my two kids would be embarrassed for me to even leave the house." The studio was confused as to how to market this unique film. Thirteen ad campaigns were considered, ranging from the obvious ("The Story of a Boy, a Girl and the Universe") to the unadulterated truth ("Never Before in Cinema History Has so Much Time, Money and Technology Been Spent. . . . Just for Fun!"). Eventually, the finished cut was submitted for release. In anticipation

of what he felt would be a disastrous reception, George Lucas literally left for Hawaii rather than face the scorn of critics and Fox.

Fortunately, Lucas's considerable talents do not extend to fortune-telling. *Star Wars* premiered on May 25, 1977. By the end of the first day, Fox knew it had a winner. Audiences stood in line for hours, and their reaction to the film was unlike anything even the most optimistic executive at the studio could have hoped for. Within days, *Star Wars* became *the* hip film to see. It crossed most demographic boundaries and appealed to people of all ages and cultural backgrounds. Lucas had fashioned a superb, old-fashioned adventure story bolstered by the best special effects ever seen on-screen. Although originally inspired by the *Flash Gordon* and *Buck Rogers* serials, more than one astute critic saw that Lucas had been inspired by—of all things—John Ford Westerns, in particular, *The Searchers*. In fact, there are so many elements of the classic Western to be found in *Star Wars* that many critics cited Harrison Ford's playing of Han Solo as reminiscent of John Wayne (who starred in *The Searchers*). Replied Ford: "If that is so, it was completely unconscious. I didn't know I was doing it, playing it like Wayne at times. I just did what was written down—that's all George's genius. If I'm like Wayne in places, it's my subconscious supplying something that's necessary."

Star Wars became the first film to sell $10 million in tickets on its opening weekend. Bolstered by critical acclaim, the movie would also garner eleven Oscar nominations. Ford and the cast received polite kudos from the press, but most of the praise was lavished on Lucas and his special effects team. Ford was immediately rewarded with being taken seriously as a leading man, and his financial problems would vanish literally overnight. He had received a small percentage of the profits and earned over $1 million from the film's initial release. He purchased a large home in Beverly Hills and furnished it lavishly. The press called him an overnight success, but, as often happens, reporters neglected to remember he had paid his dues in the industry only to be largely ignored for so many years. Characteristically, he was low-key about his newfound fame. He admitted, "I guess I'd still be building furniture if I hadn't fallen in with George Lucas. I had been around for fifteen years, doing TV, doing small roles in features until *Star Wars*. Now, a few of my problems have been solved, apparently forever—problems like how to pay the bills and like what I will do next, that kind of thing." He would later embellish his comments by saying, "I guess I owe a lot to George for bringing me back from the wilderness in terms of my career. He's been responsible for a lot of good things happening to me."

The movie would usher in the greatest merchandis-

The victors of the battle over the Empire are hailed as heroes. (20th Century Fox)

ing boom connected with a feature film since the Bond films of the mid-sixties. Not having foreseen such an occurrence, Ford did not have a percentage of the profits from licensing deals for the series. Although the studio would send him prototypes of the merchandise which bore his likeness, he showed little interest. "Personally, I had no emotional response to seeing Han Solo dolls," he said. His enthusiasm was probably dampened by the fact that the merchandising line would eventually gross over $2.6 billion, of which he was not entitled to dime one. *Star Wars* would be successfully reissued theatrically in 1978, 1979, 1981, and 1982, and its home video incarnations on tape and laser disc have earned mega-millions more. As of this writing, George Lucas is planning a major theatrical rerelease for 1997. The "Special Edition" will include some footage excluded from the original release, as well as enhanced special effects and soundtrack. In anticipation of this eagerly awaited event, a barrage of new *Star Wars* merchandise began hitting the stores in 1995.

Star Wars quickly overtook *Jaws* as the highest-grossing film of all time. Few disputed it deserved to. Ironically, not everyone connected with the movie would go on to fame and fortune. Despite starring in the movie's two successful sequels, Mark Hamill and Carrie Fisher never achieved the "above the title" marquee success which Ford did, although both have certainly earned praise through the variety of roles which *Star Wars* opened up for them. Others who benefited were George Lucas, who became a major force in the film industry (although he has not directed a single feature film in the ensuing years due to the trauma of making *Star Wars*); the team which would form Industrial Light and Magic, the best known special effects company in the world; and 20th Century Fox, which would see the value of its stock double in the short term. In the mid-nineties, George Lucas is beginning to aggressively plan the "prequels" to *Star Wars*—presumably Chapters I, II, and III. Undoubtedly, this will allow the team of filmmakers to entice a new generation with the help of the miraculous technology available today.

Perhaps the meaning of *Star Wars*'s success was best summed up by Harrison Ford in a 1980 issue of

Starlog magazine, the definitive fan magazine for sci-fi aficionados: "What *Star Wars* has accomplished is not possible. But it has done it, anyway. Nobody rational would have believed that there is still a place for fairy tales. There is no place in our culture for this kind of stuff. But the need is there; the human need to have the human condition expressed in mythic terms."

Reviews

"A magnificent film. George Lucas set out to make the biggest possible adventure fantasy out of his memories of serials and older action epics, and he has succeeded brilliantly. . . . Harrison Ford is outstanding as the likable mercenary pilot."
—DAILY VARIETY

"An escapist masterpiece, one of the greatest adventure movies ever made."
—NEWSDAY

"A grand and glorious film, the best movie of the year."
—TIME

"The most elaborate, most beautiful serial ever made. It's both an apotheosis of Flash Gordon serials and a witty critique that makes associations with a variety of literature that is nothing if not eclectic. . . . One of Mr. Lucas's particular achievements is the manner in which he is able to recall the tackiness of the old comic strips and serials he loves without making a movie that is, itself, tacky."
—VINCENT CANBY, NEW YORK TIMES

Heroes (1977)

"It was critical that I have as many roles as possible between the first and second Star Wars *films.... After* Heroes, *I felt secure that I was not going to be typecast."*

CAST:

Jack Dunne: Henry Winkler; *Carol*: Sally Field; *Ken Boyd*: Harrison Ford; *Bus Driver*: Val Avery; *Jane Adcox*: Olivia Cole; *Dr. Elias*: Hector Elias; *Gus*: Dennis Burkley; *Peanuts*: Michael Cavanaugh.

CREDITS:

Director: Jeremy Paul Kagan; *Producers*: David Foster and Lawrence Turman; *Screenplay*: James Carabatsos; *Director of Photography*: Frank Stanley; *Editor*: Patrick Kennedy; *Art Director*: Charles Rosen; *Music*: Jack Nitzsche and Richard Hazard. *Running time*: 113 minutes. A Turman-Foster Company Production; Released by Universal Pictures.

Upon completing *Star Wars*, Harrison Ford felt confident his work in the film would provide him with the breakthrough role every actor covets. While he could not foresee that the film would become a cultural phenomenon, he was concerned that it could prove popular enough to present him with the problem of being cast in only Han Solo–type roles. While preparations were being made for the film's sequel, *The Empire Strikes Back*, Ford began to look in earnest for a role which would prevent him from being earmarked as a one-trick pony in the action/adventure genre. He confessed that by playing such roles, "I might make more money. But it wouldn't be long before I'd be bored and stereotyped."

Ford's choice for his follow-up film surprised many in the industry. He accepted a decidedly supporting role in *Heroes*, a offbeat comedy-drama starring Henry Winkler and Sally Field. Ironically, there were parallels between his and Winkler's devotion to this film. While Ford featured the possibility of being typecast, Winkler was already facing such a dilemma by virtue of his overnight success as Fonzie in *Happy Days*. Winkler's character in *Heroes* was as far removed from that lovable leather-jacketed delinquent as possible.

Playing a psychologically disturbed Vietnam veteran, Winkler teamed with director Jeremy Paul Kagan, who several years earlier had inspired Winkler to give a memorable performance as a radical opposite Sissy Spacek in the critically acclaimed television movie *Katherine*. That was pre-Fonz, however, and the cultural icon the TV char-

As Ken Boyd, the volatile Vietnam vet. (Universal Pictures)

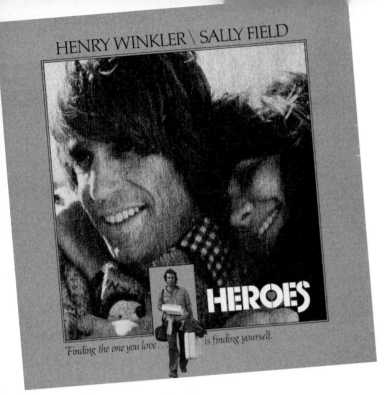

HENRY WINKLER \ SALLY FIELD

HEROES

'Finding the one you love... is finding yourself.

Heroes was primarily a vehicle for Henry Winkler and Sally Field, both of whom were trying to shed their image as television personalities. (Universal Pictures)

acter had become began to grate on Winkler. As the female lead, Sally Field also had the demons of stereotyping to escape, courtesy of her "goodie-goodie" image as Gidget and the Flying Nun. By 1977, having outgrown the perky teenager roles with which she became so identified, Field found her career on a downslide. Thus, the trio of actors in *Heroes* had a great deal riding on the film—if not financially, then certainly artistically.

The movie follows one Jack Dunne, a Vietnam vet given to implausible and occasionally outrageous behavior due to the horrors he has seen in the war. He escapes from a mental hospital, carrying the life savings of his fellow patients who are intent on investing in the worm farm Dunne plans to build in Eureka, California. Along the way, he intends to round up additional partners who served with him in Vietnam. He encounters Carol (Sally Field), a disillusioned young woman who is fleeing New York City and her forthcoming marriage. At first, the pair get on each other's nerves, but they eventually fall in love. Soon, however, Carol sees that behind Jack's charming exterior lies a bitter and disturbed man.

Harrison Ford appears for only fifteen minutes, portraying a redneck 'Nam vet who, like his friend Jack Dunne, tries to cope with haunting memories of the war. However, he dominates these sequences with a low-key assurance that was singled out by critics. Director Kagan allowed Ford the ability to improvise, and indeed, he changed his character from a midwesterner to a Missouri farmer a scant ten days prior to shooting. Ford liked the

challenge the new accent presented, and he traveled around Missouri taping conversations with locals to research his role and ensure he got the proper inflections down pat. Coincidentally, he met a young man whose passion for stock cars mirrored his character's in the film. To avoid alienating the man, Ford presented himself as a writer researching a novel. He later explained that had he admitted he was an actor, he felt it would have put "a distance between himself and everyday people."

Despite its noble if message-laden screenplay, *Heroes* was not a totally enjoyable film to make. Sally Field, who replaced Talia Shire in the only significant female role, complained about the hordes of teenagers who would besiege the set in search of "Fonzie." She griped to the press, "It was like the Hitchcock film *The Birds* or something." At one point, Field was trapped in her trailer by maniacal fans who—convinced it was Henry Winkler's dressing room—hoped to get a glimpse of the Fonz in his leather jacket (among other things). Shortly after the film's release, Field complained to the press about the artistic shortcomings of the final cut, stating that the people in charge of the film "just couldn't get their heads together about what kind of a picture they were making. What it is is a light, romantic romp along with the Vietnam war. You just don't mix the two. It may make a lot of money, but it's a far cry from wonderful."

Field's comments were fairly accurate. *Heroes* never quite jells, due to its inconsistent screenplay. One moment the audience is watching the schtick between the cute-as-a-button Field and the boyishly charming Winkler. The next moment we are witnessing a brutal barroom brawl and horrible flashbacks to Vietnam. The uneven story line is somewhat mindful of Blake Edwards's earlier *Soldier in the Rain*, but that film had a certain poignancy that *Heroes* lacks. In fairness, Winkler tries hard, and he does succeed in stepping out from the long shadow of the Fonz. However, one is always aware that he is trying with desperation to show his diversity as an actor. He is burdened by a character who is overdeveloped and more annoying than lovable. When Field encounters his obnoxious antics on a cross-country Greyhound trip, one can only wonder what she eventually sees in him. Traveling with Winkler's Jack Dunne is like having a manic-depressive version of comic Rip Taylor next to you on a bus ride from hell. At this point in his career, Winkler simply did not have the dramatic screen presence to carry a complicated role like Jack Dunne. However, he never embarrasses himself, and he does lend a genuine sincerity to the role, especially in the film's most moving sequence— a tragic visit to the home of an old army buddy. Field is as watchable as ever but does little here to shed her overgrown pixie image. Her acceptance as a leading lady would still be several years away. As for Harrison Ford, he overshadows his costars by *underplaying* his role—a trait he has wisely kept throughout his career.

Although *Heroes* generated decent box-office grosses, it was not the blockbuster Henry Winkler and Universal had hoped for. Like so many other television stars, Winkler never found an audience that followed him into the movie theaters. Despite the film's shortcomings, however, it is worth remembering that it boldly dealt with the emotional impact of Vietnam at a time when it was not fashionable to do so. Indeed, *Heroes* preceded such Vietnam-inspired classics as *The Deer Hunter*, *Coming Home*, and *Apocalypse Now*. While hardly in the same league as those Oscar-winners, *Heroes* deserves a certain respect for at least attempting to be original.

Reflecting on *Heroes* after its release, Harrison Ford criticized the way his character had been developed in the script, claiming he initially believed in the role "but it didn't tell the whole truth. The only kind of belief I can have is something that's well rounded, and this was not that kind of a role. But I had a chance to create a completely different image from Han Solo. I knew that *Heroes* would be very quickly released and would show me in something totally different, and thus give some proof of my versatility." By all accounts, *Heroes* did just that.

Ken (*Ford*) becomes the object of Jack's (*Winkler*) suppressed anger. (Universal Pictures)

Reviews

"Ford gives us an inkling of what this movie might have been. Behind his good old boy behavior, you feel the toll that war has taken on this man. When Ford is on-screen, the tiny echoes of old movies die away and Heroes *takes on—briefly—the resonance of real life.*"
—HOLLYWOOD REPORTER

"An excruciatingly obvious film . . . brings to the motion picture theater all the magic of commercial television except canned laughter. Well, no truly rotten movie is perfect. . . . Ford is effective in a supporting role too small to make the picture worth seeing."
—VINCENT CANBY, NEW YORK TIMES

Sharing dreams of grandeur over the proposed worm farm with Field and Winkler. (Universal Pictures)

"Poorly written melodrama. . . . Winkler [gives] a good, though flawed performance. Plot peg is standard—boy and girl, running from separate problems, meet 'cute' and fall in love, with some ups and downs enroute. Speaking of the writing 'cutes,' there's a plague in this screenplay, mainly in the Winkler character and actor's performance. Since the character has a history of mental malaise, the kooky bits are many and just awful. See Winkler confound his doctor. . . . See him escape from the hospital. See him run and jump and streak and shout."
—VARIETY

THERE HAS NEVER BEEN A FORCE LIKE

From "Jaws" & "The Deep"
ROBERT SHAW
deeper in danger than ever before

From "Star Wars"
HARRISON FORD
defending himself in a different kind of War

From "A Bridge Too Far"
EDWARD FOX
going as far as he can to blow more than a bridge

From "Spy Who Loved Me"
RICHARD KIEL
sinks his teeth into the action

From "Spy Who Loved Me"
BARBARA BACH
the Spy everyone still wants to love

From "Rocky"
CARL WEATHERS
fighting on rough ground again

From "The Pirate"
FRANCO NERO
as the treacherous Lescovar

FORCE 10 FROM NAVARONE

SAMUEL Z. ARKOFF and OLIVER A. UNGER Present A GUY HAMILTON PRODUCTION

ROBERT SHAW

starring

HARRISON FORD   BARBARA BACH   EDWARD FOX

and FRANCO NERO as 'Lescovar' in

"FORCE 10 FROM NAVARONE"

CARL WEATHERS   RICHARD KIEL   ALAN BADEL   Based on the novel by ALISTAIR MacLEAN

Screen Story by CARL FOREMAN   Screenplay by ROBIN CHAPMAN

Produced by OLIVER A. UNGER   Co-produced by JOHN R. SLOAN and ANTHONY B. UNGER   Directed by GUY HAMILTON

Music Composed and Conducted by RON GOODWIN   Filmed in Panavision® Technicolor® Prints by Movielab   [DOLBY SYSTEM]   A Navarone Productions Limited Film

PG PARENTAL GUIDANCE SUGGESTED
SOME MATERIAL MAY NOT BE SUITABLE FOR CHILDREN

RELEASED BY AMERICAN INTERNATIONAL PICTURES

© 1978 American International Pictures, Inc.

10

Force 10 From Navarone (1978)

"I did Force 10 From Navarone *for the wrong reasons.... The film gave me billing above the title.... It also upped my price. That is important because in order to be considered for certain parts in Hollywood you have to have a certain price tag attached to your name. If you're in the high-priced category, you've got a head start."*

CAST:

Major Mallory: Robert Shaw; *Lt. Col. Mike Barnsby*: Harrison Ford; *Sgt. "Milly" Miller*: Edward Fox; *Maritza Petrovitch*: Barbara Bach; *Nicholai Lescovar*: Franco Nero; *Sgt. Walter Weaver*: Carl Weathers; *Captain Drazac*: Richard Kiel; *Lt. Doug Reynolds*: Angus MacInnes; *Major Petrovitch*: Alan Badel; *Major Schroder*: Michael Byrne.

CREDITS:

Director: Guy Hamilton; *Producer*: Oliver A. Unger; *Executive Producer*: Carl Foreman; *Screenplay*: Robin Chapman; *Based on the novel by* Alistair MacLean; *Screen Story*: Carl Foreman; *Director of Photography*: Chris Challis; *Editor*: Ray Poulton; *Art Director*: Geoffrey Drake; *Music*: Ron Goodwin. *Running time*: 118 minutes. Columbia-EMI/Navarone Productions; Released in U.S. by American International Pictures.

Advance teaser poster which capitalized on the stars' previous successes. (American International Pictures)

One of the longest-delayed sequels in movie history, *Force 10 From Navarone* hit theater screens seventeen years after the premiere of its classic predecessor *The Guns of Navarone*. Despite its makers having almost two decades to fashion a quality film, *Force 10* feels as though it were conceived by people who O.D'd on old John Wayne trailers over a long weekend. It is appropriate that the British-made *Force 10* would be distributed in the U.S. by American International Pictures, the studio known for force-feeding such upper-crust epics as "Beach Blanket Bingo" to hapless audiences worldwide. (If AIP had made *Gone With the Wind*, Frankie Avalon and Annette Funicello would have played Rhett and Scarlett under the skilled direction of Ed Wood.

Force 10 is a film of jaw-dropping ineptness which strives for greatness. Although the production values were high by AIP standards (the studio did not finance the film but merely distributed it), it is the cinematic equivalent of fast food. Label it a "McEpic." There's enough penny-pinching evident throughout to make one suspect Leona Helmsley was the producer. The film does achieve one impressive feat: it manages to squander the considerable talents of some well-respected actors, Harrison Ford among them. Ford plays Mike Barnsby, a U.S. officer who is assigned to lead a secret mission into World War II Yugoslavia. Among his *Force 10* commando squadron are

real capacity. He flies, he fights, he's got brains . . . an interesting character. I think it'll work." He obviously had been mistakenly reading the script for *The Guns of Navarone*, because this character in this mess has no such qualities. After the film's release, Ford admitted, "I did have doubts as to whether *Force 10* would work. I was promised a rewrite on it, promised a lot of things which didn't come through." He later complained, "There was no reason for my character being there. I had no part of the story that was important to tell. I had a hard time taking stage with the bullshit that I was supposed to be doing."

Filming *Force 10* proved to be almost as arduous as viewing the final cut. Although ailing dictator Marshal Tito placed the Yugoslavian army at the filmmaker's disposal (for a price, of course), even he could not command the weather. The unrelenting rain and fog forced the company to eventually relocate to England. Prophetically, a series of severe storms followed, wreaking havoc on the production once again. The dreary atmosphere seemed to have permeated the set, as the demoralized cast and crew gamely went through the motions of completing a film that seemed to boast an endless production schedule. Watching the finished film, one can only be saddened by the waste of a talented cast, which by accident or design includes a number of veterans from the James Bond films: Robert Shaw (*From Russia With Love*), Richard Kiel ("Jaws" from *The Spy Who Loved Me* and *Moonraker*), and Kiel's *Spy* costar Barbara Bach. The interesting angle of casting Kiel and Bach as adversaries once again could have had intriguing results, but they are not allowed to build any chemistry, and their character names—Drazac and Maritza—sound disturbingly like new miracle pain killers from Johnson & Johnson. Another 007 veteran, Guy Hamilton, directed *Force 10*. Hamilton initially gained fame as the man who helmed the best of the Bond epics, *Goldfinger*. Sadly, *Force 10* is more reflective of his work on

Mallory (Robert Shaw) and Miller (Edward Fox), two British officers who have recently destroyed the massive Nazi gun batteries at Navarone. The group is to locate a traitor among the Yugoslav partisans and assassinate him, and in their spare time demolish a strategic bridge.

The screenplay reads like an encyclopedia of clichés: the Brits and Yanks are always at each other's throats until they learn to respect each other under fire; the token black commando (Carl Weathers) spouts enough platitudes about racial injustice to have made the late left-wing attorney William Kunstler join the Ku Klux Klan; and every time someone lays a trap for the Nazis on the most isolated roads imaginable, an enemy convoy conveniently comes along within seconds and falls victim to the scheme. The shortcomings in the script are not helped by the muddled camerawork, and the amateurish editing appears to have been accomplished with a Ginsu knife.

Harrison Ford initially explained what attracted him to the role in this ill-fated venture: "Barnsby's a man of

the later films in the series, such as the anemic *Man With the Golden Gun*. Only old pros Robert Shaw (in one of his last screen appearances) and Edward Fox escape unscathed, in roles played by Gregory Peck and David Niven in the original *Navarone*. Franco Nero is entertaining as a charismatic villain, but the plot twist involving his character is telegraphed from minute one. Carl Weathers, a usually engaging screen personality, is given an embarrassingly patronizing role. (Although it's hard to imagine *anyone* shouting lines like "Hey! That's some heavy-duty dog doo!" with any sense of dignity.)

As for Harrison Ford, one can only say that this is the least animated performance of his career. He seems so . . . grouchy. That's understandable, considering his character has to bark clichés that had moss on them in the forties ("This place is crawlin' with Krauts!"). He looks completely—and appropriately—uncomfortable. However, while his character is a bore, Ford keeps his dignity intact and keeps the stale dialogue from generating unintentional laughter from the audience. The lion's share of criticism must be borne by screenwriter Robin Chapman, who gave up writing creatively and began merely typing after page two of the script. No help is rendered by director Hamilton, who admittedly must cope with cheesy special effects. (A rock slide seems to be accomplished by rolling a few pebbles in front of the camera, and the climactic destruction of the bridge looks like a Lego set was knocked over by a careless toddler. At least the rocks could be recycled for AIP's forthcoming disastrous—oops—disaster film *Meteor*, which was inflicted upon audiences the following year.) Ron Goodwin's bombastic score—probably the only upbeat element of the film—simply accentuates the fact that this is a pseudo-epic. Fittingly, the most gripping moments of the movie occur over the beginning credits—when we see clips from the original *Guns of Navarone*.

Force 10 did not impress critics or audiences. While it did nothing to further Ford's career, neither did it damage his reputation as a rising young leading man. In fact, by achieving his goal of getting "above the title" billing, it catapulted him into permanent star status. The movie itself strives nobly to emulate the great war films but falls somewhat short of *Hogan's Heroes*. Ford elaborated on his disappointment with the finished film: "It was a job I did for the money. . . . I can't do that, and I won't ever do that again. It wasn't a bad film. There were honest people involved making an honest effort. But it wasn't the right thing for me to do." With all due respect to his reasoning, *Force 10 was* a bad film, though a well-intentioned one. A more suitable summation of the movie could be found in critic James Agee's timeless review of the 1949 John Wayne bomb *Tycoon*. His entire critique stated simply, "In

A rare moment of bliss on an otherwise dreary set, with Barbara Bach. (American International Pictures)

this movie several tons of dynamite are set off—none of it under the right people."

Reviews

"The plot is banally improbable. Hamilton's direction is sluggish and the camera work . . . makes the least of the picturesque locations. . . . There is, moreover, an unmistakable air of haste and cost-cutting that suggests that most of the production budget went to high-priced stars."

—Tom Buckley, NEW YORK TIMES

"Ford, required to look grim and determined throughout, hasn't decided if he's playing the story of G.I. Joe or Terry and the Pirates."

—NEWSWEEK

"Guy Hamilton builds Force 10 *into a straight-forward, man-sized adventure—a nostalgic toast to the good old war years, when we unequivocally rooted for our side to win."*

—Bruce Williamson, PLAYBOY

"Awful sequel, poor in all departments, although Shaw, Ford, and Nero try to give it a lift. [They] attempt to blow a bridge vital to Nazis. They blew the film instead."

—LEONARD MALTIN'S MOVIE AND VIDEO GUIDE

11

Hanover Street (1979)

"I don't choose films on the basis of whether I think they're going to be commercially successful. I'm recalling this bit of advice that Noël Coward gave to David Lean: 'Do what pleases you and if people don't like it, get out of show business.'"

Cast:
David Halloran: Harrison Ford; *Margaret Sellinger*: Lesley-Anne Down; *Paul Sellinger*: Christopher Plummer; *Major Trumbo*: Alec McCowen; *2nd Lt. Jerry Cimino*: Richard Masur; *2nd Lt. Martin Hyer*: Michael Sacks; *Sarah Sellinger*: Patsy Kensit; *Harry Pike*: Max Wall; *Col. Ronald Bart*: Shane Rimmer; *Lieutenant Wells*: Keith Buckley; *Sgt. John Lucas*: John Ratzenberger.

Credits:
Director and Writer: Peter Hyams; *Producer*: Paul N. Lazarus III; *Director of Photography*: David Watkin; *Editor*: James Mitchell; *Production Designer*: Philip Harrison; *Music*: John Barry. *Running time*: 109 minutes. Hanover Street Productions; Released by Columbia Pictures.

Ford with Down. *Hanover Street* proved to be one of the more underrated films of their careers. (Columbia Pictures)

Hanover Street was a landmark film in at least one respect: it represented the first time Ford received top billing in a major production for a top studio. Unfortunately, the film's rocky road to completion extended to the movie's theatrical release. Director-writer Peter Hyams had been impressed by Harrison Ford since seeing his charismatic turn as Han Solo. "He jumped off the screen for me. . . . [He] possessed a fierce, burning sexual energy." Hyams had lobbied for Ford to be cast in the starring role of his forthcoming film *Hanover Street*, a forties-style soap opera/adventure/espionage thriller set in World War II London. Columbia, which was financing the rather expensive production, vetoed Ford for the lead and insisted upon having Kris Kristofferson as the dashing American flyer who has a passionate but illicit affair with a British nurse. Genevieve Bujold was set to play opposite Kristofferson, but as so often happens, the best-laid plans of mice, men, and Hollywood executives often go awry. Kristofferson began to have second thoughts about the project and, in a much publicized spat with the studio, "ankled" the film. Bujold followed suit, and Hyams was left with a start date approaching and a conspicuous shortage of leads. Eventually, Columbia relented and agreed to approach Ford, who was then shooting in Yugoslavia. Hyams personally flew to the set to meet with the exhausted actor, who was not initially receptive to taking on another big-budget war film set in Europe.

Reluctantly assisting Christopher Plummer in infiltrating Gestapo headquarters. (Columbia Pictures)

with overcoming his own mediocre status in life. A sizable budget was spent recreating wartime London, and the film succeeds in conveying a sense of atmosphere of the era. While no one faulted the art direction, gorgeous cinematography, and the wonderfully lush John Barry score, Hyam's script came under fire for its lack of believability. Ford plays a U.S. fighter pilot stationed in London who fearlessly leads bombing raids over Germany on a daily basis. He is courageous only because his loneliness prevents him from having a fear of death. In true storybook manner, his life suddenly finds meaning after he has a chance encounter with Down. The two flirt and, over afternoon tea, fall in love. While Down returns Ford's feelings, she mysteriously refuses to discuss her personal life and will not even tell him her name. He discovers she is married, and the two grudgingly part company. Seconds later a convenient air raid of devasting destruction lands them both in each other's arms. For a moment, it is as if they are the only two people in the world, as the bombs explode around them. Suffice it to say that from this point, the couple shares more than crumpets. The story jumps back and forth between Ford fighting both the Nazis and his obsession for Down, and Down trying to play loving wife and mother while fantasizing over her erotic escapades with Ford. Refreshingly, Down's husband is not portrayed as the stereotypical abusive spouse, but rather as a sophisticated, gentle, and decent man (played with typical understated charm by Christopher Plummer). Although the script piles up a

Recalled Ford, "I did at first say no. I was still making *Force 10*, which was running a month over schedule, and I needed a break." However, he changed his mind after finding he had a rapport with Hyams: "We were night shooting a fight scene on top of a windy bluff overlooking the ocean [for *Force 10*]. Peter and I talked all night in my trailer. I was impressed with his monomaniacal attitude." Ford also explained that he had a more practical reason for doing the film: "My motivation for doing *Hanover Street* was because I had never kissed a female human being on the screen before. The characters I played were totally sexless, and here was a movie that was being touted as a romance. That was a clear, obvious reason for doing it."

With Ford on board, Hyams succeeded in casting Lesley-Anne Down as the female lead. Down's star had risen considerably in recent months as the result of her amusing performance (and memorable erotic sequences) opposite Sean Connery in *The Great Train Robbery*. Christopher Plummer rounded out the leads as Down's husband—a man obsessed

Ford idolized in a Japanese fan magazine. (Jerry Ohlinger's Movie Material Store)

84

Assisting a critically wounded Plummer to the safety of the partisans. (Columbia Pictures)

stack of clichés longer than Betty Grable's gams, the sequences in which Down finds herself emotionally torn between two worthy men in her life—as well as her little daughter—ring true.

As long as the story deals with this ménage à trois, the situations are believable. Suddenly, however, the script makes a sharp turn and tries to disguise its soap opera origins by becoming an espionage thriller. Plummer decides to prove his manhood to his wife by undertaking a dangerous mission to infiltrate Gestapo headquarters to steal some vital documents for the Allies. Through one of those miraculous cinematic coincidences, guess who is assigned the job of flying Plummer over enemy lines? You got it. Naturally, the plane is shot down, conveniently killing everyone but Ford and Plummer. By necessity, Ford must accompany his companion on his "mission impossible." The two men succeed but are discovered and must flee for their lives. In a fierce battle with the Nazis, the French Underground rescues them, and Ford escorts a badly wounded Plummer back to England. Naturally, by this point, Ford learns through yet another coincidence that Plummer is married to Down. Nice guy that he is, Ford refuses to divulge the affair and informs Down upon his return that they must part company for good. Although she is heartbroken, Down's newfound respect for her husband's courage leads one to believe the couple will live together happily ever after. The lesson here is clear for any males whose wives doubt their virility: simply embark on a suicide mission, infiltrate a foreign power's police headquarters, steal secret documents, and

get yourself virtually blown in half. Chances are "the little woman" will get off your back for a while, too.

Despite the clichés and unabashed influences from old wartime tearjerkers, *Hanover Street* is an engrossing and moving story. In less capable hands, the film would generate more unintentional laughs than *Plan 9 From Outer Space*. However, director Hyams is far more impressive than screenwriter Hyams, and he manages to blend the awkward mixing of several genres successfully. The film also benefits from the charisma of its three principals. Ford cuts a dashing figure in his leather flight jacket and cap, cigarette dangling from his lips. Another actor would look like he was pretentiously trying to recreate a 1943 Lucky Strike advertisement in *Life* magazine, but Ford's disarming naturalness avoids this. It's a good, solid performance allowing him to display a wide range of emotions. He benefits from lovely Down's equally low-key and charming performance. Her character is a good, old-fashioned woman who both welcomes and dreads the romantic predicament in which she finds herself. Down conveys the inner demons which haunt her in a believable way, leaving the audience sympathetic with her plight. Christopher Plummer's scene-stealing capabilities are in ample evidence as the archetypal upper-crust British gentleman who discovers he would rather die than remain dull. His scenes provide *Hanover Street* with some much-needed levity amidst all the teary-eyed encounters. Surprisingly, the movie also works well on the level of a war film. Although the transition to an action/adventure story line is anything but seamless, Hyams does a good

As Halloran, escaping the Nazi dragnet at the farm. (Columbia Pictures)

Although *Hanover Street* is often like *Brief Encounter* with swastikas, time has been kind to it. It may have been a failure, but it was a worthy film on many levels. As for Ford, the movie remains an unhappy memory. Shortly after its release, he lamented, "I don't even like to think about *Hanover Street.* . . . I've never even seen the film."

Reviews

"Ford, who excelled as a dazed veteran in Heroes, *gives the pilot a kind of glum, almost sour intensity."*

—CHARLES CHAMPLIN, *LOS ANGELES TIMES*

"Every now and then a film comes along of such painstaking and overripe foolishness that it breaks through the garbage barrier to become one of those rare movies you rush to see for laughs. . . . I've no idea whether the film will do anything for Mr. Ford's screen popularity. He's more a comic strip character here than he was in Star Wars, *which was a live action cartoon. . . . In his last movie,* Capricorn One, *which was about a faked space mission, Mr. Hyams was exposing fraud. In* Hanover Street, *he's practicing it."*

—VINCENT CANBY, *NEW YORK TIMES*

*"*Hanover Street *demonstrates that sugary dialogue doesn't work any better than in the '40s. . . . Only when Down takes a back seat and Ford is thrown together with her cuckolded husband, British Secret Service topper Christopher Plummer, does* Hanover Street *manifest any vital signs of life. The last third of the picture becomes a model of efficient war filmmaking, but then it's back to tears and stiff upper lips."*

—*VARIETY*

"Ford, as a romantic leading man, is fairly stolid and one-dimensional, laboring hard to simulate the kind of casual charm that Redford, Newman, and a dozen other male actors must work hard to conceal when they want to be taken seriously. Hyams gives us a pair of lovers who seldom appear to enjoy each other very much."

—BRUCE WILLIAMSON, *PLAYBOY*

job of handling the action. Plummer and Ford's infiltration of the Gestapo headquarters is genuinely suspenseful (even if we are to believe that it is the most ineptly guarded building since the Mayberry Savings and Loan), and the resulting chase sequence and battle scene move at a brisk pace. The film also benefits from one of composer John Barry's most haunting scores.

Unfortunately for Harrison Ford, *Hanover Street*, like most of the films he would make in the years immediately after *Star Wars*, was not a critical or box-office success. Reviewers scoffed at the dated story line and credibility gaps in the script. Columbia found it a difficult film to market. The main ad campaign stressed the romantic elements of the story, but this did not lure audiences. While not winning many enthusiastic reviews, the able cast was spared from personal attack.

Although Ford continued to grow as an actor with each film, skeptics began to ponder whether his success in *Star Wars* would ever translate into mainstream movies. In later years, Ford made it clear that even he was disappointed with the final cut of *Hanover Street*. He had lobbied extensively for certain script changes but at that time did not carry enough clout to ensure the rewrites were done. Yet, as for so many of his other films, Ford's criticism seems to have been unnecessarily harsh.

12

The Frisco Kid (1979)

"It's such a wonderful script!"

CAST:
Avram Belinski: Gene Wilder; *Tommy Lillard*: Harrison Ford; *Chief Rabbi*: Leo Fuchs; *Mr. Jones*: Ramon Bieri; *Chief Gray Cloud*: Val Bisoglio; *Darryl Diggs*: George Ralph DiCenzo; *Rosalie*: Penny Peyser; *Matt Diggs*: William Smith; *Samuel Bender*: Jack Somack.

CREDITS:
Director: Robert Aldrich; *Producer*: Mace Neufeld; *Executive Producer*: Howard W. Koch; *Screenplay*: Michael Elias and Frank Shaw; *Director of Photography*: Robert B. Hauser; *Editors*: Maury Winetrobe, Irving Rosenblum, and Jack Horger; *Production Designer*: Terence Marsh; *Music*: Frank DeVol. *Running time*: 122 minutes. Released by Warner Brothers.

ollowing *Hanover Street*, it was Harrison Ford's intention to take a much needed hiatus from the rigors of moviemaking for at least six months. However, when the opportunity arose to costar with Gene Wilder under the direction of Robert Aldrich in the lighthearted Western *The Frisco Kid*, the temptation to continue his workaholic lifestyle proved too much. Eager to showcase his seldom-seen talent for comedy, Ford was enthused about the project from the very beginning. He also welcomed the opportunity to work stateside for a change, on location in Arizona and Colorado, after having been abroad for an extended period of time making his last few films.

Ford's role in *The Frisco Kid* is very much a supporting one, as the vehicle was a showcase for Gene Wilder, who was riding high during this period as the star of *Blazing Saddles* and *Young Frankenstein*. Wilder portrays Avram Belinski, an inept rabbi in 1850 Poland, who is sent to America to organize a growing Jewish community in San Francisco. He relishes the challenge, specifically the inevitable journey through the Wild West enroute to his destination. However, immediately after he sets foot on these shores, his good nature and gullibility are exploited by a gang of thugs who pretend to be his friends and protectors. He is beaten, robbed, and left alone in the desert. Helpless as a babe in the woods, he is befriended by an Amish clan whom he mistakes for fellow Hasidim. He later finds a genuine protector and friend in Tommy

Ford and Gene Wilder in an apparent Old West version of a Calvin Klein ad. (Warner Bros.)

Lillard, a small-time bandit who sympathizes with the rabbi. Lillard grudgingly admires Avram's determination to fulfill his obligation to the Jews in San Francisco, regardless of the personal risks he must endure. Along the way, the duo encounter shoot-outs, fistfights, and any number of other obstacles. They also form a genuine friendship, reinforced by each man saving the other's life.

The Frisco Kid was a change of pace not only for Ford but for director Robert Aldrich as well. Aldrich was primarily known for offbeat dramas like What Ever Happened to Baby Jane? and macho epics such as The Dirty Dozen and Attack! Here, Aldrich shows a surprisingly deft ability to handle the script's gentle humor in a dignified way. Equally impressive is Ford's performance as Tommy Lillard. Though knowing full well he would be the straight man of the film, he was inspired to take the role by his son Ben (twelve at the time). Ford had a tradition of seeking Ben's advice as to which roles would serve him best, and the boy inspired him by comparing the Tommy Lillard character to Ford's favorite straight man, Bud Abbott. Ford works wonders with the role, holding his own against veteran scene-stealer Gene Wilder. The two men have a wonderful chemistry, and one regrets that Ford so infrequently has gotten a chance to show his lighter side on-screen. The screenplay vacillates between light drama and Mel Brooks–type slapstick, but somehow the end result works. Wilder is at his best here, and he

has many memorable sequences, such as the one in which he tries to hide his Yiddish accent and pretend he is a Texas cowboy in deceiving a beautiful girl. The film is filled with Jewish stereotypes that would probably never appear on-screen in these politically correct times. However, they are good-natured and never demeaning. Without them, The Frisco Kid would be devoid of most of its charm.

The movie was a bittersweet experience for Ford. While he enjoyed the filmmaking process, his personal life was in turmoil. He and his wife Mary eventually decided to divorce, albeit amicably. Addit-

The shootout on the beach with Avram's assailants. (Warner Bros.)

(*Above*) Bad guys get the drop on an amused Avram (Wilder) and Tommy (Ford). (Warner Bros.)

(*Below*) The role of gunfighter Tommy Lillard gave Ford a rare opportunity to show his comedic talents. (Warner Bros.)

ionally, the movie was not particularly successful. By 1979, Ford had not yet established himself as a major box-office force, and Wilder's leading-man status was fading. Nevertheless, *The Frisco Kid* remains an underrated film that deserved a better reception. Undoubtedly, many of Ford's fans have enjoyed its many pleasures on home video.

Reviews

"*The two pivotal characters are played by Gene Wilder and Harrison Ford with an amiability and zest that are hard to resist.*"

—Motion Picture Digest

"*A movie based on a great idea that, when realized, isn't. . . . Aldrich is not much at home in the kind of lovable comedy this film wants to be. The comic timing is always a couple of beats off. . . . There's no shortage of talent in* The Frisco Kid, *but it's the wrong talent for the wrong material. . . . [Ford is] required to be little more than a stalwart straight man to the star.*"

—Vincent Canby, New York Times

"*Excellent counterpoint is provided by Ford, who finally lives up to the potential he displayed in* Star Wars. *As a cowboy who reluctantly adopts the green-horn for their westward journey, Ford provides the perfect foil for Wilder's gaffes, and their scenes together play wonderfully.*"

—Variety

89

13

Apocalypse Now (1979)

*"It's just the one scene—the laundry list scene. It told the
audience all they needed to know for the rest of the movie.
And when George [Lucas] saw it, the scene was halfway over before
he recognized me. That was exactly the way I wanted it."*

CAST:

Col. Walter Kurtz: Marlon Brando; *Lt. Col. Kilgore*: Robert
Duvall; *Captain Willard*: Martin Sheen; *Chef*: Frederic
Forrest; *Chief*: Albert Hall; *Lance*: Sam Bottoms; *Clean*:
Larry Fishburne; *Photojournalist*: Dennis Hopper; *General*:
G.D. Spradlin; *Colonel Lucas*: Harrison Ford.

CREDITS:

Producer and Director: Francis Ford Coppola; *Screenplay*:
John Milius and Francis Ford Coppola; *Suggested by the
novel* Heart of Darkness *by* Joseph Conrad; *Narration
Written by*: Michael Herr; *Director of Photography*: Vittorio
Storaro; *Production Designer*: Dean Tavoularis; *Editor*:
Richard Marks; *Music*: Carmine Coppola and Francis Ford
Coppola. *Running time*: 139 minutes. An Omni Zoetrope
Presentation. Released by United Artists.

Images of Captain Willard's journey into "the heart of darkness."
(Elektra Records)

To classify *Apocalypse Now* as a "Harrison
Ford film" would not only be an overstate-
ment but an injustice to the movie itself.
Not that Ford doesn't contribute to its overall success in his brief scene early in the
story. However, *Apocalypse Now* is truly a
collaborative effort in which every participant shines, yet
no one dominates.

The towering figure behind this bold, audacious,
somewhat insanely ambitious epic is director-producer-
screenwriter Francis Ford Coppola, who fulfilled his long-
standing dream of adapting Joseph Conrad's *Heart of
Darkness* into a cinematic metaphor for the Vietnam War.
Like other gargantuan epics such as *Cleopatra*, *The
Alamo*, the 1962 remake of *Mutiny on the Bounty*, and
Heaven's Gate, so much has been written about the struggles and disasters in the making of *Apocalypse Now* that
the finished film itself seems only slightly more dramatic
than the logistical problems encountered in bringing it to
the screen. Unlike the aforementioned epics, however,
Apocalypse Now was both a critical and box-office success. Despite its artistic merits, however, the movie will
always be remembered primarily as Coppola's personal
triumph over a series of incredible hardships which
threatened his health and sanity. Indeed, so compelling
was the story *behind* this film that a highly acclaimed fea-
ture-length documentary, *Hearts of Darkness*, would be
devoted to the trials and tribulations of making this project a reality.

Willard's reluctant crew: (*clockwise from upper left*) Chief (*Albert Hall*), Chef (*Frederic Forrest*), Clean (*Larry Fisburne*), and Lance (*Sam Bottoms*). (United Artists)

Coppola's involvement with *Apocalypse Now* can be traced back to his days as a young filmmaker in the late sixties. Disillusioned with the war, and officially designated as a conscientious objector, Coppola felt the project would be appropriate to launch his newly formed American Zoetrope production group. Frustrated with the mechanics of the studio system, Coppola hoped to develop a close-knit group of young actors and technicians with whom he could create the types of experimental movies the majors would never agree to finance. Coppola became friendly with a group of talented young filmmakers, each sharing his dream of artistic freedom in the cinema. Among the group were University of Southern California film students George Lucas and John Milius. With Coppola, they discussed the feasibility of adapting Joseph Conrad to the screen. His novel dealt with the adventure of a man named Marlowe who travels up the Amazon to locate Kurtz, a famed ivory hunter who has gone insane and established himself as king of a tribe of natives. Marlowe finds horror and enlightenment when he finally encounters the mythical Kurtz, who blends intellectual observations with a penchant for wanton violence.

Coppola and company were not the first moviemakers to attempt to bring Conrad's bizarre tale to the screen. In 1939, Orson Welles announced he would make

his motion picture debut with an ambitious production of *Heart of Darkness*. However, after incurring the skyrocketing costs of building a small number of the required sets, the studio canceled the project for fear that the costs would quickly snowball out of control. Welles turned his attention to *Citizen Kane*. The Conrad story remained untouched by Hollywood for decades.

Initially, it was decided that John Milius would write an original screenplay, loosely based on *Heart of Darkness*, wherein an army captain in Vietnam would be sent by the government to dispose of Col. Walter E. Kurtz, a renowned Green Beret who has gone mad and now reigned as leader of a tribe of murderous Montangard natives in Cambodia. Kurtz is waging an indiscriminate war against both friend and foe, and the army brass wants him "terminated with extreme prejudice" before his madness becomes public knowledge. En route, the self-doubting Willard finds himself obsessed with his target, even though he has never met him, and views their ultimate encounter with a mixture of fear and adulation. This sketchy outline for a screenplay was to serve as the genesis of a film which George Lucas would direct and Francis Coppola would produce for American Zoetrope. Immediately, however, artistic differences became apparent. Lucas and Milius viewed the film as a low budget, cinema verité experience which would be shot on location in Vietnam amidst actual battles! Coppola insisted upon making the movie a large-scale production with major stars. Ultimately, the project was shelved when Lucas turned his attention to *THX 1138* and *American Graffiti*. Coppola became the cinematic superstar of the early 1970s with *The Godfather* and *The Godfather, Part II*. Coppola would win five Oscars for these acclaimed epics and found that he could literally write his ticket in Hollywood. In 1975, he announced he would resurrect the *Heart of Darkness* project, now retitled *Apocalypse Now*.

Coppola managed to secure a $13 million budget from United Artists, for distribution rights for the film. In order to retain complete artistic control, however, Coppola had to personally guarantee any overages in the budget. Plans were to shoot on location in the jungles of the Philippines, thanks in part to dictator Ferdinand Marcos's pledge to allow full use of the military for the film's extravagant battle sequences. George Lucas warned Coppola to back away from the project. He feared that the logistics of shooting in such a remote location would be too difficult to overcome. Complicating matters was the fact that the Philippines was in the midst of a civil war. However, Coppola was obsessed with *Apocalypse* and felt confident enough to brag that he would create the first film to possibly win a Nobel Prize.

The original schedule called for a sixteen-week shoot,

commencing in March 1976. However, from the moment Coppola set foot in the jungles, his enthusiasm would be tested by a series of disasters which would tax the resolve of even the most determined filmmaker. His first problem had been to secure the right cast for the demanding roles. To his frustration, virtually every major star had rejected the part of Kurtz, including Robert Redford, Jack Nicholson, Steve McQueen, and Al Pacino. Finally, Coppola succeeded in casting Harvey Keitel as Willard and Marlon Brando as the enigmatic Kurtz. Brando agreed to film for only three weeks, with Coppola incurring steep financial penalties for any additional time before the cameras. Robert Duvall (who, like Brando, had worked for Coppola in *The Godfather*) would have a brief but important role as Colonel Kilgore, a gung-ho, possibly insane Air Cavalry officer whose penchant for surfing leads him to attack a village simply to be able to utilize its beaches.

After shooting for several weeks, Coppola began questioning Harvey Keitel's interpretation of the role of Willard. In a controversial decision which exemplified the creative clout the director enjoyed, Coppola fired Keitel, thereby rendering useless weeks of expensive footage. Tongues started wagging back in Hollywood that Coppola was already in trouble, but he assured United Artists that all was under control and that Martin Sheen would be assuming the role of Willard. Coppola's next challenge came when, in the midst of one of the most detailed and expensive battle sequences ever filmed—the assault of Kilgore's helicopters on a Vietnamese village—the Philippine army commandeered their "choppers" to fight the rebels in the surrounding hills. When Coppola did get the helicopters back, they were inevitably manned by new pilots who were unfamiliar with the scene's requirements. As a result, the massive battle scenes went overschedule and overbudget. The delay meant a postponement of Marlon Brando's sequences. However, Brando let it be known that he was reluctant to accommodate his director and threatened to keep the $1 million advance he received regardless of whether he was in the film or not. After much pleading and cajoling, Coppola persuaded his former "Don Corleone" to reconsider, and even elicited a promise from him to study Conrad's novel thoroughly so he would be prepared to shoot his sequences as expeditiously as possible.

Coppola's relief would be short-lived. Morale on the set began to decline as the cast and crew tried unsuccessfully to cope with sweltering heat, a lack of modern conveniences, and an endless array of exotic—and rather unattractive and hungry—insects. Coppola rented a large house near the location and found himself entertaining his workers, as they had had nowhere else to go and nothing else to do to amuse themselves. Coppola would

soon learn that the least of his worries was being a constant host for dinner parties. He continued to be unsatisfied with much of the footage he was shooting. He scrapped an entire sequence in which Willard and his men dine with the remnants of French aristocracy in a remote mansion in the jungle, thus rendering the costly and time-consuming scene an exercise in futility. The film was already seriously behind schedule when Mother Nature decided to test Coppola's resolve. A typhoon destroyed the expensive sets which the crew had labored so hard to construct, and the production was closed for two full months. The resulting delay began to generate industry buzz, speculating that Coppola was in so far over his head—logistically and financially—that *Apocalypse Now* might have to be abandoned.

Publicly, Coppola assured the press and the studio that everything was under control. Privately, he confided to his wife, Eleanor (who was making a documentary about the filming for publicity purposes), that he was losing control of the film and could not even visualize a definitive climax for it. With the budget ballooning to a projected $20 million, he called his epic "shit." No sooner were the sets rebuilt and filming resumed than Coppola received another staggering blow: Martin Sheen had suf-

Robert Duvall's towering, Oscar-nominated performance as the surf-crazy Colonel Kilgore. (United Artists)

Ford in his cameo as Colonel Lucas in what he calls "the Laundry List Scene." (United Artists)

fered a massive heart attack on location and was in real danger of dying. With his lead actor fighting for his life, Coppola tried gamely to shoot around him and use body doubles. However, it soon became apparent that he could only "cover" for Sheen so much without losing the impact of certain sequences. After five full weeks, Martin Sheen returned to the production tan and fit. However, Coppola secretly worried that the rigorous schedule might place Sheen back in harm's way.

As the production staggered forward, Coppola admitted he could not continue to direct and do rewrites on the script, which were necessitated by the constantly changing logistical problems. And besides, he was attempting to recut his *Godfather* movies into a miniseries for NBC long distance! He hired John Milius to make the necessary changes in the story to accommodate the daily crises. The pivotal climactic scenes between Kurtz and Willard were still being refined, and Coppola was unsure of which direction the ending would take. He was not comforted by the arrival of a severely overweight and bald Marlon Brando on the set. The actor had ballooned to a size which had made him self-conscious and uncomfortable. Coppola and Milius had to quickly rewrite key sequences in order to de-emphasize Brando's weight. The decision was made to turn the issue into an advantage and to photograph Brando in the shadows. This would not only downplay the actor's portly physique but also add an element of mystery to the character. Brando's second "surprise" was not so easily overcome. Coppola became convinced that the eccentric actor had never even read the Conrad novel and

had no idea what his character's motivations were. In his fanciful autobiography, Brando claims he did read the novel but does admit he "bullshitted" the gullible Coppola on many occasions. Nevertheless, Coppola was stuck in the middle of the jungle with the ultimate "Method actor" endlessly discussing character traits which should have been decided months before.

Coppola nervously watched the clock as the three precious weeks to which Brando had committed were slipping away even as the actor sat pensively about the set dwelling on "motivations" for Kurtz. Ultimately, Coppola became so desperate that he included Dennis Hopper in the Kurtz scenes. Hopper, who was to play a small role as an insane photojournalist who idolizes Kurtz, was not so far removed from the mental status of his character at the time. Although he has made a remarkable career comeback recently, during the filming of *Apocalypse,* Hopper was still spaced-out from the effects of the wild lifestyle he had lived in the sixties. This put Coppola in the unenviable position of dealing with a moody, slow-moving, portly leading man who had no concept of the script and a supporting actor who could not stop talking senseless gibberish. Coppola finally just turned on the cameras and let Brando improvise fascinating but self-indulgent speeches which he hoped could be of some value in the final cut. Most of these were cut from the film, despite Brando's recent claims that they represented the deepest commitment he had ever made to a characterization. By his own admissions, however, the speeches were too far out even for the ramblings of the insane Kurtz.

With the press cynically referring to the film as "Apocalypse When?" Coppola's epic lumbered toward completion after 238 days of principal photography, during which over 1.5 million feet of film was shot. The final budget had more than doubled to over $30 million (of which Coppola was personally responsible for $16 million). Initially convinced he had a disaster on his hands, the director began to feel more confident in the editing stages. Eventually, Coppola embraced *Apocalypse Now* with such intensity that he insisted on screening the film's rough cut in competition at the 1979 Cannes Film Festival. The movie shared the coveted Palme d'Or that year with *The Tin Drum,* but controversy still ensued, with charges being leveled that the festival's judges were bullied by Coppola into voting for his movie.

Coppola insisted that *Apocalypse Now* be premiered in a grand way. The film opened in 70mm in select theaters in August 1979. Initially, the idea was to treat the movie as though it had the prestige of a Broadway play. There would be no beginning or end credits, and the audience would receive a program providing information on

94

War's paradoxes: a priest leads a prayer service while a tank destroys an enemy position only yards away. (United Artists)

the production and the cast and crew. Even these plans did not escape criticism, as unions and guilds forced Coppola to add end credits to the general release engagements of the film. In doing so, Coppola placated foreign exhibitors who were lobbying for an explosive ending to the film. He ran the end credits over unused footage of the bombing of Kurtz's compound—a sequence he had decided not to use because he felt it made the climax feel like a conventional war movie. By the time it opened, *Apocalypse* was easily the most anticipated film of the year, perhaps of the decade.

It has been said that "victory has many fathers, but defeat is an orphan." The hypocrisy of the Hollywood establishment was never more apparent than when *Apocalypse Now* finally premiered. Suddenly, the legions of writers and industry executives, once salivating at the thought of Coppola being disgraced by a wretched film, began to call the director a genius and his film a work of art. *Apocalypse Now* was clearly not everyone's cup of tea, but even those who detested the story admitted that Coppola had accomplished the impossible by bringing a film of this proportion to completion. Most of the reviews were enthusiastic, although more than a few critics complained that the anticipated assault on Kurtz's compound in the finale is never shown. They accused the film of ending on a whimper, not a bang. Coppola argued that he wasn't making a war film, but rather a thought-provoking statement about the Vietnam War's psychological toll on the national conscience. In any event, the offbeat epic became a cinematic milestone, and it ultimately grossed

over $150 million. (Sadly, Coppola *would* have to declare bankruptcy in the years to come, ironically not because of *Apocalypse* but a big-budget musical misfire named *One From the Heart*.) The movie received many Oscar nominations but not surprisingly lost to the more conventional and less disturbing *Kramer vs. Kramer* in the prestigious Best Picture category.

Apocalypse Now is a rarity—a truly original motion picture which dares to combine spectacular action sequences with an intimate portrayal of two men whose psyches lead them to a common confrontation with their own personal demons. Coppola never did get the definitive ending he so wanted for the movie, but the film benefits because of the vagueness of its finale. It can be interpreted differently by each member of the audience and becomes more mesmerizing with every viewing. The final dying words of Brando's tragic Kurtz—"The horror. The horror."—linger in the mind. Yet *Apocalypse Now* is certainly in the great tradition of all movie epics. The sheer sweep of the film is staggering, and the movie is filled with so many memorable sequences that there isn't space to recount them. However, the highlights are well known to most movie lovers: the phenomenal and surrealistic helicopter attack, set to the music of Wagner; the psychedelic night battle at the bridge, which illustrates the madness of war with a power not experienced since Kubrick's *Paths of Glory*; the haunting image of Willard being salvaged from a self-destructive drinking bout only to be used as a reluctant assassin by the army brass; the poignant and heartbreaking reaction of Willard's crew to

Marlon Brando as Kurtz, the renegade Green Beret officer whom Willard is to "terminate with extreme prejudice." (United Artists)

he realization that they have inadvertently slaughtered an innocent Vietnamese family; the entrance of Willard's men into Kurtz's secret jungle compound—a place which reeks of death and is inhabited by the ghostly army of Montangard tribesmen.

The performances are uniformly excellent. Martin Sheen is a vague but stoic Captain Willard. We never learn much about the character, and that is intentional. This movie is not about Willard. Although he is on-screen in virtually every scene, he is merely our guide on a journey into revelation and terror. Robert Duvall steals the film with a brief but Oscar-nominated role as the gung-ho officer who loves "the smell of napalm in the morning" and values surfing over his own life. Frederic Forrest, Albert Hall, Sam Bottoms, and fourteen-year-old Larry Fishburne are outstanding as Willard's drugged-out, battle-weary crew. As Kurtz, Marlon Brando gives the most bizarre performance of his career. Depending on who you ask, his acting is an example of either over the top, pretentious self-indulgence, or a masterful job of portraying a tragic figure of mythical proportions. As with all of Brando's work, however, he dominates the screen and fascinates the audience.

Harrison Ford had a relatively small role in this

prestigious production. He plays the officer who explains the mission to Willard and instructs him to "terminate" Kurtz. Ford found working with Coppola refreshing and rewarding. "Francis lets you make a choice and then moves everything to support you, to make it work for you," he said. "He's really delightful." One improvisation of Ford's which Coppola kept in the script was calling his character "Col. G. Lucas," an inside joke referring to George Lucas's original intention to direct the film. He dismissed his overall contribution: "Most of my scenes were shared with Martin Sheen. It wasn't a big role for me, just a nine-day cameo as a U.S. Army Intelligence Colonel. I had my hair cut short, and presented another image—Vietnam style." In fact, Coppola had initially offered Ford a larger role, but the actor was also up for the part of Han Solo in *Star Wars*, which George Lucas was then gearing up to film at the same time. Ford weighed the options then settled on accepting the Lucas project. He would later say, "And I am glad, because some guys went to the Philippines to make *Apocalypse Now* for three months and stayed a year." Ultimately, *Apocalypse* coproducer and longtime Ford champion Fred Roos was able to squeeze the actor into the mammoth production with the small role of Colonel Lucas. Aside from allowing him to be part of one of the most high-profile films of the decade, *Apocalypse* marked the first meeting of Ford and his future wife Melissa Mathison, who was working as an assistant to Coppola.

The technical achievements in *Apocalypse Now* are textbook examples of cinematic perfection that allow viewers to wonder in amazement how this massive undertaking ever came together at all. Yet, ultimately, it is Francis Coppola's triumph. *Apocalypse Now* may have been a mad undertaking, but it is what moviegoing should be all about: thought-provoking, entertaining, and visually fascinating. It is disturbing and often unpleasant. But then again, so are many other works of art. It is a motion picture for the ages.

Apocalypse Now Redux (2001)

In 2001, Francis Ford Coppola released a highly anticipated "definitive cut" of the film, titled *Apocalypse Now Redux* and featuring 49 minutes of footage he had to eliminate from the initial version due to running-time considerations. The "lost footage" is a mixed bag. The legendary "French plantation" sequence, in which Willard and his men encounter a stubborn family of French aristocrats determined to cling to their crumbling personal empire, is fascinating in many respects, but Coppola was correct to cut it from the original version. It is slow, talky, and includes a superfluous love scene between Willard and

Willard (*Sheen, center*) and Chef (*Forrest, right*) arrive in Kurtz's compound, guided by an insane American photojournalist (*Dennis Hopper, left*). (United Artists)

the wife of one of the Frenchmen. An amusing but overlong sequence features Willard's crew trading much-needed fuel for sexual favors from the Playboy Bunnies, who are now stranded and isolated. More successful is an extension of the final scene with Robert Duvall's surf-crazy Colonel Kilgore. In the *Redux* version, we see a rare playful side of Willard as he steals Kilgore's beloved surfboard. The most mesmerizing addition to the film is a gripping sequence in which Kurtz visits the jailed Willard and lectures him about the deceitful way the military is reporting on the progress of the war. The scene goes a long way in explaining Kurtz's motives and makes him seem far less an unpredictable madman. *Redux* was released theatrically and played to strong box-office results, mostly in upscale urban theaters, before an eagerly awaited DVD release. As a testimony to its enduring impact, many critics cited it as one of the best films of 2001. Interestingly the advertising campaign now featured Harrison Ford's name above the title—despite the fact that he only appears onscreen for several minutes.

Reviews

"Watching Apocalypse Now *is like having a series of doors opened for you, each revealing the phosphorescent imagery of hell. You walk out of it shaken up, all powers of judgment jettisoned. Because it is visually, sonically, and emotionally unlike any other movie, it radically changes the perceptions and responses you bring to movies. And because it creates new standards of film-making, new standards of criticism have to be brought to it. Descriptions of 'good' or 'bad' are pointless:* Apocalypse Now *is such an awesome, man-made piece of work—a kind of colossus—that it goes far beyond tedious considerations of personal taste."*

—LAWRENCE O'TOOLE, *MACLEAN'S* (CANADA)

"When it is . . . evoking the look and feelings of the Vietnam War, dealing in sense impressions for which no explanations are adequate or necessary, Apocalypse Now *is a stunning work. It's as technically complex and masterful as any war film I can remember, including David Lean's* The Bridge on the River Kwai. . . . Apocalypse Now, *though, wants to be something more than a kind of cinematic tone poem. Mr. Coppola himself describes it as 'operatic,' but this, I suspect, is a word the director hit upon after the fact. Ultimately, [it] is neither a tone poem nor an opera. It's an adventure yarn with delusions of grandeur, a movie that ends—in the all too familiar words of the poet Mr. Coppola drags in by the bootstraps—not with a bang, but a whimper. . . . [The assassination plot] which seems to have been imposed on the film from above, keeps interrupting the natural flow of Mr. Coppola's perfectly sound, sometimes incredibly beautiful meditation upon war. . . . With the exception of Mr. Brando, who has no role to act, the actors are superlatively right. . . . Vittorio Storaro [is] responsible for the extraordinary camerawork that almost, but not quite, saves* Apocalypse Now *from its profoundly anticlimactic intellectual muddle."*

—VINCENT CANBY, *NEW YORK TIMES*

"There, thanks to the marvel of glorious Technicolor and deafening Dolby sound, is Vietnam in all its sound and fury, recaptured in boldly executed sequences of such stunning force that they leave the audience emotionally shattered and completely overwhelmed."

—KATHLEEN CARROLL, *NEW YORK DAILY NEWS*

14

More American Graffiti (1979)

CAST:
John Milner: Paul LeMat; *Terry Fields:* Charles Martin Smith; *Laurie Bolander:* Cindy Williams; Debbie Dunham: *Candy Clark;* Carol ("Rainbow") Morrison: *Mackenzie Phillips;* Eva: *Anna Bjorn;* Joe: *Bo Hopkins;* Andy: *Will Seltzer;* Lance: *John Lansing;* Newt: *Scott Glenn;* Teensa: *Mary Kay Place; and Ron Howard as* Steve Bolander; *Featuring* the voice *of Wolfman Jack;* Officer Falfa: *Harrison Ford (uncredited).*

CREDITS:
Director and Writer: B.W.L. Norton; *Executive Producer:* George Lucas; *Producer:* Howard Kazanjian; *Based on characters created by:* George Lucas, Gloria Katz, and Willard Huyck; *Director of Photography:* Caleb Deschanel; *Editor:* Tina Hirsch. *Running time:* 111 minutes. A LucasFilm Ltd/Coppola Company Production; Released by Universal Pictures.

Ford's brief, uncredited appearance as "Officer" Bob Falfa, seen here arresting Candy Clark's boyfriend for smoking pot. (Universal Pictures)

"You can't go home again" goes the old adage, and *More American Graffiti* amply demonstrates the wisdom of this timeless bit of advice. Six years after the release of George Lucas's classic coming-of-age comedy-drama, virtually all the creative forces were reunited in what must have seemed like an irresistible project from both a production and financial standpoint. However, like so many sequels, this one proved to be too much of a good thing. Lucas's original was a masterpiece of economic filmmaking. Those involved in the film—made on a shoestring budget with a largely unknown cast—were hungry for a hit. Despite—or perhaps because of—the low budget and claustrophobic atmosphere, audiences could concentrate on getting to know the main characters and the complexities of their interwoven relationships. *More American Graffiti*, on the other hand, is kind of like the small-town kid who makes it big and finds he can't identify with his roots any longer. Although the main members of the cast return in fine form, their characters are mere shells of the people we met in the original film. Worse, no one is given anything very interesting to do.

Director-screenwriter B.W.L. Norton tries to emulate the appeal of the earlier film by having various story lines intermingled. However, while this effect was startlingly effective the first time around, it proves to be an annoying distraction here. The script traces developments in the lives of the characters over four consecutive New Year's Eves. We follow the exploits of John Milner (Paul LeMat), the hotshot race car driver as he mingles wom-

Paul LeMat as the ill-fated John Milner, res-urrected from the original (*left*). (Universal Pictures)

fire. With the exception of Terry Fields, who bumbles his way through Vietnam, none of the characters generate much interest.

Paul LeMat's John Milner is no longer the charismatic know-it-all who inspired such fascination in the earlier film. He's now reduced to acting like Elvis Presley in *Speedway*, changing a seemingly endless number of spark plugs and tires in preparation for some of the dullest auto races ever filmed. He flirts with a vivacious foreign exchange student (Anna Bjorn), but since her character does not speak a word of English, it gives you a pretty good idea how creative their dialogue is. Charles Martin Smith is still very engaging as Terry ("The Toad") Fields, and while he's *still* a klutz, incapable of imposing a self-inflicted gunshot wound, Vietnam has made him a bit more self-confident and a lot more cynical. Occasionally, the war sequences threaten to have an impact, but one is always distracted by the obvious use of

anizing with his quest to become a legend on the track in 1964. Cut to Vietnam circa 1965, where the nerdish Terry Fields (Charles Martin Smith) attempts various unscrupulous methods—including trying to inflict his own wounds—in order to be sent back to the States. Cut to 1966 and his equally lovable but far more annoying paramour Debbie (Candy Clark), who, presuming Terry is dead, rambles through a series of unrewarding relationships with abusive men. Cut to Steve and Laurie Bolander (Ron Howard and Cindy Williams), the white-bread couple of 1967, whose relationship has gone from storybook romance to living hell, making *Who's Afraid of Virginia Woolf?* look like an example of domestic tranquillity. Other supporting cast members from the original *Graffiti* repeat their roles, but their only purpose is to serve as ballast for this cinematic mis-

Ron Howard as Steve Bolander in the original film (*left*), and in the sequel. Sadly, Howard appears only briefly in the sequel. (Universal Pictures)

stock news footage edited into the battle scenes. Candy Clark, so watchably goofy in the first movie, whines her way through the years like Peg Bundy on LSD. The sequences that generate electricity are the domestic disputes between Ron Howard and Cindy Williams. It's quite shocking—in a refreshing sort of way—to see the stars of *Happy Days* and *Laverne and Shirley* stretch their dramatic talents in scenes that are smartly written and genuinely tense.

While the first movie was completely apolitical, this one is so left-wing that one suspects that writer B.W.L. Norton is a pseudoynm for Abbie Hoffman. However, the script does not have the courage of its convictions and paints a formulaic, sugarcoated look at the mid to late sixties, as though not wanting to offend anyone who actually lived through the era. The Terry Fields character gripes a lot about insubordination, but aside from dropping the contents of a latrine on some officers as a joke, he seems about as politically active as Gomer Pyle. John Milner remains oblivious to the tensions of the times and indulges himself solely in his passion for cars and women. That chauvinist husband Steve Bolander and aspiring feminist wife Laurie will be reunited is never in doubt. However, when they find their common bond is civil disobedience (the riots at Berkeley awaken them to the horrors of police brutality), it seems their idea of rebellion is limited to knocking over some trash cans with their van. Having "survived" these shocking forms of protest, one assumes they graduate to calling in phony pizza orders and playing "ring and run." The screenplay never rises above a shallow and pretentious level. It strives to invoke memories of the Chicago Seven but ends up recalling *My Three Sons*. Director Norton does invoke some innovative camerawork, often showing various related sequences on screen at one time. However, the device is never utilized to any great effect, and it becomes annoying after the first half-hour.

Harrison Ford appears briefly in an unbilled cameo as the motorcycle cop Officer Falfa. Hidden behind sunglasses and a helmet, he is all but unrecognizable—however, the voice is unmistakable. Evidently "graduating" from racing his hot rod on the strip (as depicted in the original film), Falfa is now the consummate cop with a fixation on busting small-time dope users. Ford's short sequence involves arresting Candy Clark and her on-screen hippie boyfriend for possession of marijuana. There is little that is memorable about the scene itself, although it does play a pivotal role in the rambling events which follow. Ford injects some much needed laughs into the film by playing his role like a Jack Webb clone. If only the filmmakers had had the foresight to engage his services beyond this all too short sequence, the movie might have risen above the level of a sitcom.

Even the poster campaign for the film seemed confusing and misguided. (Universal Pictures)

More American Graffiti was executive-produced by George Lucas, and possibly because the cast was grateful for what the original film did for their careers, all were willing to return to the fold (save for Ford and Richard Dreyfuss). The most difficult aspect of the production was scheduling the stars around their other commitments: Cindy Williams was appearing in *Laverne and Shirley*; Ron Howard was not only the star of *Happy Days* but was pursuing his budding career as a director as well (which probably explains his all too limited time on-screen). The movie strives to be an epic, but its cost-cutting measures are quite apparent: it was shot entirely in California, with even the Vietnam sequences filmed on a farm in Modesto (giving credence to all the locals who have always warned "It's a jungle out there"). In certain shots, suburban homes can be seen in the distance. Since not many Viet Cong families resided in ranch-style houses, one assumes their presence in the film is the result of sloppy continuity work. The soundtrack music of the era is quite effective, but the producers have surprisingly omitted any archival news footage, which would have added greatly to the sense of authenticity. Instead, we get endless padding in the form of rock numbers from Country Joe and the Fish, among others, none of which are particularly memorable.

When *More American Graffiti* opened in 1979, it was skewered by critics and ignored by audiences. A less-

The gang's all here—apparently to prove "you can't go home again": Howard, Williams, Clark, Smith. (Universal Pictures)

than-creative ad campaign did not help, and the film quickly faded from theaters. While one is tempted to lay blame on director Norton, it must be said that any imaginable sequel to *American Graffiti* was misguided and destined for failure, as it is one movie that tied up most of its loose ends satisfactorily. The lasting impact of those updates on the characters which appeared before the end credits of the first film are repeated here virtually verbatim. But to what avail? We learn nothing interesting about these characters' lives, after having seen them in greater detail, other than the fact that Terry Fields did not die. He simply feigned his death and walked out of Vietnam as an act of defiance. (Just how far a nerd in a Hawaiian shirt is going to walk in the midst of a battle zone is anyone's guess, but the implication is he survives.) Even this development cheapens the impact of the original film, as we learned in the closing minutes of that story that Fields was reported "missing in action." That such a likable small-town boy could be the victim of a faraway war generated the desired audience reaction in a wonderfully understated way. This time around, not only do we find he's alive and well, but the previous movie's subtleties about war are replaced by a sledgehammer approach. Reviving Fields is a cheap trick not equaled until they reincarnated Superman after his much-vaunted "death." There is, however, one moment that does linger a bit in the mind beyond the closing credits. Prior to being reminded that John Milner was killed by a drunken dri-

ver, we see him drive into the sunset while an oncoming car seems to be heading directly toward him. We brace ourselves for the crash, but the film fades out. The audience is left wondering whether this is the moment in which Milner meets his death, but—in contrast to the rest of the script—the answer is not spelled out for us. If only the rest of the movie demonstrated this much class. As audiences and critics agreed, this time around *More* was less.

Reviews

"Grotesquely misconceived, so much so that it nearly eradicates memories of the original."
—Janet Maslin, New York Times

"More American Graffiti may be one of the most innovative and ambitious films of the last five years, but by no means is it one of the most successful. . . . B.W.L. Norton overloads the sequel with four wholly different cinematic styles. . . . While dazzling to the eye, the flirtation with split-screen, anamorphic, 16mm and 1:85 screen sizes does not justify itself in terms of the film's content. . . . Part of Norton's presumed goal, of course, is to show how the 1960s fractured and split apart. But without a dramatic glue to hold the disparate story elements together, Graffiti is too disorganized for its own good."
—Variety

15

The Empire Strikes Back (1980)

"[Han Solo] is not a cardboard character for me at all. He's real as anything else. I have never thought of the character as having only two dimensions until the critics said so. And they're wrong. The third dimension is me. It's part of me. I intentionally keep my interpretation simple...I can't conceive of any negative aspect of playing a role like Han Solo."

CAST:

Luke Skywalker: Mark Hamill; *Han Solo*: Harrison Ford; *Princess Leia Organa*: Carrie Fisher; *Lando Calrissian*: Billy Dee Williams; *Ben (Obi Wan) Kenobi*: Alec Guinness; *C-3PO*: Anthony Daniels; *R2D2*: Kenny Baker; *Chewbacca*: Peter Mayhew; *Darth Vader*: David Prowse (*Voice*: James Earl Jones); *Yoda*: Frank Oz.

CREDITS:

Director: Irvin Kershner; *Producer*: Gary Kurtz; *Executive Producer*: George Lucas; *Screenplay*: Leigh Brackett and Lawrence Kasdan; *Based on a story by* George Lucas; *Production Designer*: Norman Reynolds; *Editor*: Paul Hirsch; *Director of Photography*: Peter Suschitzky; *Art Directors*: Leslie Dilley, Harry Lange, and Alan Tomkins; *Sound Design and Supervising Sound Effects Editor*: Ben Burtt; *Special Effects Co-Supervisors*: Brian Johnson and Richard Edlund; *Music*: John Williams. *Running time*: 124 minutes. A LucasFilm Ltd. Production; Released by 20th Century Fox.

Despite the record-breaking international grosses for *Star Wars*, George Lucas managed to resist any temptation he might have had to bring a "quickie" sequel to the screen. On the contrary, the success of the original only reconfirmed his commitment to create future "chapters" of his science fiction epic with painstaking preparation. By this point, however, Lucas was determined that another director would helm the project, thus allowing him to concentrate on virtually every other aspect of the mammoth production. (However, Lucas did direct one brief scene in which Luke Skywalker talks with the droid Too-Onebee while he suits up for the Hoth battle.) Emboldened and enriched by the grosses of *Star Wars*, Lucas vowed to become increasingly independent from the major studios. He announced that although the sequel would be distributed by Fox, all of the financing would come from his own production company. Considering the complexity of the epic he wanted to create, coupled with the public's lukewarm response to most sequels, Lucas's decision was not without risk. It was his dream to use the profits from this new film to finance construction of the Skywalker Ranch, a state-of-the-art studio which would be totally under his ownership and control.

Lucas had one distinct advantage on this project, which he had titled *The Empire Strikes Back*—with the elements and characters in the story having been estab-

C-3PO and R2D2 join the rebel forces in their ice cave headquarters. (LucasFilm Ltd.)

a hell of a better movie. I mean it would just be infinitely more exciting and interesting and fascinating. Because with the first one you're in a foreign environment. You just don't know what's going on. And it's the same thing for the author as it is for the audience."

Lucas had entrusted screenwriter Leigh Brackett (primarily known for her work in Westerns) to flesh out his script outline to a full-fledged screenplay. Brackett had done extensive work on the project and completed a first draft, then notified Lucas one weekend that she was entering the hospital for a few days of tests. Unbeknownst to Lucas, Brackett was suffering from terminal cancer. Tragically, this prolific writer would pass away during her hospital stay. Shaken by the death of his screenwriter, Lucas could not afford much time to mourn. Pressure was mounting to finalize the script for *Empire*. Lucas worked on some rewrites himself but then hired Lawrence Kasdan to work full time on the screenplay. Although not well-known in Hollywood at the time, Kasdan had been engaged by Steven Spielberg to write the script for *Raiders of the Lost Ark*, the forthcoming adventure film which Spielberg would direct and Lucas would produce. Kasdan was astonished that Lucas would entrust him with a project of such personal importance as *Empire* without having seen any of his work. Lucas attributed his

lished in the previous movie, the filmmakers would not have to start from "ground zero." As he told the *New York Times*, "We may have had to invent 5,000 new things, but we could build on the 5,000 things we established in *Star Wars*. . . . We can do things we only hinted at in the first movie." He reflected in the documentary *From Star Wars to Jedi*: "It took so much effort to get up to speed, which was essentially to make the first movie. And I created this great world but I didn't have the fun of being able to run around in it. Now that I knew the world and I could see it was a real thing, it brings up all kinds of ideas and things, funny moments and adventures you could have in that environment that you've created. And I never got to exploit that. I always felt that if I went back and made another film in that environment using those characters, I could make

Luke Skywalker battles his long-lost father, Darth Vader, in the shattering conclusion. (LucasFilm Ltd.)

confidence to his "feeling" that Kasdan would not disappoint him. Kasdan did not question Lucas's instincts, although years later he would remain bewildered about why he got the job.

The next major task was to select a director who could not only coordinate the massive logistical problems the film would provide, but to also remain true to Lucas's determination to not let the characters get lost amidst the technology. Ultimately, Lucas made another unorthodox decision, hiring Irvin Kershner, whose own sequel *Return of a Man Called Horse* had impressed him (although not audiences or critics!). At the time, *Empire* producer Gary Kurtz justified the decision by saying: "[Kershner] hasn't gotten a chance to do science fiction before. He's very enthusiastic about it, which is important. He has a good attitude toward the characters on a legitimate basis. He wasn't cynical when we met him. He has a very real interest in science fiction on both its serious and humorous level. We found out during our various interviews with directors that it was more difficult than we had thought to find someone that seemed to be right in terms of their *attitude* toward the material."

Although most of the cast of *Star Wars* eagerly enlisted for the sequel, there was nervousness about the willingness of Alec Guinness and Harrison Ford to participate. Guinness, whose recent eye surgery almost precluded his presence in the film, ultimately let it be known that he would be available. Ford initially balked at becoming part of an ongoing series, as it reminded him somewhat of the bad old days when he was a contract player for the major studios. (He later reflected, "I wasn't going to make that mistake again!") A fruitful discussion with George Lucas changed his mind, however, when Ford was assured that the role of Han Solo would have far more depth to it this time around. This factor was important to Ford, who wanted the character to develop into more than merely someone who presses buttons and ducks from laser beams. He told *Starlog* magazine, "it's part of the natural progression, really. You'd expect development of characters in a second act. I was expecting it and wasn't surprised when I saw a different version of Han Solo in the script. We got to know him better." Ford was also awarded a higher salary and a percentage of the gross, which put him on equal par with costars Mark Hamill and Carrie Fisher.

Harrison Ford and the cast and crew began to earn their raises from minute one on *The Empire Strikes Back*. The first sequence to be filmed would be the ferocious battle between the Darth Vader forces and that of the rebels on the ice planet Hoth. The location was Finse, Norway, a remote village 5,000 feet above sea level, with a population of only one-hundred hardy souls, was virtu-

Lando Calrissian (*Billy Dee Williams*) greets old friend Han Solo (*Ford*) along with Princess Leia (*Carrie Fisher*) and Chewbacca (*Peter Mayhew*). (LucasFilm Ltd.)

ally inaccessible during the best of conditions. To their horror, the filmmakers found that they had to contend with one of Norway's harshest winters in recent memory. Blizzards confined many of the cast and crew to their quarters, while Kurtz, Kershner, and Hamill found themselves having to be rescued when stranded while on location. By the time Harrison Ford arrived to begin filming his first scenes, he found the weather conditions still appalling. Ultimately, he was trapped inside a train within a snow-clogged tunnel. Told to use whatever resources he could muster to make it to the film site, he hired a special train with a snow plow equipped to get him through the next leg of his journey—which still left him twenty-three miles short of his ultimate goal. Ford then utilized a private snowplow to drive him through drifts of up to fifty feet until he arrived on the set. To everyone's astonishment, he was right on time when shooting began the next morning. He explained with characteristic modesty: "Part of professionalism is showing up on time and knowing your lines. But I have never before learned them in an avalanche, or reached a set in a snowplow!" Unit publicist Alan Arnold recalled that Ford "looked a bit dazed and bleary-eyed. He had gotten very little sleep, but he could not have been more courteous. His manner reminded me of something I had not encountered since dealing with

Reissue one-sheet. (LucasFilm Ltd.)

menting that he felt the film would bear more of his personal imprint. A total of sixty-four sets were to be utilized—twice as many as in *Star Wars*. The special effects would be equally ambitious, and the number of individual F/X shots would far exceed those in the previous film. The production team quickly realized that there was not an abundance of studios which could provide the space required. Only Britain's Pinewood Studios had a stage large enough to accommodate their needs. This was the famed "007" Stage, built by James Bond producer Albert R. Broccoli in 1976 for *The Spy Who Loved Me*. However, the necessity of in-house staffing at Pinewood made the overhead prohibitively expensive. Lucas and producer Gary Kurtz eventually utilized virtually every square foot of England's Elstree Studios (which was not booked at the time). The venerable Elstree had lost much of its luster in recent years, but it offered enough vacant space to allow the *Empire* team the breathing room required. Here, one of the largest sets in film history was erected to simulate the rebel base on the ice world of Hoth and later, Yoda's home amidst the bogs on the planet Dagobah. Not even Lucas's California home was off-limits, as the producer's swimming pool was filled with mud and used for the sequence in which a swamp creature drags R2D2 under the muck. A full-scale Millennium Falcon spacecraft, measuring 65' x 16' x 80', was created by a shipbuilding company. The dimensions of this creation were so daunting that the vehicle had to be transported to Elstree in sixteen sections, only to be reassembled and floated into position on hoverpads. Literally every foot of available stage space would be utilized, and certain scenes were being filmed amidst ongoing construction on the very sets being used.

As with *Star Wars*, the filming of *Empire* would be beset by a string of unlucky events that would unnerve even the ever cool George Lucas. The crew was waiting for Stanley Kubrick to complete work on his version of *The Shining* at Elstree, so that production of *Empire* could finally get underway. Immediately prior to filming, a severe fire erupted on Kubrick's set, forcing a postponement in wrapping *The Shining*. Consequently, *Empire* had to incur the substantial cost and logistical nightmares of a delayed shooting schedule. Once production did get underway, it became apparent that the director could not singlehandedly oversee every aspect of the epic story. A second unit was created to help expedite filming of certain sequences. John Barry, commonly known as one of the best production designers in the business, was second-unit director for studio sequences, helping to fulfill

actors from the past, romantic stars like Cary Grant. I have seldom seen it in the younger generation of actors who tend to be self-conscious. Yet, here was Harrison—urbane, self-assured, and charming after having been up half the night. What a pleasant change!"

Any illusions that filming *Empire* would be any less arduous than filming its predecessor were quickly dispelled. So enormous was the scope of the film that Irvin Kershner had to prepare a book of storyboards to help plan each sequence. By the time he was finished, the book was over nine inches thick. Kershner provided a copy of the sketchbook to George Lucas, who would be overseeing the production from the California offices of Industrial Light and Magic. While Lucas would approve most of the major decisions, his absence from the set allowed Kershner some flexibility in deciding day-to-day matters. The director was pleased with this arrangement, com-

A posed publicity shot on the "frozen" rebel base set. (LucasFilm Ltd.)

Yoda, the Jedi Master: one of the film's many unforgettable characters, created by Frank Oz. (LucasFilm Ltd.)

felt it wasn't working at all. I was running out of money and I had a movie I thought was no good." Before long, the $15 million budget had exceeded $33 million, and the film was six weeks behind schedule. In a desperate attempt to stop the flow of money, the cast and crew were required to rehearse on their own day off each week. George Lucas eventually come on the set to oversee the editing process and did all he could to get the production back on track. Kershner was under increasing pressure to get quality results quickly, but this was easier said than done. Lucas had created a number of new characters such as Yoda, the impish trainer of Jedi knights. Lucas was determined that the pint-sized rubber creature have all the characteristics and movements of a human being. However, the logistics of this deprived the crew of sleep. Yoda was pivotal to the script, yet it was feared that he would look like a cheap puppet on-screen. Muppeteer Frank Oz saved the day by devising a complicated method of controlling Yoda's movements. The results were nothing less than miraculous, and despite Yoda's bizarre appearance, one is never under the impression that the Jedi trainer is anything other than a living creature.

In addition to all the technical problems, the filmmakers and studio worried endlessly about plot devices or special effects information being leaked to the press. The script for *Empire* was ambitious in scope and offered a multitude of surprises. The story (Chapter V) begins with the rebel forces fighting a losing battle against the overwhelming armies of the Empire, under the merciless Darth Vader. A key element to the story has Luke under the spiritual guidance of Ben Kenobi (who perished in a battle with Vader in the previous film). Ben directs Luke to train under Yoda to become a Jedi knight. Despite his astounding achievements as a potential knight, Luke disregards his mentor to attempt a suicidal mission to rescue Han Solo, Princess Leia, and Chewbacca from the clutches of Vader. The film climaxes with a thrilling light saber duel between Luke and Vader, in which the latter reveals that they are father and son. Ultimately, Luke, Princess Leia, and Chewbacca escape Vader's trap with the help of a renegade adventurer named Lando Calrissian. The movie's controversial cliff-hanger ending leaves a key element of the plot unresolved: the fate of Han Solo, who has been placed in suspended animation by Vader and is taken by the bounty hunter Bobba Fett to the clutches of the notorious gangster Jabba the Hut.

With so many startling elements to the story, it was pivotal that the audience not be tipped off to these developments in advance. Lucas had the crew rehearse bogus dialogue and scenes to thwart any information leaks. Not even the actors were totally sure at all times of the film's direction. The Vader/Luke relationship was known only to

his long-term dream of being a creative force in the directing field. (On location in Norway, the second-unit director was Peter MacDonald, who would later direct *Rambo III*.) Barry had opted to pass on Lucas's offer to be production designer for *Empire*, so that he could direct his own first film, *Saturn 3*. Ironically, he was fired from that project, thus allowing him to work on *Empire* in a most unexpected way. Sadly, Barry died shortly after starting work on the film. The cast and crew grieved, and George Lucas made the decision to cancel an entire day of filming (at a cost of over $100,000) so that the stars and technicians could attend the funeral. Gary Kurtz took over the reins of the second unit until Harley Cokliss replaced Barry on a full-time basis.

When filming did resume, logistical problems began to mount. Before long, the film was behind schedule and over-budget. To make matters worse, Lucas was not pleased with the footage he was seeing. He recalled, "I

Mark Hamill. David Prowse, the actor behind Vader's mask, was given superfluous dialogue which was later changed and redubbed by James Earl Jones. The element of surprise did not prove to be a problem for Harrison Ford, who voluntarily opted to read only the pages of the script in which he had dialogue. Ford was determined to view the film with the same freshness as moviegoers would.

Ultimately, *Empire* crawled toward completion, although there were some bruised egos. Despite the tension between Kershner and Lucas, the latter was enormously pleased with the finished film. He told the press: "It's a tragedy, a traditional second act. In the second act, you always give your characters a problem. Luke's problems are resolved in the third act, *The Return of the Jedi*. There are no real winners in *Empire* as

there were in the first film, and, for the characters, it's an emotional tragedy. I think it's a better film than the first one." Not everyone was pleased, however. Screenwriter Lawrence Kasdan would later reflect that he was unhappy with the many changes made to his script. He griped, "Han and Leia's relationship is not all what I envisioned. I could be the only one who feels this way, but I thought their romance had a touch of falseness about it. Han and Leia's scenes were among what I was proudest of in my script, but they barely remained." Kasdan cited Kershner and the actors as the main culprits in allowing improvisation to override his written words. He also indicated that while he was pleased with Harrison Ford's performance as Indiana Jones, "I was one of those people who wasn't crazy about him in *Empire*."

Lawrence Kasdan's grumblings aside, *Empire* is a superb piece of cinematic entertainment. Lucas's meticulous ability to tell a story in a unique and exciting fashion has never been more apparent, and in many ways, *Empire* is a more fully developed and enriching story than its noble predecessor. The hardware is still dominant in most sequences, and it would be hypocritical to say that the actors always overcome this obstacle. However, the characters' on-screen relationships are far more intriguing this go-round, and the creatures which inhabit the screen are even more fascinating this time around. The introduction of Yoda makes for one of the most delightful creations in all of the sci-fi genre. Also, the Darth Vader character becomes much more than a one-dimensional villain, thanks to Lucas's insistence upon exploring the relationship with Luke Skywalker.

The trio of stars is far more comfortable in their

Han and Leia finally show their true emotions amidst the battle against the evil Empire.

there's no question that he's added much to the role. When the story gets a little too arch, too corny or old-fashioned, Harrison will express exasperation or skepticism. He represents a portion of the audience that's too sophisticated to see the story from a young person's viewpoint." It would be impossible to cite all the creative geniuses responsible for making *Empire* the science fiction classic it is. Suffice it to say that Irvin Kershner overcame tremendous odds and delivered a film of which the entire cast and crew could be proud.

On the financial front, Lucas could breathe easier. Interest in the film was so high that prepaid exhibitor guarantees placed *Empire* in the black before it had even premiered. Following an international barrage of publicity, the movie opened on Memorial Day 1980 (three years after *Star Wars* had premiered on the same holiday weekend). It broke house records, dispelling the old adage that sequels are never worthy of their predecessors. Not

roles, and each gets a great scene in which to shine. Ironically, Harrison Ford had to fight to allow his improvisation of a key scene to be retained. This occurs when Han Solo is about to be lowered into the carbon freezing chamber by Vader. Princess Leia finally shouts "I love you" to him. Solo replies rhetorically, "I know!" Ford recalls Lucas saying. 'It's a laugh line. I'm not sure it belongs there. This is a serious, dramatic moment." He responded by telling Lucas, "It relieves a grim situation without generating laughs or diverting the drama. It also serves to make Solo's plight more poignant and memorable." Ford won out, and the dialogue had the desired effect on the audience. (According to Kasdan, Ford's original line of dialogue was to be "I love you, too.") Ford and Kershner had formed a mutual admiration society, with the actor praising his director's willingness to let him improvise, and the director saying of the actor, "Harrison I adored. He was so creative and so much fun." Mark Hamill was also impressed by Ford's ability to make innovative and creative suggestions. He commented, "Harrison's ideas are usually superb. He has more freedom to bring bits to Solo;

Luke (*Mark Hamill*) depicted in action in a German lobby card. (LucasFilm Ltd.)

only did audiences give the film enthusiastic word of mouth, but most critics did, too. The movie was the cinematic blockbuster of the year. A few nay-saying critics complained that the film left audiences hanging with its serial-like ending, in which it is unclear whether Han Solo lives or dies. Harrison Ford took issue with them: "I have no real defense for that argument but what obligation is there to tie up every question with an equal answer? The cliff-hanger is because the trilogy was really constructed in the classic form of a three-act play. Naturally, there are going to be questions in the second act which have to be resolved in the third. I guess it really depends on what you go to a movie for. I figure there was at least eleven dollars worth of entertainment in *Empire*. So if you paid four bucks and didn't get an ending, you're still seven dollars ahead of the game." No one in the moviegoing audience seemed inclined to disagree with Ford's assessment.

On the set with Williams. (LucasFilm Ltd.)

The Empire Strikes Back proved to be the film virtually everyone had hoped for. The impact it had on Harrison Ford's career is impossible to overstate. Suffice it to say that it cemented him as one of the cinema's most popular leading men. However, Ford had little time to relish his success or to relax. George Lucas was beckoning him once more for an even more arduous project—one that would take him from an era of space ships and alien beings back to another time of high adventure. All courtesy of a new legend in the making named Indiana Jones.

Reviews

"A worthy sequel to Star Wars, *equal in both technical mastery and characterizations. The only box office question is how many earthly trucks it will take to carry the cash to the bank."*

VARIETY

"I especially like the handling of Han Solo in this outing. Han not only grows in stature, but his romantic passages with Princess Leia seem more urgent and heartfelt than in the earlier chapter."

ARTHUR KNIGHT, HOLLYWOOD REPORTER

"Smashing sequel manages to top the original in its embellishment of leading characters' personalities, truly dazzling special effects and nonstop spirit of adventure and excitement."

LEONARD MALTIN'S MOVIE AND VIDEO GUIDE

"Instead of trying to match the original film's momentum, [it] concentrated on laying groundwork for a more extended story. . . . Compared to [its] predecessor, [it] is just as polished and technically proficient, but seldom as lighthearted and seldom as fun. . . . This time Harrison Ford's Han Solo steals the show. Mr. Ford slips easily into the film's comic-book conversational style, and he also brings a real air of tragedy to Han's fate, which is another thing we won't exactly know about until next time. So he goes to what may or may not be his doom with a grand show of nobility, flinging his head back and staring bravely ahead."

JANET MASLIN, NEW YORK TIMES

"Hamill, Fisher, and Ford flounder in roles that are certain to doom their careers, regardless of the series' success."

CINEFANTASTIQUE[1]

[1](Authors' Comment: This perceptive reviewer undoubtedly went on to predict landslides for Mondale and Dukakis!)

111

16

Raiders of the Lost Ark (1981)

"I saw the opportunity to do a character who was instantly attractive to people. The script described something so exciting, and the opportunity to work with Steven Spielberg was undeniable. The whole thing was a major dream. And we had such a good time doing it!"

CAST:
Indiana Jones: Harrison Ford; *Marion Ravenwood*: Karen Allen; *René Belloq*: Paul Freeman; *Toht*: Ronald Lacey; *Marcus Brody*: Denholm Elliott; *Sallah*: John Rhys-Davies; *Dietrich*: Wolf Kahler.

CREDITS:
Director: Steven Spielberg; *Producer*: Frank Marshall; *Executive Producers*: George Lucas and Howard Kazanjian; *Screenplay*: Lawrence Kasdan; *Story*: George Lucas and Philip Kaufman; *Director of Photography*: Douglas Slocombe; *Production Designer*: Norman Reynolds; *Editor*: Michael Kahn; *Visual Effects Supervisor*: Richard Edlund; *Music*: John Williams. *Running time: 115 minutes. A LucasFilm Ltd. Production; Released by Paramount Pictures.*

The role of Indiana Jones confirmed Harrison Ford as an international superstar. (LucasFilm Ltd.)

Although the names Steven Spielberg and George Lucas are known today to all but Tibetan monks, there had been a time when these prolific talents were not yet the darlings of the American cinema. Although they would later emerge—along with Francis Ford Coppola—as the premier movie directors of the 1970s, they suffered the uncertainties which inevitably come with a career in filmmaking. By the midseventies, Spielberg had established himself as a popular director, courtesy of the critical and popular success of *Jaws*. However, he had yet to prove he could deliver a successful film without the benefit of summer audiences eager to be devoured by the cinematic terrors of a great white shark. His "soon-to-be-released" *Close Encounters of the Third Kind* was a mega-budget gamble, and advance word of mouth was mixed. George Lucas was nervous about the release of his own *Star Wars*, convinced the sci-fi epic would destroy the momentum his career had gained since his Oscar-nominated *American Graffiti* in 1973.

Worried over the expected failure of their two high-profile films, Spielberg and Lucas vacationed in Hawaii to allow the latter to escape the premiere of *Star Wars* on the mainland. It was during this trip that they discussed their mutual love of old movie serials and their desire to revive the genre in a spectacular way. Lucas had long been a fan of the old Republic serials, while Spielberg had lobbied previously—without success—to direct a James

ferent perceptions of Jones's alter ego. Lucas favored making him a playboy who is financed by museums which buy the antiquities he "confiscates" on his death-defying missions around the globe. Spielberg wanted him to be a somewhat sleazy character with an alcohol problem. A compromise was reached whereby Jones would be a seemingly dull American professor of archaeology, circa the 1930s. Jones "weekends" as a daring adventurer, traveling the globe in search of elusive treasures and artifacts.

A central problem faced the production team: which leading man had the charisma and physical attributes to bring Indiana Jones to life? Initially, Tom Selleck was the number-one choice. Selleck was tied to CBS for the *Magnum P.I.* series. The network was prepared to release him from his contract, but—ironically—the offer to do

Bond film. The two planned to combine elements of both genres into a future project. Lucas then received the buoyant news that *Star Wars* was breaking box-office records stateside. Not wanting to lose momentum, he dove into *The Empire Strikes Back.* Spielberg, who would relish his own success with the release of *Close Encounters* later that year, chose the bloated comedy *1941* as his next film. Both men agreed that the "serial project" would have to be put on the back burner.

In 1980, following the successful release of *Empire* and the unexpected flop of *1941*, Spielberg and Lucas began work on their dream project, now titled *Raiders of the Lost Ark.* Armed with a $20 million budget from Paramount, director Spielberg and executive producer Lucas began the search for an actor to play the film's hero, Indiana Jones. Like Superman, Indy would lead a double life. Originally, Spielberg and Lucas had dif-

Professor Jones argues a point with Brody (*Denholm Elliott*). (LucasFilm Ltd.)

Raiders renewed interest in him, and the show went back into production, thus eliminating Selleck from the role of a lifetime. A frustrated Spielberg attended a screening of *The Empire Strikes Back* and immediately had a revelation: Harrison Ford would be the perfect Indiana Jones. Recalled Spielberg: "Harrison was so obviously right for Indiana Jones that George Lucas and I approached him the next day." Initially reluctant to accept a script with Tom Selleck's fingerprints on it, Ford met with Spielberg. He was instantly agreeable to doing the film, citing the fact that the director seemed as though "he would be fun to work with."

Concerned about typecasting, Ford insisted that the Jones character be distinctive from Han Solo. "I think there is a similarity between Solo and Jones, but they're as unlike each other as they are alike. They're both fast-talking, smooth guys in a certain way. But Han Solo is less complicated than Indiana, a less sophisticated person. Jones is a character who has some other dimensions. He's kind of a swashbuckling hero type, but he has human frailties, fears, and money problems, and therefore is more down to earth. He does brave things, but I wouldn't describe him as a hero. He teaches, but I wouldn't describe him as an intellectual."

Ford took an active interest in the film behind the scenes as well as in front of the camera. On the flight to England (where much of the film would be shot), he and Spielberg fine-tuned the story line for ten hours. He read every thirties book about archaeology he could find and contributed ideas to virtually every aspect of the film, from choreographing action sequences to making suggestions about the wardrobe. (He never did feel comfortable, however, with Indy's trademark fedora, which kept blowing off his head during the filming of action sequences. He joked that the hat had to be kept on "with carpet tacks!")

According to Steven Spielberg: "Harrison contributes so much to the writing of the scripts, to just the general feeling of the films. He's one of the most inventive actors I've ever worked with. He deals on a level that is so human, so identifiable. His ideas are all our ideas. In one pure flash, Harrison will come up with something and it's absolutely right." Ford also spent countless hours mastering the bullwhip, which Indy wields with such precision in the film. While Batman has his utility belt, Jones had to rely on only his wits and the logical tools of a thirties archaeologist to help him escape the numerous death traps he would encounter.

To make actors who were auditioning for supporting roles feel more relaxed, the producers held casting calls in the kitchen of LucasFilm. Here, the aspiring stars would recite their lines while helping to prepare meals. The bizarre ploy worked well, and a cast of charismatic and talented individuals began to form. Karen Allen, a relatively unknown actress, immediately impressed Lucas and Spielberg and quickly landed the role of Marion Ravenwood, who shares life-and-death adventures with Indy.

Locations for *Raiders* extended from Elstree Studios in Britain to Hawaii, France, and Tunisia. The latter site,

Relaxing on the set. (LucasFilm Ltd.)

Ford took intensive training courses in how to handle a bullwhip. (LucasFilm Ltd.)

which was to represent Egypt, proved to be hell on earth for the cast and crew. Here, six hundred members of the crew had to dig an excavation site in boiling temperatures that ranged from a high of 130 degrees in the day to a "bonechilling" 110 degrees after sunset. Nature also contributed the occasional sandstorm or unexpected deluge. The logistical challenges of bringing supplies to the set were daunting. Literally every block of stone or piece of wood had to be brought in by truck, since the company was forty miles from the nearest village. Water consumption topped ten thousand gallons a day. Before long, many in the production company were hit with severe dysentery. While Harrison Ford had little trouble defeating virtually the entire Third Reich on film, he was no match for the "Tunisian Revenge." However, the ever-inventive actor used his suffering to improvise the film's most memorable scene, in which Indy "offs" an Arab swordsman. Originally, the two men were to engage in a rugged duel between sword and bullwhip, but after five weeks of stomach viruses, Ford did not relish the idea of filming the sequence. He recalled how necessity became the mother of invention when his illness became so debilitating that he could barely stand up: "I'm riding to the set at 5:30 A.M., and I can't wait to storm up to Steven with this

idea I'd worked out so we could save four whole days on this lousy location. Besides which, I think it was right and important, because what's more vital in the character's mind is finding Marion. He doesn't have time for another fight. But, as is very often the case, when I suggest this to Steven—'Let's just shoot the sucker'—he said, "I thought of the same thing this morning." The improvised scene is a highlight of the film. It also demonstrated the rapport and chemistry which Ford and Spielberg had begun to develop.

Despite his lingering illness, Ford managed to stagger onto the set each day to continue with what he referred to as "the hardest job I'll ever have." Complicating matters was his insistence upon doing as many of his own stunts as possible. Indeed, in all but the most death-defying sequences, Ford performed the action himself—including ten takes of the film's famous opening scene wherein Indy must outrun a gigantic rolling boulder. Recalled Spielberg: "He was lucky and I was an idiot for letting him try!" Ford faced other perils on the set: the scene in which he narrowly escapes a tribe of natives by clinging to the bottom of a seaplane nearly ended in disaster when the aircraft crashed. During a sequence in which Indy fights a Nazi guard beneath the rotating propellers of a plane, Ford slipped and nearly had his leg crushed by the plane's tire. On another occasion, a fire threatened to go out of control when the Tunisian Fire Department's *hoses* went up in flames! For the spine-chilling scene wherein Indy and Marion are menaced by a tombful of snakes, over six thousand poisonous cobras and pythons were imported. An antidote for the venom had to be kept close at hand. If not taken within two minutes after being bitten, death would have occurred. (Fortunately, the only casualty was a boa constrictor which was bitten by a cobra—although this was small comfort to the boa constrictor!) Unlike his on-screen alter ego, Ford did not have undue fear of snakes, although—ironically—he was bitten by one in his own garden upon returning from filming *Raiders*.

Raiders of the Lost Ark is one of the great achievements in moviemaking, not only from an artistic viewpoint but from a logistical one as well. Spielberg labored furiously to complete the film in a scant seventy-three days. He not only brought the film in twelve days early but also underbudget—much to the delight of executive producer Lucas and the Paramount brass. A film of this scope could easily have cost twice as much, even in 1980 dollars. (Indeed, the notorious *Heaven's Gate*, which was filmed the same year, staggered toward completion at a budget of $40 million.) The sheer sweep of *Raiders* is awe-inspiring, and everyone connected with the movie felt it was destined to be a winner.

Indy (*Ford*) defies death to steal a "cursed" treasure . . . (LucasFilm Ltd.)

ers in the *Star Wars* films were the droids, the space creatures, and the special effects. With Indy, Ford could display a wider range of human emotions. He is sexually charged in the love scenes and mild-mannered as the schoolteacher and possesses a wry wit during the most dangerous situations. Indeed, the rapport between Ford and Paul Freeman (who plays the charismatic villain Belloq) is good enough to remind us of those wonderful encounters of verbal one-upmanship between Basil Rathbone's Sherlock Holmes and the various players who portrayed Professor Moriarity. Ford receives considerable support from Karen Allen, who is wonderfully refreshing as the oft-endangered Marion. Equally memorable are Ronald Lacey as the notorious Gestapo agent, John Rhys-Davies (in a role originally offered to Danny DeVito) as Indy's able assistant Sallah, and Britain's always delightful Denholm Elliott as the museum's "Mr. Waverly" figure, who commissions Indy for his perilous assignments.

John Williams's appropriately bombastic score takes its place beside his *Superman* and *Star Wars* work as one

. . . and lives to regret it! (LucasFilm Ltd.)

The plot centers on Jones being commissioned by the Allies to prevent Adolf Hitler from gaining access to the Ark of the Covenant, purported to be the vessel in which the Ten Commandments were placed by Moses. As the Ark allegedly grants its possessor supernatural powers, it is imperative that Jones find it before the agents of the Reich place it the the Führer's hands. Jones plays an international game of cat-and-mouse with his longtime nemesis Belloq, a French archaeologist in league with the Nazis. Accompanied by Marion Ravenwood, the tomboyish daughter of his mentor, Indy travels the globe and barely escapes death countless times in his quest for the Ark. Eventually, the Germans capture both Indy and Marion, as well as the Ark, before the supernaturally driven climax wreaks havoc on the villains.

Raiders succeeds on almost every level. Cinematically, audiences had rarely seen an adventure of this scope. Special effects and jaw-dropping locations never override the chemistry between the characters. For Harrison Ford, the role of Indiana Jones made him an international screen icon. While the role of Han Solo had won him enormous popularity, the real scene steal-

Indy and Sallah (*John Rhys-Davies*) among the snakes. (LucasFilm Ltd.)

"The stuff that raucous Saturday matinees at the local Bijou once were made of, a crackerjack fantasy-adventure. Ford marks a major turning point in his career as the occasionally frail but ever invincible mercenary-archaeologist, projecting a riveting strength of character throughout."

—VARIETY

"One of the most deliriously funny, ingenious, and stylish American adventure movies ever made. . . . Great fun as much for the things it explains as for the explanations it withholds."

—VINCENT CANBY, NEW YORK TIMES

Japanese theater poster. (LucasFilm Ltd.)

of the great signature pieces of motion picture music, and all other technical aspects of *Raiders* are equally impressive. With this film, Steven Spielberg reestablished himself as one of the foremost filmmakers of his era. Audiences responded to the movie with predictable enthusiasm, reinforced by virtually unanimous critical praise. (The film would be nominated for numerous Oscars, including Best Picture.) Despite opening against such surefire hits as *Superman II*, *The Cannonball Run* (remember, this was 1981, and Burt Reynolds's ascots were still in style!), and *For Your Eyes Only*, the film became the top-grossing box-office attraction of the year. *Raiders* has spawned two sequels to date, and another is in development as of this writing.

By all accounts, Harrison Ford played a major role in insuring that Indiana Jones became one of the screen's legendary heroes. Perhaps Tom Selleck, obviously harboring no grudges against his successor for the role of Indy, said it best: "It's hard to imagine anyone better than Harrison. He was quite wonderful."

Reviews

"Ford emerges as a matinee idol of old, with a touch of the Errol Flynns. . . . Ford, with his strong offbeat features and light cynicism, has the potential to become a grand romantic hero in the line of Clark Gable."

—PHOTOPLAY

118

17

Blade Runner (1982)
Original Release Version

"I was desperately unhappy with it. I was compelled by contract to record five or six different versions of the narration, each of which was found wanting on a storytelling basis. The final version was something that I was completely unhappy with. The movie obviously has a strong following, but it could have been more than a a cult picture."

CAST:
Deckard: Harrison Ford; *Roy Batty*: Rutger Hauer; *Rachael*: Sean Young; *Gaff*: Edward James Olmos; *Bryant*: M. Emmet Walsh; *Pris*: Daryl Hannah; *J. F. Sebastian*: William Sanderson; *Leon*: Brion James; *Zhora*: Joanna Cassidy; *Tyrell*: Joe Turkel.

CREDITS:
Director: Ridley Scott; *Executive Producers*: Brian Kelly and Hampton Fancher; *Producer*: Michael Deeley; *Screenplay*: Hampton Fancher and David Peoples; *Based on the novel* Do Androids Dream of Electric Sheep? by Philip K. Dick; *Narration Written by*: Roland Kibbee (uncredited); *Director of Photography*: Jordan Cronenweth; *Production Designer*: Lawrence G. Paull; *Special Effects*: Douglas Trumbull; *Supervising Editor*: Terry Rawlings; *Music*: Vangelis; *Running time*: 118 minutes. A Ladd Company Film in association with Sir Run Run Shaw; Released by Warner Brothers.

Despite its lofty status as one of the most analyzed and "hip" cult films, *Blade Runner* proved to be a nightmarish experience for many of those involved with bringing the offbeat sci-fi story to the screen. Among all the movies in which Harrison Ford has starred, it remains the only one with which the actor has repeatedly stated his dissatisfaction. Indeed, on paper, it would appear to be a viable property for a movie. The genesis of the film's troubled road to theater screens began innocently enough in 1968 when author Philip K. Dick published his science fiction story *Do Androids Dream of Electric Sheep?* Dick's innovative story, written under the influence of amphetamines, dealt with the efforts of a futuristic society to terminate renegade robots who are virtually indistinguishable from human beings. Martin Scorsese first expressed an interest in adapting the tale to film in 1969, but not yet a "name" in the movie business, he could not get studio backing. The option eventually went to Herb Jaffe, who completed a script in 1973 which left the author "horrified." He accused Jaffe of trivializing his book and reducing it to pulp fiction. Unable to get the project off the ground, Jaffe gave up his option in 1977. Former actors Hampton Fancher and Brian Kelly (the father on TV's *Flipper* series) were enthusiastic about the book, and Fancher wrote a script (eventually

Deckard (*Harrison Ford*) hunts the replicants amidst the decay of Los Angeles. (The Ladd Company)

written by David Peoples) which was submitted to Michael Deeley, the producer of *The Deer Hunter*. The project, then known at various times as *The Android*, *Mechanismo*, *Dangerous Days*, and *Gotham City*, proved to be a hard sell to potential financial backers. Among the unenthused was Philip K. Dick, who expressed his reaction after seeing one of the first scripts: "When I read it, I thought, 'I will move to the Soviet Union where I am completely unknown and work making light bulbs in a factory and never even look at a book again and pretend that I can't read.' " Hardly an auspicious beginning for a high-profile motion picture.

Eventually, the script regained many of the elements of Dick's original and the author became more muted in his criticisms. Deeley approached director Ridley Scott with the script, now titled *Blade Runner*. Scott, who had recently made a name for himself as a visionary director on the basis of his 1979 science fiction epic *Alien*, was intrigued with the story and felt the project might make him the John Ford of the sci-fi genre. With Scott on board, the producers succeeded in getting a distribution and financing deal with Filmways. An enormous amount of time was spent on preproduction: building futuristic vehicles and commissioning paintings and storyboards as models for the big-budget set designs. (Among those contributing in this area was Mentor Huebner, who in the fifties had created the final design for Robby the Robot in *Forbidden Planet*.)

Scott's most immediate concern was casting the lead role of Deckard, the retired "Blade Runner"—a quasi–police officer who hunts down and destroys rebellious androids in Los Angeles circa 2019. The plot would focus on Deckard's increasing aversion to killing these superpowerful robots or replicants, who are for all intents and purposes human beings with built-in lifespans of up to four years. When several of the androids tire of being used as slave labor and become desperate to prolong their "lives," they travel back to earth, where they go on murderous rampages and must be destroyed. Deckard's problem is in identifying the replicants and resisting the urge to treat them with the same compassion one might extend to a human being. If he becomes too

Ford as Deckard, with Sean Young as Rachael—the alluring replicant. (The Ladd Company)

movie at an audience, people were familiar with Harrison. I thought it was double-edged. It was a great choice, you know, because I knew Harrison wanted a change of pace . . . ."

Scott visited Ford on the set of *Raiders of the Lost Ark* and promised that the production could be filmed in Los Angeles. Scott reiterated that the Deckard character would be entirely different from Han Solo, and indicated he would allow Ford to participate in the creative aspects of the movie. When Ford ultimately signed for the film, Scott found that Ford's involvement with a movie goes far beyond his work as an actor. "After going over the story-line, [Ford] will turn to the details. He wants to know not only what the character looks like but what he'd wear, right down to the kind of shoes, and the type of gun he would carry; where he would live and how." Ford explained his philosophy of filmmaking: "I've no desire to have films written for me or to produce my own projects. I prefer to find something that already has a life of its own, to which I can then add my contributions. That way, we can go further."

Soon after Ford signed for *Blade Runner*, the film

"attached," it will be that much harder to destroy them. The moral dilemma is made worse when he falls in love with one of his targets—Rachael—an android so indistinguishable from an actual person that she possesses an artificial memory and real emotions.

Ridley Scott first talked with Dustin Hoffman about playing the brooding hero. Hoffman declined, saying the role called for an actor more associated with macho action roles. The only other actor deemed appropriate for the perfectionist director was Harrison Ford. Scott had been an admirer of Ford and felt the actor would fit his vision of a "thirty-year-old Robert Mitchum." Ford, too, declined the offer, saying it would have required him to film yet another major motion picture in England, a land of whose climate and customs he was rapidly growing weary. Ford was also concerned that the character of Deckard might be too similar to that of Han Solo—an image he was trying desperately to avoid being typecast as. Scott would later tell *Starlog* magazine: "I knew Rick Deckard was so different from Han Solo that it represented a kind of challenge to Harrison. He would most certainly have played against the central character that we know him for, plus the fact that, from my point of view as a filmmaker and someone who is actually trying to aim a

Deckard finds his gun is useless against Batty. (The Ladd Company)

The thriller's ultimate status as a cult film was due to enthusiastic coverage by sci-fi magazines such as *Starlog*.

faced its first crisis when Filmways, reeling from financial problems, could not guarantee the movie's $15 million budget. With the cast and crew on the verge of being disbanded, producer Michael Deeley succeeded in arranging backing from the Ladd Group. Ford was originally enthused about the project, telling the press, "It's totally unlike anything I've ever done before. *Star Wars* and *Empire* were science fiction, but they were space fantasies. *Blade Runner* is a traditional, big-city detective story, transplanted into a science fiction environment. It's real and gritty." His devotion to his role extended to giving Deckard an identifiable characteristic—a short cropped haircut. Ford agreed to be shaved almost bald, so that his hair would have a choppy, motley-looking quality when it began to grow in—something he felt would help define the down-and-out ex–Blade Runner he would be portraying. The cast and crew jokingly referred to Ford as "Daddy Warbucks," and in a sign of potential conflicts of style to come, director Scott's insistence upon overseeing the haircutting turned the process into a four-hour ordeal.

Both Ford and Scott made references to the fact that the script reminded them of a Raymond Chandler novel set in the future. Ironically, filming was done on the same Warner Brothers lot where *The Maltese Falcon* and *The Big Sleep* were shot. The production proved to be arduous from day one, and Ford began to realize how much his improvisation-driven, no-nonsense approach to filmmaking contrasted with the perfectionism of his director. Scott enjoyed directing the movie by looking through the actual camera lens, a habit which unnerved Ford. He was relieved when the camera-operators union put an end to the practice. Ford griped to the press, "Scott likes to watch the performance through the lens. As an actor, I'm glad he wasn't able to do that. I think that when a director is looking through the camera, he's watching the edges to

be sure where everything is. I want a director to be helping me with the whole scene, the performance." Adding to the tension was the necessity of shooting this film noir at night. This, too, did not settle well with the cast or crew, and Ford complained, "Night filming does tend to drive everybody a little wacko after a while. Lunch was served after midnight and shooting would wrap around four or five A.M." The company endured four months of twelve-hour workdays. The environment was every bit as depressing as the futuristic society Scott wanted to depict on-screen: there was a deep chill on the set, caused by the omnipresent drizzle from seven sprinkler systems. Before long, the hardened industry veterans who made up the cast and crew were calling *Blade Runner* the toughest job of their careers.

With the tensions between Scott and Ford having surfaced, the crew was divided into "pro-Ridley" and "pro-Harrison" camps, with each one citing the other's man as a prima donna. Actress Sean Young, who portrayed Rachael, the replicant with whom Deckard falls in love, recalled that Ford seemed more at home with the technicians than the other actors: "It's where he can feel earthy. That's where he feels safest." She added, "I don't think people know that he's really a very good comedian." Unfortunately, Ford had little cause to show his lighter side. A colleague of Ford's would tell *Premiere* magazine years later: "It was a grueling movie and Ridley demanded so many takes that it finally wore Harrison out. I know he was ready to kill Ridley." The actor became particularly annoyed when filming the climactic chase through a flooded room. Here, the crew tossed sixty pigeons in Ford's direction, leaving him rather unceremoniously "decorated" with their droppings. At other times, he complained of the lag time between scenes on some of the high-tech films he had worked on—*Blade Runner* included: "I sit and stare at the walls or walk around in my trailer. Either I'm thinking about the next scene or I'm in a state of mental suspension. I can't read or concentrate on anything else. It's the worst thing about being an actor for me."

Nevertheless, Ford and Scott were both professionals, and they toiled tirelessly to overcome their differences and make *Blade Runner* the film they envisioned. Ironically, the one point both men would agree upon later was that they did not succeed. Who was at fault for the emergence of the "flawed" original release version of the film is open to debate, but in assessing the blame for the movie's faults, one can harken back to a quote from blacklisted writer Dalton Trumbo when he recalled the McCarthy hearings: "It will do no good to search for villains or heroes or saints or devils, because there were none; there were only victims." Indeed, the wrong-headed judgments surrounding the initial release of the film were made, as always, by people with the best of intentions. In the case of *Blade Runner*, however, the controversial changes to Scott's film were done reluctantly and, in hindsight, perhaps with good reason. Scott had fashioned a bizarre movie that was unlike any science fiction film before—or since. Virtually everyone agreed the film was visually stunning and a masterpiece of set design. Like other filmmakers who dealt with futuristic story lines, Scott foretold a bleak outlook for man's destiny. His vision of urban America in the not-too-distant future is one of hopelessness, despair, and violence. Most of the action takes place at night, in futuristic Los Angeles. Here, high-tech spacecraft fly above a crowded metropolis; the population, comprised primarily of Asians, speaks a strange street language derived from various cultures; the settings are claustrophobic. The depressing atmosphere is unrelenting, and the script does not provide any humor whatsoever.

Criticisms that Scott's preoccupation with atmosphere weakened potential interest in the characters was borne out. The central flaw in the film is that none of the characters is very interesting—including Deckard, from whose viewpoint all of the strange developments unfold. Scott had hoped to make a thought-provoking film which would encourage audiences to speculate about the characters and their backgrounds and not spell out the answers as traditional films do. In essence, he hoped to accomplish on the big screen what Patrick McGoohan had done on television two decades before with *The Prisoner.* Unfortunately, for all its visual splendor and technical marvels, much of *Blade Runner* proved to be slow moving, confusing, and—most harmful of all—dull. Scenes drag on far too long, as though Scott cannot bring himself to pull the camera away from the marvelous sets and special effects, let alone shut the camera off. The potentially

As Deckard—one of the most controversial roles of his career. (The Ladd Company)

fascinating story line involving Deckard's increasing reluctance to treat his prey as subhuman robots never really gains any emotional momentum, and his forbidden love affair with Rachael never strikes a responsive chord with audiences. The movie does build to a shattering, nerve-racking conclusion in which Deckard finds himself at the mercy of Batty, the seemingly indestructible replicant leader (superbly played by Rutger Hauer). These sequences fulfill the potential which *Blade Runner* never quite reaches throughout the first three-quarters of the film.

However, the movie's most legendary flaw cannot be blamed on Ridley Scott. Following some test screenings, Warner Brothers was horrified to find that audiences had an overwhelmingly negative reaction to the sci-fi epic. Clearly, the public was expecting another "feel good" space movie with Harrison Ford cracking jokes in between blasting aliens with a ray gun. What they got was an antiseptic, downbeat detective story that apparently

As Deckard, facing almost certain death at the hands of a replicant. (The Ladd Company)

would not play in New York or Los Angeles, let alone those all-important drive-ins in the Midwest.

Panic-stricken executives called for immediate strategy sessions to "rescue" *Blade Runner* before it escaped into general release. The studio insisted upon two major changes, and Ridley Scott, who did not have rights to the final cut, was made to comply. The first decision involved having Harrison Ford record some extensive narration to clarify sequences which had left audiences confused. Scott protested that confusion was exactly what he hoped to create, and reminded the studio brass that the delicate subtleties which he labored to create would be destroyed by the narration. On this point, he and Ford agreed. However, neither could sway the decision-makers, so Ford was contractually forced to do the narration. Upon seeing *Blade Runner* for the first time, one is astonished at how badly Ford performs the voice-over. He sounds like someone doing a Jack Webb imitation with a lampshade on their head at the office Christmas party or like Howard Cosell suffering from insomnia. Confidants of Ford argue that the actor intentionally made a mockery of the narration in the hopes that the studio would find it unusable. If this was his motive, it was not successful. The narration was incorporated into the final cut—warts and all.

The next crucial change concerned the fate of Deckard and Rachael. Throughout the film, hints are dropped that Deckard himself may be a replicant, although it is never actually stated. The studio felt that this point should be addressed more directly, and Ford's narration includes a line which seems to imply that he is

indeed a replicant. More importantly, audiences seemed to be turned off by the film's original ending, which found Deckard and Rachael clearly in love but uncertain about their future since she (and possibly he, if he is a replicant) has a very limited life span. The first version of the film left all the loose ends untied, and the audience had to speculate as to how the couple fared. The studio insisted that an epilogue be shot which presumably would leave audiences more upbeat. Virtually at gunpoint, Scott and Ford filmed a sequence in which Deckard and Rachael fly off into the sunset (actually this was unused stock footage from Stanley Kubrick's *The Shining*), with the hokey narration now miraculously and conveniently informing us that Rachael is the only replicant without an artificially shortened life span. Presumably, she and Deckard live happily ever after.

While no one can fault Warners for taking action to counter the negative response to *Blade Runner* in its test screenings, it is ironic that the elements of the film which elicited the most criticism upon its release were the narration and the epilogue! Critics scoffed at having the script explained to them by the Deckard character—especially since most of the narration simply stated the obvious. The film's conclusion was the most lambasted "feel good" ending since Hitchcock was forced to water down *Suspicion* to show Cary Grant as a hero. Audiences were no more impressed with the "new, improved" *Blade Runner* than they had been with the original cut. The movie opened strongly, largely due to the fact that Harrison Ford was again appearing in a sci-fi epic. However, the initial fears that audiences would be turned off by the bizarre style of the movie and the depressing atmosphere proved to be well-founded. *Blade Runner* did not have "legs" at the box office, and the grosses declined rapidly in the ensuing weeks. The film was not a financial disaster, by any means, and did recoup its cost on its initial release. However, Warners, which had every right to expect a blockbuster considering the talent they were employing, was greatly disappointed.

While Harrison Ford has distanced himself from *Blade Runner* from day one, Ridley Scott has praised his star for contributing to the many admirable aspects of the film. He told the press: "Harrison has an immense understanding of the entire moviemaking process. You can't fool him at all—he always knows exactly what's happening. His contributions were tremendous, on a story level as well as to his own character. He brought many ideas to me—in fact, it got bloody embarrassing they were so good, there was no way I could wriggle out of using them." Despite Ford's aversion to the movie, and Scott's well-publicized denouncement of the original release as not being the "director's cut" he envisioned, *Blade Runner* did become a legitimate cult film, particularly among science fiction aficionados who reveled in the magnificent sets and virtuoso special effects. However, marketing the film to this audience segment was akin to preaching to the choir. The "unconverted" among the general population remained so. As with so many high-profile movies which have been altered at the insistence of studios, fans of the film began to lobby for release of the version which Scott had originally intended for general release. The following section details the resurrection of *Blade Runner* and its subsequent success with both audiences and critics. Unlike the contrived epilogue in the first version of the film, the restored *Blade Runner* would have a genuinely happy ending.

a wonderfully meticulous movie and marvel at the comprehensiveness of its vision. Even those without a taste for gadgetry cannot fail to appreciate the degree of effort that has gone into constructing a film so ambitious and idiosyncratic . . . . But Blade Runner is a film that special effects could easily have run away with, and run away with it they have. And it's also a mess, at least as far as its narrative is concerned. Almost nothing is explained coherently and the plot has great lapses . . . . Mr. Ford is, for a movie so darkly fanciful, rather a colorless hero; he fades too early into the bleak background. And he is often upstaged by Rutger Hauer."

JANET MASLIN, *NEW YORK TIMES*

"A case could be made for Blade Runner *as the best sci-fi film of the past decade."*

STARLOG

"Philip Marlowe meets Frankenstein."

BRUCE WILLIAMSON, *PLAYBOY*

Reviews

"Ford is perfectly cast as the scruffy hunter, a character he endows with enough personality and vulnerability to create all the necessary audience identification and caring."

HOLLYWOOD REPORTER

"A triumph of production design, defeated by a muddled script and main characters with no appeal whatsoever."

LEONARD MALTIN'S MOVIE AND VIDEO GUIDE

"Scott's creepy, oppressive vision requires some sort of overriding idea—something besides spoofy gimmicks, such as having Deckard narrate the movie in the loner-in-the-big-city manner of a Hammett or Chandler private eye. This voice-over, which is said to have been a late addition, sounds ludicrous and it breaks the visual hold of the material."

PAULINE KAEL, *THE NEW YORKER*

*"*Blade Runner *is crammed to the gills with much more information than it can hold. Science fiction devotees may find [it]*

In the film's shattering climax, Deckard is relentlessly pursued by the seemingly indestructable Batty (*Rutger Hauer*). (The Ladd Company)

1991 Director's Cut

(Running time: 117 minutes)

In the years since its initial release, *Blade Runner* had overcome the stigma of its disappointing performance at the box office to become a high-profile cult film. In addition to launching the careers of Rutger Hauer (at least in America) and Sean Young, it cemented Harrison Ford—reluctantly or not—as the idol of sci-fi groupies. Nevertheless, Ford never warmed to the movie and generally continued to dismiss it as a painful memory and an exhausting experience. Director Ridley Scott had given up any notion that his original version of the movie would ever be seen, and had to content himself with continuing to disavow the cut which went into general release in 1982. However, the strange saga of *Blade Runner* would become even more bizarre when a Warners executive accidently discovered a rare 70mm print of the film on a fateful day in 1989. The studio was persuaded to screen the movie at a festival of 70mm films in Los Angeles. To the amazement of the audience, this turned out to be Ridley Scott's original work print, which had some key differences from the version originally released.

Significantly, the newly discovered *Blade Runner* did not have the narration which incited such hostility among the critics, the public, and the filmmakers themselves. Even more startling was the fact that this version included Scott's original ambiguous ending, which has Deckard and Rachael absconding together despite the fact that Rachael has a limited life span. As they leave Deckard's apartment, presumably to escape the authorities and find a new life together, the elevator door simply closes on them, and we see the end credits. While this version clearly leaves the audience hanging regarding the fate of the lovers, this is precisely what Scott had hoped to achieve. Gone was the infamous studio-imposed "happy ending," with Deckard absurdly reassuring the audience that Rachael was the only replicant not programmed for a short life span as the couple literally fly off into the sunset. (It should also be noted that nowhere in Philip K. Dick's source story was it ever insinuated that Deckard was a replicant himself.)

While Scott was delighted that this version was still intact, he refused to endorse it because it lacked a short sequence which the studio had never allowed him to film: a simple, fleeting moment in which Deckard dreams of a unicorn. While designed to seem inconsequential and baffling to the audience, the sequence also was intended to hint at the finale of the movie. In both versions of the film, Deckard interacts with a detective named Gaff (Edward

The director's cut was enthusiastically received when released to theaters and home video. (The Ladd Company)

James Olmos), a strange man who talks in CitySpeak, a strange combination of several languages. Gaff seems to play no significant role throughout most of the film, although he does display a penchant for making little origami figures from paper and matches. At the end of the film, when Deckard survives his battle to the death with Batty, Gaff informs Deckard that he is aware of his forbidden love for Rachael but will turn a blind eye toward their relationship. Curiously, he compliments Deckard by telling him, "You've done a man's job, sir." This could be construed as a nod toward Deckard's macho image, but, combined with some other subtle clues strewn throughout the film, it might also imply that Deckard himself is a replicant. The significance of the unicorn sequence was to become clear in the final seconds of the movie, when Deckard discovers an origami figure of a unicorn in his apartment as he and Rachael are about to flee. In the original release version, this unicorn figure simply seems to alert him that Gaff had been in the apartment and had given his blessing to the affair with Rachael. Had the unicorn dream sequence preceded this scene as Scott had intended, the meaning of the origami figure would have been far more obvious. It would have clearly hinted that Deckard was indeed a replicant, because Gaff had access to his programmed dreams and memories.

Warners decided to release this work print at two theaters in California to see if the "new" version had commercial appeal. Encouraged by its reception, the studio chose to get Scott's blessing for a definitive version of the film, which would be rereleased theatrically in major cities, followed by a heavily promoted release on video. Scott agreed to be a consultant on the project but insisted that the unicorn dream sequence be inserted into the film. Although the studio had originally vetoed the inclusion of the unicorn, this time Warners agreed. (Rumor has it that Scott may have utilized some footage from the film he was currently shooting, *Legend*, which coincidentally featured unicorns!) With the disputed sequence at last included in the master print, Scott finally consented to calling this version the "Director's Cut" of *Blade Runner*. Curiously, the "definitive" version lacks some footage from the original videotape release, which was mastered from European prints. Most of the cuts center on Batty's murder of Tyrell, which is far more graphic than in the original U.S. theatrical release. (The scene depicts a gory close-up of Tyrell's eyes being poked out.) In addition to this cut, an abbreviated scene in which Pris lifts Deckard by his nostrils in their brutal fight is trimmed. Warners couldn't get master prints of this footage in time for the premiere of the "Director's Cut." The absence of these shots has no dramatic impact on the story. On the other hand, the inclusion of the unicorn adds significantly to the plot and, combined with the deletion of the sappy narration and happy ending, allows Scott to succeed in creating a thinking man's sci-fi epic.

The "Director's Cut" of *Blade Runner* was shown theatrically and generated a good deal of publicity as well as impressive grosses at the box office. The video release was even more successful, and Warners had the good sense to master both the tapes and laser discs in letterbox format to preserve the film's original aspect ratio, thus allowing the magnificent sets to be seen in all their depressing glory. (Prospective viewers are hereby warned to stay away from the traditional pan-and-scan video versions of *Blade Runner*, which severely crop the image. To add insult to injury, many of the tapes being sold at bargain prices are in the slower and grainier LP or EP modes, which seriously dilutes the quality of the film.) Yet the question remains: is Scott's version of *Blade Runner* significantly more satisfying than its predecessor? The answer is yes—with some reservations. There are still sequences which extend far too long. And despite Scott's admirable insistence upon making the audience think, the script is still needlessly confusing. Yet while *Blade Runner* remains very much an acquired taste, it succeeds in captivating the mind and the eye. The controversy which has surrounded the film has also added to its mystique and allowed the work to be analyzed more thoroughly than it might have been if the original version had been the definitive one. The absence of the uninspired narration greatly enhances Harrison Ford's performance, although the scene-stealing trophy still belongs to Rutger Hauer, who—in the tradition of all memorable movie villains— has the flashiest role. It's probably safe to say that those who hated *Blade Runner* the first time around won't be swayed by the "new, improved" edition. This includes Harrison Ford, who has commented, "I have no interest in seeing the 'Director's Cut.' Making the movie was an unpleasant experience I do not wish to relive." However, for those who are more objective, a second look at this strange but fascinating epic would be time well spent.

Deckard learns too late that the mannequin is actually a murderous replicant (*Daryl Hannah*). (The Ladd Company)

18

Return of the Jedi (1983)

"If I hadn't made other movies in between I might have felt differently about coming back, but as it stands I'm delighted to be in on the third act. In any case, I don't condemn sequels when they're done with the pride that George Lucas brings to them."

CAST:
Luke Skywalker: Mark Hamill; *Han Solo*: Harrison Ford; *Princess Leia Organa*: Carrie Fisher; *Lando Calrissian*: Billy Dee Williams; *Ben (Obi Wan) Kenobi*: Alec Guinness; *C-3PO*: Anthony Daniels; *R2D2*: Kenny Baker; *Chewbacca*: Peter Mayhew; *Anakin Skywalker*: Sebastian Shaw; *Emperor*: Ian McDiarmid; *Yoda*: Frank Oz; *Darth Vader*: David Prowse; *Voice by*: James Earl Jones; *Wicket*: Warwick Davis.

CREDITS:
Director: Richard Marquand; *Executive Producer*: George Lucas; *Producer*: Howard Kazanjian; *Co-Producers*: Robert Watts and Jim Bloom; *Screenplay*: Lawrence Kasdan and George Lucas; *Story*: George Lucas; *Director of Photography*: Alan Hume; *Editors*: Sean Barton, Marcia Lucas, and Duwayne Dunham; *Visual Effects*: Richard Edlund, Dennis Muren, and Ken Ralston; *Music*: John Williams. *Running time*: 133 minutes. A LucasFilm Ltd. Production: Released by 20th Century Fox.

Being comforted by Chewbacca (*Peter Mayhew*) as both face certain death at the hands of Jabba the Hut. (Albert Clarke, courtesy LucasFilm Ltd.)

There was never a doubt among fans of the *Star Wars* saga that George Lucas would fulfill his promise to complete the first trilogy in what he viewed as an ever-evolving series. What was in doubt was whether Harrison Ford would enlist for another go-round as his on-screen alter ego, Han Solo. The first two films had been a boost to the careers of everyone involved. However, among the cast, only Harrison Ford was catapulted into the elite superstar stratosphere. Lucas had foreseen the possibility that he might ultimately become "too big" for the one-dimensional role of Solo and therefore created the controversial cliff-hanger ending of *The Empire Strikes Back* in which Solo is frozen in suspended animation and sent to the clutches of his murderous enemy, Jabba the Hutt. The feeling was that if Ford elected not to return for the next *Star Wars* film, the character of Solo could be explained away by saying he was still in the hands of Jabba or perhaps had been killed by him. Mark Hamill, the series' Luke Skywalker, explained at the time: "Look at what's happening to Harrison. He wasn't at all sure whether he wanted to repeat his role and he's not at all committed to doing it a third time. So George has left him in limbo and given him the option. Solo is not vital to future stories. It's up to Harrison, I guess, as to whether Han comes back into the saga."

Much to the delight of George Lucas and devotees of the series, Ford decided to sign up for the third episode in the series, then called *Revenge of the Jedi*. This, despite

In his role as Han Solo for the third time. (LucasFilm Ltd.)

the fact that *Jedi*, more so than the other films, is very much the story of Luke Skywalker. In this conclusion to the trilogy, Luke and Princess Leia lead a ragtag army of confederates—including Chewbacca, C-3PO, R2D2, and the charismatic renegade Lando Calrissian—on a rescue mission to the lair of Jabba the Hutt. Here they manage to free Han Solo from his frozen tomb, while destroying Jabba the Hutt in the process. The evil Emperor is building a new Death Star—a high-tech militaristic space station even more menacing than the one which Luke and the Rebels had previously destroyed. However, the "new, improved" Death Star will feature so much weaponry and troops that it virtually guarantees the destruction of the Rebel forces. Skywalker and his friends lead the rebel army on a crusade to demolish the Death Star before it can be put into full operation. In an intriguing plot twist, Luke learns that Princess Leia is his sister. He also must try to sway his father, Anakin Skywalker (alias Darth Vader), from the path of evil he has chosen. He must accomplish this by strictly adhering to the code of the Jedi, so that he may finally earn his place as the last of the Jedi knights.

Harrison Ford confessed that he had reservations about the script, since *Jedi* made Han Solo very much a secondary character. He related to *Los Angeles Times* movie critic Charles Champlin in *George Lucas: The Creative Impulse*: "I didn't think I was really involved in the story, so I had no idea of what to do with my character. We had tough discussions about that. Part of the brouhaha was that I thought my character should die. Since Han Solo had no momma and no poppa and wasn't going to get the girl anyway, he may as well die to give the whole thing some real emotional resonance. But George wouldn't agree to it." Despite this, Ford publicly announced his enthusiasm about working with Lucas and said he trusted Lucas's judgment. He told the press, "I'm so confident in Lucas's control of the story that I really don't spend a second thinking about what direction Han Solo should go in."

Ford was not the only veteran of the *Star Wars* saga who initially had some reservations about signing on for *Jedi*. Screenwriter Lawrence Kasdan, who had written the scripts for *The Empire Strikes Back* and *Raiders of the Lost Ark*, was by now a well-established director in his own right. Kasdan explained that he ordinarily would not have welcomed returning to the role of being exclusively a screenwriter. He told *Starlog* magazine, "I'm doing this because I feel I owe George a lot. Besides, I like working with him. There's also a certain satisfaction in finishing the trilogy. Additionally, writing *Jedi* will, of course, be very financially rewarding. . . . If anyone besides George had asked me to just write a screenplay, I never would have done it. This is a very special situation. . . . The only disadvantage to my doing *Jedi* is that it will push back the start of whatever I direct next by a few months."

With Kasdan and Ford aboard, Lucas had accomplished the remarkable task of once again reuniting all of the principal players from the first two films. Ford's costars were somewhat surprised at his participation, as his star status far eclipsed that of the other cast members. (Ford even consented to second billing under Mark Hamill, as he had done in the first two films.) Hamill had nothing but compliments for him, saying, "He has still not received the recognition he deserves as an actor. He's a very funny guy, witty and spontaneous. It's difficult for me to separate my admiration for the character of Han Solo and for Harrison Ford. Maybe, because in our relationship, it's very easy for me to look up to him. That's part of Lucas's genius, casting actors who are close to their characters. Harrison has always been strong and supportive. 'Hey, kid,' he'd say. 'Your part's much tougher than mine.' He's very gracious that way."

Carrie Fisher was also enthused about working with Ford once again. She had become quite close to him and his wife Melissa and had even vacationed with the couple

Luke, Han, and Chewie, about to be cast into the dreaded Pit of Sarlacc. Lando (*far left*) awaits his chance to save them. (LucasFilm Ltd.)

immediately prior to the *Jedi* shooting. She reflected on her relationship with him in a 1990 interview. "In any encounter he's always the senior and you're always the freshman. I think he always felt I was too loud, a little out of control, and he's the kind of guy who'd kick me under the table or fix me with a withering look to let me know it. I respect Harrison. He's well read, thoughtful. Just don't wear the wrong clothes around him, because he'll get you! At times like those, he turns into your dad."

To direct *Jedi*, George Lucas hired British director Richard Marquand, who had gained critical acclaim for his television documentary series *The Search for the Nile* and the 1981 Ken Follett thriller *Eye of the Needle*. Lucas had been impressed by the latter film and the way two different stories had been seamlessly merged to build to a startling climax. He felt that Marquand could bring the required balance of suspense, humor, and high-tech wizardry to the project. Lucas said at the time, "One of the most important things is to create

an emotion in the audience. The movie can be funny, sad or scary, but there *has* to be an emotion. It has to make you feel good or laugh or jump out of your seat." As with the two previous films, *Jedi* would aspire to all of these emotions. As director, Richard Marquand would soon learn that the logistics of insuring that these goals were met would test even the patience of a Jedi knight.

Marquand expressed confidence that, with Lucas's support, he could bring *Jedi* in on schedule and within the budget. "I'm an actor's director, rather than a shots man," he said. "And having George Lucas as an executive producer is like directing *King Lear* with Shakespeare in the next room!"

From a production standpoint, *Jedi* had one distinct advantage over the two preceding films: it was shot in accessible and "friendly" locations, as opposed to the deserts of Tunisia. Lucas had decided that many of the major desert loca-

Leia (*Carrie Fisher*) and Han battle Darth Vader's forces outside the imperial bunker. (Ralph Nelson Jr., courtesy LucasFilm Ltd.)

131

tions could be replicated in a remote valley near Yuma, Arizona. Here, the crew labored to remove any sign of vegetation, so the barren and "dead" landscape could serve as the desert world of Tatooine, domain of the villainous Jabba the Hutt. One problem the filmmakers had was contending with the thousands of dune buggy enthusiasts who descend on this area every weekend. At one point, over 35,000 people were racing the buggies, making it a nightmare to shoot around them. It was at this location that a spectacular set was built, consisting of Jabba's enormous sail barge with which he transports Luke, Han, and Leia to be sacrificed to Sarlacc, a grotesque creature consisting of a gigantic gaping mouth extending from below the sand—complete with octopus-like tentacles for snatching its victims.

The Sarlacc set and Jabba's barge required the production team to labor for five months, logging over 5,500 hours in hotel rooms. (Hopefully, Lucas used his frequent visitor card to acquire valuable points!) Over 14,000 *pounds* of nails were utilized, not to mention hundreds of thousands of dollars worth of wood. The barge was 212 feet long and 80 feet high, with a platform measuring 30,000 square feet. The laundry list of materials continued to pile up as shooting began: 4,000 yards of sailcloth, two million gallons of water (used to dampen the only access road to the remote location). The logistics of operating Jabba, a massive, repulsive, sluglike villain whose evil is exceeded only by his gluttony, was daunting—as was the task of building his exotic "Throne Room." It took three operators inside the body of Jabba to control his lifelike movements. Television monitors had to be installed inside the creature so the technicians could get feedback on their performance. (Originally, the character of Jabba the Hutt was to have appeared in *Star Wars*, and Lucas indeed shot a sequence in which Han Solo confronts Jabba, demanding his payment. In this sequence—which Lucas excised from the final cut—Jabba is a rather rotund but otherwise unremarkable human being. The scene appears in the documentary *From Star Wars to Jedi*.)

The technicians who had to operate the special effects for the elevated barge as well as the Sarlacc creature felt that it might be less painful to be fed to the fictional beast than continue to work in the stifling heat. Phil Tippett, the designer and operator of the Sarlacc creature, told *Starlog* magazine, "We were working the creature at the bottom of a gorge, so we got no breeze. Sand constantly fell down upon us. And we were covered with glue from the costume. I almost cracked on that one. I think I cried, it was so terrible." It was at times like these that the production crew may very well have wished their executive producer had an obsession with musicals, as opposed to science fiction epics. The crew wanted to vent their frustrations by actually dynamiting the $1.2 million barge for the explosive battle scene between the heroes and Jabba the Hutt. To their frustration, Lucas insisted that miniatures be used for the sequence. (However, the crew did get the satisfaction of dismantling the dreaded barge and Sarlacc set and seeing it sold as scrap to Mexico with the stipulation that the materials *not* be sold as souvenirs.)

Despite the frustration caused by a few sandstorms, production on *Jedi* went much smoother than had been the case on the two previous films. Interior scenes were once again shot at Elstree Studios in England, where one stage alone occupied over 1.5 million square feet. Meanwhile, many of the actors went through their paces in front of "blue screens" at the California offices of Industrial Light and Magic, where the special effects sequences were filmed. (The entire F/X process would take over a year of work.)

Much of the story takes place in a forest inhabited by Lucas's latest bizarre group of lovable creatures, the Ewoks. These short, furry, teddy-bear-like beings become valuable allies to the heroes in a spectacular battle set among towering redwood trees. Since not even George Lucas can duplicate a redwood forest, the scenes were shot on location among the ancient redwoods near Crescent City and Smith River, California. Regulations regarding fire prevention prohibited shooting the explosive action scenes in national parks, so Lucas used a private forest belonging to a lumber company. The *Jedi* production was welcome news to the locals, whose economy had been suffering. In addition to the revenue the film generated in local businesses, two hundred citizens were hired as extras for the battle sequence. The Ewoks' scenes required the most impressive and challenging special effects of the film, including the famous high speed chase between Luke, Leia, the Ewoks, and the forces of the Empire on airborne Speeder Bikes—which whiz through the forest at incredible speeds. (The irony of this sequence is finding the primitive Ewoks besting the high-tech soldiers of the Empire with their own gadgetry. The scene calls to mind the triumph of Robin Hood and his Merry Men over the better-equipped troops of the Sheriff of Nottingham.)

As usual, every attempt was made to insure that details of the plot did not leak out to the public. Lucas went so far as to create T-shirts with bogus film titles ("Blue Harvest," "Horror Beyond Imagination") for the crew to wear, in hopes of convincing curious onlookers that a B horror film was being shot. The press saw through the ruse, however, and the cast and crew had to suddenly contend with hordes of fans who descended upon the set to glimpse their favorite star or perhaps get an advanced "scoop" about the plot. Nevertheless, the script continued to be protected as though it were a state secret. Actors were only given their own portions of the script to read, and irrelevant dialogue was occasionally included in order to stop anyone from figuring out the entire story line. Carrie Fisher recalled, "The days when we would shoot the secret scenes, they would ask the crew not to listen. It's fun, like the Academy Awards!" The film was also shot out of sequence, as were its predecessors. Fisher reflected on the challenge this provided to the cast and crew: "These movies are shot way out of sequence. Few films are done out of continuity to this degree. They have to keep it in their minds, and sometimes they would have to remind us: 'Remember, this is a scene you shot last month and you're coming in from this point.' We would come to the door in England, and step through it in Yuma!"

Refreshingly for George Lucas, who'd had to tolerate the logistical nightmares inherent in bringing *Star Wars* and *The Empire Strikes Back* to the screen, *Jedi* came in on time and within the $32.5 million budget—a significant achievement for director Marquand. While in postproduction, the film underwent a well-publicized title change to *Return of the Jedi* when Lucas was reminded by many fans that Jedi knights do not give in to feelings of vengeance. Therefore, the word "Revenge" in the original title was at odds with the Jedi philosophy of peaceful coexistence. Lucas agreed and changed the title but has maintained that the word "Revenge" was intentionally used to deceive the public from guessing the key theme of the movie. He maintained it was his intention to change the title eventually anyway. (Nonetheless, thousands of "teaser" one-sheet posters had been distributed with the "Revenge" logo. These became instant collector's items, and despite Lucas's attempts to flood the market with reprints of the "rarities" to prevent price gouging on the part of memorabilia dealers, the original "Revenge" poster can still command hundreds of dollars.)

How does *Return of the Jedi* compare to its predecessors? Well, as one reviewer said of *The Godfather Part III*, "One of them had to be third best." *Return* is the least satisfying entry in the series, but that is not meant in an entirely negative way. It is still spectacular entertainment and fully deserves to be placed alongside the first two entries in the series. However, this time around, the filmmakers' obsession with state-of-the-art special effects

R2D2 (*Kenny Baker*) and C-3PO (*Anthony Daniels*) in harm's way (as usual) during the battle for the imperial bunker. (Ralph Nelson Jr., courtesy LucasFilm Ltd.)

and elaborate sets and incredible action sequences frequently overwhelms the human elements of the story. At every turn, it seems that the heroes are captured, escape, and are recaptured only to provide a plot device for another round of fights or chases. All of the hallmark *Star Wars* elements are present, including some of the most impressive creatures ever created for a film. (Jabba the Hutt remains one of the most memorable screen villains of recent years.)

Yet it is precisely the expertise and wizardry in the areas of special effects which ultimately make *Jedi* a less absorbing tale than the previous stories. There are so many new characters introduced—each with outrageous physical characteristics—that the effect is eventually more wearying than impressive. And the Ewoks, despite their cute and curious appearance, are somewhat overused as well. A few minutes of these lovable bearlike creatures would have sufficed. On-screen too long, they distract the audience as merely people in costumes. One suspects their market potential as a lucrative toy line may have been a factor in their significant screen time. Ultimately, the filmmakers made the same error that affected many of the later James Bond films: they allowed the gadgetry to overwhelm the human elements of the script.

The story does get back on track exactly when it needs to—in the riveting conclusion of the film, in which Luke battles the evil Emperor for the soul of Darth Vader. The scenes between the estranged father and son are both suspenseful and moving and allow Mark Hamill to exhibit emotions earlier denied him. Even this sequence is inter-cut with a spectacular battle against the Death Star, which is bigger and more technically proficient than simi-lar scenes in the other films, but not necessarily as engrossing. There are, however, a wealth of individual scenes and set pieces which impress: the entire Jabba the Hutt sequence; the touching cameo appearance by the beloved Yoda, who gives new meaning to the term "death with dignity"; the moving "deathbed" speech of Anakin Skywalker, as he requests that his life-sustaining mask be removed by Luke so that he may look upon his son with his own eyes; the all-too-brief appearances by Alec Guinness as Ben (Obi Wan) Kenobi; and the very sentimental last scene in which the visions of Ben, Yoda, and Anakin Skywalker (the reformed Darth Vader) give their tacit approval to Luke, who has finally earned the title of Jedi knight. The special effects are, not surprisingly, even more amazing this time around and, unlike the first two films, do not seem the least bit dated in today's high-tech age.

With the exception of Luke and Anakin Skywalker, there is little character development for the key players in the story. As Ford feared, the part of Han Solo is large-ly superfluous to the story. He is still dashing and heroic, but unlike in the other films, he does not have any scenes that are particularly memorable because of him alone. Ford gamely goes through the motions, but little is required of him here other than shooting on target and keeping the spaceships on course. Carrie Fisher's Leia fares marginally better, primarily due to the plot device involving her discovery that she is Luke's sister. Billy Dee Williams returns as Lando, but the character remains frustratingly opaque. Given Williams's charisma and abili-ty to perform the requisite derring-do, one would have hoped that he would have been given something pivotal to do. Instead, he sits behind a control panel through much of the script, barking orders to fire at enemy aircraft.

Nevertheless, *Return of the Jedi* is certainly a wor-thy entry in the *Star Wars* canon. If Lucas is guilty of any-thing, it is giving the audience *too* much for their money.

Director Richard Marquand does an admirable job of keeping the action flowing at breakneck speed, and he handles the few quiet sequences with sensitivity and skill. (Sadly, this talented filmmaker would pass away in 1987 at the age of forty-nine.) John Williams, who has come to virtually corner the market on musical scores for epics like this, does his usual magnificent work. His contribu-tions to films such as the *Star Wars* saga, *Superman*, *Close Encounters of the Third Kind*, the Indiana Jones movies, and *Jaws* cannot be overstated. It would be impossible to single out the individuals whose special effects and makeup skills are so vividly displayed in *Jedi*. Suffice it to say that they are such geniuses in their fields that we tend to take their talents for granted.

Return of the Jedi was perhaps the most eagerly awaited movie of 1983. It premiered on May 25 of that year—six years to the day since *Star Wars* exploded onto theater screens. Unsurprisingly, the film was a success, grossing a (then) industry record of $6 million in ticket sales on opening day alone. *Jedi* soon skyrocketed past *The Empire Strikes Back* to become the third most popu-lar film ever made—behind *E.T.* and *Star Wars*. As with its predecessors, *Jedi* inspired a tidal wave of interna-tional merchandise tie-ins. To date, over 250 million *Star Wars* action figures have been sold, and although Lucas's plans to begin production on the next chapter (with all new characters) are still only on the drawing board, LucasFilm has been receiving at least thirty-five licensing offers a week since 1993! However, fans of the "old" *Star Wars* will eventually be treated to revised and enhanced versions of the first three films, which Lucas intends to rerelease theatrically in the years to come.

Reviews of *Return of the Jedi* were generally positive but unenthusiastic. While many critics groused at the emphasis on technology, most praised Lucas and his team for maintaining the dignity of the series and giving movie-goers a spectacular ride for their money. The film was nominated for five Oscars (all in the technical categories) and received a special Academy Award for its special effects.

For Harrison Ford, the main benefits of his partici-pation in the film were financial. Now a major star, he could command a lucrative percentage of the gross in addition to a sizable salary. His name on the marquee certainly made him worth every cent of these fees, and *Jedi* helped him maintain his status as one of Hollywood's most prominent leading men. However, it became appar-ent to actor and audience alike that this would be his last appearance as Han Solo. The character had never been fully or satisfactorily developed, and it was primarily due to Ford's charisma and skill as an actor that he became an integral part of the success of *Star Wars*. With *Jedi* seemingly wrapping up most of the loose ends of these chapters of the *Star Wars* saga, there was no sensible way for Solo and the other characters to continue without becoming shallow imitations of their original personas. Lucas seemed to recognize this and has been in no hurry to bring the series to its next plateau. When he does, it may very well be the vehicle that introduces moviegoers to another great action star. It's doubtful, however, that they would eclipse the record of Harrison Ford. As Richard Marquand said of his leading man, "Ford is a pure cinema actor. He works beautifully with the camera . . . . He's terrific as an ally, someone who understands the craft of being a movie star."

Reviews

"Jedi is the conclusion of the middle trilogy of George Lucas' planned nine-parter and suffers a lot in comparison to the initial Star Wars, *when all was fresh. One of the apparent problems is neither the writers nor the principal performers are putting in the same effort. . . . Even worse, Harrison Ford, who was such an essential element of the first two outings, is pre-*

The dynamic trio: Ford, Fisher, and Hamill. (LucasFilm Ltd.)

Love grows on the moon of Endor. (LucasFilm Ltd.)

sent more in body than spirit this time, given little to do but react to special effects. And it can't be said that either Carrie Fisher or Billy Dee Williams rise to previous efforts. But Lucas and director Richard Marquand have overwhelmed these performer flaws with a truly amazing array of characters, old and new, plus the familiar space hardware."

—*VARIETY*

"A sheer delight. Some lazy performances are compensated for by ingenious new characters and Oscar-winning special effects. More sentimental and episodic than its predecessors (and probably incomprehensible if you haven't seen them both)—but carried out in the best tradition of Saturday matinee serial, from which it draws its inspiration."

—*LEONARD MALTIN'S MOVIE AND VIDEO GUIDE*

"Doesn't really end the trilogy as much as it brings it to a dead stop. The film is by far the dimmest adventure of the lot. All the members of the old Star Wars *gang are back doing what they've done before but this time with a certain evident boredom. . . . The film's battle scenes might have been impressive but become tiresome because it's never certain who is zapping whom with those laser beams and neutron missiles. The narrative line is virtually nonexistent and the running time, though only slightly more than two hours, seems longer than that of Parsifal."*

—*VINCENT CANBY, NEW YORK TIMES*

≠J-TD-7295

19

Indiana Jones and the Temple of Doom (1984)

"George [Lucas] is a very practical and conscientious filmmaker and Steven [Spielberg] is one of the best directors alive today. They are my allies. I have no fear they'll muck it up. The only anxiety I feel is like…like I'm waiting for Christmas. I want to see the finished film as much as anyone else."

CAST:

Indiana Jones: Harrison Ford; *Willie Scott*: Kate Capshaw; *Short Round*: Ke Huy Quan; *Mola Ram*: Amrish Puri; *Chattar Lal*: Roshan Seth; *Captain Blumburtt*: Philip Stone; *Lao Che*: Roy Chiao; *Wu Han*: David Yip; *Shaman*: D.R. Nanayakkara; *Chieftain*: Dharmadasa Kuruppu; *Little Maharajah*: Raj Singh.

CREDITS:

Director: Steven Spielberg; *Executive Producers*: George Lucas and Frank Marshall; *Producer*: Robert Watts; *Associate Producer*: Kathleen Kennedy; *Screenplay*: Willard Huyck and Gloria Katz; *Director of Photography*: Douglas Slocombe; *Production Designer*: Elliot Scott; *Special Visual Effects*: Dennis Muren; *Editor*: Michael Kahn; *Music*: John Williams. *Running time*: 118 minutes. A LucasFilm Ltd. Production; Released by Paramount Pictures.

Still defiant in the face of death. (LucasFilm Ltd.)

With production of *Return of the Jedi* completed, Harrison Ford looked forward to some vacation time. His divorce to Mary was being finalized, and he had become romantically involved with screenwriter Melissa Mathison of *E.T.* fame. However, the lure of a film offer he could not refuse would once again encroach on his leisure time. George Lucas and Steven Spielberg approached him to star in the sequel (actually a prequel) to *Raiders of the Lost Ark*. Spielberg had said that he only wanted a peripheral role in this film, which was originally titled *Indiana Jones and the Temple of Death*. However, after a four-day brainstorming session with the ever persuasive George Lucas, Spielberg committed to directing the film. He recounted his thoughts at the time: "I can see it already and I'd hate to let it slip through my fingers into someone else's hands. I won't be involved in the third or fourth ones but I really want to do the follow-up." Spielberg's involvement was instrumental in Ford's immediate agreement to pick up Indiana Jones's now legendary bullwhip for a second time. Ford told *Starlog* magazine, "Of course I'm doing the second *Raiders* film. With great pleasure. . . . Steven Spielberg is going to direct it. So this is very exciting for me. It was one of the best working relationship experiences of my life working with Steven." Despite his enthusiasm, Ford did react with a bit of surprise when he learned that a total of five Indy films

Ford as the man with the most recognized hat in the world.
(LucasFilm Ltd.)

characterizations. Not surprisingly, most of these suggestions were eventually utilized. The script was retitled *Indiana Jones and the Temple of Doom* perhaps to signify the somewhat "lighter" mood of the story—although, ironically, the final cut would be chastised for its violent content.

At this point, the team of Lucas, Spielberg, and Ford was considered to be money in the bank by Paramount. A hefty budget of $27.5 million was secured for the elaborate production. The film shot on location in Sri Lanka (doubling for India, whose government was too restrictive and whose rivers were too polluted for the film's extensive water sequences), in Macau (doubling for 1935 Shanghai), and at Elstree Studios in England. Producer Robert Watts recalled, "I still remember when we looked at the script in the early days and we all said, 'How the hell are we going to do this?' We *always* feel that way about each new movie. But somehow or other we do it. It gets done. Don't ask me how!" Executive producer Frank Marshall felt that the overwhelming logistical problems inherent in shooting in such distant locations were overcome by the coming together of the Lucas/Spielberg "stock company" on the set: "Making this film was like a reunion. Almost everyone on the production had also worked on *Raiders*. We arrived at Sri Lanka—a very foreign place—and there were all the same faces! We knew what kind of movie we were making from the first day onward, and I think that very secure feeling allowed us to extend ourselves beyond the first movie."

This time around, Indiana Jones would not be seeking out international artifacts on behalf of a museum. Instead, the plot finds him accidentally coming to the assistance of the natives of an impoverished village in India. In addition to being on the bottom of their nation's caste system, these poor souls have their only precious resources stolen from them—their children, and a sacred religious stone. A modern-day version of the ancient Thugee religious cult has kidnapped the kids to be used as slave labor to locate another precious stone hidden in the local mines. This would give the cult all three of the stones needed to gain supernatural powers, which they will use to dominate the world. As the children are worked virtually to the point of death to locate the missing gem, the evil cult chieftains perform human sacrifices. It is Indy's mission to infiltrate the cult, save the children, and return the missing stone to the tribe. Naturally, all of this sounds much easier than it is to accomplish, and Indy and his companions must cheat death at every turn in order to emerge victorious.

As usual, the casting of Harrison Ford's costars would be a time-consuming process for the filmmakers. Kate Capshaw landed the role of Willie Scott, the talent-

were on the LucasFilm drawing board. He stopped short of committing to those, saying, "Actually, I'm only committed to one film at the moment . . . . I really enjoy working on them. And I really enjoy the character very much. And certainly I couldn't hope for any better company than Lucas and Spielberg. But having done one, I don't think I'd do four more of anything. They must be talking to Roger Moore. . . . One at a time for me!"

Lucas and Spielberg succeeded in securing the services of virtually everyone who had worked on *Raiders*, with the exception of screenwriter Lawrence Kasdan, who was now preoccupied as a director in his own right. Lucas hired the writing team of Willard Huyck and Gloria Katz (who penned *American Graffiti*) to create the screenplay for the new Indy film, telling them that he wanted a much darker tale than the preceding film, with elements of black magic thrown in to ensure a good number of scares for the audience. Huyck and Katz delivered the first draft of the script in six weeks, then submitted two more drafts over the next three months. Harrison Ford was initially disturbed by the overwhelming somberness of the story. He made a great many suggestions regarding the insertion of humor and the development of

free lounge singer who inadvertently gets caught up in Indy's pursuit of a sacred stone. (Capshaw certainly formed a close working relationship with Spielberg—they eventually married.) For the pivotal role of Short Round, the young Oriental boy who acts as Indy's sidekick and resourceful accomplice, Spielberg hired Ke Huy Quan, a twelve-year-old who had never heard of his illustrious coworkers. Quan confessed, "I had heard of Han Solo before, but I didn't know his real name was Harrison Ford. And I knew someone had made *E.T.*, but not who." Ford showed there were no hard feelings about being an "unknown" to Quan, and the actor formed a very close working relationship with the boy—which included teaching him how to master the bullwhip. Quan responded to the kindness by saying of Ford, "He's very nice. A generous man, and a noble actor." Amrish Puri, an Indian actor and veteran "villain" in numerous Hindi films, was cast as Mola Ram—Indy's most despicable nemesis. Incidentally, there are some interesting cameos in the airport sequence early in the film. Dan Aykroyd briefly greets Ford as he is about to enter a plane, and two "missionaries" on the scene are better known as George Lucas and Steven Spielberg.

While budget considerations were a concern on the original *Raiders* film, there was no such problem this time around. In fact, Spielberg and Lucas were able to utilize two key sequences for *Temple of Doom* which were originally planned for the first Indy adventure. (They were not used then due to cost factors and other constraints.) The first scene involves Indy's innovative use of a gigantic rolling gong to avoid machine-gun bullets during the spectacular nightclub shoot-out in the opening scenes. The second sequence depicted the three lead actors using a life raft to cushion their jump from a plane which is plummeting out of control. This leads to a spectacular scene wherein the heroes fall off a mountain and land in rapids for a thrilling white-water adventure. *Raiders* screenwriter Lawrence Kasdan explained why the scene had been eliminated from the first film: "We took that scene out because we thought it would be too unbelievable." However, this time around, Frank Marshall rationalized, "It's more of a roller-coaster ride—if you can imagine that—than *Raiders* was." He also justified the use of the "unbelievable" raft sequences by saying, "With this movie, we knew we could stretch things further, so we put them

Original one-sheet poster. (LucasFilm Ltd.)

in." Believable or not, the scene in question is one of the most spectacular action set pieces imaginable, and it gets the movie off to a rousing start.

The climax to *Temple* also proved to be an enormous logistical challenge. The scene features Indy trapped on a rickety suspension bridge above a crocodile-infested river. With enemies closing in on him, Indy cuts the bridge cables, sending many of his pursuers into the water below. The bridge then smashes against the side of a mountain, where Indy and the bad guys engage in hand-

139

Trapped with Short Round (*Ke Huy Quan*) in the death chamber. (LucasFilm Ltd.)

to-hand combat in a frantic attempt to climb to safety. Frank Marshall explained, "We were lucky enough to find an accessible gorge right nearby, a construction site where a British company was building a large dam. There, we had top-notch engineers and workers with convenient equipment to string the bridge with steel and cable. Once the bridge was up, we dressed it to look old and rickety." To the delight of the filmmakers, the engineers volunteered many hours of manpower, thus ensuring the film kept on schedule and within budget. To simulate the falling bodies of the villains, air-powered dummies were created with valves connected to their "limbs" to make their arms and legs flail as they fall. To achieve the necessary camera angles, another suspension bridge was built which hung below the bridge with the actors. Despite these precautions, Spielberg knew there would be only one opportunity to get the action right. Fortunately, the old "Ready when you are, C.B." scenario did not materialize, and the sequence went perfectly.

For close-up shots for this spectacular sequence, two smaller bridges—rising only fifteen feet off the

Trying to look comfortable atop an elephant with Ke Huy Quan. (LucasFilm Ltd.)

ground—were built in Sri Lanka and at Elstree Studios. However, Harrison Ford was still required to perform on the real suspension bridge, 250 feet above the gorge. Spielberg was understandably nervous about letting his star do his own stunt work. As with the original *Raiders*, wherein Ford persuaded his director to allow him to outrun the gigantic boulder in the booby-trapped cave, the actor succeeded in doing many of his own stunts on *Temple*. He confessed that Spielberg would not originally allow him on the bridge. "So before anyone could do anything, I just ran across it. In fact, it was dangerous as hell." Ford rationalized taking such risks by saying, "There are many opportunities for characterization in physical action. Really, that *is* the character—in these moments of action, you see Indiana Jones most clearly." He did allow that "I'm almost looking forward to getting older parts that won't call for me to be bounced off walls every ten minutes!" Naturally, Ford has to use a stuntman for the most dangerous sequences, but he does so reluctantly. His longtime stunt double Vic Armstrong (who bears such a strong resemblance to the actor that Ford's own son Malcolm once mistook him for his father) explained that Ford is "a very physical actor, a natural athlete, and he wants to do it all. I say to him, 'Harrison,

worked tirelessly to wrap up the scenes in Sri Lanka. By the time the unit had moved to Elstree Studios in England, Ford could not endure the constant pain. Initially, he feared he would have to undergo an intensive operation called a laminectomy, but doctors experimented with a new procedure in which papaya is injected into the body and eats away at the problem disc. The procedure worked, but Ford was forced off the set for six weeks to recuperate. Spielberg went into "disaster control" and rearranged sequences to shoot around Ford—not easy to do since the actor was in most of the scenes. Despite Spielberg's innovations, hardships were suffered, and ultimately an insurance claim of $1 million was filed.

Ford's friend Howard Becker visited him in the hospital and described the actor's concentrated efforts to hasten his recuperation: "After the operation, he used a relatively tenacious and disciplined rehabilitation—stretching, a type of yoga, if you will. He was working his muscles very hard. I was worried. I kept telling him to slow down. As a former athlete—I had a track scholarship at college—I know that strong people can sometimes come back too fast. But he healed completely, and did it faster than the doctors expected. He's a very strong-willed person." Back on the set, Ford confessed to being a bit nervous about resuming the intense physical demands of his role. He described his first action sequence following his recuperation: "At one point, the guard throws me into a mine car, and since I'd just come back from back surgery, I had second thoughts about being the throwee!" Nevertheless, in true Indiana Jones spirit, Ford accomplished what was required of him. He kept up his physical training on the set by hiring famed fitness instructor Jake ("Body by Jake") Steinfeld to train him on a daily basis. This was complemented by doing workouts with Steven Spielberg at a local gymnasium.

Despite his ability to continue filming action sequences, it was clear to the cast and crew that Ford was still in significant pain. To cheer him, the production company orchestrated a rather elaborate prank. During a key sequence in which Ford is chained up by Thugee cult members, Barbra Streisand was ushered onto the set, dressed in a kinky leather outfit and brandishing a whip, which she proceeded to use on Ford. "That's for *Hanover Street*—the worst movie I ever saw!" she ranted, to the hilarity of onlookers. In the midst of this bizarre scenario, Carrier Fisher ran in and threw herself protectively on her *Star Wars* costar. To cap off the practical joke, Irvin Kershner, the director of *The Empire Strikes Back*, ambled onto the set berating Spielberg, shouting, "Is this the way you run your movies? I would never let this happen on one of my sets!" The entire affair was allegedly filmed, and if it were ever to be

we cannot afford to get you smashed up in this scene because we've got a whole crew here that needs to make a living.' And he says, 'Yes, you're right,' and does the scene anyway. He could have made a great stuntman himself."

Ironically, Ford did suffer a major injury while filming *Temple*—but it did not come from swinging from a bridge or jumping from an airplane. Rather, he was hurt while trying to master the art of riding an elephant. The actor had complained throughout the filming that he never felt comfortable atop these creatures, telling the press, "Riding an elephant is very uncomfortable. I developed an antipathy towards elephant riding. You ride with your legs in a hyperextended position to accommodate the girth of the animal right over its shoulders. First one leg, then the other is pulled forward, which tends to spread you apart—like being stretched on a medieval rack, I imagine." He later quipped to the *New York Times*: "The only fun thing about riding an elephant is getting off!" Perhaps Ford should have stopped griping, as the elephant had the last laugh. During one sequence, Ford ruptured a spinal disc which had already been weakened due to a stunt sequence earlier in the film. He gamely continued to go through his scenes, as a production team of 120

Ford with the future Mrs. Spielberg. (LucasFilm Ltd.)

released, it would undoubtedly be Harrison Ford's top-grossing movie.

There was nothing humorous about the vast numbers of insects which figure prominently in the *Temple of Doom* plot. Animal handler Mike Culling was assigned the unenviable task of gathering thousands of creepy, crawly critters for several key sequences set inside the palace, which harbors the secret passageway to the temple. Here, Indiana Jones and his cohorts discover a modern version of the ancient Thugee-cult which engages in exotic torture and human sacrifice. Frank Marshall complained that handling bugs proved to be far more difficult than "directing" the snakes in *Raiders*: "The bugs were much harder to work with than the snakes we used for [that one]," he commented. "You can "arrange" a pile of snakes—add one here or there. That's impossible with insects. Believe me, we had a couple of terrible days at Elstree due to bugs; days when we'd grind film all day and night and get nothing usable. They hate bright light, so the minute you dump them in front of the camera, they run. If you don't get everyone's hands out of the way the minute you put them in, the shot is ruined. Mike Culling would come on the set and I'd say, 'We need more bugs! Not enough bugs!' He'd groan, 'I just put two thousand down there!' I found, too, that people were much more scared

by the insects than they were by snakes. Every once in a while I'd hear this shriek because one of the bugs crawled through from the bug tunnel to the tap dance rehearsal stage next door. Of course, this was a bad place for any bug to be—thirty-two girls tap-dancing away—so both the insects and the girls would run like hell. Mutual fear!"

Other logistical problems continued to challenge the filmmakers. For the extensive chase sequence in which Indy commandeers a mine car and travels at high speed through the bowels of the Temple of Doom, four full-size mine cars were utilized. Each had an electric motor, controlled by hidden motorcycle twist grips, as well as their own braking system. Steel flanges were installed around the wheels to keep the speeding cars from flying off the track during hairpin turns. Spielberg also had an entire mine car set built to insure getting specific shots. The smaller cars had still cameras mounted on them to capture the action. Simultaneously, plans were being made for the creation of the lava pit, which claims several victims of the Thugee human sacrifice ceremony. The use of actual lava was considered, but the heat it generates would have melted any equipment that came near it. Ultimately, the special effects team settled on colored glycerin. The lava pit was actually a set built to half-scale (although it still measured thirty feet in circumference). Giant pumps circulated the boiling liquid, with three-foot puppets doubling as the sacrifice victims.

Incredibly, *Temple* finished on schedule—no mean feat considering its star had been out of commission for weeks. Per assistant director David Tomblin: "I take my hat off to Spielberg, because we never stopped shooting in those three weeks, and it wasn't stuff that one would say, 'Oh, that's a double.' Then, Harrison came back, and we shot more material. I defy *anyone* to know who's the double and who's Harrison. . . . I have great admiration for Steven Spielberg. He is a very unusual and talented director and he *overcomes* hurdles—not only does he overcome them, he makes something *good* of them, which is a rare talent."

Spielberg summed up his own feelings about the film upon completion of principal photography: "We take a lot more chances with this latest movie; the mood shifts from

Between a rock and a high place.
(LucasFilm Ltd.)

one scene to the next. One minute you're literally laughing yourself sick, the next you're screaming yourself sick. It's more of a roller-coaster ride. The common elements? The sense of adventure, the same joie de vivre, the devil-may-care feeling of Indiana Jones as a character who differs from, say, a James Bond, because while you can never stop Bond, Indy *can* be stopped. That's what makes him more vulnerable to audiences and I think this was Harrison Ford's contribution to the character. Indiana Jones doesn't take himself too seriously. When he gets hurt, he shows it. He has a fear of snakes. He is tough, but vulnerable. And that's something that holds true in both movies."

Indiana Jones and the Temple of Doom opened to the expected stratospheric box-office grosses. Nearly thirteen million people saw the film in its first week. However, this time around, the reception from critics was less enthusiastic. Virtually every reviewer denounced the abundant gore and grotesque images in which the film almost revels. Although there is ample humor on display, this was clearly the

(*Above*) Invitation to the New York premiere party at Studio 54.

darkest film Spielberg had made to date. The MPAA rating board was caught in a dilemma: to give the film an R rating would exclude the all-important young people who were so much a part of the Indiana Jones following. However, it was very possible that the sequences featuring Indy coping with thousands of bugs, as well as an exotic dinner in which everything from live eels to chilled monkey brains is served, could have been upsetting to impressionable kids. The Board took the extraordinary step of creating a new rating—PG-13—as a compromise. The rating finds the film suitable for most young people but warns of certain "over the top" images which might result in a few nightmares for younger viewers. Despite the advance publicity which foretold of *Temple*'s grim content, critics were furious, and most felt the movie had a good many distasteful scenes. Some accused Spielberg of betraying his audience.

These were somewhat valid criticisms. However, the director and star took issue with those who found the violence gratuitous. Spielberg responded: "The film isn't called 'Indiana Jones and the Temple of Roses' . . . . There are parts of this film that are too intense for younger children, but this is a fantasy adventure. It's the kind of violence that does not really happen, cannot really happen, and cannot really be perpetuated by people leaving the cinema and performing these tricks on their friends at home." Harrison Ford con-

143

Indy (*Harrison Ford*) holds Willie (*Kate Capshaw*) hostage to escape the killers inside the nightclub. (LucasFilm Ltd.)

curred, telling the press: "I do believe that repeated acts of violence inure one to further violence. But in that, I'm talking about real violence, where journalists minutely examine an assassination, or revel in the details of a murder." Curiously, however, Spielberg seemed to weaken in his defense of *Temple* over the years and has made comments indicating he was disappointed with the overall film, saying that it was indeed a far grimmer tale than he had envisioned.

The debate over the violence in the film is reminiscent of the similar outcry which greeted director Sam Peckinpah's *The Wild Bunch* in 1969. In both cases, the overall film was virtually overlooked as reviewers dissected individual acts or sequences. Yes, *Temple* is a dark tale. Yet it is also one that is filled with enormous wit and humor. Ford and Spielberg's defense—that the type of violence seen in the film is exaggerated to such a degree that it poses no harm to younger viewers—is completely accurate. Not surprisingly, in the years which followed the movie's release, there has not been an notable upsurge in real-life preteen Thugee human sacrifice rites. *Temple* is remarkable in that it is so completely distinctive from *Raiders*. The ability to show so much more of Indy's emotional range (particularly in the sequence in which he is drugged and hypnotized into joining the villainous cult) gives Harrison Ford the chance to show us a fascinating side to the Jones character. Unlike so many other screen supermen, this one is filled with human

frailties, and it is only through chance that he is stopped from making Willie a human sacrifice victim. Kate Capshaw gives a wonderfully ditzy performance as the archetypal "dumb blonde" and gives the film a much-needed balance towards humor. Young Ke Huy Quang proves to be one of the most watchable child actors of recent years. He steals scenes from Ford and Capshaw, which is no mean feat for a youngster. Amrish Puri is frighteningly memorable as one of the most bloodthirsty and vicious screen villains in memory.

Temple boasts some incredible stunt work and continues the tradition of making the Jones films "thrill-a-second" experiences. Spielberg is guilty of dwelling on distasteful scenes with an almost pornographic delight. The aforementioned palace feast sequence would make an effective Weight Watchers training film. In fact, this notorious sequence is just an elaboration on an almost identical scene from *Octopussy* (1983), in which the villain devours a goat's eyeball during a grand meal. Nevertheless, art does not always have to be tasteful or original. *Temple* is memorable and distinctive because of such scenes. Likewise, the actual sacrifice sequences require a strong stomach—especially when a human heart is literally wrenched from the victim's chest. Certainly, no adult will lose sleep over these scenes, and adventure films should not all be watered down simply to cater to children. Even if offensive to some, *Temple* should be judged on its many other qualities—from the amazing set decoration and stunt work to the wonderful John Williams score. Obviously, audiences did not hold a grudge against Spielberg and Ford. *Temple* became one of the biggest hits of the eighties and was nominated for three Oscars (although, unlike the first Indy film, none were in the major categories). The film also initiated a tidal wave of licensed merchandise, including fedoras, ski pajamas, comic books, lunch boxes, and greeting cards. Per Maggie Jones, a vice president at LucasFilm: "We would all love to see an endless series of Indiana Jones movies. Consumers see the film and really want something in which to recreate its fun and adventure. So, we try to come out with products which represent what happens in the movie. And we try to be accurate." If any readers can locate a "chilled frozen monkey brain dessert kit," please notify the authors of this book.

Reviews

"Exuberantly tasteless and entertaining . . . endearingly disgusting and violent . . . . Unlike Raiders, *the new movie's script never quite transcends the shlocky B-movie manners that inspired it. Though it looks as if it had cost a fortune, [it] doesn't go anywhere, possibly because it's composed of a succession of climaxes. It could end at any point with nothing essential being lost. Watching it is like spending a day at an amusement park . . . . Ford has become very good at this sort of characterization in this sort of film. He gives an exceptionally skillful comic performance. [The film] is too shapeless to be the fun that* Raiders *is, but shape may be beside the point. Old-time, fifteen-part movie serials didn't have shape. They just went on and on, which is what [this movie] does with humor and technical invention."*

—VINCENT CANBY, NEW YORK TIMES

"Great Spielberg! [It] is a wonderful film. The result of Spielberg's genius is an epic melee that seems choreographed by some crazy mutation of Mack Sennett and Twyla Tharp."

—NEWSWEEK

"Headache-inducing prequel to Raiders *. . . only this time [Indy's] got a weaker story and a wimpier heroine. Recreates (and outdoes) a bunch of great cliffhanger stunts, but never gives us a chance to breathe . . . and tries to top the snake scene in* Raiders *by coming up with a variety of 'gross-out' gags."*

—LEONARD MALTIN'S MOVIE AND VIDEO GUIDE

"Steven Spielberg has packed even more thrills and

Poster magazine which promoted the film. (LucasFilm Ltd.)

chills into this follow-up than he did into the earlier pic, but to exhausting and numbing effect . . . . There isn't a quiet moment in the entire picture. Ford seems effortlessly to have picked up where he left off when Indiana Jones was last heard from, although Capshaw, who looks fetching in native attire, has unfortunately been asked to react hysterically to everything that happens to her."

—VARIETY

"Four Stars–Highest Rating. One of the greatest Bruised Forearm Movies ever made . . . . That's the kind of movie where your date is always grabbing your forearm in a viselike grip. This is the most cheerfully exciting, bizarre, goofy, romantic adventure movie since Raiders, *and it is high praise to say that it's not so much a sequel as an equal. It's quite an experience. You stagger out with a silly grin—and a bruised forearm of course."*

—ROGER EBERT'S VIDEO COMPANION*

20

Witness (1985)

"One of the real important things about this film is the moral context. That's what makes it work. Without the Amish serving as a kind of parameter [to the violence], it would have been the usual indulgence. That is what attracted me to the project . . . I think the film had something to say."

CAST:
John Book: Harrison Ford; *Rachel Lapp*: Kelly McGillis; *Paul Schaeffer*: Josef Sommer; *Samuel*: Lukas Haas; *Daniel Hochleitner*: Alexander Godunov; *McFee*: Danny Glover; *Eli Lapp*: Jan Rubes; *Elaine*: Patti LuPone; *Carter*: Brent Jennings; *Fergie*: Angus MacInnes.

CREDITS:
Director: Peter Weir; *Producer*: Edward S. Feldman; *Coproducer*: David Bombyk; *Screenplay*: Earl W. Wallace and William Kelly; *Story*: William Kelly and Pamela Wallace and Earl W. Wallace; *Director of Photography*: John Seale; *Production Designer*: Stan Jolley; *Editor*: Thom Noble; *Music*: Maurice Jarre. *Running time*: 112 minutes. Released by Paramount Pictures.

With McGillis and Haas. (Paramount Pictures)

While Harrison Ford willingly and enthusiastically agreed to once again don a Stetson hat and wield a bullwhip for *Indiana Jones and the Temple of Doom*, he became more determined than ever to develop a diversified body of work which would not pigeonhole him as "King of the Action-Adventure Blockbusters." While in the midst of filming *Temple*, he was sent a script entitled "Called Home," a crime thriller centering on a young Amish boy named Samuel who witnesses a brutal murder committed by corrupt police officers in Philadelphia. Marked for death by the killers, the lad finds a protector in Detective John Book, an honest cop who is also on the hit list after discovering that his boss is the ringleader of the bad guys. Wounded in a shoot-out with his would-be assassins, Book is sheltered in the Amish community by Samuel's mother Rachel and her father. Eventually, Book and Rachel fall in love, only to have their forbidden relationship threatened by the arrival of the killers, who engage them in a struggle to the death amidst the otherwise idyllic beauty of the Pennsylvania Dutch countryside.

If the plot of this offbeat romantic thriller seemed a bit familiar, it was with good reason. The script is a virtual contemporary remake of the John Wayne–Gail Russell 1947 Western *Angel and the Badman*. However, Ford saw potential in the project from the very beginning. He would later tell writer Pat Broeske, "It was the kind of film I

As John Book, finding refuge amidst the Amish. (Paramount Pictures)

Feldman decided to offer the director's chair to Australian Peter Weir, who had gained acclaim for such art house hits as *The Last Wave*, *Picnic at Hanging Rock*, and *The Year of Living Dangerously*. Their feeling was that, being from a distant land himself, Weir could sensitively depict the cultural differences so intrinsic to the story. Weir's original intention at that time was to concentrate on filming *The Mosquito Coast*, but he could not secure the financing. Weir, a meticulous researcher, generally labored for up to two years in preproduction on his films. For this, his first major Hollywood project, he was given eight weeks to prepare and fine-tune the script.

Ironically, one of Peter Weir's concerns centered on Harrison Ford's ability to convey the subtleties required for the role of John Book. He would later say that while he considered Ford "one of three or four actors who are simply capable of being a leading man, who have all those qualities that the screen loves. . . . I was interested that Harrison wanted to extend his range. Then, it was a matter of whether we personally got on, which we did right off, because we had similar concerns for the film." Weir's initial doubts quickly subsided when Ford reiterated his determination to broadly extend the range of his character from a hard-boiled "loner" cop to the gentle, compassionate protector of an Amish woman and her son. Weir and Ford found they shared many common traits, and the two immediately established an excellent, creative working relationship. Recalled Weir: "[This] was my first Hollywood picture after five feature films in Australia, and I had a certain devil-may-care feeling. I think [Ford] had the same quality at that time. Once he was satisfied with the details of the screenplay, then it was like, 'Let's be loose about it. Let's see what happens but not be uptight about it.' So we'd ad-lib or invent scenes as we went along, knowing we had a solid structure to bounce off. And that kind of looseness you might not expect from someone in his position, because often major film stars can become extremely inhibited as their success mounts. It can make working a painful process."

The first order of business for the filmmaker and star was to address Paramount's concerns that the title—"Called Home" (an Amish expression for death)—simply lacked box-office potential for the $12 million production. The studio had been less-than-enthused about the project or Ford's ability to carry a film without big-budget special effects. The studio offered a small reward for whoever suggested a more appropriate title. Ultimately, the winner proved to be *Witness*, which overcame such dubious competition as "The Year of Living Amishly." The second order of business was to make some dramatic improvements in the original script. Ford and Weir had liked the basic premise, but the former would

thought was about ninety percent there, which is a higher grade than I give most film scripts when I first get them. But, I felt if we didn't have a really good director it wouldn't gain anything but would most likely lose something in the translation. I was only interested in the project if we could attract a really fine director."

Ford had been approached to star in the film by its producer Edward S. Feldman, who said the script brought back memories of the classic Civil War drama about the Quakers, *Friendly Persuasion*. According to Feldman: "I thought of [Gary] Cooper wearing that Quaker outfit and I asked myself, 'Who today is a reactive kind of actor who would also look funny in an outfit like that?' The name Harrison Ford came to mind immediately." With Ford onboard, Feldman and his star began the search for an appropriate director. Both men agreed that a Hollywood "outsider" could bring a refreshing viewpoint to the unusual story line. In the wrong hands, the movie would be reduced to "Dirty Harry Meets the Amish." Ford and

later say, "It was a stupid, overly violent script. I would never have done it if Peter Weir and I hadn't been given the chance to rework it." The new, improved *Witness* has been described as a love story first, a moral drama second, and a thriller third. Ford was determined to make the character of John Book more than just another wise-cracking, head-splitting big- city cop. Surprisingly, the fact that Book was more than a one-dimensional character made the role less challenging for Ford than some of the other heroes he has portrayed. He said of the role, "You might say there's more range in *Witness*, but that's the easy part. When you have more range, it's far easier to seduce the audience, because you have more tools to work with. The more limited the character, the greater the challenge. For instance, how much does anyone know about the family background of Indiana Jones? *Witness* may seem like an advance in complexity in my film roles, but I have been able to do other complex parts as well. They just haven't been as successful artistically or commercially as the other films."

The obstacle of finding a suitable lead actress for the role of Rachel was solved when Ford and Weir decided to offer the part to Kelly McGillis, whose feature film experience was limited to one movie (*Reuben, Reuben*). It had been two years since that film, and in between, McGillis paid the rent by appearing in soap operas and movies-of-the-week, and waitressing. In fact, she was employed in a Greenwich Village coffee shop when the part of Rachel came her way. McGillis recalled the time that both Ford and Weir showed up at her job to discuss the film with her. "I wasn't done yet, so I made them wait about twenty minutes. The whole time, everyone is whispering, 'Harrison Ford is here!' And then after my shift, I sat down with him and they all said in the café, 'Who the hell does she think she is, sitting with Harrison Ford?' It was unbelievable. I was very intimidated by him at first, because he's such a star. I discovered that he's just a regular guy. He's just like everybody else. He's not anything to be terrified of, but for a long time, I was very scared of him."

As is his custom on his films, Ford began an intensive period of research pertaining to his role. Since he was portraying a hard-boiled Philadelphia detective, he gained permission to work with real-life cops on their nightly tours of duty. Ford was startled by the dangers faced by the police on a daily basis. He admitted, "All I knew about cops was what I had seen on television and in

the movies, and suffice it to say, it ain't like that. I held all the liberal predispositions against the use of unreasonable force, and I came to understand what the value of 'up against the wall' was. When these guys kicked in the door and went in, it totally disarmed the people who were inside, to the point where they offered no resistance, which is the idea . . . it was a little scary. In fact, it was damned scary!" Ford socialized with the cops after work, slugging down beers with them in the local gin mills. He was also exposed to the more grisly aspects of the job, such as the occasion in which a coroner showed him slides of the previous week's unsolved murders. "The first corpse was shocking," he recalled, "and the fifth was just as shocking."

A farewell to arms: Book turns his gun over to Rachel so that he may adopt peaceful Amish customs. (Paramount Pictures)

While Ford was busy studying police procedures, Peter Weir and Kelly McGillis had the even more challenging assignment of trying to become experts on Amish culture—despite the fact that the Amish themselves were prohibited from cooperating on the film due to their strict religious beliefs. For a while, McGillis lived with an Amish family who were unaware that she was an actress. She would also shop the local stores, recording the Amish conversations with a Walkman. The tapes were then used to help McGillis perfect her dialect. When her true identity was revealed, her host family asked her to leave the premises.

Ironically, although Weir was determined to present the Amish in a respectful and evenhanded way, he could not even secure their services to act as extras in the film. This was due to the Amish restriction on being photographed, due to their belief that it violates the Biblical commandment "Thou shalt not make unto thyself a graven image." Weir succeeded in hiring John King, a former member of the Amish religion, as a technical adviser. King's advice proved invaluable once shooting began in the heart of the Amish country—Lancaster County, Pennsylvania. However, even King could not persuade local Amish to lease their property for filming purposes. Eventually, the filmmakers succeeded in getting a Mennonite family to rent their sprawling farm as the central location for the movie. The Mennonites and Amish often dispute each other's religious philosophies.

Director Weir discusses a scene with McGillis, Jan Rubes, and Ford. (Paramount Pictures)

Whereas the Mennonites might be similar to the Amish in attire, their religion is somewhat more liberal, allowing them to utilize electricity, cars, and such. Gradually some of the Amish began to relent in their hostility toward the moviemakers. Occasionally, some Amish would offer advice on certain sequences, but all remained steadfast in not appearing in the movie. Word spread that Weir and Ford's intentions were not to exploit the Amish but to present them favorably. This swayed the opinion of some of the locals to their side. However, these people were chastised by other church members for participating in a project which they felt threatened the Amish way of life, no

matter how well-intentioned it may have been. This Hollywood-induced "War Between the Amish" persisted long after the film had been completed and released, as Amish newspapers continued to report on both sides of the "*Witness* Controversy."

Politics and religion aside, children are still children, and Amish youngsters would routinely watch the film production through binoculars. One Amish woman confessed that her children were creating scrapbooks of photos of Harrison Ford, even though the family had never previously heard of the actor. "Somebody told us he was in *Star Wars*, but that doesn't mean anything to us!" she said proudly. For his part, Ford kept his distance from the Amish culture to enhance his characterization of John Book. He said, "I very carefully kept my naïveté about them [the Amish]. Part of the character is that the Amish culture is foreign to him."

One of the highlights of the film is the now famous barn-raising sequence in which Book, hiding out from his pursuers by posing as an Amish farmer, helps the local citizenry construct an entire barn in one day—an old Amish tradition which persists to this day. Originally, the script called for Book to slip from the top of the barn and be saved by Daniel (Alexander Godunov), a legitimate Amish farmer and rival for Rachel's affection. The barn-building itself was to be seen only as an establishing shot of walls being erected, while the majority of this sequence centered on Book's salvation at the hands of Daniel. Weir drastically rewrote the sequence, doing away with the Book/Daniel lifesaving theme and instead centering on the actual ritual of construction. The rivalry between the two men is still there, but it is represented in a subtle and humorous way as they try to outdo each other's carpentry skills. The scene works magnificently, and backed by Maurice Jarre's wonderful and inspiring score, it has become a memorable sequence. The scene also gave Ford an all-too-infrequent opportunity to show off his carpentry abilities. He quipped on the set, "I always knew I could make more than $12.50 an hour doing this!" (Ironically, the beautiful barn, which was built on an empty tract of land, was dismantled immediately after filming.)

Ford's relationship with Peter Weir remained an

excellent one throughout the shooting. Weir encouraged him to do what he does best—improvise—and the film is all the richer for it. Among Ford's suggestions: the use of the pop ballad "What a Wonderful World" for the lovely sequence in which he slow dances with Kelly McGillis to the tune on a car radio, and the hilarious line "Honey, that's great coffee!" which he spontaneously quips to the Amish family during a meal—to a conspicuously unimpressed audience. (Ford's spoof of a television commercial was prompted by his having been rejected in an audition for a similar ad.) Ford praised his director, saying, "Peter lets me interpret ideas intellectually rather than kinetically. Before *Witness*, all directors ever seemed to want from me was the forward propulsive action and the sly wink. . . . My relationship with Peter worked more than it ever has with a director before." Weir returned the compliment, saying of his star, "He's an enormously likable man. I was impressed with his lack of interest in show business and power and status. He is for me in the great tradition of Hollywood heroes—the strong, silent type."

Witness represents a milestone in Ford's career. It became the first major hit in which he truly "carried" the film on the basis of his box-office appeal and acting skill. Nary a review so much as mentioned the *Star Wars* and Indiana Jones films, and Ford gained praise from all quarters. As a film, *Witness* is an example of moviemaking at its finest. It refreshingly makes the character of John Book a vulnerable man who is subject to the same misjudgments and mistakes as everyday people. The gradual love affair with Rachel is delicately handled and beautifully conveyed, with only Kelly McGillis's one nude scene—while tastefully done—seeming somewhat exploitive. The most rewarding aspect of the film is not the crime story—which is a rather predictable affair populated by standard cop-movie characters (i.e., the corrupt superior officer, the partner who turns out to be the film's sacrificial lamb, the black gangster who is mistakenly rousted by cops in their obsessive search for the murderers). Rather, what makes *Witness* unique is its painstaking and loving depiction of life among the Amish. There is no more fascinating subculture in America, and Weir does a remarkable job of capturing the dignity of these people's everyday lives. These sequences, in which Book has to adjust to this foreign lifestyle, also provide the grim story line with some much-needed humor: Ford awkwardly wearing the standard Amish apparel; Ford having to learn to milk a cow, while making an off-color joke which even Rachel's father finds humorous; Ford beating a moronic bully to a pulp, only to have Daniel explain to an incredulous onlooker that Ford is from "the Ohio Amish" to justify the violence which the sect so adamantly avoids. The film also benefits from glorious

This Japanese ad campaign stressed the dramatic elements of the film. (Paramount Pictures)

cinematography by John Seale and the beautiful musical score by Maurice Jarre.

Witness boasts so many letter-perfect performances that it is difficult to single out specific actors for praise. Ford is wonderful in the role of John Book, bringing a sensitivity and depth to his characterization that no previous role had allowed him to do. If there were any doubts about his ability to carry an adult drama, *Witness* dispelled them once and for all. Kelly McGillis plays the part of Rachel in an impressive, understated manner that never strains credibility. It's a difficult and challenging role—one that requires a sensuousness, while making the audience retain the belief that this woman has been sexually repressed her entire life because of her religious beliefs. McGillis's task was made all the more difficult when it was decided to cut a great deal of expository background from the script and film. When we first meet Rachel, in the final cut of the film, she is attending her husband's funeral, although it is never clear what type of farming accident

151

In a scene deleted from the final cut, Book and Rachel continue their forbidden love affair in the field. (Paramount Pictures)

caused his death or what type of marriage they had had. In the original script, it is explained that Rachel has been having doubts about her Amish lifestyle for quite some time. This precipitates her trip to her sister's house in Baltimore, where she hopes to reevaluate her options in life following her husband's death. (Again, the final cut eliminates the emotional reasons behind her trip.) Of course, Rachel's fateful stopover at the Philadelphia train station and her son Samuel's subsequent involvement with the murder changes those plans and the course of her life. McGillis's performance is all the more impressive because the final film does away with much of this background information about her character. (Curiously, the footage which had been cut from the theatrical release was reinstated when CBS broadcast the movie in 1992.) The supporting cast is equally good, especially Lukas Haas as the eight-year-old Samuel. Haas is an actor whose naturalness and charm are reminiscent of the young Ron Howard. The scene-stealing trophy goes to veteran actor Jan Rubes as Rachel's stern but admirable father-in-law. It's a wonderful performance that shows the harshness and humor of the Amish farmer without ever making the character seem foolish. The late Russian ballet star Alexander Godunov makes an impressive screen debut with an appropriately understated, serene performance as Daniel, John Book's friendly rival for Rachel's love.

Peter Weir wanted the climax to *Witness* to downplay the violence and stress the love affair between Book and Rachel. However, producer Edward S. Feldman convinced him that the film had to end with an exciting sequence if it were to please audiences. Ultimately, Feldman prevailed, and the finale to *Witness* is satisfying on two levels. The first pertains to the action/adventure element of the sequence, which finds Book single-handedly fending off his corrupt boss and his two confederates, who have come to kill the detective before he can expose them. The scene borrows liberally from *High Noon* and *Outland* (which was in itself a sci-fi version of that classic Gary Cooper Western), as Book uses ingenuity to outwit his pursuers one by one. On a second level, the finale is satisfying because there is no corny, pretentious goodbye scene between Book and Rachel. Once Book emerges victorious over his foes, he realizes he must return to his world and Rachel to hers. The only concession to a happy ending is in the dignified closing scene in which Book drives off Rachel's farm and passes Daniel, who is obviously now going to fill the void in Rachel's life. Yet we know both Book and Rachel will remain haunted for the rest of their lives by the "what-if" element to their relationship. It's a realistic and satisfying conclusion to a memorable film.

Witness became one of the most acclaimed films of 1985. More significantly, it was a box-office hit and earned eight Oscar nominations, including nods for Harrison Ford (Best Actor), for Peter Weir (Best Director), and for screenwriters Earl W. Wallace and William Kelley (who took the award for Best Original Screenplay). However, more than a few critics saw the irony in this, since the film is so obviously inspired by *Angel and the Badman*. (Their argument was that *Witness* should have been nominated in the Best Adapted

Screenplay category.) Ford and Weir were not always certain the film would find such a reception. Both men were nervous that Ford's fans would be disappointed when they did not get a film or character in the Indiana Jones/*Star Wars* mold. Weir recalled the first test screening Paramount held, which drew lines around the block: "The anticipation for a *Raiders 3* was terrifying. At first, one could sense that they were puzzled because they were expecting more action; but by the middle of the film, they were loving the humor. Whether that became some sort of substitute for the expected shootings, I don't know, but they got lost in the story and were obviously entertained."

The film also generated interest among the public regarding the Amish culture. Tourism boomed in Lancaster County, Pennsylvania, and the resulting onslaught of cars, buses, hotels, and shopping outlets almost caused a major highway to be constructed to handle the tidal wave of visitors. (Fortunately, the measure was voted down when it was discovered that such a project would have divided the Amish heartland and reduced the amount of previously farm acreage. Existing roads were upgraded instead.) Only in the last few years has the tourism frenzy caused by *Witness* subsided. However, the film will continue to inspire interest in the Amish culture for decades to come.

Although Harrison Ford did not carry home an Oscar for *Witness* (William Hurt won for *Kiss of the Spider Woman*), he admitted that the success and acclaim he received from it was most gratifying. He said, with characteristic understatement, "The reviews were among the finest I'd had as an actor, although that's what I'd always been doing." Longtime Ford friend and booster, producer Fred Roos, concurred. "People started saying [with *Witness*] 'He's really good.' But he was always that good."

Reviews

"The best role of [Ford's] career."
—Rex Reed, New York Daily News

"Witness furnishes Ford with the perfect vehicle for proving he's more than a mere macho, whip-cracking hipster . . . he couples the surface cool of Indiana Jones with a refreshing, deep-rooted warmth."
—Cosmopolitan

"An electrifying and poignant love story . . . . [Peter Weir] has a strong and sure feeling for places, the land, for the way that people build their self-regard by the way they do their work. In the whole middle section of this movie, he shows the man from the city and the simple Amish woman within the context of the Amish community. It is masterful filmmaking. The

Preparing for a scene as director Peter Weir (*right*) observes. (Note Ford's T-shirt, which jokingly refers to an Amish Indiana Jones.) (Paramount Pictures)

love story itself would be exciting. The ways of life in the Amish community are so well-observed that they have a documentary feel. But all three elements work together so well that something organic is happening here; we're inside this story. Harrison Ford has never given a better performance in a movie."
—Roger Ebert's Video and Movie Guide

"Witness is at times a gentle, affecting story of starcrossed lovers limited within the fascinating Amish community. Too often, however, this fragile romance is crushed by a thoroughly absurd shoot-'em-up, like ketchup poured over a delicate Pennsylvania Dutch dinner . . . . Witness warms up as the attraction builds between Ford, McGillis, and Haas—all performing excellently through this portion. Admirable, too, is Ford's growing admiration for the people he's been thrown among."
—Variety

21

The Mosquito Coast (1986)

"I'm a father and a son, so I can recognize the dynamics of that relationship. I'm a person who has worked with his hands, so I can understand that part of it. And I don't accept things the way they are, so I can relate to the criticisms of how American life has come to be. There's no lack of understanding between myself and Allie Fox. It's really a matter of degree: he goes much further than I might go."

CAST:

Allie Fox: Harrison Ford; *Mother*: Helen Mirren; *Charlie Fox*: River Phoenix; *Jerry Fox*: Jadrien Steele; *April Fox*: Hilary Gordon; *Clover Fox*: Rebecca Gordon; *Mr. Haddy*: Conrad Roberts; *The Reverend Spellgood*: Andre Gregory; *Emily Spellgood*: Martha Plimpton; *Mr. Polski*: Dick O'Neill; *Mrs. Polski*: Alice Sneed; *Mrs. Spellgood*: Melanie Boland; *Clerk*: Jason Alexander; *Ma Kennywick*: Butterfly McQueen.

CREDITS:

Director: Peter Weir; *Executive Producer*: Saul Zaentz; *Producer*: Jerome Hellman; *Screenplay*: Paul Schrader; *Based on the novel by* Paul Theroux; *Director of Photography*: John Seale; *Production Designer*: John Stoddart; *Editor*: Thom Noble; *Music*: Maurice Jarre. *Running time*: 117 minutes. The Saul Zaentz Company; Released by Warner Brothers.

As Allie Fox, in a triumphant performance. (Warner Bros.)

Harrison Ford has never been content to find comfort in a single screen persona. Among contemporary superstars of the American cinema, he is perhaps the most diversified in terms of the body of work he has produced. There is no "typical Harrison Ford film," just as there is not a standard mold for the characters he has portrayed—except for the fact that inevitably they are heroic, likable, and self-reliant. With the role of Allie Fox in the screen adaptation of Paul Theroux's novel *The Mosquito Coast*, Ford found a way to transcend even those minor stereotypical elements of his screen image. Among all the films he has made since achieving superstardom, it is his least-seen performance and, paradoxically, his best."

The long, tortuous history of bringing *The Mosquito Coast* to the screen began shortly after Theroux's novel was published in 1982. The story centered on Allie Fox, a stubborn, disillusioned man who is, by everyone's estimation, a genius—at least when it comes to inventing amazing but commercially unattractive devices. Fox is the patriarch of a family consisting of a wife, two sons, and twin daughters. His dictatorial, autocratic rule is grudgingly accepted by his long-suffering family, and particularly by his ever-supportive wife. The plot finds Fox—

Allie informs his wife of his plans to abruptly abandon the only life they have known. (Warner Bros.)

ery being a wilder manifestation of blind cowardice, and most inventiveness being self-serving."

Despite the heavyweight credentials of those involved, not one major studio showed an interest in financing a film version of *The Mosquito Coast*. The reasons given were predictable: too offbeat; too depressing; the central character lacked sympathetic traits; and the property in general was too uncommercial. Hellman recalled, "We were turned down everywhere, most places three or four times." Hellman traveled extensively to continue his personal "pitches" to studios, but the estimated $16 million budget and Peter Weir's lack of a track record at the box office were negatives which were impossible to overcome. The script, which was originally in development at Warner Brothers, eventually had the fingerprints of executives from Goldcrest Films, Embassy Pictures, and 20th Century Fox on it before it wound up back in Hellman's hands. He recalls, "It was a period in which every studio was going through management changes. No sooner had an executive approved it for production than he or she headed elsewhere, leaving Peter and me shopping for another home." By early 1984, Hellman realized that the seasonal demands of the film would postpone production for at least another year, even if the script was purchased by a studio.

The delay proved to be a blessing in disguise. During this period, Peter Weir agreed to direct *Witness* for Paramount, thus gaining an opportunity to attach himself to a truly commercial property. In collaborating with Harrison Ford on the film, which would prove to be a critical and box-office winner, Weir discovered he had a wonderful rapport with the actor. Weir now had a bankable record in the industry, and the very studios which had rejected the script for *The Mosquito Coast* were now clamoring for it. However, Hellman decided to go an unconventional route this time. He sought—and received—financing from Saul Zaentz, the maverick independent producer who had previously championed such "uncommercial" Oscar winners as *One Flew Over the Cuckoo's Nest* and *Amadeus*. Zaentz agreed to raise the $20 million–plus required to film on location in the jungles of Belize (which would double for the actual Mosquito Coast). Ironically, the film was to be distributed by Warner Brothers, the studio which Hellman and Weir had tried so hard to interest in the script several years before.

Initially Jack Nicholson was sought for the role of Allie Fox. However, Nicholson's demands for salary and perks would have sent the budget into the stratosphere. Instead, he chose to take the role of the horny, aging astronaut in *Terms of Endearment*. Although Nicholson would win an Oscar for *Terms*, he was not the first choice

convinced America is slipping irretrievably into decay—spontaneously moving his family to the remote jungles of the Mosquito Coast, a strip of land in Central America which extends from Guatemala to Panama. Here, Fox hopes to start a new civilization amidst the poverty-stricken, illiterate natives. Although his goal is to "save" his family from the perceived declining social structure of the United States, he is at least partially driven by an egotistical desire to be regarded as the heroic "savior" of the simple people he hopes to live among. Despite achieving some remarkable goals, Fox's quest ends tragically when the civilization he so despises encroaches on his jungle paradise.

Producer Jerome Hellman purchased the screen rights to Theroux's novel as soon as the book was published. In 1983, he hired screenwriter Paul Schrader (*Taxi Driver, Raging Bull*) to turn out a script. He also got a commitment from Australian director Peter Weir to helm the film. Weir met with Theroux, who offered his own insights into the character of Allie Fox: "I think the key to Allie is showing all sides of his personality and, at times, showing how one lies just beneath the other—loud bullying being a feature of a rather inward shyness, brav-

for that role. It was originally written for Burt Reynolds (who, showing the instinct for hot properties for which he has become known, turned down the role in order to make a flop titled *Stroker Ace*). The *Terms* role was later offered to Ford, who sensed the part was potential Oscar material but passed on the opportunity because he felt he was simply not right for the character. Ironically, Ford ended up agreeing to star in *The Mosquito Coast*, thus flip-flopping properties with Nicholson. Ford was enthused about the character of Allie Fox from the moment he read the script. He called the part a dream role and observed, "Allie says more in one scene than characters I've played said in the whole film. . . . There's a lot to commend him. But he's also a pain in the ass."

One person who did not share Ford's enthusiasm for the role was his longtime agent Patricia McQueeney. She told the *Hollywood Reporter* in a 1994 interview, "[Ford] says, 'I'll do these other films, but once in a while I've got to do one for me.' He loved what his character, Allie Fox, had to say. Harrison is very much into the environment and antipollution and all of those good things that Allie Fox was also into. But what I didn't like was the torture that he puts his wife and his kids through. And I said, 'The audience thinks you're a hero. They aren't going to want you to be this mean guy who drags these people through the jungle.' We often have friendly fights, friendly arguments, but with that one we really had a knock-down-drag-out!" Nevertheless, Ford remained adamant, despite the objection of McQueeney, whose guidance of his career had usually been impeccable. His enthusiasm for the script was too great to be compromised. He told one interviewer that his reaction upon seeing the script was "I can play this. . . . [Allie Fox] is complicated, he's fucking complicated. I *love* that!" He later elaborated by saying, "Allie is a complicated person, and it's a complicated job for the audience to figure him out. He's a good father and a bad father. He's a monster, a clown, a fool, a genius. It was necessary always to preserve enough compassion for him so the audience could understand why he does the things he does." Author Paul Theroux gave

Ford his own personal "thumbs up" for the role, stating, "Harrison had it all. Even the quietly smoldering gaze and the serious grin. He was Allie to the fingertips." For better or worse, *The Mosquito Coast* had found its star in Harrison Ford.

Ford was enthused about the opportunity to do another film with Peter Weir on the heels of the blockbuster reception given to *Witness*. He explained his perception of their working relationship this way: "We have lots of fun. There's a real spontaneous flow of ideas. And it seems that there's some mysterious continuity of experience between us. I feel a sureness and support of ideas I'm going for when I work with Peter. We question one another, test and expand each other's notions, and stop the other one when we think he's wrong." Weir returned the compliment, saying of his leading man, "He evokes a very American quality—strength, leadership—just by walking onto the screen. All of which made me believe we would follow him into the jungle and believe what he said."

Despite the excellent working relationship, *The*

Disillusioned with life in America, Allie gripes to son Charlie (*River Phoenix*). (Warner Bros.)

Mosquito Coast would prove to be almost as arduous for the cast and crew as it was for the characters in the script. Weir wisely chose to shoot entirely on location, a decision which gives the film the necessary sense of beauty and danger. The heat in the rain forest was stifling and unrelenting. As Ford's British costar Helen Mirren said at the time, "To actually experience the heat, the bugs, the mud, and the rain was a million times better than playing it on a studio backlot with a few palm trees." In order to keep the morale as high as possible, a wide range of modern conveniences were brought into the jungle locations, including VCRs, computers, a cappuccino machine, and a regular delivery of bagels flown in from

En route to the Mosquito Coast, Allie debates the Reverend Spellgood (*Andre Gregory*) about the values of religion. (Warner Bros.)

Miami! The fictitious town of Jeronimo, which Allie Fox develops from a few shacks into a thriving community, had to be constructed from scratch. Interestingly, in the course of doing so, the crew unearthed an unrecorded Mayan temple—a discovery which would have made Indiana Jones proud. The $7 million which the producers invested in the local economy made the film company the third biggest industry that year in Belize (following sugar and marijuana!). Over three hundred citizens were hired to build roads, carry supplies, and transport the all-important dailies.

Paul Theroux noted that, once on the set, Harrison Ford began to submerge himself into the character of

Allie Fox, going so far as to act cantankerous about the lack of amenities on the set. Appalled at the living conditions (he half joked he'd trade his hotel for a cargo plane), Ford rented a 122-foot air conditioned yacht upon which his wife Melissa Mathison worked steadily on her script for the Gen. George Custer TV movie, *Son of the Morning Star.* Gripes about accommodations aside, Ford bonded well with the cast and crew and impressed all by his lack of star attitude. From force of habit, he would help the crew with the "dirty work" and pitch in to get the job done more efficiently. He explained, "I'd rather help than just stand around and wait for them to do it themselves. If I can't stand in front of the camera until all that crap gets moved to the other side of the river, I grab a box. To everyone's absolute amazement and amusement, I'm just used to being part of a working group of people. The collar around my neck is blue."

The labors that went into making *The Mosquito Coast* were worthwhile—at least from an artistic standpoint. The film is something all too rare in today's cinema—an original. Much of the credit for making what could have been a depressing and unwatchable work seem so fascinating lies with Peter Weir's flawless direction. His ability to make the most of unusual geographic settings is never more apparent than in this film. The movie could have degenerated into a modern *Swiss Family Robinson* clone, but instead it succeeds in combining the beauty and danger of a remote land with the personal relationships of the people who try to live within its borders. It remains one of the most visually impressive films of recent years. Compromises were made to soften the character of Allie Fox just enough to not totally vilify him. These changes were made with the full approval of Paul Theroux, who remained on the set through much of the production. In the finished film, Allie remains an arrogant egotist, but his intentions are good, and we can't help but have grudging admiration for him. When everything he works for is destroyed, in a tense sequence in which he must outwit the forces of evil, his sheer determination to pick himself up and rebuild his life is an inspiration. Unfortunately, in doing so, Fox consistently exposes his family to the ravages of nature and risks their lives to justify his own obsessions.

With director Peter Weir (*in hat*), producer Jerome Hellman, and costar Helen Mirren. (Warner Bros.)

The Mosquito Coast has a remarkably talented cast, of which several members stand out in particular: Helen Mirren as Allie's weak-willed but ever-loyal wife; River Phoenix as the equally loyal son who tries to balance his love and idolization for his father with the encroaching realization that he is somewhat mad; Andre Gregory as the fire-and-brimstone missionary who unwittingly precipitates the tragedy which befalls the Foxes; and Conrad Roberts as the native friend to the family whose kindness is repaid with Allie's insults. However, most of the burden of carrying the film falls squarely on Ford's shoulders. Had his interpretation of Allie Fox been anything but letter-perfect, the character would have seemed repulsive. Thanks to his yeoman work, the fine line between hero and villain is achieved throughout the film, and Ford should have been nominated for an Oscar, along with Weir and screenwriter Paul Schrader.

Unfortunately, *The Mosquito Coast* would not garner any Oscar nominations or even become a favorite with critics. Because of the complex nature of the story line, the film was difficult to market. The one-sheet poster and newspaper ads played up Ford's star presence, but the actor was all but unrecognizable behind a pair of glasses, his hair combed back and dirty. Certainly this was not the image moviegoers had of their hero from *Star Wars* or the Indiana Jones films. The title also told the audience nothing about the theme of the film. Sadly but almost inevitably, *The Mosquito Coast* failed to gain much attention. Despite some isolated glowing notices from critics, it was generally dismissed as an ambitious failure. The normally low-key Harrison Ford was disheartened by the treatment of his movie in the press. He wrote a letter to the *Philadelphia Inquirer* in which he complained, "I have never seen a serious film treated so badly by the critics. And I think they're wrong. The picture is well worth seeing. It's a very complicated and ambitious piece and I would like people to see it. I would like to do whatever I can to help that happen."

Ford's comments were more than those of a frustrated actor venting about the rejection of his film. It is ironic that one of Ford's best performances was seen by so few of his fans. In 1993, Ford reiterated his pride in the film, telling *Empire* magazine: "It's the only film I have done that hasn't made its money back. I'm still glad I did it. If there was a fault with the film, it was that it didn't fully enough embrace the language of the book by Paul Theroux. It may have more properly been a literary rather than a cinematic exercise. But I still think it's full of powerful emotions."

Allie finds his dream has turned into a nightmare for his family (*Helen Mirren, River Phoenix, and Hilary Gordon*). (Warner Bros.)

Reviews

"A very hard movie to like. I could appreciate the good acting here, and I could admire the way Harrison Ford allowed his character's insanity to take over, [but] it was so clear that this man was not a visionary, not a mystic, but simply nuttier than a fruit-cake. The hero's bizarre behavior kept me on the outside, looking in."

—ROGER EBERT, *SISKEL AND EBERT*

"I found myself on the inside with him, because in the beginning, I didn't think he was nuttier than a fruit-cake. The guy seriously thinks there are problems in the land, and wants to do something about it. It reminded me of the sixties notion of making it a better world . . . . This movie is quite compelling in showing that descent into madness out of good intentions. This movie is about how noble wishes and noble desires can be misled."

—GENE SISKEL, *SISKEL AND EBERT*

"One of the most important films of the year . . . an exhilarating, pulse-pounding film of excitement and originality."

—REX REED

"Though Harrison Ford offers a hypnotizing portrayal of a man covering despair with lunatic optimism, hysteria with bravado, and rigid self-control, a fatal preju-dice lingers in the audience: we do not want to spend a couple of hours with Allie more than we would if he were, heaven forbid, our next-door neighbor."

—TIME

"Utterly compelling, novelistic saga of iconoclastic inventor and idealist (Ford in a knockout perfor-mance). . . . Not for all tastes, since Ford's character is unsympathetic (though he was even worse in Paul Theroux's novel!). Beautifully crafted with fine screen-play by Paul Schrader. A serious and emotionally gripping film."

—LEONARD MALTIN'S *MOVIE AND VIDEO GUIDE*

"Though Allie is played with a good deal of eccentric force by Harrison Ford, the effect is quickly numb-ing. . . . In spite of its authentic scenery, this *Mosquito Coast* is utterly flat. Even its exotic melo-drama fails to excite the imagination. The problem is not in the performances but in the way they have been presented, most of the time in a cool, dispas-sionate, third-person narrative style, stripped of Charlie's [Allie Fox's teenage son who narrates the film—Ed.] troubled thoughts and feelings that give the book its emotional force. Mr. Ford, who no longer needs to be identified as one of the more impressive and durable spin-offs of Star Wars, looks and feels right. Yet, the audience can never understand the hold he has over his loyal wife and Charlie."

—VINCENT CANBY, *NEW YORK TIMES*

22

Frantic (1988)

"The frustration and anxiety I had to create had a serious residual effect on me. I took it home every night in a way I never had done before. I usually get that out of my system, but this one was unremitting, relentless. . . . It felt good to stop being Dr. Walker. It was more of a strain than I thought."

CAST:
Dr. Richard Walker: Harrison Ford; *Michelle*: Emmanuelle Seigner; *Sondra Walker*: Betty Buckley; *Williams*: John Mahoney; *Gaillard*: Gerard Klein; *Shaap*: Jimmie Ray Weeks; *The Kidnapper*: Yorgo Voyagis; *Peter*: David Huddleston.

CREDITS:
Director: Roman Polanski; *Producers*: Thom Mount and Tim Hampton; *Screenplay*: Roman Polanski and Gerard Brach; *Director of Photography*: Witold Sobocinski; *Production Designer*: Pierre Guffroy; *Editor*: Sam O'Steen; *Music*: Ennio Morricone. *Running time*: 120 minutes. A Mount Company Production; Released by Warner Brothers.

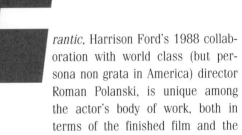

Frantic, Harrison Ford's 1988 collaboration with world class (but persona non grata in America) director Roman Polanski, is unique among the actor's body of work, both in terms of the finished film and the way in which the project materialized. During the 1985 Christmas season, Ford's wife Melissa Mathison flew to Paris to meet with Polanski regarding a script she was writing for his proposed movie based on the famous Belgian cartoon hero "Tin-Tin." The film (which, as of this writing, has yet to come to fruition) was to be produced by Steven Spielberg, for whom Mathison had written the script for *E.T.* Ford was worried about his wife's well-being while abroad. Not only had there been an upsurge in European terrorism, but there also were more personal concerns as well: Mathison was pregnant at the time. He decided to accompany her on the trip, acknowledging, "I'm always worrying about her. That pretty much defines my reality."

Ironically, while the Mathison/Polanski/Spielberg project would not materialize, Polanski found he had a chemistry with Harrison Ford. Polanski gave Ford the script to *Frantic*, a film he was planning to shoot in the near future, and asked him if he would consider starring in it. As Ford could not read French, Polanski decided to convey the essence of the story line in a most unique way: he jumped up on a table and began to enact the various

With director Roman Polanski in Paris. (Warner Bros.)

Walker (*Harrison Ford*) and Michelle (*Emmanuelle Seigner*) tempt death to retrieve a replica of the Statue of Liberty which contains the key to his wife's disappearance. (Warner Bros.)

characters. An hour and a half later, Ford committed himself to the project. This represented an uncharacteristically spontaneous decision for a top star. Ford is noted for taking a good deal of time to contemplate prospective projects, and few could argue with his methodology, as most of his films have proven to be hits. This time, however, he was impressed with Polanski's enthusiasm, as well as the fact that the story had a special meaning to the director. The plot centers on a man who finds himself unable to protect his wife when she mysteriously vanishes from their Paris hotel room. Polanski has always been haunted by his own wife Sharon Tate's gruesome death at the hands of the Charles Manson cult in 1969.

Ford said of the director's one-man performance of the script, "He played everything but the weather. And he was great. . . . It was clear that this was deeply emotional for Roman. To think how I'd feel if the circumstances had happened to me was, well. . . . When [Polanski's "performance"] was over, I said, 'If that's what it's going to be like when it's written down, I'll do it.'" The decision was a bold one. Polanski, one of the most acclaimed directors of the sixties and seventies, had found his career at the time in a downward spiral, both artistically and on a personal level. He had not had a major hit in years and was banned from ever entering the United States due to a scandalous

sexual encounter with a thirteen-year-old girl in the early 1980s. With Ford's participation, Polanski hoped to regain a degree of credibility and was able to secure a U.S. distribution deal with Paramount.

Frantic is a thought-provoking thriller with more than a few Hitchcockian overtones. Ford plays Richard Walker, a prominent cardiologist who arrives with his wife in Paris, where he will be the keynote speaker at an international medical seminar. The film quickly hooks the audience by presenting the classic Hitchcock scenario: an ordinary man reluctantly thrust into an extraordinary situation which tests the very essence of his character. In this case, the situation Ford encounters is terrifying because it cannot be rationally explained. He is taking a shower in his hotel suite as his wife dresses in the other room. He observes her talking on the telephone but cannot hear her, and nothing unusual is occurring. By the time he emerges from the shower, she is gone. Thinking she stepped out to buy something, he is not alarmed. However, as the hours pass, he begins to panic. How could someone vanish in plain sight? This eerie premise establishes a truly intriguing story line. The things that frighten us the most are those that we cannot rationally explain—the things that go "bump" in the night, or incidents which defy all logical explanations. We don't know much about her at the time of her disappearance, but we believe his wife is a straitlaced, loyal woman with no reason to disappear on her own. Yet how can a woman vanish from the safety of her own room in a crowded metropolitan hotel?

When the script sticks to Ford's maddening search for the answers, *Frantic* is as riveting as any Hitchcock film. However, as he begins to find the answers, through some conveniently available witnesses and clues, the film becomes merely a conventional thriller. Ford learns that his wife has been abducted because she has mistakenly been given a piece of luggage containing the detonating device for a nuclear bomb. Terrorists will hold her hostage until Ford can deliver it to them. He is given reluctant assistance by Michelle, a young punk rocker who had been hired to smuggle the device into France. Due to her mistake, Ford and his wife were given the suitcase which contains the detonator. Now Ford and his companion must play a cat-and-mouse game with a ruthless gang of murderers.

Frantic betrays itself by providing conventional answers to an unconventional premise. We learn too soon of Ford's wife's fate, when his frustrating pursuit of the facts had been the plot device which held the audience spellbound. The fear of the unknown is quickly replaced with a clichéd threat—that of some nameless terrorists from Central Casting. From this point, *Frantic* rests

An American in Paris: Ford in a festive mood on the set. (Warner Bros.)

entirely on the skills of its star and director. Fortunately, they are up to the task, and while the film never reaches its potential, it is still superior to most movies in the thriller genre.

The role of Dr. Richard Walker mirrored traits in Harrison Ford's own personality, most notably his obsession with orderliness and meticulousness. He admitted, "My wife and kids think I'm nuts—and people in the film business indulge me. . . . I am a great nuisance to art directors and others when I'm on a film set. I am always asking questions—'Why and where?' It is the only way I can really be happy at home and at work. I only do my best work when I consider the surroundings to be absolutely correct." He later confessed, "My brain does not easily relax. I'm always trying to keep myself from obsessive behavior, without much success." An example of Ford's dedication to the small details can be found in the fact that, despite his character not having any scenes which involved detailed knowledge of medicine, Ford nevertheless kept company with real-life cardiologists. He told *Playboy*, "It seemed important in order to better understand the character—even if it didn't show up in the

Reluctant allies: Walker and Michelle on the trail of the kidnappers. (Warner Bros.)

film. I met with a couple of heart surgeons and I spoke to other surgeons about heart surgeons. I learned there's a certain degree of authority they have in their world that they seem to want to take to the outside world. . . . I also found a certain elegance or vanity of gesture that was common to these guys. Lots of hand movements. I already gesture enough with my hands, so that wasn't a challenge."

Ford found that playing an everyday, unremarkable man was a welcome change from the larger-than-life heroes he was primarily identified with. "[Walker] is someone I haven't played before," he remarked. "He's not Indiana Jones. He's an ordinary man who faces a terrible ordeal and can't find anyone in authority to help him. He's an upper-class, straitlaced guy." Ford became so engulfed by his on-screen character that he found he brought many of Walker's characteristics home with him from the set. "To imagine how terrible someone would feel if his wife were kidnapped wasn't hard. My wife and I are very close. After we've viewed a day's filming, I'll ask her, 'Was that scene really dogshit?' and she'll say, 'Yeah, that really was dogshit.' My problem is my wife often found me in the same frustrating mood as my character, a mood I thought I'd been able to drop."

If Ford's behavior off the set was irritating to his wife, he could at least take comfort in the fact that during filming, his relationship with Roman Polanski was more enjoyable than he could have imagined. Polanski not only indulged Ford in his habit of suggesting improvisations but actually encouraged him to do so. Ford praised his director. "Roman is actually pretty free in the shooting process. If he can see it working before him, he doesn't care as much as other writing directors I've met that he get word-by-word interpretations." He later added, "He's very creative, and he improvises right on the set. When I work with Steven [Spielberg] or George Lucas, well, those kind of films have already been preplanned down to the smallest detail. People have been working on them for a long time before I start. There is no deviation from the screenwriter and director's vision. Roman, in the typical European style, was much more loose about that, and we sort of made parts of it up as we went along."

Polanski was equally generous with praise for Ford: "Often when Harrison read a line, it was a different reading than I anticipated, but it worked. Somehow, it was more inspiring or original than what I had in mind." He summed up his feeling for Ford by calling him "a fantastic actor. . . . As a human being, he's interesting, very straightforward, very direct and very honest." Coproducer Thom Mount characterized the odd-couple teaming of Ford and Polanski thusly: "Polanski's this mischievous little Polish devil and Harrison's a thoughtful American guy. And so you had a kind of creative and philosophical Mutt and Jeff."

As usual, Ford's insistence upon doing many of his own stunts caused concern among the crew. Per Thom Mount: "We weren't shooting him out of a cannon or anything. But it was stuff that you and I would not be thrilled about doing." The most challenging sequence involved Ford climbing over a sloping rooftop, thirty feet high. According to editor Sam O'Steen: "Polanski and Harrison were up on that steep roof climbing around like a couple of ten-year-olds, trying to work out the shots. Had either of them slipped, they would have been killed. I watched three takes and had to leave the set, it was so scary." The perilous sequence took six full days to shoot, even though it only lasts several minutes on film. Yet this scene illus-

As the obsessed Dr. Richard Walker. (Warner Bros.)

Yet we never learn much about these people. Refreshingly, Walker is an aboveboard, old-fashioned kind of guy who does not allow himself to be distracted by Michelle's blatant sexuality and promiscuity. However, we know nothing of the background of his marriage, and his wife remains a cardboard character who merely serves as the catalyst for the main plot device. Similarly, we know very little about Michelle, other than that she dabbles in drugs, has a penchant for dressing in leather, likes Grace Jones records, and is motivated primarily by money. The terrorists are given no background or motivation whatsoever. Because there is no central menace, the plot is seriously weakened by Ford having to outwit villains who generate no interest whatsoever. As critics Gene Siskel and Roger Ebert have repeatedly pointed out, a thriller is only as strong as its villains, and in *Frantic*, the bad guys remain far too sketchy. The script also introduces the mandatory hapless bureaucrats from the U.S. Embassy, who follow in the long line of other hapless bureaucrats from other cinematic U.S. Embassies. (Can't *any* of these people ever be presented in a sympathetic or professional way? Next to fat redneck sheriffs, they are among the most belittled group seen in modern movies.)

Ford found working with Polanski to be an extraordinarily rewarding experience. (Warner Bros.)

trates the accuracy of Ford's long-standing belief that seeing the star in a death-defying situation sans stuntman maximizes the suspense. Indeed, Ford's precarious climb across the rooftop is a highlight of *Frantic* and succeeds in matching similar scenes in Hitchcock's *Vertigo*, a film which was obviously a source of inspiration for this sequence.

While *Frantic* emulates Hitchcock successfully on one level, it fails to satisfactorily develop characters the way Hitchcock's films did. This is the central weakness of the movie. None of the characters is fully realized, including Ford's Richard Walker—despite the fact that he is on-screen virtually every minute of the film. The screenplay is devoted almost completely to Ford's dogged search for his wife and his reluctant partnership with Michelle, the woman who inadvertently caused her abduction.

Walker and his wife (*Betty Buckley*) grieve over the body of Michelle). (Warner Bros.)

Despite its many flaws and a failure to live up to its initial promise, *Frantic* consistently holds the viewer's interest. Polanski makes the most of the Parisian locations and succeeds in making the charming "City of Lights" appear dark and menacing. Ford's performance is solid and earnest, but the actor seems uncomfortable throughout. It appears as though he is having trouble finding a consistent manner in which to play Walker. This is primarily the fault of the script, which allows the character's personality traits to sway from a dull but devoted husband to a quick-thinking, charming man of action. The inconsistency of the character is best illustrated in an implausible sequence in which Walker saves Michelle from being tortured by posing as her naked lover—complete with a strategically placed teddy bear hiding his private parts. The scene is amusing but completely out of place for both the character and the situation. The plot is remindful of any number of Hitchcock classics, but his 1956 version of *The Man Who Knew Too Much* springs most prominently to mind. Instead of Jimmy Stewart and Doris Day searching furiously all over London for their kidnapped son, we have Harrison Ford and Emmanuelle Seigner scouring Paris for Ford's wife. Yet we never care

about the latter characters the way we do about Stewart and Day in the earlier film. And when the violent climax materializes, it is so clichéd that it betrays the many original moments which have preceded it.

Ford gets able support from Ms. Seigner, a twenty-two-year-old actress making her film debut in *Frantic*. She conveys a sexuality and confidence that commands the attention of the audience. (Seigner was Polanski's real-life girlfriend at the time.) The supporting cast is relatively unremarkable, with American actors John Mahoney and David Huddleston making brief appearances among the otherwise predominantly French company. Betty Buckley (from TV's *Eight Is Enough* and Broadway's *Cats* and later *Sunset Boulevard*) never gets an opportunity to emote very much as Ford's victimized wife, a fact which weakens the overall relationship between the two characters and renders their reunion in the film's climax somewhat hollow. Director Polanski deftly directs some inventive action set pieces but tends to go a bit over the top at the expense of logic. (Ford's pursuit by car of the kidnappers through the streets of Paris, while a dead man sits behind the wheel of the car, is more ludicrous than thrilling and calls to mind a similarly silly sequence in *A View to a Kill*.)

Still, *Frantic* is an interesting addition to the Harrison Ford canon. It deserved better than the cool reception it received when it premiered in 1988. The studio pressured Polanski to reshoot the ending, much to the chagrin of Ford, who advised them to "not change a fucking thing!" The running time was also trimmed by fifteen minutes. Whether these changes were responsible for the abundance of negative reviews and almost total disinterest on the part of the audience will never be known. Suffice it to say that *Frantic* was a rarity among Harrison Ford films: a flop. The star acknowledged years later that "I knew it would have a limited appeal to non-European audiences. But it's a film I think will hold up in the years to come. I have no regrets about making it." Ford did have a theory that the film's title may have been inappropriate: "I always knew calling it *Frantic* was a mistake. The script never had a frantic pace. I told Polanski we should call it 'Moderately Disturbed.' He was not amused."

Curiously, the French/Dutch film *The Vanishing*, made several years later, takes a similar premise—the inexplicable disappearance of an everyday, nondescript person—and lures the audience into a fascinating and nightmarish thriller that climaxes with a scene that is shocking, horrifying, and yet splendidly original in its determination to avoid a "feel good" ending. If only *Frantic* had stayed on course, it, too, could have had a similar impact. Yet the movie was packaged as a typical American thriller, primarily due to the presence of its larger-than-life American star. The compromises which were made reduced the final film from a classic thriller to a merely satisfactory one.

Ironically, when *The Vanishing* was remade for American audiences in 1993, its ending was changed in an attempt to leave audiences feeling upbeat. Like *Frantic*, it, too, was a critical and box-office failure. Perhaps someday studios will allow U.S. audiences the luxury of thrillers which have not been watered down for popular consumption. In 1988, however, not even Harrison Ford had enough influence to make such a goal a reality.

Reviews

"Keeps you on the edge of your seat with tension and suspense."

—REX REED, *AT THE MOVIES*

"A plodding rip-off of Hitchcock."

—*PHILADELPHIA INQUIRER*

"Ford makes you realize what a movie star really is— someone whose every on-screen move is totally enjoyable, an indefinable synthesis of his own person- ality and the role he's playing."

—*NEWSWEEK*

"Ford is superb, with an intriguing blend of innocence and guilt, and a watchability that brings to mind none other than James Stewart."

—*PHILADELPHIA DAILY NEWS*

"Frantic generates its suspense precisely because it appears so reasonable, because it takes such a calm, methodical approach to the maddening events that lure Dr. Walker into the maelstrom. . . . Harrison Ford plays the doctor in a tough, cool, single-minded way. He's able to convey great determination, as well as a restraint that barely masks the character's mounting rage, and he makes a compelling, if rather uncomplicated, hero."

—JANET MASLIN, *NEW YORK TIMES*

"Frantic is a thriller without much surprise, sus- pense, or excitement. . . . Ford sweats a lot while conveying Polanski's view that anxiety is the natural state of the human condition."

—*VARIETY*

"Every scene of this film feels like a project from Polanski's heart—a film to prove he is still capable of

A revealing moment for Ford, as he poses as Michelle's lover. (Warner Bros.)

generating the kind of suspense he became famous for. And every scene, on its own, seems to work. It is only the total of the scenes that is wrong; the movie goes on too long, adds too many elaborations, tacks on too many complications, until the lean and eco- nomical construction of the first hour begins to drift into self-parody. . . . The nature of the mystery becomes clear to the audience some time before it becomes clear to Ford [and] the movie begins to lose its tightly wound tension about the time the Seigner character enters the plot. Until then, it develops with chilling logic, one step at a time. . . . Even with its excesses, Frantic is a reminder of how absorbing a thriller can be."

—ROGER EBERT'S *VIDEO COMPANION*

＊全女性必見——

一流会社のアイデア秘書が、あなたと恋人に贈る爽快オフィス・ドラマ！

A MIKE NICHOLS FILM
Working Girl

マイク・ニコルズ監督作品

ワーキング・ガール

20世紀フォックス提供／ハリソン・フォード／シガーニイ・ウィーバー／メラニー・グリフィス

マイク・ニコルズ・フィルム "ワーキング・ガール" ■音楽カーリー・サイモン ■ドラマ音楽ロブ・マウンジー ■編集サム・オースティーン

製作総指揮ロバート・グリーンハット／ローレンス・マーク ■脚本ケビン・ウェイド

製作ダグラス・ウィック ■監督マイク・ニコルズ

23

Working Girl *(1988)*

"It had a lot of serious things to say about modern male-female relationships, and how women are treated in the workplace. I found it all very interesting."

CAST:

Jack Trainer: Harrison Ford; *Tess McGill*: Melanie Griffith; *Katharine Parker*: Sigourney Weaver; *Cyn*: Joan Cusack; *Mick Dugan*: Alec Baldwin; *Oren Trask*: Philip Bosco; *Lutz*: Oliver Platt; *Ginny*: Nora Dunn; *Personnel Director*: Olympia Dukakis; *Bridesmaid*: Ricki Lake

CREDITS:

Director: Mike Nichols; *Executive Producers*: Robert Greenhut and Laurence Mark; *Producer*: Douglas Wick; *Screenplay*: Kevin Wade; *Director of Photography*: Michael Ballhaus; *Production Designer*: Patrizia Von Brandenstein; *Editor*: Sam O'Steen; *Music*: Carly Simon. *Running time*: 113 minutes. Released by 20th Century Fox.

Japanese pressbook showcased Ford, Melanie Griffith (*left*) and Sigourney Weaver. (20th Century Fox)

To no one's surprise, *Working Girl*, was one of the top hits of 1988. What did surprise many was the fact that, although he is given first billing, Ford is very much a supporting character in this witty, contemporary look at Machiavellian business practices in today's large corporations. What also surprised many was Ford's presence in a gentle comedy–love story, with nary a bullwhip or laser gun in sight. Ford reacted to these observations a bit testily, reminding everyone that "I'm always doing comedy. It's a point of view about life." He explained that he felt the Indiana Jones films would be unwatchable if comedy were not such a prominent part of their appeal. He also reiterated that *Star Wars* was a comedy. "I look for comedy all the time." Ford's point was astute. The praise from critics regarding his deft handling of the broad comedic challenges of *Working Girl* was meant to be a compliment, but Ford took it as a backhanded one. For years, his screen presence had taken the edge off of films that might otherwise have been dismissed as overly violent or sadistic. In this respect, he shared a common "Bond" with Sean Connery, who did much the same thing with the character of 007—only to have his comedic talents overlooked entirely by the critics. "He's just playing himself," they would say, when in fact the man had nothing in common with the hero he portrayed on-screen.

Ford found himself victimized in a similar manner. No sane person could believe that his real-life persona could in any way resemble that of Indiana Jones or Han

169

Katharine (*Weaver*) makes Jack an offer he can refuse. (20th Century Fox)

sonal secretary of incoming executive Katharine Parker (Sigourney Weaver), who turns out to be a real bitch. Tess feels she will have a sympathetic ear from a fellow female and not be subjected to the sexual innuendoes in this male-dominated industry. Tess astonishes Katharine with her knowledge of the stock market, and she suggests a key business strategy to assist Katherine in landing a major account. Katherine seems impressed but tells her the deal has been rejected by the prospective client. When Katharine is disabled in a skiing accident while on a romantic vacation out of the country, Tess manages her affairs and discovers to her horror that the business plan she suggested is very much alive—but now being touted as her boss's idea. Tess utilizes Katharine's empty office to embark on an ambitious plan to conclude the deal by posing as an executive. She courts the services of Jack Trainer (Harrison Ford), a high-powered figure on Wall Street, to help conclude the deal. With Trainer's help, they induce the client (Philip Bosco) into making a verbal agreement to sign the deal. In the process, Tess and Jack fall in love. Complications arise when Katharine returns sooner than expected, and Tess discovers *she* is Jack's lover. All hell breaks loose, with Tess being discredited and Katharine almost stealing away the deal—and Jack. However, Tess is able to prove she was the mastermind behind the strategy that will enrich the client, and he hires her as an executive. Jack drops Katharine, who is

Solo, yet his performance in *Working Girl* seemed like a revelation to even his hard-core fans. Like Connery, Ford's talent was extensive enough to make moviegoers believe he didn't have to "stretch" to impress in the memorable characterizations he achieved on-screen. In short, the consummate actor made it look all too easy.

Working Girl traces a few chaotic weeks in the life of Tess McGill (Melanie Griffith), an attractive and extremely competent secretary from Staten Island with a seemingly dead-end job at a major Wall Street brokerage firm. Tired of being judged as a brainless sexpot, Tess is delighted when she is transferred to another department to be the per-

Tess (*Griffith*) and Jack (*Ford*) impress the "suits" on Wall Street. (20th Century Fox)

On the set with Melanie Griffith (*left*) and Sigourney Weaver. (20th Century Fox)

publicly humiliated and fired. As the film closes, Tess has gained the respect she so desired—based on her intellect rather than her looks. To top it all off, she and Jack resume their love affair.

In other hands, *Working Girl* could have looked like pretentious propaganda in which the business establishment is made to look like the heavy. However, the film's criticism of sexual harassment is delivered in a humorous and very believable way. We sympathize with Tess and realize that there are probably millions of underutilized, overqualified employees out there who are ignored on a daily basis because they pose a threat to their bosses or are simply not taken seriously. The movie, under Mike Nichols's direction, is a tour de force for the two female leads, and both Melanie Griffith and Sigourney Weaver play their roles for maximum effect. Griffith is a beautiful actress of rather limited range who has done more than her share to render any number of dramas laughable. (If you believe her as the World War II heroine behind Nazi lines in *Shining Through*, for example, then you probably think the plans for the D-Day invasion could have been entrusted to Gracie Allen). In *Working Girl*, however, Griffith's performance is right on the money. She embellishes Tess with some wonderfully realistic personality traits, and we relate to her naive dreams that one can

climb the corporate ladder based entirely on knowledge and work ethic.

The scene-stealing honors belong to Sigourney Weaver as the "boss from hell." Weaver plays Katharine in an "over the top" performance that nevertheless does not strain credulity. She is every employee's worst nightmare—an egotistical, patronizing phony who exerts her power to cover up her own insecurities. Perhaps the two actresses carried their roles to the extreme, as it was reported that there was no love lost between them on the set. Weaver dispelled this notion, albeit in a rather mild fashion, by telling *US* magazine in 1992: "There was some comment in the press about how much we hadn't gotten along. That was pretty much nonsense. Melanie sometimes was taken aback by how much I enjoyed playing the villain. And I was sometimes taken aback by how sensitive she was when I teased her. I tease people I like. Not all actors are used to that." (One can only hope Griffith became desensitized before reading the reviews of her performances in *Shining Through* and *A Stranger Among Us*. Undoubtedly, those reviews made Weaver's barbs look likc testimonials!)

Originally, the role of Jack Trainer was to be relatively marginal. Alec Baldwin was slated for the part, but in the first of a number of amazing career coincidences

Jack and Tess confront Katharine with the evidence that will destroy her. (20th Century Fox)

involving films in which Harrison Ford would later be associated, Baldwin was relegated to the relatively minor role of Tess's blue-collar boyfriend. He reacted gallantly, saying, "The minute Harrison Ford shows up, you drop everything and sign up Harrison Ford." (Baldwin would not be so accommodating when Ford would later inherit the Jack Ryan and Richard Kimble characters, both of which Baldwin was originally going to play.) Producer Douglas Wick explained why he sought Ford for the role: "We wanted a guy who looked like he could be a winner on Wall Street, but who also had the look of burnout around the fringes. Harrison has that funny warmth and softness that goes against the grain of his personality." With Ford onboard, the Trainer role was expanded to allow him more screen time. Still, the part is decidedly secondary to Griffith's and Weaver's. He told the press he had no reservations about taking a supporting role, saying it was a nice change of pace. However, he reiterated that he didn't want to make a habit of it: "I'd rather be home. If I'm going to leave the ranch at all, I would prefer it be for a big piece of work in a successful film. I certainly don't mind taking on a secondary role. Sometimes, the secondary roles are when you find really interesting characters who might not have a whole movie of their own." (Ford then cited his satisfaction with his supporting work in *Heroes* and *Judgment: The Court Martial of Lt. William Calley*.)

Ford interacted well with his costars but did admit some sensitivity over Sigourney Weaver's complaint that, despite his limited screen time, his paycheck for the film was considerably larger than hers or Melanie Griffith's. Ford agreed that the system reeked of sexism and confessed, "I'm slightly embarrassed. It's not within my control, but I'm certainly sympathetic to her point of view—she's right." Political correctness aside, neither Weaver or Ford would comment on the obvious—that the disparity in paychecks had less to do with sexism than with the ability of a star to "open" a film at the box office. Despite her indisputable talents, Weaver is simply not the draw with audiences that Harrison Ford has proven to be.

Ford plunged himself into the role of Jack Trainer with characteristic professionalism. Immersing himself in the unfamiliar world of Wall Street, he spent considerable time at New York brokerage houses acquainting himself with the people in the industry. He even sat in on meetings between investment bankers and their clients to insure he had the proper feel for his character. Unfortunately, he had to cease this practice when it became apparent that the presence of one of the world's biggest movie stars had more than a slight influence on the behavior of the participants in these meetings. Although not fond of large urban areas, Ford decided that, while on location in New York, it would be beneficial to have a residence in the city. He purchased a $2 million apartment overlooking Central Park from actress Debra Winger, indicating that perhaps he found the deal-making environment of Wall Street somewhat addictive.

Upon its release, *Working Girl* was greeted with overwhelmingly favorable notices and became the year's hottest "date" movie. The film crossed all demographic boundaries and appealed to virtually all audiences. Artistically, director Mike Nichols managed to keep the comedy flowing without ever being tempted to turn the slightly exaggerated characters into cartoons. The film also has its share of pathos, and it's difficult not to empathize with the character of Tess when her entire world seems to cave in upon her. Melanie Griffith and Sigourney Weaver make the most of their scenery-chewing roles (even if Griffith does indulge in an annoying habit of clearing her throat either prior to or immediately after delivering almost every line). Harrison Ford more than holds his own in the realm of light comedy and again demonstrates his often overlooked ability to get a laugh by underplaying a scene. Executive producer Robert Greenhut promised, "You haven't seen Harrison in a sophisticated comedy of this type. He's the closest we've got to Cary Grant in the talent pool these days." Extravagant praise from a not exactly impartial party, but accurate nonetheless.

Working Girl earned several key Oscar nominations, among them nods for both Griffith and Weaver. Not surprisingly, Ford was overlooked, not because his performance wasn't admired, but, again, probably because he made it look too damned easy. If the Academy did not see fit to honor Ford's work in the film, Melanie Griffith felt differently. She would later tell TV Guide, "He was so easy to act with, because you look in his eyes and there's a real person there. He listens, he reacts, he gives a lot. He helped me enormously." Director Mike Nichols also heaped praise on his leading actor, quipping that he regarded Harrison not as a Ford but as a Ferrari. With characteristic modesty, he shrugged off the accolade by pointing out, "That means I'm difficult and expensive to maintain!"

Working Girl provided Harrison Ford with a rare comedic role. (Andrew Schwartz, courtesy 20th Century Fox).

Reviews

"Ford is marvelous. He's so identified with action movies that it comes as a shock to see him doing tremendously interesting work in a romantic comedy with a coat and tie on. He's put on a coat and tie a lot lately, and he's been getting more impressive with each film."

—BUFFALO NEWS

"Ford's comic abilities are a total surprise; he's been so good recently that a critical re-evaluation is due."

—USA TODAY

"Enjoyable, even when it isn't credible, which is most of the time. The film, like its heroine, has a genius for getting by on pure charm. . . . The screenplay has a sly wit, but it is surprisingly primitive. So the plot contains distracting holes and the details of Tess's scheme to succeed seem crude, even for a film as lighthearted as this. Mike Nichols also displays an uncharacteristic blunt touch, and in its later stages, the story remains lively but seldom has the perceptiveness or acuity of Mr. Nichols's best work. . . . Mr. Ford, who plays Jack in a foggy and rather faraway manner, never sets off many sparks with Miss Griffith, but perhaps that's not the point. One of the many things that mark Working Girl as an '80s creation is its way of regarding business and sex as almost interchangeable pursuits and suggesting that life's greatest happiness can be achieved by combining the two."

—JANET MASLIN, NEW YORK TIMES

24

Indiana Jones and the Last Crusade (1989)

"I insisted we complicate the character. I wanted not only the adventure, the environment, to be good, but I wanted the audience to have the opportunity to learn something more about the character. The device of introducing his father played by Sean Connery was a stroke of genius."

CAST:
Indiana Jones: Harrison Ford; *Prof. Henry Jones*: Sean Connery; *Elsa*: Alison Doody; *Sallah*: John Rhys-Davies; *Marcus Brody*: Denholm Elliott; *Walter Donovan*: Julian Glover; *Young Indy*: River Phoenix; *Vogel*: Michael Byrne; *Kazim:* Kevord Malikyan.

CREDITS:
Director: Steven Spielberg; *Executive Producers*: George Lucas and Frank Marshall; *Producer*: Robert Watts; *Screenplay*: Jeffrey Boam; *Story*: George Lucas and Menno Meyjes; *Based on characters created by* George Lucas and Philip Kaufman; *Director of Photography*: Douglas Slocombe; *Production Designer*: Elliot Scott; *Editor*: Michael Kahn; *Special Effects Supervisors*: George Gibbs and Michael J. McAlister; *Music*: John Williams. *Running time*: 127 minutes. A LucasFilm Ltd. Production; Released by Paramount Pictures.

Ford did his own stunts during the dangerous tank chase sequence. (Murray Close, courtesy LucasFilm Ltd.)

Although it had been four years since the release of *Indiana Jones and the Temple of Doom*, Steven Spielberg was determined to direct a grand finale for the series, partly to counter the hostile reaction the previous film had received from critics—and many moviegoers as well. Although it had been a box-office smash, there was a general feeling of disillusionment with the final cut. Reflecting on the second Indy adventure, Spielberg would later admit, "I wasn't happy with that film at all. It was too dark, too subterranean, and much too horrific. . . . There is not an ounce of my personal feeling in [it]." Ford would admit to having the same opinion, saying he felt it was excessive in its brutality. He lamented, "Occasionally, I rose to protest, but moviemaking is a collaborative effort and while my attitude was noted, it did not prevail."

Spielberg, Ford, and executive producers George Lucas and Frank Marshall agreed that the series had to recapture the humor and fun of *Raiders of the Lost Ark*, but they could not decide on how to make the film fundamentally different. The team hired screenwriter Jeffrey Boam (*Lethal Weapon 2*) to fashion a script which would incorporate all of the elements which originally made Indiana Jones a classic movie hero. Boam had some very definitive ideas and was quite vocal in how his story would differ from the preceding films: "For me, the first two movies just didn't have enough *character*. Indiana

Jones has always been a great character, but he has always been this *being* presented full-blown with his fedora and bullwhip. I felt that, given the opportunity, I could bring an added dimension to the Indy character and basically get inside him and let the audience find out *how* Indiana Jones becomes Indiana Jones.... By the time the film is over, Indiana Jones won't have too many secrets left."

The hook which the filmmakers decided upon to differentiate this movie from its predecessors would be the introduction of Indy's father, a famous, eccentric archaeologist named Professor Henry Jones. The plot would center on Indy and his dad engaged in a life-and-death struggle with the Nazis to locate the sacred Holy Grail—the cup from which Jesus allegedly drank during the Last Supper. The story line was suggested by Adolf Hitler's well-known belief in the supernatural, as well as his quest for immortality. As legend holds that the person who drinks from the Grail lives forever, it would seem only natural that the Führer would embark on a relentless pursuit of the sacred cup. In Jeffrey Boam's script, Indy's father is a man who has devoted his entire adult life to locating the Grail. Ironically, he has been captured by the Nazis just as he has finally learned its location and is being forced to lead the Gestapo to its hiding place in Egypt. The elder Jones manages to get word to his estranged son Indiana, and the two men narrowly defeat the forces of the Third Reich while simultaneously learning to respect and love each other for the first time in their lives.

Initially, the part of Professor Jones was to be a crotchety, aristocratic type of English gentleman—the type of character one would envision being played by John Houseman. However, Steven Spielberg came up with a bold and inspiring idea. Since Indiana Jones was his answer to

Indy (*Harrison Ford*) and Elsa (*Alison Doody*) pursue the Holy Grail in catacombs beneath the streets of Venice. (Murray Close, courtesy LucasFilm Ltd.)

Still bickering after all these years: Indy pauses for a debate with his dad (*Sean Connery*). (Murray Close, courtesy LucasFilm Ltd.)

James Bond, why not have the man who created 007 on-screen play Indy's dad? The idea of getting Sean Connery for the role was met with skepticism by George Lucas, who feared that in the unlikely event Connery accepted

176

the part, his presence would be far too formidable to be accepted as a bookish, eccentric professor. Spielberg countered, "I figured Sean would give Harrison a run for his money. . . . I couldn't imagine anyone with less screen power than Sean Connery to be the famous Indiana Jones's father. Ford takes up a lot of screen, and I didn't want Harrison diminishing any father in screen presence."

Having convinced Lucas that approaching Connery was a worthwhile endeavor, the next hurdle was to convince the actor himself that the part was worth accepting. Spielberg admitted he felt the chances were slim of succeeding: "I didn't think Sean would want to play Indy's father. Obviously, Sean had his trademark on the James Bond movies, and we were a kind of James Bond movie ourselves." Spielberg's reservations were wellfounded, as Connery's problems with the Bond films were well-known. While they initially brought the struggling young Scottish-born actor fame and fortune, he soon discovered that they also thrust him into a goldfish bowl of scrutiny by the press and public. When the Bond films hit their peak popularity in the midsixties, Connery—an intensely private man—could no longer bear the pressure. The producers allowed him to "retire" from the 007 role one film earlier than his contract called for, and in 1967, Sean left the role of a lifetime to the unknown George Lazenby. Four years later, frustrated by public and critical rejection of his non-Bond films, Connery reluctantly made a return to the role in *Diamonds Are Forever.* In 1983, he faced a similar dilemma and made his last appearance as Bond in *Never Say Never Again.* Since that time, Connery had been on a winning streak and had successfully distanced himself from the 007 films. In 1988, he was awarded the Oscar for Best Supporting Actor for his superb performance in *The Untouchables.*

Would the popular but moody actor really consider starring in a film whose origins were so obviously inspired by the Bond films? To the relief of all, the answer was a resounding yes—provided that Connery could have considerable creative input into defining the character of Professor Jones. He explained his dissatisfaction with the role as originally written, which presented Professor Jones as a "Yoda-like," gnomish, wise old man: "It didn't add up in my book. I was after something a bit more Victorian and flamboyant, like one of the explorers—Sir Richard Burton and Mungo Park, who went off to the hinterlands and were missing for months. . . . That's what we got."

Connery made a number of suggestions which were readily accepted by the Indiana Jones filmmakers. When Jeffrey Boam was questioned as to whether it really was in character for Professor Jones to have slept with Indy's

Once more, it's Indy to the rescue. (LucasFilm Ltd.)

love interest, he replied, "No way. . . . But Sean Connery would!" Connery concurred that humor was essential to this film, praising his director and costar in the process: "The nice thing about Indiana Jones is the humor, and the fact that it's back to an older age, not an age of hardware and spacecraft, but cars and airplanes and trains and horses. I'm always looking for the humor in a situation and Harrison Ford has a nice, sly sense of humor. I'm very impressed by Steven Spielberg; he's very inventive, very quick." Connery also explained the appeal of his character: "He's got skin and that's what I think captures an audience for this type of story and that's what the James Bond films had, too. Indiana Jones, in some ways, is a Bondian character because he always ends up in terrible situations which always have to be resolved with some invention or humorous action. That's the only solution he ever has, whether it's jumping into a plane and he says he can fly it but that he doesn't know how to land it. Yes, he's very Bondian."

Indy is mistaken by Der Führer for an autograph seeker. (LucasFilm Ltd.)

confessed, "I didn't know quite how it would work. But there is the most wonderful chemistry between the two of them; it's a little like the Newman/Redford chemistry in *Butch Cassidy* and *The Sting*. It's a real sparkle of screen magic." He also mentioned the awe in which the cast and crew held the two stars: "When Sean and Harrison arrived on the set, everyone got quiet and respectful. The two are like royalty." Surprisingly, both Ford and Connery—neither of whom is known for their outlandish senses of humor—engaged in a great many practical jokes which tended to "break up" the other man. Spielberg commented at the time, "The biggest thrill was putting Harrison and Sean in a two-shot and calling 'Action!' and trying not to ruin the take by laughing."

The pair's anarchic sense of fun was displayed most prominently during the filming of the sequence in which Indy and his dad attempt to escape the Nazis by posing as tourists aboard a Zeppelin. The temperatures on location in Spain were easily in excess of 100 degrees—a condition which was particularly unpleasant for Connery, who was clad in a three-piece tweed suit. Ford didn't fare much better, attired in Indy's customary leather jacket. Because the actors were seated at a table and would only be shot from the waist up, Connery simply removed his pants to minimize the heat. At first, Ford was shocked, but as the sweat poured down his own face, he did the same. The two pros continued their dialogue without missing a beat.

Filming of *Last Crusade* took place in Almeria, Spain; Venice, Italy; Jordan, and at George Lucas's adopted home base in England, Elstree Studios. The film required some of the most challenging stunt work ever to appear in a Harrison Ford movie. Characteristically, Ford wanted to perform most of his own stunts to enhance the reality of the scenes. The most elaborate of these was Indy's dangling from the side of a Nazi tank while being crushed against the side of a ditch. The scene, which was shot in Spain, took two full weeks to film at a cost of $200,000 per day. Although Ford allowed his longtime stunt double Vic Armstrong to make the fourteen-foot leap onto the moving tank, the actor insisted upon hanging from the tank himself, thus risking serious injury. Upon concluding this amazing sequence, Ford did confess that

Harrison Ford confessed to not having been an afficionado of the 007 films, with the exception of *From Russia With Love*, Connery's second Bond movie and, coincidentally, his own personal favorite. However, he was an enormous admirer of Sean Connery's acting skills. He said of his legendary costar, "When I got to be an actor, I could see that Sean was one of the good ones. I thought he was great in *The Man Who Would Be King*, *Robin and Marian*, and *The Wind and the Lion*." He would later add, "Sean is, of course, such a terribly experienced actor, and that made it interesting to work with him. He's an awfully nice guy, too. I've enjoyed knowing him as well as working with him." Ford admitted that Connery, who was only twelve years older than he, was nonetheless so convincing in his paternal role that Ford was constantly reminded of his relationship with his real father: "It was great to work with Sean. And it was really interesting to relate to him as my father. I think it gave us the opportunity to explore how much I'm like my own father. All those things that always drove me crazy about my father have started showing up in my personality. My sons haven't had to deal with that yet. That comes when you are forty or so."

The possibility for a clash of egos between two present-day screen icons was apparent to Steven Spielberg. He was delighted that the pairing instead resulted in Ford and Connery forming a mutual admiration society. He

178

Indy utilizes his ever-present bullwhip to save himself and Elsa from the Nazis. (LucasFilm Ltd.)

the sequence was "one of the hairiest stunts I've ever been involved with."

For another scene, Ford wanted to jump from a sixteen-foot ledge, knock a villain from a horse, take the reins, and gallop off. According to Vic Armstrong, "The only way I could dissuade him was with a little white lie. I dragged him to one side and hissed that if he did stunts he would do me out of money. Harrison was horrified and said, 'Sorry, Vic. I just didn't realize. Of course, I'll shut up.' " Ford maintained that the stunts he did perform were so well planned that he was not courting any real danger: "Bumps and bruises go with the territory. It's what distinguishes an Indiana Jones movie from another adventure film. You sit there in the theater and know I'm doing it."

Not all of Ford's "stunts" were confined to action sequences. He showed a great deal of chemistry with actress Alison Doody, who plays Elsa, the sensual archaeologist who turns out to be a Nazi agent. The two exuded a marvelous chemistry, with Doody's performance helping to make the unrepentant Elsa the most intriguing female character in the Indiana Jones trilogy. Doody recalled Ford's thoughtfulness on the set: "If there was a moment where I was tense or something, he would joke around, which is very nice because he was doing it to try and ease the tension. . . . Working with Harrison was such a pleasure. He's a great man to work with; he helped me a great deal in my scenes. . . . He would talk scenes through. And if I had a problem at all, he was always there and willing to try and sort it out and my life on the set was much easier." One important sequence in which Ford's sense of humor played a pivotal role involved a sequence in which Indy and Elsa kiss passionately. Doody was rather uncomfortable with the pure sexuality of the scene, so Ford tried to ease her tension by puckering his lips and making silly kissing noises off-camera, cooing all the while, "Alison, I'm ready!" Ford also advised her how to cope with the inevitable questions the British press would ask about what it was like to do a love scene with him. He told her, "Tell them that Harrison Ford is so famous he doesn't even use his own tongue!"

Some of Ford's other "costars" were not quite so glamorous. At Elstree, he and Doody had to film a sequence set in the underground catacombs of Venice. Here, Indy and Elsa encounter thousands of rats, which (in a scene inspired by *From Russia With Love*) are driven to stampede by a raging fire. The scene required one thousand mechanical rats and six thousand of the real thing. Although the rats were allegedly "safe" because they had been bred in captivity, this was not enough to prevent any timid crew members from leaving the set. The sequence manages to be chilling without the over-the-top grotesqueness of the "bug scene" in *Temple of Doom*. Steven Spielberg lamented, "Same thing with the snakes [in *Raiders*]. We lost half the crew on the first movie, and we lost three-quarters of the crew with the bugs [in *Temple*]." Harrison Ford stoically announced, "That kind of stuff doesn't bother me. It's people I'm scared of!" Perhaps Ford's hobby of breeding rats as a young boy explained his courage in the sequence.

Last Crusade benefited from the best cast of any of the three Indiana Jones films. Assisting Ford, Connery, and Doody were the wonderful Denholm Elliott as the bumbling but brave Marcus Brody, Indy's friend and mentor; John Rhys-Davies as Sallah, Indy's loyal and resourceful Arab adventurer and con man; and Julian Glover, excellent as the cultured but evil Walter Donovan. With the exception of Harrison Ford and Denholm Elliott, all have appeared in at least one James Bond film.

The film also features River Phoenix as the teenaged Indy in a superb opening sequence. The scenes, which feature Indy as a Boy Scout trying to prevent the theft of a sacred artifact by scavengers in a deserted gold mine, is

179

River Phoenix as a young Indy in the film's memorable opening scene. (Bruce Talamon, courtesy LucasFilm Ltd.)

a marvel of flawless screenwriting, directing, and editing. Indy's battle with the thieves takes him from inside the mine, to a chase on horseback, to a cat-and-mouse game aboard a circus train loaded with deadly animals. Within a few precious minutes, the scene manages to explain the origins of everything from Indy's fear of snakes to his acquisition of his trademark Stetson hat. The sequence beautifully segues to twenty-six years later, when we see a grown Indy once again caught in a life-and-death struggle to save the same artifact from greedy opportunists. It's an example of the kind of action scene which Steven Spielberg does so well, and it moves so quickly that you feel that whatever follows will be anticlimactic. Fortunately, this is not the case. *Last Crusade* retains the "thrill-a-second" pace of the previous films, but this one has far more heart. It is arguably the most satisfying entry of the series.

Although the movie abounds with the technology of the era it portrays, the technology never

overshadows the characters. The script allows Ford and Connery to define what cinematic chemistry is all about. There are exchanges of dialogue between the two, such as when Indy accuses his father of never communicating with him. The old man replies that Indy left home just when he was getting interesting. The transition between father and son being adversaries to being loving family members is done in an understated and unsentimental way that is nevertheless quite moving. The action sequences are woven into the story to allow Indy and his dad to demonstrate their own types of resourcefulness: Indy with strength and force, his father with ingenuity and wit. The humor is omnipresent and often hilarious. The funniest moment in the film involves Connery and Ford tied back-to-back on a chair, when the former inadvertently starts a fire. The resulting sequence (reminiscent of many adventure flicks from the thirties and forties), in which the two men try to escape the flames by using a revolving hidden door connected to Nazi headquarters, is a highlight of the film. The incredible ending manages to blend mysticism, religion, and spectacular action far more successfully than the conclusions of the first two films. All of this is accompanied, of course, by John Williams's wonderful and familiar score.

Last Crusade opened on Memorial Day weekend, 1989. The $36 million epic immediately set two then-box-office records: collecting the most receipts ever in one day ($10 million) and having the biggest opening week in film history (a total gross of $50 million). Critics were unstinting in their praise, thus forgiving Steven

In the fierce battle with the mysterious Kazim (*Kevork Malikyan*). (Murray Close, courtesy of LucasFilm Ltd.)

Spielberg for the somber tone of *Temple*. Virtually every reviewer cited the casting coup of a Harrison Ford–Sean Connery teamup. *Last Crusade*, along with *Batman* and *Lethal Weapon 2*, dominated the summer box office and made short work of the competition, which included such high-profile sequels as *The Karate Kid, Part II, Ghostbusters II*, and *Star Trek V*. Ironically, one of the films "victimized" by *Last Crusade*'s staying power was the 007 thriller *License to Kill*.

Ford saw *Last Crusade* as his last appearance as Indiana Jones. He reflected on the role with some sentiment: "I'll miss the whole thing. There is a lot of pleasure in this character for me. I enjoy the kind of humor that we have in these films and I love doing the physical stuff. It makes me feel like a kid. I'll miss the particular fun of playing the character but I think three films is enough." When asked about any possibility of continuing the role in the future, Ford responded, "I'll be in my fifties pretending to be thirty-five, and I'm afraid it's going to get to a point where it's too hard to get out of bed in the morning! I just won't be able to do the things I used to do." However, he did add, "Well, if there's *anything* I learned from Sean, it's to never say never again!" Indeed. As of this writing, Ford, Spielberg, and Lucas are considering reviving Indiana Jones for one more "last" crusade.

Clowning on the set with Steven Spielberg and Connery. (Murray Close, courtesy LucasFilm Ltd.)

Reviews

"*More cerebral than the first two Indiana Jones films, and less schmaltzy than the second, this literate adventure should entertain and enlighten kids and adults alike. The Harrison Ford–Sean Connery father-and-son team gives* Last Crusade *unexpected emotional depth, reminding us that real film magic is not in special effects.*"

—*Variety*

"*Take a good look at this movie. In fact, go back four or five times and take four or five good looks. In this imperfect world, you're not likely to see many man-made objects come this close to perfection.*"

—Ralph Novak, *People*

"*No, it's not as fresh and exhilarating as* Raiders, *but how could it be? Here's an antidote for anyone who sensed sequel sluggishness in* Temple of Doom. . . .*"

"*One of the best ideas in this second sequel was recruiting Sean Connery. Connery and Ford are a testy father-son duo sharing quips, imminent danger, and even the favors of a gorgeous Nazi. . . .* Last Crusade *is an adult comic strip, hyperkinetic high adventure that scarcely pauses for breath. . . . Grab a crash helmet and go.*"

—Bruce Williamson, *Playboy*

"*Though it cannot regain the brash originality of* Raiders, *in its own way,* Last Crusade *is nearly as good, matching its audience's wildest hopes.*"

—Caryn James, *New York Times*

"*This thrice-told tale gives you your money's worth. Now it's time to hang up the bullwhip and move on.*"

—David Ansen, *Newsweek*

Trivia Note

• *Harrison Ford did officially appear again as Indiana Jones in an episode of the* Young Indiana Jones *television series titled "The Mystery of the Blues," which aired on ABC on March 13, 1993. A bearded Ford appears briefly as an older and wiser Indy in the opening sequence, which then segues into flashbacks of Indy's adventures as a teenager. Originally, the show's producer, George Lucas, wanted Ford to play Indy as a ninety-three-year-old man, but the actor felt it would be more effective to be seen the way audiences had come to recognize him, albeit a little older.*

25

Presumed Innocent (1990)

"I had an emotional reaction to the character. He's different from what I've played recently, and to work with Alan J. Pakula, a director I admire, made the whole project appeal to me."

CAST:
Rusty Sabich: Harrison Ford; *Raymond Horgan*: Brian Dennehy; *Sandy Stern*: Raul Julia; *Barbara Sabich*: Bonnie Bedelia; *Judge Larren Lyttle*: Paul Winfield; *Carolyn Polhemus*: Greta Scacchi; *Detective Lipranzer*: John Spencer; *Tommy Molto*: Joe Grifasi; *"Painless" Kumagai*: Sab Shimono; *Nico Della Guardia*: Tom Mardirosian.

CREDITS:
Director: Alan J. Pakula; *Executive Producer*: Susan Solt; *Producers*: Sydney Pollack and Mark Rosenberg; *Screenplay*: Frank Pierson and Alan J. Pakula; *Based on the novel by* Scott Turow; *Director of Photography*: Gordon Willis; *Production Designer*: George Jenkins; *Art Director*: Bob Guerra; *Editor*: Evan Lottman; *Music*: John Williams. *Running time*: 127 minutes. A Mirage Production; Released by Warner Brothers.

As Rusty Sabich. (Warner Bros.)

Despite his success in genre films like the *Star Wars* and Indiana Jones series, Harrison Ford continued his career-long quest to have a diversified body of work. Like *The Mosquito Coast*, his starring role in *Presumed Innocent* was a substantial risk, as this would be a dialogue-heavy, complicated courtroom drama with nary an action sequence throughout its two-plus hours. Although Ford was a box-office icon by 1989, there was a question that his audience would accept him in the role of a morally ambiguous man who is filled with self-doubt. A similar gamble paid off artistically with *Mosquito*, but that film failed to find favor with Ford's hard-core fans. Would an intellectual, thought-provoking story like *Presumed Innocent* be able to compete with the slew of action/adventure films flooding the market? The major studios apparently thought so, as the screen rights to author Scott Turow's best-seller were the subject of a hotly contested bidding war which found Warner Brothers the victor—at a cost of over $1 million.

Presumed Innocent was a literary sensation upon its publication in 1987. Scott Turow, an attorney with no previous professional writing experience, became the center of one of the great Horatio Alger stories in American publishing. His novel was an instant smash, entrenching itself on the *New York Times* best-seller list for forty-four weeks. It was a sordid but fascinating story focusing on Rusty Sabich, a married, seemingly straight-laced, pillar-of-the-community-type chief deputy assistant

Redford for Rusty. Pollack and Redford had a relationship extending back to the early 1970s, and the two had collaborated on seven different films. However, Pollack became convinced that the role required a younger actor. While contemplating who his leading man would be, Pollack sent Turow's book to director Alan J. Pakula, who had received acclaim for making successful movies out of presumably "unfilmable" books such as *Sophie's Choice* and *All the President's Men*.

Presumed Innocent would be no less a challenge. The debate between Pakula and Pollack centered on two different directions for the film. The first scenario, which Pollack favored, concentrated on the sexual nature of the story line (i.e., a rational man abandoning his high ideals for the sake of an ill-fated affair with an irresistible yet dangerous woman). Pakula wanted to make the passion angle secondary to a story about the justice system and the irony of a man of presumably high morality being victimized by the very system he has served so diligently for so many years. Ultimately, Pakula's vision won out.

Director Pakula and producer Pollack needed a leading man who could convincingly convey Sabich's deeply repressed emotions, while at the same time remaining sympathetic to an audience who would be pondering the question of his guilt. In essence, Rusty Sabich was a hero in the Hitchcock mold: innocent of the crime for which he is accused, but guilty of some other moral transgression. A flawed but likable man with whom the audience can identify. Pakula did not need to ponder his choice for long. He reflected at the time: "We wanted an all-American leading man, the kind that personifies truth, honesty, and integrity. Harrison Ford was right up there as someone you don't want to believe could be embroiled in this type of mystery, plus he's an icon." He expanded on what qualities he felt made Ford more appropriate for this role than most other leading actors: "The movie has to have someone you could identify with as a lead. Warren Beatty is a movie star who happens to be a person. Harrison Ford is a person who happens to be a movie star. The ordinary male viewer

D.A, who finds his life in turmoil when he becomes the prime suspect in the murder of a voluptuous fellow prosecutor named Carolyn Polhemus. The two had been engaged in a torrid affair, which Polhemus broke off when she found she no longer needed Rusty to advance her political career. Rusty continues to carry a torch, despite the fact that his wife Barbara confronts him about the affair. When Carolyn's body is found, all evidence points to Rusty. The murder is particularly scandalous because of its kinky nature: Carolyn's naked body is found tied in a position which indicates she may have been lured into an S&M game which went out of control. She has been raped, and Rusty's semen and blood type are found within her body. Indicted and disgraced, with no other suspects available, the straight-arrow prosecutor finds his career and life on the line as he begins preparing for his most important courtroom appearance ever.

The novel seemed far too explicit for the broad movie public. Turow's manuscript included descriptive scenes of bondage, sadomasochism, and anal sex. The first challenge for Warner Brothers was to find the right talent to keep the essence of the story without allowing it to be overly offensive to mainstream audiences. Producer Sydney Pollack initially wanted his old friend Robert

thinks he could be like Harrison Ford."

Despite his enthusiasm for Ford, Pakula did admit he had doubts as to whether the actor could truly convey the dark side of a character and make the audience actually begin to wonder if he just might be capable of obsession and murder. Several colleagues had advised Ford against taking the part on the basis that it could be construed boring and indicative of limited range. Rusty is a rather passive character—a man who holds back his emotions. Although he figures in virtually every scene of the movie, he appears to be a bystander in his own life—someone who reacts to the actions taken by others and is never proactive. Indeed, throughout the entire second half of the screenplay (the actual trial sequences), Rusty is reduced to brooding in silence while secondary characters get the best dialogue. It was essential that, despite these factors, the audience still regard Rusty as the center of attention. The role therefore called for an actor who could emote through facial expressions and gestures—body language as opposed to dialogue. Pakula flew to Ford's ranch in Wyoming to discuss the role. Ford continued to waver but ultimately agreed. He did not keep his reservations and concerns a secret, calling it "a scary, complicated role. It's not going to be easy to play this repressed character, but yeah, let's jump in."

Once committed to the film, Ford began his usual practice of extensively researching his role to insure he fully understood what made the character tick. As the film's primary location shooting would take place in Detroit (with other key sequences filmed in Newark and Allendale, New Jersey), Ford was granted complete access to the Detroit and Wayne County Prosecutor's office. His liaison, Chief Assistant Prosecutor George Ward, was amazed at the actor's commitment. Ford quizzed lawyers during lunch, took files back to his hotel to study them, and watched training films to ensure he understood the world in which Rusty Sabich lived and prospered. Ward recalled one meeting in which a question arose regarding relative heights of a gunman and his victim. "Harrison

Rusty is confronted by his boss, Raymond Horgan (*Brian Dennehy*) about his affair with the murdered Carolyn Polhemus. (Warner Bros.)

was the only one who knew the answer," he said. "Because he had studied the pictures. He really did his homework." Ford tried to be inconspicuous as he continued to research his role. However, the presence of the famous movie star proved to be somewhat distracting even to hard-bitten law professionals. Suddenly, attorneys, clerks, witnesses, reporters, and even judges were discovering they "coincidentally" had urgent business in the courtroom where Ford was sitting. The scene became so chaotic that on one occasion a deputy had to tape a note on the door which read "HARRISON FORD HAS LEFT THE COURTHOUSE."

Ironically, it was not the court cases themselves which interested Ford. Rather, he was observing the daily grind of lawyer's lives. He studied their dress and their conduct with their peers and the judges. He even studied their mannerisms in handling files and paperwork. He told an interviewer at the time, "I needed to ground it in some reality. To see what their offices looked like, how hot it was, how tired they were, what was in their briefcases, what it felt like. I hate it when people just give me a briefcase from props. You have to tell the prop person you want heavy stuff in it because they're liable to take pity on you and take all the stuff out. Feeling that case is heavy is something you shouldn't have to act."

ative suggestions and told the *Dallas Morning News* that he felt Ford would make a great director: "He has enormous technical skills. I've worked with two actors who went on to win Oscars as directors—Warren Beatty and Robert Redford. Believe me, Harrison is in that category." Despite the compliments, Ford seems disinclined to expand his talents into the field of directing. He admitted to an interviewer, "What I love about my job is that I'm able to come on to a project, work intensely for a finite period of time, then I'm off." The rigors of directing would extend that work schedule for many months and also require that he spend more time in Hollywood. For this very private man, neither option seems likely.

If Ford favorably impressed the director, his costars on *Presumed Innocent* were no less enthusiastic about his abilities and his low-key methods of making those around him regard him as an instant friend. Bonnie Bedelia, who plays Ford's wife, commented to *Vanity Fair*: "A lot of it became just Harrison and Bonnie, which is the way it should be, but not always the way it is. All you really have in your relationship onscreen is the amount you're willing, as actors, to expose to each other. To look in someone's eyes and have them right there with you—I've worked with a lot of big stars, and I can't stress how often that's not the case." She expanded her praise in another interview, saying, "Who *couldn't* feel the chemistry with Harrison Ford? You'd have to be half kangaroo or something. He's like the ultimate man—as a human being, as just a male person. I'm completely in love with him. I haven't told him yet, but I think Melissa might know!" Ford also gained praise for his sensitive handling of a love scene which required Greta Scacchi to appear nude for several minutes. Knowing the actress would probably feel uncomfortable, Ford took special pains to ease her tension and bring out the humor in the scene. Costar Paul Winfield recalled studying with Ford in 1964 at Columbia University during those years of racial tension: "Harrison was my only friend, the only one who

Ford's commitment to the role extended to a visit to author Scott Turow in Chicago. He explained he wanted to "meet the mind behind this brilliantly constructed text. It was like seeing a magnificent building and wanting to meet the architectural mind behind it." (Ford had not read Turow's novel until after he had absorbed the screenplay, as he didn't want to be prejudiced by first impressions of the book.) For his part, Turow was equally enthused about the casting of Ford. He said, "Harrison looks just like Rusty as I envisioned him. I don't think anybody could have done it better." Turow even noted that Ford possessed the required flat, midwestern accent for the role.

Filming began in Detroit in the summer of 1989, following a three-week rehearsal period for the cast. Harrison Ford's presence caused some commotion among the local citizenry. At one point, a bystander proved his intellect by shouting, "Isn't this the movie where Indiana Jones kills his wife?" (The same fellow would probably have referred to Laurence Olivier in *The Jazz Singer* as "the film where Hamlet sings Yiddish songs!") Alan J. Pakula, like other directors with whom Ford had worked, was impressed by his leading man's ability to make cre-

took me at face value. He was a breath of fresh air, very nonjudgmental in his dealings with people. Very open. I don't think he's changed very much as a human being since." Brian Dennehy found Ford's work in this film to be a career highlight for the actor: "It's a tremendous performance by Harrison. And not in an easy framework. Because he essentially plays catch. In other words, he's surrounded by actors, all of whom are bouncing off him. And yet you can't take your eyes off him. It's riveting and very moving, and tremendously effective. It's a terrific picture and a hell of a performance." Ford responded to the love-fest on the set by saying, "Working with professionals like that is the way you keep on learning."

Presumed Innocent is certainly one of the "deepest" of Ford's films to date on every level—story, characterization, and performance. In watching the film, one is aware of the risks Ford takes with the role of Rusty Sabich. It is true that a lesser actor may have allowed his character to become of secondary importance once the more colorful ones are introduced in the film's second half. However, Ford emotes with such understated strength that his eyes and gestures often speak more powerfully than any dialogue. Cast against type here, Ford is playing a happily married man who makes just one tragic mistake, succumbing to the temptations of a selfish, manipulative woman. He is smart enough to know he is being used for her own selfish purposes, but naive enough to think their relationship can resume after she has casually tossed him away. The vulnerability of his character allows Ford to make mistakes and show weaknesses that would be unthinkable for most of the characters he had portrayed in the past. While we want to believe he is innocent of his lover's murder and that he has truly rehabilitated himself as a family man, there is some doubt among the audience that he may not be quite what he seems. Refreshingly, the character of Rusty admits humiliating behavior as his court case drags on: he repeatedly has called his lover, Carolyn, after assuring his wife the affair has ended; he admits to asking a detective to overlook potential evidence which might implicate him; he conveniently avoids telling his boss about having had a sexual relationship with the woman whose murder he has been assigned to solve. In essence, Harrison Ford is playing an everyday man—basically decent but capable of spontaneous acts of selfishness when confronted with an overwhelming sexual temptation.

The film makes the audience consider excesses and temptations and how strong anyone's resolve is in avoiding them. The fact that Rusty reluctantly reaches his breaking point and succumbs provides Ford with the opportunity to turn in a yeoman performance as a man whose life is shattered by the one transgression he has

Ford and Bonnie Bedelia momentarily play surrogate parents to little Brian Cellary, on location at the family's New Jersey home. (The Cellary Family)

allowed himself to make. Alan J. Pakula recalled Ford's work in the film's climactic scene, in which his character listens to his wife's moving monologue, the key to the entire plot. In the sequence, Ford was merely supposed to watch intently as Bonnie Bedelia delivered the heart-wrenching dialogue. However, he gradually breaks down in tears, thus embellishing the scene with strong emotional impact. The situation reminded Ford of the heartbreak he and his first wife Mary endured during the collapse of their marriage. He said at the time, "I found that tears rolled each time within five words of the previous take." Pakula was unprepared for his leading man's breakdown on-screen, but he knew the reaction would only add to the emotional impact of the scene: "The pain in him was so real, he totally gave himself to that character's feelings. There's a lot of movie stars/actors who would feel that that's unmanly, showing that kind of vulnerability, that kind of pain. It's not manly to cry and I didn't ask him to cry. To not worry about his image, to just play it honestly as an actor, was a great gift to the film. It took a lot of courage to do and a lot of faith in being his own man."

The cast of *Presumed Innocent* would satisfy any producer's wish list for talent. Not often does a drama contain as many memorable performances and characters. Bonnie Bedelia is wonderfully touching as Ford's long-suffering wife—a woman who has forgiven her husband for his affair, but who has lived in the shadow of his irresistible lover for far too long. Brian Dennehy once again shows himself to be one of the screen's most dynamic supporting actors. His work as the tired, despondent district attorney is quite possibly his best screen performance to date. Raul Julia appears late in the film as the defense attorney whom Ford hires to prove his innocence. The fact that the two characters were one-time arch rivals in the courtroom adds a fascinating plot device to the script. Greta Scacchi, seen only in brief flashback sequences, ignites the screen with a letter-perfect performance as the brilliant "bitch" attorney who uses both her body and brains to further her insatiable quest for power and success. Rounding out the outstanding supporting cast is Paul Winfield as a judge who may not be all he appears to be, and Joe Grifasi and John Spencer as Ford's foe and friend, respectively.

It takes a skilled director to make such a complicated and dialogue-heavy story maintain a high level of interest for the audience. Alan J. Pakula proved to be up to the task. If anything, *Presumed Innocent* builds in intensity as the dialogue increases, leading to a riveting series of courtroom scenes and a shock ending that will probably leave any viewer numb. In fact, the film did receive some criticism for ending the story before the novel did. Ford responded by saying, "We felt we had to get out of it at a

ハリソン・フォード

魅惑。欲望。欺き。殺人。——完全に無罪の人は誰もいない。

推定無罪

PRESUMED
INNOCENT

Japanese theater poster. (Warner Bros.)

certain point and not answer certain questions that the moviegoer might want to mull over for himself. But I think [the ending] suggests a resolution akin to the one in the novel." It's difficult to disagree with Ford's assessment, as it is refreshing for a film to allow the audience to think for itself and not fill in all the blanks.

Despite advance word that *Presumed Innocent* was a high-quality film, industry eyebrows were raised when Warner Brothers decided to release it amidst the heavyweight action films which traditionally dominated the summer marketplace. Although Ford's star power was beyond question, there was a substantial risk in allowing this type of film to be released at a time when only a few dominate the box office. Nevertheless, Ford supported the release date and the marketing plan, telling *US* magazine "I think it's a good idea. We've tested well in all the age ranges. And if we had not, I think it would be very risky. But I think the film seems to appeal to a very broad audience. Even teenage girls. I couldn't be happier if that's the case. I hadn't expected it to do well with a younger audience. I think it's a film that people will think about for more than the time it takes them to get into their cars."

Ford's confidence proved on the mark. *Presumed Innocent* was a hit in the summer of 1990, holding its own against such high profile competition as *Ghost* and *Die Hard 2*. Critics were delighted to have an intellectual film to distract them from the endless series of cinematic explosions they were enduring. Virtually every reviewer commented with enthusiasm about Ford's performance, with a fair number of them calling it the best of his career. Ironically, the press spent an inordinate amount of time commenting on the unflattering, short-cropped hair Ford sported in the movie. The haircut was his idea: an attempt to show his character's complete lack of vanity and sophistication. He finally became so disgusted with having this minor issue overshadow the film itself that he uncharacteristically let off steam in the press by complaining, "Never in my life, not since carpentry became such a prominent part of my story, has one item been such a big deal. People have gone nuts about it. Completely, absolutely nuts!" Two years later, the issue still irritated him, as he reflected in an interview with Britain's *Empire* magazine: "Nearly every article and review had some reference to my haircut. That was the one time I was absolutely befuddled. I guess I finally began to understand that people felt they owned me, in a way. I understand this is a service occupation. I've never misunderstood that. But my occupation is assistant storyteller. It is not *icon*. And they were saying, 'This is not what we want our icon to look like.' And I was saying, 'Well, what about the fucking story? Do you understand that this is part of storytelling? Not about a fucking haircut!' But aside from the haircut, I don't think the audience had any trouble with me in the role. And I notice Kevin Costner got the same haircut in *The Bodyguard*."

Haircuts aside, this film proved that Harrison Ford's audience extended far beyond the action-film genre. Audiences were paying to see *him*. Ford continued to reward their loyalty by showing an ability to choose films which appealed to a broad spectrum of moviegoers. His fans know that Ford will continue to push the envelope and experiment as an actor. Perhaps Alan J. Pakula summed up the actor's appeal when he said, "Harrison has a depth to his talent that people are not altogether aware of yet. He has enormous range with a first-rate intellect behind it. You can see this at work in *Presumed Innocent*."

Reviews

"Pakula has directed an intense, enveloping, gratifyingly thorough screen adaptation of Mr. Turow's story. . . . This version is notably more subdued than Mr. Turow's, and at times its grimness and reserve risk becoming overwhelming. But this director's best work can make restraint a great virtue, turning it into a slowburning fuse. . . . Mr. Ford, who comes alive in the flashbacks recalling his tempestuous affair with Carolyn, spends much of the film with a wary, cautious expression washing all other emotions. He does this with flawless delicacy."

—JANET MASLIN, *NEW YORK TIMES*

"Harrison Ford proves once again that he is steadily developing into one of the most powerful and versatile actors in American films."

—SEATTLE POST-INTELLIGENCER

A tense encounter between Rusty and his colleague and former lover Carolyn. (Warner Bros.)

Defense attorney Sandy Stern advises client Rusty Sabich during his murder trial, as Rusty's wife Barbara listens intently. (Warner Bros.)

"Ford gives the best performance of his career."

—DAILY EXPRESS (LONDON)

"Ford is so subdued and solid that at times he begins to resemble one of the big pine beds he probably builds in his spare time."

—EMPIRE (LONDON)

189

26

Regarding Henry (1991)

"I responded to Henry. His emotion wasn't buried. After his accident, he's basically unaware of how others see him; he's like a child. As adults, we're worried about what someone else thinks about us. It was intriguing to play this character."

CAST:

Henry Turner: Harrison Ford; *Sarah Turner*: Annette Bening; *Bradley*: Bill Nunn; *Rachel Turner*: Mikki Allen; *Charlie*: Donald Moffat; *Jessica*: Elizabeth Wilson; *Rosella*: Aida Linares; *Bruce*: Bruce Altman; *Mrs. O'Brien*: Nancy Marchand (uncredited); *Dr. Sultan*: James Rebhorn; *Julia*: Mary Gilbert; *George*: John MacKay.

CREDITS:

Director: Mike Nichols; *Executive Producer*: Robert Greenhut; *Producers*: Scott Rudin and Mike Nichols; *Coproducer and Writer*: Jeffrey Abrams; *Director of Photography*: Giuseppe Rotunno; *Production Designer*: Tony Walton; *Editor*: Sam O'Steen; *Music*: Hans Zimmer. *Running time*: 107 minutes. Released by Paramount Pictures.

The Turners, happy once more. (Paramount Pictures)

As if to demonstrate that there is no "typical" Harrison Ford film, the actor chose the family drama *Regarding Henry* as his follow-up vehicle to *Presumed Innocent*. Like *The Mosquito Coast*, however, the film has the distinction of showcasing one of Ford's most impressive performances in one of his least-seen movies. It introduces us to Henry Turner, a slick, power-hungry New York attorney whose reputation for making mincemeat of his courtroom opponents has made him a legend in the prestigious law firm which he represents. At home, his style is equally Machiavellian with his wife, Sarah, and twelve-year-old daughter, Rachel. Henry consistently ignores his responsibilities as husband and father in order to ingratiate himself with the Park Avenue elite. One fateful night, Henry is wounded in the head after stumbling onto a holdup in a local grocery store. His recovery is a hard-fought one, and while he eventually regains most of his physical abilities, he suffers from amnesia. He must literally reinvent his entire life without the benefit of knowing anything about his past. The process involves Henry learning to talk and walk again. Ironically, the "new" Henry proves to be a far more loving and compassionate man than his former self. The film traces his psychological torment as he tries to return to his normal high-paying job as an unscrupulous attorney, while coping with his newfound devotion to his wife and daughter and doing what is in the family's best interest.

The script for *Regarding Henry* was written in seven

Rachel (*Mikki Allen*) tries to comprehend the change in her father's personality. (François Duhamel, courtesy Paramount Pictures)

days by Jeffrey Abrams, a twenty-three-year-old recent college graduate. Harrison Ford had been actively seeking a new project to work on with director Mike Nichols. The two men had enjoyed making *Working Girl* together and were eager to maintain the creative momentum they had developed. Producer Scott Rudin, who had seen Abrams's script and convinced Paramount to purchase the rights for $450,000, had intended from the start to induce Ford to star in the film. He recalled, "The script had an incredible humanity to it, and Harrison was the first actor I thought of for the role. He is one of the few guys I know who could pull it off, who could make you believe that he was both a shark lawyer and a diminished adult."

Ford read the script the night he received it and was amazed that someone as young as Jeffrey Abrams could have such insight into human nature. Calling the script "very smart, very emotional and good enough to attract the kind of people that I would want to work with," Ford immediately approached Nichols, and industry insiders were surprised at the speed with which both men attached themselves to this project. Clearly, neither Ford nor Nichols wanted to take a chance that the film would be made by others. According to Jeffrey Abrams, Nichols had been offered the chance to direct *Big* in 1988 but refused the job. Abrams said, "He and Harrison wished that they had made that film. Well, here was another film about a man's body that was essentially being filled by a child." Abrams cautioned Ford about the sensitivity of playing the complex role of Henry: "We've got to be extra

careful here. . . . This is a very deliberate subject. Henry can't be a buffoon."

Ford put more effort into researching the role of Henry than he had for any other character he had ever portrayed. He read every book about brain injuries he could find, visited a rehab center over a period of two months, and held extensive interviews with neurologists, brain surgeons, and other specialists. He would also attend patient therapy sessions when permitted and never failed to be moved by the experience. He recalled, "It got very emotional at times, watching patients with appalling disabilities who, after a period of depression, realize that there is a light at the end of the tunnel." Ford was introduced to Tom Frost, a Princeton-educated lawyer who had suffered the same type of injuries as Henry Turner. He studied Frost closely and incorporated many of his mannerisms into his performance. The actor was grateful for this opportunity, saying, "This man gave us access to his private life, and he gave me the most faith in the correctness of the choices we made in creating this character. He told us we were right on the mark and that's all I needed to know."

Since the film was shot out of sequence, Ford was worried that he might confuse which stage of Henry's development he was enacting at any given time. The character is shown to make slow but steady progress in his physical and emotional rehabilitation. As many of the indicants of his improvement are very subtle, it would have been easy for Ford to forget what stage Henry's progress was at when acting in any given scene. The methodical actor resolved this crisis by creating three stacks of index cards, each of which charted Henry's emotional state as well as his speaking skills and physical abilities. Ford numbered each card from one to ten to keep track of where his speech patterns and physical abilities were during each sequence. He wanted to play the role as realistically as possible and noticed that the patients he interacted with seemed to be concentrating on the essentials of getting from one moment to the next. He noted, "From the research I did, it seemed that people in these situations are struggling to keep up all the time. So they fixate on what's really happening. They don't have extra time for thinking about telephone calls they have to make, and that's very easy to play. You just show up and listen, which is half of acting anyway." While Ford's modest assessment of his acting abilities rivals Spencer Tracy's ("just memorize your lines and don't bump into the furniture"), his low-key yet powerful performance was as impressive in its own way as Robert De Niro's was in the similarly themed *Awakenings*.

Ford's coworkers felt the role of Henry had provided the actor with an opportunity to give one of his most fully realized performances. Rudin said, "When I saw the finished result, I knew I had made the right choice. It's rare that you get the film on screen that you envision in your head, but Harrison did it. It was a beautiful, subtle performance." Nichols was equally impressed, telling an interviewer that Ford's own personality mirrored the two different sides of Henry seem in the film: "Both of these men

As Henry Turner. (Paramount Pictures)

are in him. I've seen him make a fuss about a suite at the Savoy, and then I've seen him be wonderful with his kids and mine." Ford concurred with his director's assessment: "Both Henrys are in me, and in all of us." Mikki Allen, who played Ford's on-screen daughter, was appreciative of his ability to keep her spirits high, as well as his devotion to his own family: "He was really good to me, teasing me, keeping me happy. But he kept to himself very much. As soon as work finished, he'd rush home to be with his own boy and girl. People on the set learned to understand: as soon as his hours were over, he was home."

Regarding Henry proved an underrated film that never seemed

Enjoying the filming with director Mike Nichols. (Paramount Pictures)

With Aida Linares (*left*), Bening, and Allen. (Paramount Pictures)

and Dad, along with said puppy, "rescue" their daughter from the clutches of an oppressive private school.) While not one of the most remarkable films on either Ford's or Nichols's resumés, *Regarding Henry* is nevertheless a movie which both men can point to with pride.

Despite the presence of Ford's name on the marquee, *Regarding Henry* was a major disappointment at the box office. Since Ford had proven he could draw audiences outside the realm of action/adventure films, one can only think that the downbeat story line and abundance of suds turned off his core fans. Not helping matters was the mostly negative critical reaction, which occasionally went overboard in attacking the film as a dreary, unconvincing soap opera. While some critics astutely called Ford's performance a major achievement, others provided the actor with something he has rarely experienced in his career—negative reviews. Perhaps the larger-than-life character played by De Niro had made Ford's everyman approach to the role of Henry seem dull and uninspired, yet it was precisely what he had hoped to achieve. Despite De Niro's showier role, Ford's performance is the one we can best relate to.

Ford was taken aback by the harsh reaction to *Regarding Henry* and was particularly sensitive to the barbs aimed at Mike Nichols. "I thought it was a good movie, a gentle, relatively accurate portrayal of events," he told *Empire* magazine. "I was very surprised at the basis on which Mike Nichols was attacked. Mike was criticized because the Mike that the critics knew to be sophisticated and flinty had made a movie that was emotional, and they just said 'That's not Mike. He's just trying to take advantage of the sentimentality of the eighties.' That just infuriated me. Mike is incapable of that kind of insincerity. To have his work dismissed that way I thought was completely unfair."

Despite its mediocre reception and the critical brickbats, *Regarding Henry* is a noble—and mostly successful—attempt to show one family's triumph over incredible odds. Like *The Mosquito Coast*, it will doubtlessly be reevaluated by audiences in the years to come and find the acclaim it deserved on its initial release.

to find its audience. To be certain, it has flaws. For one, the darker side of Henry is dismissed far too early in the story, and we never really get to see what made this man tick. True, we see him acting as an intolerant, strict disciplinarian with his daughter and a hypocritical elitist when networking among New York's power players on the party circuit. However, just as interest in this side of the man is building, he is disabled in a shooting, and henceforth, we must rely on other characters' opinions of the "old" Henry to illustrate the crudeness of the man. Yet these qualms are small, and the overall film is a moving experience. Ford is wonderful as Henry, making us feel as though we share his smallest triumphs during his long road to rehabilitation. He gets excellent support from Annette Bening as his frustrated wife, whose loyalty is rewarded by the chance to rebuild a loving marriage with the new Henry, a man she feared no longer existed.

The supporting cast is equally able, with Bill Nunn a standout as the rehab aide whose determination and ingenuity help Henry triumph over adversity. The scenes between the two men are both humorous and genuinely touching. Mikki Allen is also impressive as Henry's neglected daughter, who, like her mother, reinvents her relationship with her father with moving results. Mike Nichols, one of the least-discussed talents in directing today, keeps the talky plot consistently interesting, even when the screenplay becomes a bit too obvious. (We know Henry is now a nice guy when he buys the puppy he has always denied his daughter; in the tearjerky finale, Mom

Reviews

Henry (*Harrison Ford*) and Sarah (*Annette Bening*) try to adjust to the challenges in their lives. (Paramount Pictures)

"*Regarding Henry is an unimaginably bad movie, from none other than Mike Nichols, who appears to have lost his brain.*"

—NEW YORK

"*The story is a shallow soap opera. . . . Jeffrey Abrams's script might have been written by Henry in a childish phase.*"

—CARYN JAMES, NEW YORK TIMES

"*In the worst performance of his career, Harrison Ford isn't awful, just boring.*"

—BERGEN RECORD

"*The finest dramatic performance of Ford's career.*"

—NEW YORK NEWSDAY

"*Mr. Nichols has made a movie that is a good deal more tolerable than any such gimmick movie has a right to be. Make no mistake about it, Regarding Henry is a gimmick movie, the kind that appears to have had its genesis in a very particular, not exactly commonplace situation, for which the characters were then cut to fit—like wallpaper and as thin. . . . Invites the audience to enjoy a sudsy spectacle without being implicated in any disturbing way. . . . Here is a sentimental urban fairy tale that has been cast with actors from the A list, dressed and designed like* a fashion layout, and written and directed with such skill that its essential banality is often disguised. . . .

It doesn't help the movie that Henry is less interesting as a good guy than when he was a rat, but whether this is the role or Mr. Ford's performance is unclear; maybe a combination of the two. Mr. Ford's rehabilitated Henry behaves like a cross between Tom Hanks in* Big *and Peter Sellers in* Being There, *but with no sense of fun. It's a ponderous, toned-down golly-gee-whiz performance. . . . A most uncharacteristic Mike Nichols film. It's easy to take, but it succeeds neither as an all-out inspirational drama nor as a send-up of American manners.*"

—VINCENT CANBY, NEW YORK TIMES

Rachel becomes the teacher as her father literally has to reinvent his life. (Paramount Pictures)

195

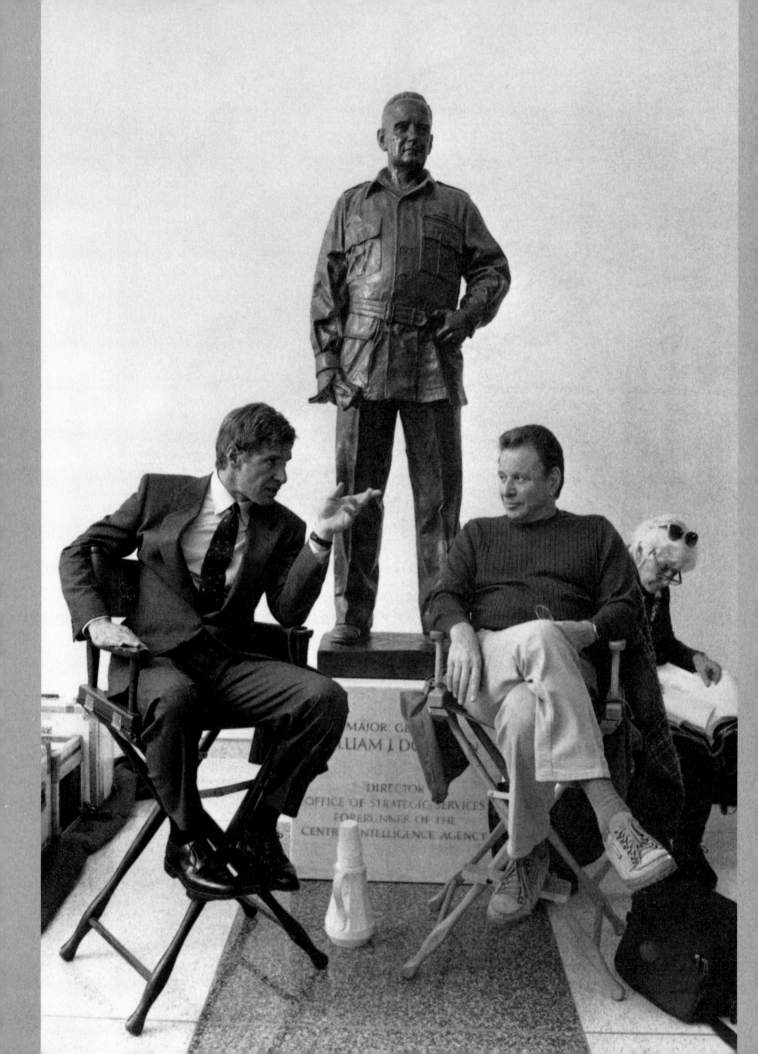

MAJOR GE...
...LLIAM J. DO...

DIRECTOR
OFFICE OF STRATEGIC SERVICES
FORERUNNER OF THE
CENTRAL INTELLIGENCE AGENCY

27

Patriot Games (1992)

"I've been doing quite a few desk jobs, and I figured it was time to roll around in the mud."

CAST:

Jack Ryan: Harrison Ford; *Cathy Ryan*: Anne Archer; *Kevin O'Donnell*: Patrick Bergin; *Sean Miller*: Sean Bean; *Sally Ryan*: Thora Birch; *Lord Holmes*: James Fox; *Robby Jackson*: Samuel L. Jackson; *Annette*: Polly Walker; *Admiral James Greer*: James Earl Jones; *Paddy O'Neil*: Richard Harris.

CREDITS:

Director: Phillip Noyce; *Executive Producer*: Charles H. Maguire; *Producers*: Mace Neufeld and Robert Rehme; *Screenplay*: W. Peter Iliff and Donald Stewart; *Based on the novel by* Tom Clancy; *Director of Photography*: Donald McAlpine; *Production Designer*: Joseph Nemec III; *Editor*: Neil Travis; *Music*: James Horner. *Running time*: 116 minutes. Released by Paramount Pictures.

On location at C.I.A. headquarters, Ford talks with producer Mace Neufeld under the watchful eye of Gen. William J. Donovan, a pioneer in the field of intelligence work. (John Seakwood, courtesy Paramount Pictures)

Following the lukewarm reception accorded *Regarding Henry*, Harrison Ford backed off his publicly stated plans to deemphasize his image as an action/adventure film icon. Clearly, he had proven his acting ability in any number of dramas and comedies, but he acknowledged that his public primarily opted to see him as a man of action. He stated his rationale with typical honesty: "I thought if I didn't use my license to do action/adventure, then pretty soon it wouldn't be viable . . . . I don't think the executives ever stopped thinking of me in terms of action/adventures. But I kept turning them down because of their overweening violence or because they lacked ambition. I wanted to deal with ideas within the context of action."

The vehicle Ford chose to return to the genre which initially made him a star would turn out to be a troubled project with a convoluted production history. It would also become the most controversial film in which he has starred. The movie was an adaptation of novelist Tom Clancy's thriller *Patriot Games*. The hero of the book, C.I.A agent Jack Ryan, had been introduced to audiences in Clancy's first novel, *The Hunt for Red October*, a cold-war epic in which a Soviet submarine commander named Ramius attempts to defect to the West and present them with his nuclear sub as a "gift." Ramius avoids the pursuing Soviet forces, with Ryan's aid, in an exciting conclusion which helped to launch Clancy's initially obscure late-eighties novel onto the best-seller lists. When the film version was released in 1990, it was a hit starring

197

Jack Ryan dashes to rescue his family (*Archer and Thora Birch*) from a devastating bomb . . . (Paramount Pictures)

. . . then heroically foils the terrorist's escape. (Paramount Pictures)

Sean Connery as Ramius and Alec Baldwin as Ryan. (Ironically, Harrison Ford originally had been offered both the Ryan and Ramius roles but declined them both.)

Quite naturally, *Red October*'s distributor, Paramount Pictures, wanted to move quickly to capitalize on the popular success of Baldwin and the Ryan character. Studio boss Brandon Tartikoff foresaw the potential to make a series of Ryan films a "tentpole" property for Paramount, as the James Bond films had been for United Artists and MGM. The public's appetite for espionage thrillers catapulted the film version of *Patriot Games*, Clancy's next Jack Ryan best-seller, to the front burner at Paramount. Initially, John Badham was set to direct, but ultimately Tartikoff took a chance on Phillip Noyce, whose only notable credit had been the underrated thriller *Dead Calm*. While the studio opened discussions with Alec Baldwin to star in Jack Ryan's sophomore screen vehicle, Harrison Ford was carefully contemplating a number of projects which had been offered him. Among those he was considering was a Philip Marlowe story to be directed by Sydney Pollack; a comedy called *Good Behavior* for Mike Nichols; a tongue-in-cheek Western which would depict a fictional trip to New York City by Wild Bill Hickok and Buffalo Bill (presumably Ford and Bruce Willis); and *JFK*, the controversial Oliver Stone project in which he would have starred in the role eventually taken by Kevin

Costner. Instead, Ford decided to do *Night Ride Down*, a mystery thriller set aboard a Pullman passenger train in 1936. The story—a favorite of Ford's agent Pat McQueeney—centered on a black man working as a porter who is accused of kidnapping a Pullman executive's young daughter. Ford was to play the executive, who teams with the porter to prove the latter's innocence and solve the crime. Harold Becker (*Sea of Love*) was to direct a script by the team of Willard Huyck and Gloria Katz (*Indiana Jones and the Temple of Doom, American Graffiti*). However, the project fell through due to a ballooning budget and Ford's concerns about changes to the script.

Simultaneously, Paramount found that negotiating with Alec Baldwin was a bit more challenging than it had anticipated. The studio eventually agreed to pay him a salary of $4 million, despite his unproven record at the box office.

Jack and Cathy Ryan (*Harrison Ford and Anne Archer*). (Paramount Pictures)

(While he *had* received good reviews, there was no doubt that *Red October*'s hefty grosses had been primarily due to the success of the Clancy novel and Sean Connery's presence.) Although the "up-front" money had been negotiated, Baldwin insisted upon changes to the script—even though he had yet to formally commit to the project. He then informed Paramount of his other demands: costly perks, extra pay for overages, a definite stop date for filming, and—most bizarre—a promise not to let *Premiere* magazine anywhere near the set. (Presumably, this was because of a scathing article the magazine had done about the alleged "prima donna" attitudes he and Kim Basinger displayed on the set of *The Marrying Man*.) This time, the studio balked. Mace Neufeld, coproducer of *Patriot Games*, recalled, "Alec Baldwin had a contract with Paramount—the dollars and terms were all negotiated. But he had not approved the screenplay, even though the work was ongoing. Phillip [Noyce] and I urged him to commit. But we couldn't give him a stop date. It was finally a question of let's stop dancing and make up your mind. He was given several days to decide, and he passed." All hope of luring Baldwin back to the role was lost when the actor informed the studio that the filming schedule—which had been delayed partly because of the negotiations he had insisted upon—would now interfere with his plans to play Stanley Kowalski in a Broadway revival of *A Streetcar Named Desire*.

Brandon Tartikoff and producers Mace Neufeld and Robert Rehme now had to search for a new star. Pat McQueeney was simultaneously looking for a suitable project for Harrison Ford, since his plans to star in *Night Ride Down* had fallen through. McQueeney urged Paramount to send the Clancy script to Harrison Ford despite the studio's belief that Ford would not be interested in the three-picture deal that *Patriot Games* would entail. To the studio's surprise, Ford responded enthusiastically and signed for the forthcoming Jack Ryan films. He told *Premiere* magazine, "I'd done too many suit-and-tie jobs, and I reckoned I had to hit somebody in my next movie or lose that as an option. Most of what had been offered to me in the area of action/adventure was lacking in necessary ambition and was just an exercise in kinetics. So when this came along—the potential for complication in the character, Jack Ryan, was there." Phillip Noyce breathed easier having landed the screen's leading box-office name for his most high-profile film. He said, "Once Harrison Ford wanted to play the part, there was a great sense of relief. Because the worst thing that can happen to a film is that it doesn't have a star and you can't find the right person. Usually, in that case the film gets put on the shelf."

Controversy greeted the casting of Harrison Ford as Jack Ryan, and industry speculation was that a feud was brewing between him and Alec Baldwin. The rumor had it that Baldwin had every intention of playing Ryan and had called Paramount's bluff, only to be stunned when they signed Ford. Baldwin denied this was the case, insisting that the reason for his refusal had been the Broadway commitment. He did confess that the missed opportunity ultimately hurt: "What I loved about that character [Jack Ryan] and why I was so sad that I didn't get to play him in the other movie was that it was a chance to have a real development. To start here and end up there. . . . After I did *Red October*, I really wanted to do *Patriot Games* because I liked the idea of a guy who didn't want to be a spy. But I always felt that the chance to play that kind of part will come again. The opportunity to do Tennessee Williams on Broadway will never come again."

For his part, Ford downplayed any professional rift with Baldwin. "I've never spoken to Alec. By the time I was asked to participate, Alec had made his decision to do *A Streetcar Named Desire* on Broadway and there was no *reason* to talk to him about it. We're not *friends*, we don't have each other's phone number, and there was no issue between us, so I didn't feel it necessary to communicate with him about it." There was the usual concern, however, that occurs when any actor takes over from someone else to play an established role. However, with the character of Ryan having only made one screen appearance, Ford didn't have to contend with public perceptions the way the various actors who played James Bond did. (Indeed, most of the cynicism in the press was directed toward Baldwin, with *Premiere* magazine referring to him as the next George Lazenby, the actor who gave up fame and fortune when he walked away from the 007 role—bad career move—after one film.) Phillip Noyce addressed the issue, saying that people might "have trouble accepting Harrison Ford . . . for about two minutes. By the end of the movie, audiences will think that nobody else could play Jack Ryan but Harrison Ford." Producer Mace Neufeld, who had worked with Ford on *The Frisco Kid*, concurred: "Ford is a star for everybody. What you see in this movie is Harrison Ford using all of the combination of characters he's played in various films—the cop, Indiana Jones, Han Solo, the lawyer from *Presumed Innocent*—and he kind of rolls them all into one to give a very, very interesting Jack Ryan. When Alec left, I was very unhappy. But I guess sometimes adversity turns into good fortune."

Neufeld's sense of good fortune would be short-lived. Although he had lured Ford to star in *Patriot Games* (at a reported $9 million salary—an all-time high for Harrison

Ford to this time), Neufeld and coproducer Robert Rehme were about to feel the wrath of an author scorned. Tom Clancy immediately opposed Ford's casting, launching a verbal barrage of complaints to the press. The writer who had given birth to Jack Ryan on the printed page complained that, at age forty-nine, Ford was too old to play the role of a character in his mid-thirties. Ironically, when Ford was asked to play the Ryan role in *Red October*, Clancy sang his praises. Ford turned down the part because he felt that Ryan would end up a secondary character compared to Captain Ramius. He would later say of his rejection of the role, "I said, 'Submarine movies, uh-uh.' That's how smart I was."

Ford did not ingratiate himself to Clancy when he began making suggestions to dramatically alter the screenplay, which had been written by W. Peter Iliff and Donald Stewart. "I had some concerns about the complexity of it. I had some plot problems. I had some questions about giving the character a little bit more humor and a more specific relationship with his wife and child." Ultimately, screenwriter Steven Zaillian, who penned *Awakenings* and *The Falcon and the Snowman*, was brought in to do uncredited cosmetic work on the script. According to Phillip Noyce, Zaillian "gave a lot more texture to the characters, he also took the action out of your face and put it in your bones where you can fear it—and you don't necessarily have to see it. We de-explosioned the film, you could say." The script, which centers on Ryan being marked for death after he foils a terrorist attack on a fictional relative of Queen Elizabeth by a renegade wing of the I.R.A., had been amended from making Prince Charles and Princess Diana the targets. The filmmakers felt this might actually inspire a real-life copycat act of terrorism.

The producers received cooperation from the C.I.A., including tours for Ford and crew of the usually off-limits Counter-Terrorism Center at the agency's headquarters in Langley, Virginia. (Ford and Noyce had to first sign a secrecy agreement.) Once at Langley, Ford immersed himself in researching his character with his usual attention to painstaking detail. He observed the habits of the C.I.A. people and tried to emulate their mannerisms. He explained, "This is a film that has to be taken seriously. So we wanted it to be as realistic as possible." Attention to detail also was a key factor in Ford's advice on the construction of Ryan's house, which was actually built on a bluff at Sea World above Mission Bay, California. Paramount's art department had planned on a modern home, but Ford felt Ryan would reside in a traditional, colonial house. "I only do my best work when I consider the surroundings to be correct. . . . If we could represent my character's feelings with such a house, then I would

Ryan studies a satellite feed of a camp of terrorists who have targeted his family for death. (Merrick Morton, courtesy Paramount Pictures)

not have to act that part of me. A small detail? Sure. But that is the way I can bring out the best performance."

Ford earned his pay in filming the climactic speedboat chase and fight to the death with Irish actor Sean Bean, who plays the terrorist stalking Ryan and his family. The sequence was far too dangerous to shoot in the ocean, so a half-acre site was found on the Paramount backlot, utilizing the same tank in which Charlton Heston parted the Red Sea in *The Ten Commandments*. Over one million gallons of water were used to simulate the storm-swept sea wherein Ford and Bean play a deadly seaborne cat-and-mouse game. The cold weather added to the actors' misery, made worse by a prolonged scene in the original script which called for the two men to battle under the water. Coproducer Robert Rehme recalled, "It was winter, and the water was very cold and dirty because you couldn't filter it." Ford continued gamely to film his scenes, despite the fact that he had broken out in a painful rash, caused by an infection from the unclean water. He would later say of the experience, "[It was] torturous! It went on forever!"

Ironically, much of Ford's work in shooting this scene was for naught. Test screenings indicated that the fight beneath the waves was not received well by audiences. Ford was not surprised when he was called back after principal photography had been completed, to reshoot the climax. "I knew from the moment we began shooting it that it wasn't working, because we couldn't see well enough, and that meant that emotional moment

was hard to capture. The resistance of the water rendered everything balletic." The underwater battle was replaced with a fight to the death aboard an out-of-control speedboat, à la *Thunderball*. Soon there was speculation that the film was in trouble, especially when the reshoot ballooned the budget to $42 million, despite the fact that it only required two days of extra filming. Tabloids also spread rumors of Ford being seriously injured, when, in fact, a mishap had resulted in a minor bump on the head which did not even require a Band-Aid.

As the release date of the film grew nearer, Tom Clancy opened another salvo and criticized the movie in a front page article in the *Wall Street Journal*. "They have made a movie called *Patriot Games* that uses my characters—but it's not my story," he griped. He complained that the screenplay was filled with technical errors which violated his well-known penchant for detail. Neufeld responded, telling *Entertainment Weekly*, "I was very distressed because I felt we had treated Tom with the utmost respect. We'd spent enormous amounts of time with Tom, and there were enormous numbers of changes made as a result of good suggestions that Tom made. But in the movie business, nobody ever gets 100 percent of what he wants." Phillip Noyce supported his producer, saying most of Clancy's criticisms were about points so highly technical that the audience would be oblivious to them.

Paramount's Brandon Tartikoff tried to stem Clancy's verbal assaults by visiting him personally. Alas, he left in despair, noting with resignation, "No matter

what one does, Mr. Clancy cannot be satisfied." In fact, Mr. Clancy *would* be satisfied when Tartikoff paid him a reported $10 to $12 million for rights to future novels. Miraculously, the author said that upon seeing a rough cut of the film, he was impressed—although he still had some reservations. He lavished praise on the nuts-and-bolts depiction of intelligence work, and said of Ford: "We'll be working together. I only met Mr. Ford once. I liked what I saw then. It'd be nice to sit down with him and talk a while. In fact, that's one of the things Brandon suggested we ought to do."

No sooner did Paramount get Clancy to give his recommendations to the film, lukewarm as they were, than a tidal wave of controversy greeted its premiere. *Patriot Games* had boldly presented the I.R.A. in an unflattering light, and Politically Correct forces began to attack the script's allegedly right-wing tone. In fact, while the I.R.A. is not painted in a glowing light, the story emphasizes that the terrorism is being caused by a splinter faction which the I.R.A. itself condemns. Indeed, in the film, an I.R.A. spokesman (Richard Harris) helps Ryan eventually track down his would-be assassins. Nevertheless, controversy continued to build. Ford responded, "I *cannot* accept that this film has a right-wing point of view. Tom Clancy may have a right-wing point of view, but this film does *not*. This film is about *people* and, in fact, the amount of work that has gone into creating villains who also have a great degree of humanity—and who [audiences] have some way of understanding and feel some degree of sympathy for—is one of the things that makes this film interesting. There is *no* stamp on this film of a

political point of view and I think it would be wrong to do that.... Listen, I'm not running for president—I'm promoting a movie!"

The cause célèbre reached its pinnacle with a scathing review of the film in *Variety* by critic Joseph McBride. Sensitive to what he felt were pro-British and anti-Catholic sentiments in the movie, McBride seemed incapable of accepting the film as a simple thriller. He called *Patriot Games* "mindless, morally repugnant" and "shoddy." The resulting brouhaha caused Paramount to cancel all advertising in *Variety* for a period of time. Studio brass complained that McBride's review was clouded by his political leanings and was unprofessional in nature. Eventually, *Variety* editor Peter Bart apologized to Paramount chief Martin Davis and reprimanded McBride for reviewing politics, and not the film.

All of the controversy surrounding *Patriot Games* proved to be a tempest in a teapot, because the film is basically an old-fashioned thriller with the politics acting as a convenient catalyst for showing Ford in action. This is an exciting movie which grabs the audience from the very beginning and does not let go until the final credits roll. Because of Ford's confident and assured performance, the Jack Ryan character could indeed become a mainstay on theater screens for years to come. The film is expertly directed by Phillip Noyce, who shows a distinct flair for making a superior espionage thriller. He benefits from a terrific cast, including Anne Archer, one of the screen's more underrated actresses, as Ford's loyal but long-suffering wife; James Earl Jones, personifying dignity as the admiral who assists Ryan in taking preemptive action against the assassins; and Sean Bean, outstanding as the fanatical terrorist obsessed with avenging the death of his equally murderous brother at Ryan's hands.

If *Patriot Games* has a fault, it is that it follows the pattern set by most big-budget action films of recent years in its attempt to have one scene top the last at any price—including lapses of logic. Throughout the entire film, the screenplay meticulously details Ryan's use of high-tech C.I.A. gadgetry to outwit his pursuers. However, the controversial climax turns into a quasi–haunted house scene, with Ryan, his family, and the conveniently visiting British royal hiding in closets in their secluded, darkened home, complete with a storm raging outside. One expects Vincent Price to wander onto the scene—candelabra in hand—straight from the set of *House on Haunted Hill.* (The film also follows the age-old tradition of having the heroes protected by completely incompetent security forces who are decimated within seconds by the villains. Don't any of these people see all those movies and know that the minute the heroes' safety is assured, it's time to worry?) The climactic battle between Ford and Bean aboard the speedboat is exciting but seems rather clumsy from a production standpoint. It is quite apparent this ending was tacked on at the last minute.

Criticisms aside, however, *Patriot Games* is not an anti-Irish film. Nor is it primarily a political film. One would have to think back to *Marathon Man* and perhaps *On Her Majesty's Secret Service* to find a better espionage thriller. Critical notices were basically tepid, but audiences flocked to the film despite the wishful-thinking predictions of *Variety* critic Joseph McBride that "downbeat word of mouth [will spread] like wildfire." Although not a financial knockout by Fordian standards, *Patriot Games* was a significant box-office hit. With all due respect to Alec Baldwin, Harrison Ford had established another potentially legendary screen hero.

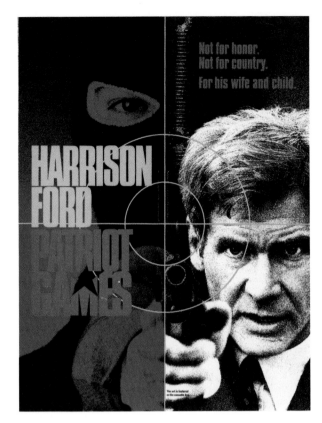

(Paramount Pictures)

Reviews

"An expensive stiff. . . . Morally repugnant, and ineptly directed to boot. . . . The novel's pontifications on the political context are shallow and biased toward the British, but the book does take the time to address the subject. That's more than can be said for the film, which takes about twenty seconds to do so in a TV soundbite of a Sinn Fein political rep (Richard Harris), whose comments can barely be heard above the Ford family chatter. Harris makes a point that should have been allowed to play much more loudly: that when Americans talk of their own uprising against their British colonial rulers, they call the revolutionaries 'patriots,' not 'terrorists.' This film has little time for such distinctions or for the nuances of the Irish cause. . . . While Ford is a solid blend of thought and action in his James Bondish role, and his need to protect his family gives the film some gripping moments, the film's moral viewpoint is strictly Neanderthal. . . . If [the producers] don't raise their standards next time out . . . Paramount's Jack Ryan tentpole may collapse prematurely."
—JOSEPH MCBRIDE, *VARIETY*

"[The movie] settles into more traditional thriller patterns, until it all comes down to people creeping around in a dark basement. . . . Patriot Games includes the usual decisions that are made only by the characters in thrillers. For example, aware that vicious hit men have targeted his family, Ryan takes his wife and daughter to their isolated home, on a wind-and-rain-swept coast. I forgive movies for decisions like this, because I know that if Ryan did the obvious thing and set up bunks for his family inside a vault at C.I.A. headquarters . . . the movie would be over. But such decisions don't make the character seem much brighter. . . . Harrison Ford once again demonstrates what a solid, convincing actor he is."
—ROGER EBERT'S VIDEO COMPANION

"For all its polish and its apparent global span, the film never really moves beyond the hollow question of whether the Ryan family will survive each new threat to life and limb. . . . Mr. Ford's restrained performance is just right for this chilly atmosphere, and he even brings some earnestness to the happy-family scenes, which are otherwise saccharine. He makes a more plausible Jack Ryan than Alec Baldwin."
—JANET MASLIN, *NEW YORK TIMES*

A murdered wife.
A one-armed man.
An obsessed detective.
The chase begins.

HARRISON FORD
IS THE FUGITIVE

WARNER BROS. Presents
A KEITH BARISH/ARNOLD KOPELSON Production An ANDREW DAVIS Film
HARRISON FORD TOMMY LEE JONES "THE FUGITIVE" SELA WARD JOE PANTOLIANO ANDREAS KATSULAS
JEROEN KRABBE Edited by DENNIS VIRKLER and DAVID FINFER Production Designed by DENNIS WASHINGTON Director of Photography MICHAEL CHAPMAN
Music by JAMES NEWTON HOWARD Co-Producer PETER MACGREGOR-SCOTT Executive Producers KEITH BARISH ROY HUGGINS Story by DAVID TWOHY
Screenplay by JEB STUART and DAVID TWOHY Based on characters created by ROY HUGGINS Produced by ARNOLD KOPELSON Directed by ANDREW DAVIS

WARNER BROS.
A TIME WARNER ENTERTAINMENT COMPANY

Read the Dell Paperback   Soundtrack Album on Elektra Entertainment

PG-13

MARCH 22

The Fugitive (1993)

"I had a strong emotional reaction to the material. When I read it I felt sympathy for this guy. I felt that the audience would be emotionally involved in the story and that's the thing I most look for. On my first reading of the script I knew it was something I wanted to do. I've said before that if I get through the script, I'm likely to do it, and I got through this one and that's why I had to begin to think seriously about it. Most scripts I am simply not able to get through.'

CAST:

Dr. Richard Kimble: Harrison Ford; *Samuel Gerard*: Tommy Lee Jones; *Cosmo Renfro*: Joe Pantoliano; *Helen Kimble*: Sela Ward; *Dr. Anne Eastman*: Julianne Moore; *Fred Sykes*: Andreas Katsulas; *Dr. Charles Nichols*: Jeroen Krabbe; *Biggs*: Daniel Roebuck; *Poole*: L. Scott Caldwell.

CREDITS:

Director: Andrew Davis; *Executive Producers*: Keith Barish and Roy Huggins; *Producer*: Arnold Kopelson; *Screenplay*: Jeb Stuart and David Twohy; *Based on characters created by* Roy Huggins; *Director of Photography*: Michael Chapman; *Production Designer*: Dennis Washington; *Editors*: Dennis Virkler, David Finfer, Dean Goodhill, Don Brochu, Richard Nord, and Dov Hoenig; *Special Effects*: Roy Arbogast; *Music*: James Newton Howard. *Running time*: 127 minutes. Released by Warner Brothers.

There was a time when television programs were considered to be beneath the contempt of any self-respecting motion picture studio. Initially afraid that TV would ultimately put movie theaters out of business, the studios have learned otherwise. In recent years, they have had varying degrees of success adapting television series to the big screen. As of this writing, plans are in development for mega-budget movie versions of everything from *Mission: Impossible* to *The Man From U.N.C.L.E.* Yet it will take a considerable effort to match the success of the most popular screen adaptation of a television series to date—*The Fugitive*.

The Fugitive series premiered on television in 1963, and for 120 episodes, audiences were glued to their screens as they followed the plight of Dr. Richard Kimble, unjustly sentenced to death for the murder of his wife. While he is en route to death row, a devastating train wreck allows him to escape and pursue a one-armed man he knows is responsible for the crime. Trailing him with a zeal that borders on obsession is police lieutenant Samuel Gerard, who is convinced of Kimble's guilt and feels responsible for his escape. This modern version of *Les Miserables*, concocted by Roy Huggins, rested squarely on the talents of its two leads. David Janssen, whose moody and somber demeanor perfectly captured the constant emotional pain and loneliness of Kimble, became one of

205

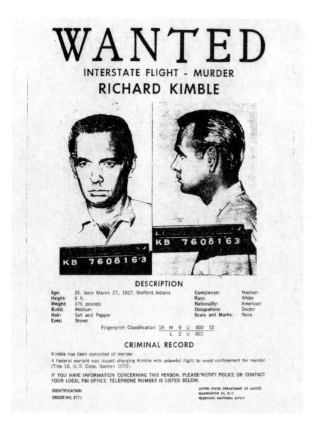

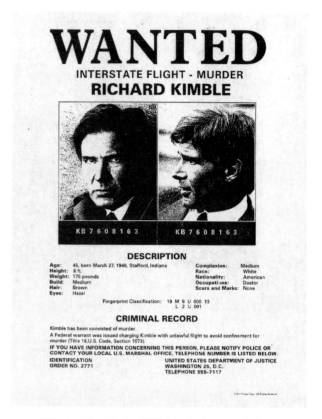

Fugitives David Janssen as TV's original Dr. Richard Kimble . . .
(ABC-TV)

. . . and Harrison Ford in the 1993 theatrical version. (Warner
Bros.)

television's most enduring and popular actors on the basis of his work in *The Fugitive*. He was given able assistance by Barry Morse, whose Gerard was the epitome of the unfeeling bureaucratic police officer. The show was among the first series to have a formal wrap-up in a final episode, and indeed the two-part finale of *The Fugitive* (telecast on August 29, 1967) still ranks among the highest-rated shows in history. For the record, the pivotal climax has Kimble finally trapping the one-armed man and having his life saved by Gerard, who suddenly realizes his innocence.

Movie producer Arnold Kopelson had wanted to option *The Fugitive* for the big screen since the 1970s. However, it was only after he teamed with high-profile entrepreneur Keith Barish that the rights could finally be secured. After signing a distribution deal with Warner Brothers, the two initially approached Harrison Ford to star in the film, but he was unenthused about the project and passed on it. The producers then spoke with Alec Baldwin and director Walter Hill about teaming with them for the project. However, the deal fell through when Hill had a meeting with Warners that left the "suits" less than impressed. Baldwin later recalled, "I can see now . . . why they didn't want to make the movie with me. . . . Walter Hill was going to direct [and] we sat down with the people

from Warner Brothers and Walter started talking about Dostoevsky and the mytho-poetic iconoclasm of the character Kimble and the guys from Warner Brothers blinked a couple of times and their eyes glazed over and it was like, 'Get these people out of here.' "

Once again, the screen fates of Harrison Ford and Alec Baldwin would intertwine. Kopelson and Barish gave Ford the script, and this time the actor responded positively. He explained his rationale for quickly signing for the role of Richard Kimble: "I wanted to work this spring, because I wanted to work twice this year and then not at all next year, so I could stay home with my family and see my kid through first grade and enjoy being in Wyoming for one whole year. I knew I wanted to do another action picture while I still had the capacity, and this was an interesting project. The character is not unique, but his circumstances are unique and compelling. He's wrongly accused of killing his wife in a particularly cruel and horrible way."

Surprisingly, Ford claimed he had never seen the original series upon which the film would be based. However, he felt this fact would benefit the film, because he would not be influenced or prejudiced by David Janssen's portrayal of Dr. Kimble. He felt his ignorance of the show would give the movie "a fair chance of having a life of its own." He stressed that the intricacies of the script would ensure that this project would not simply be a rehash of the television show. In the cinematic *Fugitive*, the one-armed man is still the murderer, but he is but a pawn of a larger conspiracy involving corrupt doctors who try to frame Kimble for murder because he is on the verge of exposing their fraudulent test results on a new drug. The doctors, in collusion with a major pharmaceutical company, are continuing to endorse the potentially deadly "miracle" drug because the effect of pulling it off the market would mean economic disaster and the loss of reputations. Ford described how portraying Kimble as the target of a conspiracy helped give the film a distinctive twist: "This was a new look at the medical mystery story, and the addition of the drug company and the testing of the drug gave it a broader moral canvas to work in."

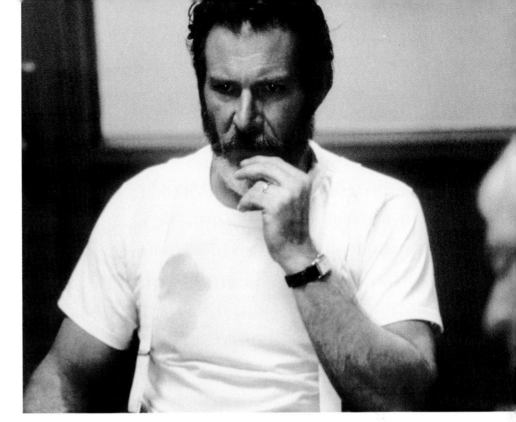

Richard Kimble (*Harrison Ford*) begins to suspect he is the prime suspect in his wife's murder. (Warner Bros.)

The antagonists from the classic television show: Janssen as Richard Kimble and Barry Morse as the relentless Gerard. (ABC-TV)

With Ford onboard, the producers next signed Andrew Davis to direct. Davis, who had impressed Barish, Kopelson, and Ford with his direction of *Under Siege*, reconsidered his own vacation plans and joined the team, saying of the project's star: "Harrison Ford has done a very good job of [playing] the common man who gets into circumstances over his head and he's probably the best there is at that. But I think that's one of the attractions about how everybody can relate to this guy [Kimble]. He wakes up one morning and this horrific event happens to him in his life and everybody watching the movie can say this could happen to me. And so they're very compassionate and drawn to this character."

The pivotal role of U.S. Deputy Marshal Gerard still had to be cast, and it was imperative that an actor with a dynamic intensity play the part. Ultimately, all of the principals involved with the film agreed that Tommy Lee Jones, whose portrayal of the lead terrorist had stolen *Under Siege* from star Steven Seagal, was the man for the job. Andrew Davis, who had directed Jones in that high-seas thriller, explained, "He's one of the most talented actors I've had the good fortune of working with; he has a unique ability to sustain intense characterizations on-screen. I think he brings a critical balance to the film in terms of his and Harrison's strengths; the dynamics of their relationship are explosive." Jones was equally enthusiastic about *The Fugitive*, saying, "I've worked with Arnold [Kopelson] before, and I've worked with Andy

The key people involved with the Kimble murder case: (*Top*) Sela Ward as the victim, Helen Kimble; Joe Pantoliano as Assistant U.S. Marshal Joe Renfro; (*Bottom*) Andreas Katsulas (*left*) as Sykes, the notorious one-armed man; and Jeroen Krabbe as Dr. Charles Nichols, Kimble's esteemed colleague. (Stephen Vaughan, courtesy Warner Bros.)

the best possible option as a location. It's a city of neighborhoods. We could get the grittiness, we could get the flash of architecture, the charm of the lake. It has it all."

Ford recalled the pressure of bringing *The Fugitive* in on a tight schedule of fifteen weeks. He told *Empire* magazine, "It was an extremely short schedule and it was a real burden on Andrew Davis, and all of us, because we didn't have a complete script to start with. . . . And also the postproduction period was so short on this movie. After shooting wrapped in mid-May, seven editors and twenty-one assistants worked around the clock to meet the deadline. There was an adequate shooting period but it was the preproduction and postproduction time that was really short." Davis agreed with Ford's assessment, adding "We were on the run—just like Richard Kimble!"

Several key sequences were shot inside the University of Chicago Hospitals. Here, Harrison Ford indulged in intensive research for his role as a physician. He accompanied actual doctors on their rounds, social-

[Davis] before, and I've never had the opportunity to work with Harrison Ford. Those are reasons enough for going to work."

Principal photography, which would take place primarily in Chicago and its environs, began in February 1993. The location was Ford's idea. Explained Andrew Davis, "Originally, I wasn't even going to try to come to Chicago. I thought that the weather would be too cold and difficult for shooting. But Harrison, having seen several of my prior films shot in Chicago, suggested doing it here. This town has a lot of character, and furthermore, we knew we would have the cooperation of the city, good crews, a rich pool of talent, great sets, and endless resources." Ford was enthused for reasons other than those given by his director. "It's nice coming back. I grew up in Chicago, went to college in Wisconsin, and came back to take summer jobs for three years. I felt this was

Kimble frantically attempts to elude police in a Chicago city jail. (Stephen Vaughan, courtesy Warner Bros.)

ized with them, and watched them prepare for surgery. He made it clear to *Film Review*, however, that his methodical approach to the role did not extend into practicing medicine. "I don't want to worry anyone! The hospital lawyers made sure I never did anything dangerous! I assisted by 'scrubbing' and 'retracting,' but it did allow me to get the feel of what it is like to be a surgeon. It allows you to move and act as if you've done things hundreds of times before. It's those little extra bits that give the audience something to believe in. I did go on rounds, I went completely unnoticed among the seven or so medical students. The seventy-one-year-old heart patient wasn't looking for a famous face, so he didn't 'see' me."

Although *The Fugitive* is a personal story of one man's obsession with finding justice and another man's obsession with upholding the law, the script allowed for several spectacular action set pieces. One occurs when Kimble tries to elude the dogged Gerard in the tunnels of a large dam. With nowhere to run, Kimble chooses to jump to almost certain death by leaping into the churning waters which flow over the dam. His determination begins to plant doubts about his guilt in the mind of Gerard. The exteriors of this suspense-filled sequence were shot at the Cheoah Dam, near Asheville, N.C. The interior tunnel shots were done on sets built in Chicago, although the section of the tunnel from which Kimble jumps was imported to North Carolina from Chicago and installed above the dam.

Ford shocked the crew by refusing to use a double for the establishing shots that clearly show him precariously close to the edge of the tunnel. He did concede to wearing a wire but confessed to being a bit uneasy. "I don't like heights very much. It takes me a minute or two to steel myself for heights, but then I get used to it real quick. . . . There are a lot of people around to assure the safety of the things I do. I don't worry about it, I have great confidence in them." The scene in which Kimble plunges over the dam was accomplished by using a dummy, albeit an expensive one costing around $12,000. In the final film, the sequence—which was filmed over two days at a cost of over $2 million—works flawlessly and sets Gerard's pursuit of Kimble into high gear. Andrew Davis explained the significance of the scene: "The fall serves as [Kimble's] baptism. That's when he becomes the fugitive."

Tommy Lee Jones in his Oscar-winning role as Gerard. (Arnold Kopelson, courtesy Warner Bros.)

The action sequence which received the most notoriety was the spectacular train crash from which Kimble escapes his journey to death row. Superbly directed, the scene is a chaotic, manic event which begins with one of Kimble's fellow prisoners knifing a guard aboard the prison van. The van goes out of control and rolls down a hillside, directly in the path of an oncoming train. Here, Kimble puts his medical ethics above his own life and helps rescue the wounded guard, leaving only a second to jump out of the way of the speeding train. The resulting crash is one of the most memorable action scenes to appear in any film. Traditionally, train wrecks depicted in films relied on miniatures. However, for this sequence, the filmmakers secured two actual, full-sized locomotives, along with boxcars, flat cars, and a "pusher train" that would make the vehicles exceed the normal, "safe" speed of 35 MPH. This was necessary because the train would literally plow into the prisoners' bus at high speed. With only one take possible, Andrew Davis devised a method of capturing the action with as many cameras as possible. On location for the scene in Dillsboro, N.C., Davis placed thirteen robotic cameras in steel boxes and set them up directly in front of the train and around the perimeter of the action. He also had engineers and insurance investigators consulted, as well as special effects experts, stunt coordinators, and anyone else who might be able to predict which direction the train would go in upon impact. "We had only one train to crash, and we had to do it right." Despite the train going 42 MPH instead of the

Dr. Richard Kimble sneaks into the apartment of the one-armed man to search for evidence which may exonerate him. (Stephen Vaughan, courtesy Warner Bros.)

planned 32 MPH—a difference which could have been potentially disastrous—the sequence went superbly. Despite weeks of preparation, the actual shoot took only one minute—at a cost of over $1 million.

There was concern about Harrison Ford's ability to physically participate in the demanding scene, which required his jumping from an eight-foot platform super-imposed over footage of the mangled bus. Earlier in the filming, he had torn a ligament in his leg. He recalled, "It was an accident. I was running toward the camera for a scene that wasn't even for the film itself. It was for the trailer. I had to keep very close to the camera and put all the weight on my right leg as I cut left. That's when it went." Later, the ligament went out again, leaving Ford in pain throughout much of the filming. (Indeed, he is seen noticeably limping throughout the movie.) Although he was scheduled for surgery two days after filming the train wreck sequence, Ford spurned a stunt double. Artistically, the risk was worth it, as the close-up of Kimble leaping from the path of the train is greatly enhanced by the audience seeing it is actually Harrison Ford doing "the dirty work." Ford again downplayed his physical contributions in the area of stunt work. "It looks like a tough film, but you've got to remember it's done one piece at a time, then I go back to my trailer and rest."

Throughout the production, Ford contributed ideas and improvisations which he felt would benefit the movie. Screenwriter Jeb Stuart said, "He becomes the soul of the whole project. After four months of working sixteen- to seventeen-hour days under a tremendous amount of pressure, when you're looking at parts of the script and have to make a decision to do it or not do it, it's important to be able to say, 'No, this isn't right,' as opposed to 'Well, let's go with what's here.' Those are tough decisions, but Harrison kept on the right course through the whole thing." Ford rationalized his perfectionism: "If the audience sees a movie with my face in it and they don't have a good time, they don't put the blame on Andy Davis, they put the blame on me. So I use whatever efforts I can to ensure that at least *I'm* happy with it."

Among Ford's improvisations are the personal characteristics of Richard Kimble. Ford was concerned that the emphasis on physical action might limit his ability to

Kimble boldly enters his former hospital to track down the identity of his wife's killer. (Warner Bros.)

show the human side of his character. He told *Empire* magazine, "We had the beginning sequence to describe him before the traumatic events of his wife's murder, but we had very little time to sketch that in and so I wanted to use as much visual information as possible. That's why the beard is there, why the flowered waistcoat is there. I wanted to create this character that is a bit outside the medical establishment. You could maybe understand that if his virtue was called into question, as it was when his wife was murdered, how he might not have as many friends as some other doctors. He might be alone. That's why I wanted to demonstrate the ego of the surgeon, the success that this man has enjoyed so that we could have some sort of departure."

"The studio was not happy with the beard," Ford explained. "They figured they paid for the face they wanted to see, so they were concerned about that." However, Ford argued that the beard "establishes the guy as slightly idiosyncratic. That, his flowered vest, and the particular kind of art on his walls describes him as a character who is a bit outside of the medical establishment, which comes into play later in the story."

Ford's determination to keep the beard was reinforced by a real-life occurrence. "One evening Andy and I were discussing doctors in a restaurant. A baby was playing at our table and I asked the maitre'd if it was his child. He said it belonged to a doctor from Northwestern and his wife, who were sitting just around the corner. We invited them over for a drink, and we learned that they are longtime friends of Andy's assistant. He appeared the way I looked. His beard and long hair substantiated my characterization. The doctor, who happened to be an art collector, invited us back to his house to view his collection. The house not only had the art I had been trying to describe, but the architecture that would best articulate the murder. I asked them if we could have our art department see their home. It subsequently became the model for the Kimble house."

Ford, who enjoys a reputation of being very giving to his fellow actors, was not the least bit concerned that the film centered almost as much on the Tommy Lee Jones character as it did on his own. He explained, "There are a lot of scenes of Kimble without contact with other people.

In a fight to the death with the one-armed man (*Katsulas*) aboard a Chicago subway. (Warner Bros.)

And that's balanced in the context of the film as a whole with what's going on on the Tommy Lee Jones side. If there had been a whole film of Kimble alone, I think it might not have worked as well." Ford was unstinting in his praise of his costar. "I would like to have had more with Tommy. He's a wonderful actor, and he's brought a great deal to his character."

The Fugitive is a mesmerizing adventure. There is nary a second of padding in the fast-moving, emotionally wrenching story, and the skilled team of filmmakers insured that every aspect of the final cut met all expectations. From its opening frames to its edge-of-the seat climax, the film leaves audiences breathless from the chase and emotionally drained in their desire to see Kimble prevail. The moving climax has Kimble expose and defeat his former friend, a noted doctor (well-played by Jeroen Krabbe) who is behind the plot to frame him. Their battle to the death atop a Chicago skyscraper is superbly staged and enacted. Best of all, the movie does not denigrate the spirit or memory of the classic show upon which it is based. If anything, the film heightened interest in the old series to such a degree that NBC made the extraordinary decision to telecast the two-part climax of the show in prime time more than twenty-five years after it left the air.

Although Harrison Ford continues to warn that his days as an action star are rapidly dwindling, one would never know it from *The Fugitive*. This is one of the most

The moment before Kimble makes his death-defying leap into the water. (Warner Bros.)

and faced formidable competition from the likes of no less than *Jurassic Park*. Ford professed not to worry about his movie getting lost in the marketplace, as did Arnold Schwarzenegger's mega-flop *The Last Action Hero*, which fell victim to Steven Spielberg's *Tyrannosaurus rex* epic. Ford said, "Each film has a life of its own and it's like comparing apples and oranges. I know this is a good ride for the audience. I've been with audiences who have seen the film and I know *they* have enjoyed it. The movie business is stronger now than it has ever been and certainly it must be because there is a batch of satisfying movies out there, so I think that if people have a good time with *Jurassic Park* they are likely to think that they're going to have a good time at another movie."

Ford's instincts were correct. *The Fugitive* became the third-highest-grossing film of 1993, trailing only *Jurassic Park* and *Mrs. Doubtfire*. The film also earned seven Oscar nominations including Best Picture and for cinematography, editing, sound, sound effects editing, and original score. Tommy Lee Jones walked away with the Best Supporting Actor award, thanking his costar in the process by saying what theaterowners have known for many years: "Above all, I thank the man who needs no support at all, Harrison Ford."

Reviews

"The surprising aspect of The Fugitive, *a supremely clever and exciting update of the old '60s TV series, is that it isn't just a high-powered summer blockbuster. It's something cannier (and rarer): a suspense thriller rooted in character. . . . The Fugitive is proof, if any were needed, that a thriller is more thrilling when we can actually believe our eyes. . . . Throughout the movie, we're wired into Harrison Ford's emotions. He doesn't actually have much dialogue, but the fear, calculation, and resolve that pass across his face are as eloquent as most actors' spoken words. Ford may be the only movie star alive who's as convincing playing a scholarly, compassionate physician as he is beating a subway goon into submission. . . . Ford humanizes conventional heroics."*

—OWEN GLEIBERMAN, *ENTERTAINMENT WEEKLY*

demanding roles of his career, not only from an acting standpoint but from a physical one as well, and the stunts and dangers inherent in playing Richard Kimble were no less challenging than those encountered by playing Indiana Jones. As for Ford's performance as a whole, because he is one of the few remaining larger-than-life heroes of the cinema, he brings instant credibility to the role of Kimble. The audience, which is used to rooting for Ford in any number of other films, instantly feels a sympathy for his character, which is essential in such an emotional story. We have to *feel* Kimble's frustration, fears, and anguish so that his final triumph is all the more satisfying. Ford's performance as Kimble was instantly ranked by critics and audiences as one of the finest of his career.

The flashier, more humorous role was that of Gerard, and Tommy Lee Jones's portrayal of the buttoned-down lawman earned him universal praise. We see Gerard evolve from an arrogant, machinelike technocrat, who doesn't care whether Kimble is guilty or innocent, into a reluctant pursuer of a man whom he suspects has been framed. Jones turns what could have been a fairly one-dimensional role into one of the more memorable screen characters of recent years, with his sarcastic wisecracks and stoicism in the face of mounting frustrations.

The Fugitive was a major summer release in 1993

"A smashing success, a juggernaut of an action-adventure saga that owes nothing to the past. As directed sensationally by Andrew Davis and acted to steely perfection by Harrison Ford, Tommy Lee Jones and a flawless supporting cast, it is a film whose every element conspires to sustain crisp intelligence and a relentless pace. Tight editing, a powerhouse score, adroit sound effects and a clever, inventive screenplay all contribute mightily to the fever pitch. To put it simply, this is a home run. . . . As it turns out, compressing four years of The Fugitive into two tight hours was a fine idea, giving the film a simple and effective plot. . . . Mr. Ford succeeds in making his character deeply sympathetic from the film's opening frames. This actor's wary intelligence is no surprise, but he projects it with particular grace in this spare, visceral story. Mr. Ford works furiously to turn his character's terror into something starkly physical. And he looks like a doctor, not like a movie star with a personal trainer."

—JANET MASLIN, NEW YORK TIMES

"Nobody plays harried better than Harrison Ford. He plays other things well, too—notably in the scene in which, as he is interrogated by the police, he comes to realize that he is their chief suspect. Grief, outrage, incomprehension, terror—what a rich mix of emotions he registers in a matter of seconds."

—RICHARD SCHICKEL, TIME

"One of the best entertainments of the year, a tense, taut, and expert thriller that becomes something more than that: an allegory about an innocent man in a world prepared to crush him. . . . Ford is once again the great modern movie everyman, dogged, determined, brave and not demonstrative. As an actor, nothing he does seems merely for show, and in the face of this melodramatic material, he deliberately plays down, lies low and gets on with business. . . . The Fugitive has the standards of an earlier, classic time, when acting, character, and dialogue were meant to stand on their own, and where characters continued to change and develop right up until the last frame."

—ROGER EBERT, CHICAGO SUN TIMES

Trivia Note

● David Janssen's mother appears as an extra in the film, seated behind Harrison Ford in the courtroom scene.

Gerard begins to doubt Kimble's guilt. (Stephen Vaughan, courtesy Warner Bros.)

NOTE: Like many classic television series, The Fugitive has a cult following. Additionally, it has spawned two active fan clubs, both of which debate the merits of the original TV show and 1993 feature film. Coincidentally, both are located in Texas.

● "On the Run," publishes a bimonthly newsletter that analyzes three different episodes from the TV series in the order in which they aired. The magazine also includes biographies and updates on cast members and guest stars, classified ads and reprints of newspaper and magazine articles pertaining to the show. For information, write to: Rusty Pollard, On the Run Newsletter, POB 461402, Garland, Texas 75046-1402.

● "The F.U.G.I.T.I.V.E.S." (Friends United for Great Intelligent Television and Inspiring Video Entertainment Series) encourages members to meet to discuss the series and hold conventions, as well as help the less fortunate in the spirit in which Richard Kimble acted in the series. Members stay in touch via a bimonthly newsletter. Information can be obtained by writing to: "Texas" Bob Reinhardt, 507 B. Bellevue Place, Austin, Texas 78705-3109

29

Jimmy Hollywood (1994)

CAST:

Jimmy Alto: Joe Pesci; *William*: Christian Slater; *Lorraine*: Victoria Abril; *Detective*: John Cothran Jr.; *Detective*: Hal Fishman.

CREDITS:

Director and Writer: Barry Levinson; *Producers*: Mark Johnson and Barry Levinson; *Screenplay*: Barry Levinson; *Director of Photography*: Peter Sove; *Production Designer*: Linda De Scenna; *Editor*: Jay Rabinowitz; *Music*: Robbie Robertson. *Running time*: 117 minutes. Released by Paramount Pictures.

(Paramount Pictures)

By no stretch of the imagination is *Jimmy Hollywood* a Harrison Ford movie. However, to be comprehensive, we have included an analysis of the film in this book. Ford appears only briefly during the last sequence, but his time on screen is a highlight and illustrates that Ford is open to taking an unbilled part just for the sheer fun of it.

Jimmy Hollywood is an offbeat, humorous look at the cannibalistic methods aspiring actors often use to get a break in the dog-eat-dog world of today's motion picture industry. Joe Pesci plays Jimmy Alto, an aging but optimistic no-talent who continues to believe he will make a sensation in the acting community if he only gets one opportunity to showcase his abilities. Accompanied by his dim-witted but loyal friend William (Christian Slater), Jimmy makes the rounds to auditions for low-budget movies, only to be rejected at every turn. He continues to get solace from his long-suffering girlfriend Lorraine (Victoria Abril), who patiently puts up with Jimmy's incessant bragging about how he will one day be a major force in Hollywood.

Desperate for attention, Jimmy enlists William to form a bogus citizens' vigilante group called S.O.S. ("Save Our Streets"), which ostensibly serves notice to criminals that they will fall victim to the group's own brand of justice. Jimmy's scheme is not motivated by a desire to stop crime as much it is by having the videos he sends to the police broadcast on the news. Disguised as "Jericho," the mysterious leader of S.O.S., Jimmy becomes addicted to his newfound fame. When the group receives widespread public support for stopping a few petty thefts and the police promise a crackdown on S.O.S., the organization takes on mythic proportions—even though the entire group consists of Jimmy and William.

With the police closing in, Jimmy goes public with his identity and thrives on becoming a popular figure. The climax of the film involves Jimmy hiding inside the Egyptian Theater as an army of police officers copes with the throngs who have shown up to support "Jericho." Jimmy plans a true Hollywood finale to his fifteen minutes of fame by dashing toward the cops with both guns blazing. However, his grand plan goes awry when the police refuse to fire back, thus denying him the death of a martyr. Seems that Lorraine has tipped them off that "Jericho" is merely a publicity-starved actor who wouldn't hurt a fly.

The ironic ending finds Jimmy freed following a brief prison stint and finally achieving his dream of stardom through a film about his life—starring Harrison Ford!

Jimmy Hollywood is the brainchild of director-writer Barry Levinson, whose credits include his Oscar-winning work on *Rain Man*, along with *Bugsy, Good Morning, Vietnam, Diner, Tin Men, The Natural*, and *Avalon*. Producer Mark Johnson explained what motivated Levinson to make such a low-key film: "I think this is a very personal movie for Barry. Hollywood has very strong emotional ties for him, and this one really got us back to the source, to what is really most fun about making movies. There's something about lower-budget films that is so satisfying. It's just as imaginative, but you have to be even more resourceful."

The film began shooting in August 1993, and locations included many legendary Hollywood sites: the Hollywood Walk of Fame, the El Capitan and Egyptian theaters, and the Hollywood Bowl. Levinson used steadicams and multicamera setups to track Joe Pesci and Christian Slater as they walked through the Hollywood area trying to remember the glory of a by-gone era of glitz and glamour that they never really knew.

Upon release, *Jimmy Hollywood* the movie was as ignored as Jimmy Hollywood the character. The film received almost universal pans from critics, and after months in release, the theatrical grosses had barely topped a measly $3 million. It's easy to see why the movie failed to become a hit: its appeal is limited to those with a true understanding of the pitfalls of trying to find fame in the present-day movie business. Like Martin Scorsese's brilliant but underrated 1983 film *The King of Comedy*, *Jimmy Hollywood* is a bit "too hip for the room."

This is not to say that this is a major work of art. The fragmented story line is an uneven blend of pathos, senti-

ment, and slapstick. The characters are never as well-defined as they should be, and at 117 minutes, the final cut seems at least fifteen minutes too long. However, the film does include a fascinating performance by Joe Pesci, who seems incapable of being anything but mesmerizing on-screen. Here, saddled with a ludicrous blond caveman hairdo, Pesci is at his most obnoxious. However, one can't help but feel an emotional attachment to his plight. Despite Jimmy Hollywood's woeful lack of talent, the audience winds up rooting for him. In the film's opening sequence, we see Jimmy trying to memorize every star on the Walk of Fame. It's a wonderful and revealing moment, which gives great insight into his character, as he tries to emulate the famous by idolizing them. Perhaps Pesci's inspired acting was due to his sympathy for aspiring thespians in real-life Tinseltown. He commented during production, "[The film] shows what's really going on in Hollywood. People think it's a magic place where dreams are made. Actually, it makes for broken dreams. It's almost impossible for a young actor today to make it."

The other cast member who gives a standout performance is Victoria Abril, the acclaimed young actress who scored in numerous foreign films prior to *Jimmy Hollywood*. In this, her American film debut, she brings a great deal of sensitivity to what could have been a throwaway part in the hands of a less talented actress. Her scenes with Pesci are both amusing and touching. Christian Slater has little to do in the role of Pesci's sidekick William, a good-natured airhead who claims to suffer from memory lapses and a childhood fear of the Universal Pictures monster, the Mummy. Still, he makes a good foil for Pesci, and it is to his credit that he allows his costar the lion's share of the laughs and the best dialogue.

Harrison Ford's brief appearance under the closing credits is without a doubt the movie's highlight. One just hopes the audience stayed in their seats long enough to enjoy it. It is a hilarious scene in which Ford tries unsuccessfully to emulate the struggling Jimmy Hollywood as he pleads for a role during an audition. Finally, Jimmy—by now a major name in the media—condescendingly puts his arm around Ford and advises him about acting techniques and the methods of getting "inside" a character. The short bit is truly inspired (as is a brief appearance by Barry Levinson as the fictional film's director). The sequence was singled out by many critics as one of the few scenes in *Jimmy Hollywood* which really worked.

Levinson's film is not a success on every level, yet it deserved a better fate. Besides, in light of the O. J. Simpson case, the film's central premise—that a brainless, obnoxious, no-talent can mesmerize the American public by being in the wrong place at the right time—no longer strains credibility. Perhaps if the film were released as *The Kato Kaelin Story*, it would do boffo business at the box office. (After all, the same hair stylist obviously created the remarkably similar "dos" for Kaelin and Alto!)

Reviews

"Barry Levinson's Jimmy Hollywood *has a wonderful opening shot in which Jimmy Alto, would-be actor, walks down Hollywood Boulevard reciting the name of every star on the pavement, by memory. There are people who can do this. And there are a lot of people like Jimmy holding on desperately to the leftover dreams of many years ago, still hoping to be 'discovered.' Pesci's own life is a case in point: he had given up hopes of an acting career and resigned himself to real life in 1980, when Martin Scorsese and Robert De Niro discovered him and cast him in his career-making role in* Raging Bull. *That stroke of luck is still awaiting Jimmy Alto . . . but he has been close to glory: 'I was up for the role of Cliff on* Matlock,' *he tells a short-order cook. 'But they felt I was a little too strong for Andy Griffith.'*

*"*Jimmy Hollywood *goes wrong when Jimmy starts pulling off stunts that would make you famous in the movies but would get you killed in real life. Once the story cuts loose from its base of realism, it doesn't matter what happens; Jimmy, William, and Lorraine, who seemed so real in her cluttered apartment, become plot devices, not people."*
—ROGER EBERT'S VIDEO
COMPANION

*"*Jimmy Hollywood *turns out to be just the kind of flimsy doodle of a movie, amusing but small in scale, you might expect from the director of* Diner *and* Tin Men. *One of the problems is that there is too much of Jimmy in it and too little of any-*

Would-be actor Jimmy Alto (*Joe Pesci*) and William (*Christian Slater*) pretend to be oblivious to Jimmy's "subtle" self promotional tactic. (Brian Hamill, courtesy Paramount Pictures)

thing else. Levinson seems to have been mesmerized by his title character. . . . The film's plot has related problems, first taking its time to kick in and grandly bypassing plausibility when it does. Still, Jimmy

Jimmy argues with his girlfriend Lorraine (*Victoria Abril*). (Brian Hamill, courtesy Paramount Pictures)

Critics agreed that Harrison Ford's unbilled cameo at the conclusion was the highlight of the movie. (Paramount Pictures)

Hollywood is such a determined character that the cockeyed fable he's lent his name and story to manages to carry you along even as it gets further and further out of hand. Maybe the guy can act after all."

—KENNETH TURAN, *LOS ANGELES TIMES*

"At the critical, defining moment in the life of Jimmy Alto, he comes up firing blanks. The same can be said of Barry Levinson's oddball attempt to mix offbeat comedy with social commentary and fringe-level char-acter study. However well intentioned, the contrary elements just don't mesh, and the picture's only possible box-office salvation—laughter—never materializes. This look at a showbiz loser will itself be a commercial castoff. . . . As a low budget indie shot on the run and then marketed cleverly, this story of terminal down-and-outers might have made some sense. As a $20 million studio undertaking, without major stars, it never stood a chance."

—TODD MCCARTHY, *VARIETY*

30

Clear and Present Danger (1994)

"[Jack] Ryan finds himself drawn into this situation that finally only he can resolve. We all have moral decisions to make in our lives and the nature of them depends on the exact detail of the circumstances. I think Ryan behaves well and admirably, not out of super patriotism or out of national zeal, but out of regard for his fellow human beings, out of compassion and intelligence and a sense of responsibility."

CAST:

Jack Ryan: Harrison Ford; *Clark*: Willem Dafoe; *Cathy Ryan*: Anne Archer; *Adm. James Greer*: James Earl Jones; *Felix Cortez*: Joaquim De Almeida; *Robert Ritter*: Henry Czerny; *James Cutter*: Harris Yulin; *President Bennett*: Donald Moffat; *Ernesto Escobedo*: Miguel Sandoval; *Judge Moore*: Dean Jones; *Moira Wolfson*: Ann Magnuson; *Captain Ramirez*: Benjamin Bratt; *Sally Ryan*: Thora Birch; *Chavez*: Raymond Cruz; *Senator Mayo*: Hope Lange.

CREDITS:

Director: Phillip Noyce; *Producers*: Mace Neufeld and Robert Rehme; *Coproducer*: Ralph S. Singleton; *Screenplay*: Donald Stewart, Steve Zaillian, and John Milius; *Based on the novel by* Tom Clancy; *Director of Photography*: Donald M. McAlpine; *Production Designer*: Terence Marsh; *Special Effects Coordinators*: Paul and Joe Lombardi; *Editor*: Neil Travis; *Art Director*: William Cruise; *Music*: James Horner; *Running time*: 142 minutes. Released by Paramount Pictures.

With *The Fugitive* still breaking box-office records throughout the world, Harrison Ford went before the cameras for one of his most elaborate and expensive action films: the $60-plus million screen adaptation of Tom Clancy's *Clear and Present Danger*, wherein Ford would resume the role of C.I.A. hero Jack Ryan. Ford, who earlier in his career had reservations about appearing in sequels, had finally grown comfortable with the fact that audiences would respond to him primarily as an actor and not necessarily as the specific character he was portraying. This confidence, coupled with his personal reservations about the final cut of the previous Ryan adventure movie *Patriot Games*, made Ford eager to develop his on-screen character beyond the level of someone who merely sidesteps bombs and bullets.

From the moment he finished *Patriot Games*, Ford seemed receptive to the idea of carrying on the cinematic legacy of Jack Ryan. He made an analogy to his portrayal of Indiana Jones and linked the two diverse fictional characters with a common characteristic: "If you're going to do it again as well as giving an entertaining story, we have to advance the understanding of the character so it's not the same old stuff. I think we did that in Indiana

219

Jack Ryan (*Harrison Ford*) reluctantly fills in for the ailing Admiral Greer as adviser to the President (*Donald Moffat, far left*). (Paramount Pictures)

Jones, through dramatic devices, and I hope to do the same with the Jack Ryan character."

Phillip Noyce, the director of *Patriot Games*, did not share Ford's commitment or enthusiasm about making another Jack Ryan thriller: "After *Patriot Games*, I swore I didn't want to be a part of the series anymore." He relented, however, when he read Tom Clancy's novel, saying, "I didn't admire the novel of *Patriot Games*—it's the opposite with this book. Clancy has written a cautionary tale about the use and abuse of power." Noyce signed on and, along with producers Mace Neufeld and Robert Rehme, completed the reunion of the creative team that had brought *Patriot Games* to the screen in 1992. Enticing the talent would prove to be the easy part, as filming *Clear and Present Danger* was to be a more challenging and arduous experience than its controversial predecessor had been.

The basic problem was how to adapt the novel to the screen, since the Ryan character barely appears in the first half of the book, and when he does, he is initially restricted to working behind a desk. Noyce recalled to *Entertainment Weekly*, "There was no place for Harrison Ford. There was a place, but the audience would have rioted." John Milius had written an initial concept which met with the approval of Tom Clancy. However, because the script remained very close to the novel, the Jack Ryan character does not appear until late in the story—an aspect that would be unfeasible for a film starring

Harrison Ford. Paramount hired Donald Stewart to do a rewrite that would make Ryan more central to the early story line. Predictably, Tom Clancy was outspoken in his objection to the new script. Finally, Ford and Noyce asked Steven Zaillian to see if he could come up with a definitive script which would allow Ryan to appear prominently throughout, while addressing some of Clancy's concerns. This version satisfied all parties—with the exception of the insatiable Tom Clancy.

John Milius's original script prompted an outcry from Clancy, who was apparently as unhappy with the pending film version of *Clear and Present Danger* as he had been with *Patriot Games*. Clancy, who does not count subtlety among his virtues, referred to the script as "really awful . . . an absolute piece of crap." Taking those comments as being somewhat negative in tone, Harrison Ford replied with equal candor, "I don't give a shit what he says." He elaborated on his disdain of Clancy's attitude, citing the author's ceaseless tirades about the script of *Patriot Games*: "I think [Clancy's] criticism did hurt the film. I don't think it should have. It's inevitable that a book changes in bringing it to the screen. It's generally accepted by those professionals that have had some experience with the process. And if one doesn't want to submit to the process, the simple expedient is not to sell your stuff."

Still, Clancy persisted with a broadside of faxes, letters, and public complaints that the new script by Donald Stewart was "really awful," which, in the scheme of things, could probably be viewed as progress. Clancy warned Phillip Noyce, "If you shoot this script, *Sliver* (Noyce's infamous box-office dud) will look like *Citizen Kane*." He rationalized, "*Clear and Present Danger* was the number one best-selling novel of the 1980s. One might conclude that the novel's basic story line had some quality to it. Why, then, has nearly every aspect of the book been tossed away?" Ford's increasingly impatient response: "You do things when you're typing that you would never do if you had to fucking stand there and deliver [the lines]." *Clear and Present Danger* would go before the cameras with or without the support of Tom Clancy. Producer Mace Neufeld, still wounded from his battles with Clancy over the earlier film, spoke with an air of resignation about his efforts to please the novelist: "I did everything in one man's power to make Tom Clancy happy. I went back time and time again after having felt battered and bloody. At this point, I question whether there is anything that will please Tom Clancy." Still, Neufeld and Ford admitted the script needed more fine-tuning, and writer Steve Zaillian was brought aboard to make key changes, as he had done with *Patriot Games*.

Clear and Present Danger is considerably different in scope from *Patriot Games* or the first Jack Ryan screen adventure, *The Hunt for Red October*. The pure adventure aspect of the earlier films was replaced by a literate and engrossing story revolving around Jack Ryan's efforts to place his personal sense of honor over the dictates of misguided and/or corrupt superiors. "I feel an obligation to expand on the role of Ryan," Ford said. "We were able to do that this time because we see him in such different circumstances than in *Patriot Games*, a tale of a man and his family being threatened. This [one] has a lot more energy to it. It's a lot more intriguing story of government and corruption and one man's attempt to stand up against the system."

The plot finds the President of the United States outraged over the murder of his personal friend at the hands of a Colombian drug cartel. In revenge, he authorizes a clandestine war against the cartel, waged by a secret unit of the U.S. army led by a renegade paramilitary expert named Clark. Jack Ryan is used as a dupe to secure funding from Congress to finance the secret war. The plan goes awry, however, when embarrassing revelations indicate that the President's friend was a major player in the drug trade. As the press begins to unravel the military operation, the President orders the war to cease and leaves the small, covert band of U.S. soldiers in Colombia to face certain death. Outraged at the seemingly endless cover-up attempts by the White House, Ryan disregards his career and personal safety and, along with Clark, leads a daring rescue mission to bring the surviving members of the secret army back from Colombia. In a dramatic confrontation with the President, Ryan expresses his disgust and makes good on his vow to expose the incredible scandal to Congress.

The addition of the climactic sequence in which Ryan is seen appearing before Congress was not in the original

(Paramount Pictures)

novel. Ford explained the rationale behind adding this scene: "I thought we would be making an insufficient entertainment if we didn't give people the satisfaction of knowing Ryan did testify. It's hard to make an ambiguous ending to a two-hour movie. The audience is not satisfied [with that]." Ford also allowed that the script deemphasized some of Clancy's right-wing beliefs. "We have softened the political bias [Clancy] brings to the subject, not because we're bleeding-heart liberals, but because we wanted to divest it of some of its baggage and let it walk on its own two legs."

Mace Neufeld recalled, "This was a very difficult film to get off the ground, easily more difficult than *Hunt for*

Red October and *Patriot Games*. There were complexities of character and logistics that didn't exist in the other films and Phillip [Noyce] did a wonderful job of pulling it all together." Among the logistical problems were finding suitable locations for filming. Puerto Rico was rejected because of tax laws; California was unsuitable because it could not properly simulate the necessary locales; and Colombia was quickly dismissed because, as Mace Neufeld admitted, "I felt in danger just *being* there!" Ultimately, it was decided that Mexico would be the most suitable spot to simulate the extensive Colombian sequences. Some location work was shot in Washington,

On the set with producer Mace Neufeld. (Paramount Pictures)

D.C., and certain footage (mostly interiors) was filmed on two large soundstages at Sony Studios in Los Angeles.

From the start, the decision to utilize Mexican locations seemed ill-advised. Neufeld despondently recalled some of the problems encountered in an interview with *Premiere* magazine: "Our timing was exquisitely wrong. We arrived in Mexico just a week after the revolution broke out in Chiapas. Naturally, the Mexican government was somewhat reluctant to issue permits for all the weaponry and explosives needed. It wasn't until two days before we began shooting that the permits were finally issued." The production company also found that Mexico's "idyllic" weather could be very elusive. Torrential rains and thick fog delayed shooting for two weeks.

Neufeld was not faring much better securing the necessary cooperation of the Pentagon and C.I.A. to utilize the high-tech gadgetry and weapons which are so instrumental to the story. The Pentagon objected to many aspects of the script, citing its oversimplification of the procedures utilized to initiate bombing raids. Out of necessity, certain changes were made in the script to pacify the Pentagon, and eventually the military granted full cooperation. The C.I.A. was far less enthusiastic, possibly because the script shows the agency in a less-than-flattering light. The crew was not allowed access to White House grounds, so the scenes of Ryan driving through the executive mansion's checkpoint were achieved using special effects and clever editing.

The filmmakers did receive considerable cooperation from the Drug Enforcement Agency, the F.B.I., and the State Department. In fact, (then) National Security Advisor Brent Scowcroft gave technical advice so that the White House meetings depicted in the film had an air of realism. The helpful attitude of the government allowed the crew to film at such diverse sites as Arlington National Cemetery, the Los Alamitos Reserve Center, the U.S. Coast Guard station in San Pedro, Nellis Air Force Base, and aboard the aircraft carrier *Kitty Hawk*. Phillip Noyce also persuaded the army to use a special forces unit specializing in stealth missions to pilot three Blackhawk helicopters for key sequences in the film. Actual military honor guards and bands were also used for the funeral scene at Arlington National Cemetery. Noyce explained the emphasis on using actual military personnel in the film: "It adds to the reality of the story. There is something to using the people who do these things everyday that cannot be substituted."

The most challenging logistical problem proved to be preparing the elaborate action sequence in which a C.I.A. caravan of vehicles is ambushed by bazooka-wielding members of the drug cartel on a residential street in Colombia. The suspenseful scene finds Jack Ryan the sole survivor of the attack, having escaped death by smashing his way to safety by driving in reverse through a devastating barrage of machine-gun fire and exploding shells. The set required eight weeks of preparation on a specially fabricated street which measured the length of two football fields. State-of-the-art technology was used to create computer-generated, fully animated storyboards which would give a detailed look as to how the scene would look on-screen. This sequence, originally planned for a five-day shoot, dragged on for eight days, thus putting the entire production behind schedule.

Throughout *Clear and Present Danger*, Ford continued his tradition of trying to do as many of his own stunts as possible, although he was characteristically low-key about this aspect of his contribution to the film, saying, "I don't do stunts. I do running, jumping, falling down. I hit people, I get hit by people, that kind of shit. Stunts are done by stuntmen. . . . You need to invest an action scene with moments of emotion. The audience is quite used to the kinetics. You can't show them too much more than they saw in *The Dukes of Hazzard* as far as rolling cars over. But if you get them to care about who's *inside* the cars, then it's a whole different thing."

Stunt coordinator Dick Ziker disagrees with Ford's statement that he does not do his own stunts. "He changes everything, trying to make it better. He always knows where the camera would be, where his face should be. That's why I have to use him all the time. We have a great stunt double for him, but [the double] never works." Indeed, for the pivotal rescue sequence in the film's climax, Ford hung suspended from a helicopter, forty feet in the air. In the aforementioned scene wherein Ryan and his C.I.A. associates are ambushed, Ford drove his "escape vehicle" backwards at 100 MPH, prompting Dick Ziker to admit, "He scares the shit out of me sometimes! Harrison does the stunts, I pay the double. That's the way he wants it." Ford had the last word on the subject, insisting that "If you fall on the ground, it's a stunt. If you fall on a pad, it's *acting!*"

In addition to the challenges the action sequences posed, the filmmakers also had to cope with the problem of boredom on the remote Mexican locations. At times, the cast and crew would drive for many miles to shop, although they had no interest in buying anything—it simply killed some time. While all of this was going on, the script was being revised daily. Mace Neufeld admitted that the stress was difficult to cope with. "After filming two films in a

As Jack Ryan. (Paramount Pictures)

series, you would think the third would be easier. But it hasn't. *Danger* has been the hardest. Harder than *Red October*, harder than *Patriot Games* . . . . For one thing, there are four major action sequences that had to be shot not only in different parts of the world, but on land, in the air, and at sea." The strain occasionally caused tension

Ryan is enraged to learn he is being framed by Ritter (*Henry Czerny*). (Paramount Pictures)

223

Ryan lies in wait for an adversary within the drug kingpin's compound. (Paramount Pictures)

pleasure with the film's climax, saying that he felt it was less exciting than the ambush sequence which occurs midway through the movie. Ultimately, he could not change the scene in any fundamental way. He later complained, "The studio gave us an ultimatum that we had to finish by a certain time, and the only way we could do that was by cutting our suit to fit the cloth. In retrospect, I'd say they made a big mistake. The ending of the film needed to be bigger than the ambush."

Despite Noyce's criticisms of the studio, Paramount did something that is uncharacteristic of most studios: it insisted that *Clear and Present Danger*'s running time be extended to a lengthy 142 minutes. Noyce had originally trimmed more than ten minutes of footage, but he admitted that when the movie was screened to audiences as a test, "[the cuts] didn't seem to make it better, just shorter. The studio constantly encouraged me to put material back. When we cut it shorter, more people found it longer than when it was long."

Clear and Present Danger does seem long at times, and in all due respect to the director, it seems as though the film could have reduced the number of characters and details which at times threaten to overwhelm the audience. This is the talkiest political thriller since *Seven Days in May* (1964), but like that film, it also stands as an example of intelligent moviemaking. The script may be far too complicated for its own good, and the dialogue does drag on occasion, but it is refreshing to find a major motion picture which does not underestimate the intelligence of the audience. Indeed, if you blink once too often, you'll probably miss several key details and become hopelessly lost. Yet every time the film threatens to bore the viewer with complications and technicalities, a major action set piece appears which keeps the audience on edge. The spectacular ambush sequence is a textbook example of superb directing, acting, editing, and cinematography. Likewise, the literally explosive scene in which a drug lord's hacienda is destroyed by a missile is stunning in its impact. (A genuine, full-size mansion was blown to bits in a sequence filmed by the second unit on the last day of principal photography. Only one take was possible, and eight cameras recorded the action, which cost over $500,000 to stage.)

between Harrison Ford and Phillip Noyce, but Ford explained such incidents as being in the film's best interest: "We had less of a script this time, so we had more to argue about—I mean argue in a responsible way, not bicker. The first time you work with a person, the debate tends to be polite. Then the marriage continues and maybe the second time you know each other better, so you conduct the argument more like a husband and wife than business associates."

When *Clear and Present Danger* finally finished shooting, the filmmakers' problems were far from over. Noyce was not satisfied with several key sequences. For one, he found that "everybody had a great entrance but Jack Ryan. And that's not good." Additionally, the ambush sequence strained credibility when an assassin on a motorcycle kills the F.B.I. man Ryan is carrying to safety. (Per Noyce: "The motorcyclist killing the F.B.I. director and not Jack Ryan—who had already shown he had more than nine lives—would have tipped the whole thing into unbelievability.") The last key scene presented problems involving the death of the villainous Cortez. According to Mace Neufeld: "We had one screening where people started to clap, but it was over before they could." Each of these scenes was rectified with two additional days of shooting on the Paramount lot. Noyce still professed dis-

Narrowly escaping death in the South American ambush of the CIA caravan. (Paramount Pictures)

For all of its action/adventure appeal, however, the real suspense in *Clear and Present Danger* comes from the interaction among its characters, as Jack Ryan exposes corruption extending all the way up the government ladder to the President of the United States. Ryan's climactic confrontation with the President (Donald Moffatt) is so well acted that one overlooks the clichéd situation in which the chief executive is portrayed as someone less than honorable. In fact, there are very few honorable people depicted outside of Jack Ryan, the mercenary played by Willem Dafoe, and Ryan's superior, Admiral Greer, again played by James Earl Jones. When Greer succumbs to terminal cancer, it is as though the gates of hell open and the entire U.S. government is suddenly a cesspool of corruption. This leads to severe tension between Ryan and two White House cabinet members,

With C.I.A. field contractor Clark (*Willem DaFoe*), infiltrating Escobedo's lair. (Bruce McBroom, courtesy Paramount Pictures)

played by Harris Yulin and Henry Czerny. The scene in which Ford engages in a desperate duel of computers to prevent Czerny from deleting incriminating files is filled with both humor and nail-biting suspense.

Clear and Present Danger is so completely different in style and scope from the two preceding Jack Ryan thrillers that it appears at times as though Ford is portraying a different character altogether. The bond to the Jack Ryan of the previous films is undermined by the script's diminishing the role of Ryan's wife. By not utilizing Anne Archer's considerable skills as an actress, the character of Ryan does not have the emotional ties to his family he demonstrated in *Patriot Games*. Here, Archer is relegated to looking exasperated and sighing each time Ryan phones in to tell her about his narrow escapes—like a less corny version of Vera Miles brooding about Big Duke Wayne in *Hellfighters*. The film does benefit from its intelligent use of the other cast members, most of whom are less well-known. Particularly good are Harris Yulin and Henry Czerny as Ford's opponents in the White House, and Joaquim De Almeida and Miguel Sandoval, both superb as the slimy but charismatic brains behind the Colombian drug cartel. Willem Dafoe gets to flex his muscles and shoot a lot of people, but unfortunately, his character is never fully developed.

Minor criticisms aside, however, *Clear and Present Danger* is a first-rate thriller that should insure the longevity of the Jack Ryan character—hopefully with Harrison Ford continuing to reprise the lead role. The film opened as Paramount's big action entry for late summer 1994. Backed by generally favorable reviews and an ad campaign that solely stressed the presence of Harrison Ford, the movie garnered a huge $20.4 million in its opening weekend. As of this writing, it has grossed over $120 million domestically, far eclipsing the considerable box-office receipts of *Patriot Games*, and proving that Ford—although now in his fifties—is still a major player in the action/adventure film genre.

As to his oft-stated concerns that he may be getting too "long in the tooth" for such physically demanding roles, Ford replied, "Some days you feel like Joe Montana—'Do I really need this?' But then something comes along which looks like it would be fun, for both me and the audience, and I can't wait to get out there again." He later told *Entertainment Tonight*, "I'll do it as long as I can. Running, jumping, falling down. There comes a point where you look silly doing it. But hopefully we haven't reached that point yet." In fact, even the hard-to-please Tom Clancy extended an olive branch to the actor, saying, "Mr. Ford and I sat down together. We had a spirited discussion that had points of disagreement, but it ended with our shaking hands. I'm happy for him to play Jack Ryan as long as he cares to."

Reviews

"Delivers everything you would expect from a top-drawer action thriller. . . . Phillip Noyce . . . wisely concentrates on human interaction rather than on wizardly gizmos or big action scenes—and that means that the explosions of masterfully shot, brilliantly edited violence that do periodically punctuate the tension, strike with far more terrifying impact than in lesser thrillers. It's only in the concluding scenes, with an over-the-top firefight and rescue followed by preachy moralizing by the hero . . . that the movie loses the realism and moral ambiguity that made it so fascinating to watch."

—MICHAEL MEDVED, NEW YORK POST

"Narrative complexity and momentum make this a true cinematic equivalent of an absorbing page-turner. Even if the excitement only occasionally reaches thrilling levels, its bestseller profile, action quotient, and Harrison Ford as a can-do hero assure muscular late summer box-office for this well-tooled entertainment . . . the most interesting of the three Clancy adaptations, at least from a content point of view."

—TODD MCCARTHY, VARIETY

"Harrison Ford is in peak form. It's the summer's smartest thriller: a gripping blend of suspense and surprising humor. There's more talk than action, but the talk is prime and the action, when it comes, is smashing . . . . Clancy never had it this good onscreen."

—PETER TRAVERS, ROLLING STONE

"Does more than provide the summer's most satisfying movie experience—which may sound like damning with faint praise, but shouldn't. It reaffirms, if reaffirmation is necessary, Harrison Ford's position as the most reliable action star around. If Danger has a problem, it is that it starts too slowly. But its key strength, and something rarer in films than good action, is plausible dialogue and acting."

—KENNETH TURAN, LOS ANGELES TIMES

"Harrison Ford, making only his second screen appearance as Jack Ryan, has already become Old Faithful in this role. [He] may be the most reticent of American movie stars, but he brings considerable subtlety to the job of humanizing Jack Ryan. . . . Mr. Ford's wary intelligence does wonders for a potentially one-dimensional character."

—JANET MASLIN, NEW YORK TIMES

31

Sabrina (1995)

"I was looking for a comedy with some . . . ambition, that was about something. Sydney nibbled at this one and I hooked him."

CAST:
Linus Larrabee: Harrison Ford; *David Larrabee*: Greg Kinnear; *Sabrina Fairchild*: Julia Ormond; *Maude Larrabee*: Nancy Marchand; *Fairchild*: John Wood; *Rosa*: Miriam Colon; *Joanna*: Elizabeth Franz; *Scott*: Paul Giamatti; *Linda*: Becky Ann Baker; *Mack*: Dana Ivey; *Elizabeth Tyson*: Lauren Holly; *Patrick Tyson*: Richard Crenna; *Ingrid Tyson*: Angie Dickinson.

CREDITS:
Director: Sydney Pollack; *Producers*: Scott Rudin and Sydney Pollack; *Screenplay*: Barbara Benedek and David Rayfiel; *Based on the 1954 film written by*: Billy Wilder, Samuel Taylor, and Ernest Lehman; *From the play by*: Samuel Taylor; *Director of Photography*: Giuseppe Rotunno; *Production Designer*: Brian Morris; *Editor*: Frederic Steinkamp; *Music*: John Williams. *Running time*: 127 minutes. A Mirage/Scott Rudin/Sandollar Production. Released by Paramount Pictures.

Not content to stay with the "safe" and successful confines of the action-adventure genre, Harrison Ford surprised the film industry when he announced his screen project for 1995 would be a contemporary remake of the 1954 romantic comedy *Sabrina* for Paramount (which, not coincidentally, released the original version). "I wanted something light," he said, "where I didn't have to hit anybody or have anybody hit me." He added, "I've been looking for a comedy for a long time, one with some ambition and I thought this had it. I responded emotionally to the character, the dilemma, the circumstances. I also thought it would be the kind of movie that an audience would love to see."

The original screen version of *Sabrina* was produced and directed by Billy Wilder and featured recent Oscar winners Humphrey Bogart, Audrey Hepburn, and William Holden. Hepburn starred as the title character, the daughter of the chauffeur to irresponsible society playboy Holden. "Plain Jane" Hepburn loves Holden but can't seem to get him to respond until she returns from a life-altering trip to Paris and emerges as a sophisticated, cultured, and beautiful young woman. She now attracts Holden, but his family tries to break up the relationship by forcing him to marry a "proper" girl of wealth. Holden's older brother, played by Bogart, initially tries to distract Hepburn by pretending to fall in love with her. Naturally, he really does; this comedic ménage à trois became one of the most popular films of 1954.

Classic Good Looks

With both *Sabrina*s in house, it afforded Paramount some interesting promotional opportunities.

For the remake, Harrison Ford was cast in the role originally played by Bogart. The search for his leading lady received widespread international coverage, as seemingly every major young actress, including Wynona Ryder, Meg Ryan, Demi Moore, and Julia Roberts, was rumored to be under consideration. Eventually, the role of Sabrina went to Julia Ormond, the acclaimed rising star of *Legends of the Fall* and *First Knight*. The thirty-year-old Ormond seemed awestruck at having landed the part and admitted, "I watched [the original *Sabrina*] four times before I auditioned. . . . Then, I got the role and . . . I've watched it three or four times. I'm going to have to stop."

Although such heavyweight talents as Tom Cruise, Alec Baldwin, Kurt Russell, and Val Kilmer had been rumored for the William Holden role, the part went to television talk show host Greg Kinnear (NBC's *Later* and E!'s *Talk Soup*), whose wit and engaging personality overcame his lack of acting experience.

Producer Scott Rudin, who had convinced Paramount chief Sherry Lansing to green-light the remake, asked Ford for input as to who should direct the picture. Ford said, "The film needed strong emotional values and good comedy chops. Sydney [Pollack] was the one who came to mind for me." Pollack, the acclaimed direc-

tor of *Tootsie* and *Out of Africa*, was hesitant, but Ford eventually persuaded him. "It took a while to talk him into it," Ford recalled. "I don't think he was sure until he could find a way of telling the story that interested him." Pollack later said, "I had never met Harrison Ford before and I'd always been a big fan. He called personally and said, 'Come on, man, let's go and have some fun' and I couldn't say no." He later detailed his initial reluctance, saying, "In the beginning, I thought it was just the world's worst idea. I was horrified at the idea of a remake in general, and particularly a remake of a Billy Wilder movie. But by struggling so hard to get out of doing something, you end up, while you are defining why it is you don't want to do it, sometimes stating a challenge that you find irresistible."

Pollack approached Billy Wilder for his advice on the film, only to find that Wilder was a bit miffed that Paramount had not consulted him about the remake. Nevertheless, he was flattered that Pollack respected him enough to ask his opinions and gave some general advice. Pollack began filming in the summer of 1994 in New York City and on the North Shore of Long Island, then followed with a three-week shoot in Paris. Pollack realized almost immediately that it would be difficult to have a finished cut of the film ready for its anticipated summer release. He had just worked miracles with *The Firm* (also for producer Rudin), barely managing to get the movie into theaters by its premiere date, and didn't relish working under such pressure again. Ultimately, he convinced the studio to give him more breathing room by moving *Sabrina*'s release date to the winter of 1995.

Going into production Harrison Ford was well aware of the perception that the original *Sabrina*, although still loved by fans, had not aged very well. "I hadn't seen the original when I read the [new] script [but] then I was disadvantaged in talking about the script by not having seen the original, so I went and looked at it. I thought Audrey Hepburn was extraordinary as a presence, a personality. I loved Bill Holden. I felt as uncomfortable watching Humphrey Bogart as I think he was being there. The movie had a very dated period feel to it. [Billy] Wilder is a great director, so it's unsuccessful now mostly just because of the passage of time." Still, Ford felt that the script could be successfully updated to appeal to contemporary audiences.

Ford got along well with his costars, although Greg Kinnear admitted to being a nervous wreck over the prospect of making his film debut opposite the world's most popular movie star. Kinnear had auditioned for the

As the hugely successful businessman Linus Larrabee (Paramount Pictures)

role three months prior to finally receiving the word that the part was his. Still in awe, and still in disbelief at landing the role, he arrived on the set feeling very much like an outsider. Ford immediately put him at ease. "It seems to me that the bigger they are, the more powerful they are, you get a sense that they can be any way they want," Kinnear reflected. "Sometimes that can be very dark and negative . . . but Harrison is the exact opposite . . . he's unbelievably gracious, nice, and down-to-earth. He didn't have to go out of his way to make this an easy experience for me, but he did from the very first day. I was standing around and it seemed everybody knew everybody else, except for me. I was just the guy standing in the corner eating a bran muffin. I felt very awkward. All of a sudden, up walked Harrison and he said, 'So, you're my brother, huh? Goddamned good looking, isn't he?' And everyone started laughing. I will be eternally grateful to him for that."

The fact that the cast and crew interacted so enthusiastically made *Sabrina* a rewarding experience for all concerned. How does the film fare as entertainment, as well as in comparison with the original? Very well, indeed. The filmmakers wisely chose to update the screenplay, but not in any obvious or overt ways. The new incarnation of *Sabrina,* which was regarded as an old-fashioned love story back in 1954, seems even more nostalgic today. Amazingly, the dialogue remains tasteful and we are not subjected to any sequences of gratuitous sex—a virtual impossibility in contemporary cinema. Ford acknowledged that all of this was intentional: "I think this is a family picture, which I haven't done in a while. There is no swearing, no ill treatment of women, no gratuitous sex or violence. I think it could be a film that women make their men go see. But once there, men will be engaged by it."

The original *Sabrina* has been criticized as being rather lightweight, with much emphasis placed on what many felt was the miscasting of Humphrey Bogart in a role clearly suited for a much younger man. (Interestingly, Bogart was fifty-five when he played Linus, while Ford, at fifty-three, appears much more youthful and the romance between Linus and Sabrina much more believable.) Yet, it remains sterling entertainment, evok-

ing a time in which movies with sparkling wit and interesting characters were the norm. The 1995 version captures all the charm of its predecessor and impresses with an equally capable cast.

Sabrina is very much an ensemble piece, with each star getting plenty of opportunities to shine. It's a real pleasure to see Harrison Ford's not inconsiderable comedic talents put to use; he underplays the role of what is essentially a cold and cranky character, and makes him gain our sympathy. Ford doesn't need one-liners to get laughs. He plays his role in a low-key manner (much as Bogart did, albeit more "comfortably") and evokes more laughs with a facial expression than most actors can get with a pratfall. He displays genuine chemistry with Julia Ormond, who is quite wonderful and radiant in the title role. The scene stealer, however, is Greg Kinnear, in a surprisingly accomplished screen debut. The memory of William Holden's amusing performance in the same role is quite strong, and to Kinnear's credit he does equal justice to the part. Also registering well are Nancy Marchand as the obnoxious but somehow likable family matriarch, and John Wood, wonderfully dignified as the loyal family chauffeur.

The script remains very close to the original, even

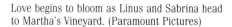
Love begins to bloom as Linus and Sabrina head to Martha's Vineyard. (Paramount Pictures)

unique way and she makes the 1995 *Sabrina* shine just as much as Hepburn did forty years earlier. The movie performed rather unspectacularly at the box-office (topping out at around $54 million in America), perhaps because in an age of big budget summer action extravaganzas, audiences are too impatient for a deliberately paced, intelligent comedy. In any event, on an artistic level, *Sabrina* is a worthy effort by all concerned and a movie whose charms are certain to be appreciated more in the years to come than at the time of the film's release.

Reviews

"Sabrina is the cinematic equivalent of comfort food—it soothed when you were younger and, in its familiarity, it soothes again. . . . Harrison Ford only occasionally [looks] as miserable as Humphrey Bogart apparently was when making the original. . . . Ford's own enormous sense of gravity is perfect for the dour Linus, except that you have to wonder how such a handsome guy could have such unquenchable dry mouth around women"

—JAMI BERNARD, NEW YORK POST

"The guilty pleasure of this holiday movie season. . . . The new film gives more emphasis to Linus Larrabee. . . . Now, as played more invitingly by Harrison Ford, this becomes a Robert Redford role. As in the many times in which Mr. Pollack has directed Mr. Redford, the leading man is aloof, guarded, and so quietly dashing that others are willing to overlook his unfriendliness and coax him in from the cold. Mr. Ford shares the Redford knack for suggesting all this with a twinkle in his eye."

—JANET MASLIN, NEW YORK TIMES

"It's said that they don't make movies like Sabrina anymore. . . . This 1995 version shows that they occasionally do. . . . The new version is just as satisfying, if not as dry and cynical, as the original."

—ROGER EBERT, SYNDICATED

leaving some of the original lines intact, possibly because the filmmakers were wise enough not to attempt to improve a Billy Wilder movie. There are a few minor changes and plot devices added, but like the 1954 version, this is a film which truly sparkles with wit and is never the slightest bit boring, despite the fact that it is virtually all talk and very little action. Due to his popularity, Ford's character is given more screen time, and he gets to flex his comic chops and to display a soft side to this somewhat obsessed businessman. The new version has a visual splendor lacking from the original, which symbolized Paris in a comedic way by showing an obvious backdrop of the Eiffel Tower through the window. In Ford's *Sabrina*, much is made of Paris being the world's most romantic city, and director Pollack fully capitalizes on the City of Light's charms by shooting extensively on location. After seeing this film, viewers want to immediately pack their bags and head to France.

Critics were kind to *Sabrina* and the film received generally solid, if not enthusiastic reviews. Ford's performance was well received and he was nominated for a Golden Globe award. However, Julia Ormond found that she was consistently compared with the legendary Audrey Hepburn's larger-than-life benchmark performance. This is unfortunate, as Ormand is equally charming in her own

32

The Devil's Own (1997)

*"I didn't want to make an apology or an argument for the I.R.A.
I just wanted to be seen wrestling with the question."*

CAST:
Tom O'Meara: Harrison Ford; *Francis "Frankie" McGuire/Rory Devaney*: Brad Pitt; *Sheila O'Meara*: Margaret Colin; *Edwin Diaz*: Ruben Blades; *Billy Burke*: Treat Williams; *Peter Fitzsimmons*: George Hearn; *Chief Jim Kelly*: Mitchell Ryan; *Megan Doherty*: Natascha McElhone; *Sean Phelan*: Paul Ronan; *Harry Sloan*: Simon Jones.

CREDITS:
Director: Alan J. Pakula; *Executive Producers*: Lloyd Levin and Donald Laventhall; *Producers*: Lawrence Gordon and Robert F Colesberry; *Screenplay*: David Aaron Cohen, Vincent Patrick, and Kevin Jarre; *From a story by*: Kevin Jarre; *Director of Photography*: Gordon Willis; *Production Designer*: Jane Musky; *Editors*: Tom Rolf and Dennis Virkler; *Music*: James Horner. *Running time*: 107 minutes. A Lawrence Gordon Production. Released by Columbia Pictures

Perhaps no other political issue has been as difficult to present on screen than the situation in Northern Ireland. Yet "the troubles" (as the Irish refer to the bloody decades of anti-British I.R.A. activities) are an irresistible subject matter for socially conscious filmmakers. Because of the passionate and divisive feelings which arise at the very mention of the I.R.A., screenwriters have been drawn to the subject as the inspiration for a number of acclaimed cinematic achievements dating back to 1935's *The Informer*. Memorable films of a more recent era dealing with the subject include 1992's *Patriot Games*. The last proved to be a difficult and controversial project to bring to the screen despite the fact that it was marketed primarily as a Harrison Ford action-adventure film. Among the key controversies: heated debates about whether the script was too sympathetic to the British point of view.

Despite all the trials and tribulations that engulfed the filming of *Patriot Games*, Ford became intrigued just a few short years later by another high profile script centering on the Irish "troubles." *The Devil's Own* had been a pet project of producer Lawrence Gordon (*Die Hard, 48Hrs.*) and his partner Robert F. Colesberry for nearly ten years. The story centered on the relationship between a young, charismatic I.R.A. member named Devaney who is wanted by British authorities for a series of high profile slayings of soldiers and policemen in Northern Ireland. Forced to flee to New York, he is boarded by police officer Tom O'Meara. The two men become fast friends until

231

ous points, but at Pitt's suggestion, Harrison Ford was approached, who surprised them by enthusiastically agreeing to sign on. With Ford's involvement, however, *The Devil's Own* entered a whole new realm, evolving into a major "event" film.

The teaming of Ford, the world's greatest box-office attraction, with up-and-coming phenomenon Pitt was initially regarded as a major coup for Columbia—despite the fact that the combined salaries exceeded the entire estimated budget. (Ford would receive a whopping $20 million and 15 percent of the gross, while Pitt had to make due with $9 million, later upped to $12 million, and 10 percent of the gross). The next step was to find a director agreeable to both stars, each of whom wielded considerable clout. Ultimately, Alan J. Pakula, who had directed Harrison Ford in *Presumed Innocent*, signed on for $5 million. At this point, the budget for salaries alone for this once modest character study had ballooned to $37 million . . . without a single frame of film having been shot.

Ford and Pitt were genuinely eager to step into roles which each represented a stretch compared to their normal screen personas. For Pitt, playing an I.R.A. member would help him shed his image as a pretty boy idol. Of his role as ordinary police officer Tom O'Meara, Harrison Ford said, "I don't pretend to be younger than my age. When I run, I get out of breath and I limp after hurting my leg." He later added, "I liked this part because it was different from any part I've played recently. He's a blue collar guy, a responsible family man whose world completely changes as a result of complications that ensue from taking this young man into his home."

As usual, Ford delved into a period of intense research to ensure he played his part with conviction. He spent weeks riding in squad cars with New York City police officers. "I've already seen it all," he said. "Robbings, stabbings, shootings, drugs, you name it." Ford even experimented by growing a mustache for the role, but decided to shave it before filming began. Pitt was also committed to making Devaney a believable, three-dimensional figure. He traveled through Ireland and hobnobbed with the citizenry to gain insight into how the I.R.A. was perceived. While abroad, he studied with dialect coach Brendan Gunn and returned with a very convincing Irish brogue.

With Ford having signed aboard, the role of Sgt. O'Meara would have to be expanded upon to capitalize on his star power. However, it was Kevin Jarre's original script which had first enthused Pitt years earlier. A gritty, unsentimental tale, it presented two characters who

O'Meara discovers Devaney's background. This knowledge thrusts him into a moral dilemma: as a police officer, he is compelled to arrest Devaney before he can complete a major arms deal, but being of Irish ancestry and knowing the tragedy Devaney has faced in such a short life, he sympathizes with the young man's cause. The tortured relationship between the two men is the basis of the script, although in the original version O'Meara was very much a supporting character.

As early as 1991, Lawrence Gordon persuaded Brad Pitt to star as Devaney. The film became a personal crusade for both men, but no major studio would touch the hot potato subject matter. Ultimately, the duo convinced Columbia Pictures chief Mark Canton to allocate an estimated $30 million for the production. The studio was of the opinion that Pitt—pre–*Legends of the Fall* and *Interview With the Vampire*—could not carry a major film alone, so they were looking to flesh out the character of O'Meara and to cast a major star in the role. Both Gene Hackman and Sean Connery had been considered at vari-

Buddies Diaz (Ruben Blades), O'Meara (Ford), and Devane (Brad Pitt) (Columbia TriStar)

would not exactly endear themselves to the audience. O'Meara was especially unsympathetic, presented as a hard-nosed, foul-mouthed cop. The character of Devaney had most of the screen time and had his own demons to bear, including drug addiction. Additionally, Devaney was depicted as being a rather vicious person who slaughters British soldiers without the slightest hint of remorse. Ultimately, Jarre's script was to receive radical changes from screenwriters Vincent Patrick and David Aaron Cohen. Thus began an odyssey of troubles that became the talk of the film industry.

The new scripts had to please Ford, Pitt, and Pakula. However, it became clear that Pitt's vision of the film differed substantially from that of his costar and his director. Consequently, as the movie went into production, the script was being rewritten on a day-to-day basis—a precarious situation for all parties involved. Columbia executives became increasingly nervous as costs skyrocketed. Rumors spread that Pitt began to resent Ford and Pakula's attempts to move the script in their own direction, fearing it was becoming "Patriot Games II." He griped, "I'm used to working on movies where the script gets written *beforehand.*" He would later say, "The first draft we had was full of leprechaun jokes and green beer. I had this responsibility to represent somewhat these people whose lives have been shattered. It would have been an injustice to Hollywoodize it. It was coming very close to shooting time. It made me very uneasy. . . . I know how it gets on a set. It costs $150,000 a day to shoot and we have to shoot something the next day and if we don't have it written down, things get sloppy."

Despite all of the obstacles, principal photography began on location in New York City in January, 1996. Even the weather proved problematic, as the region had suffered through record snowfalls during the season. Still, Harrison Ford was enthused about filming in the Big Apple. "You can't replicate New York," he said. "It's unlike any place in the world. The combination of the architec-

ture and the people who live here is so distinctive as to be unreproducable anywhere else." The company shot at a number of intriguing locations including the Cloisters museum, the Staten Island Ferry, Wollman Rink in Central Park, and numerous Irish bars. Interiors were shot in Kaufman Astoria Studios in Queens and additional location photography was done in Brooklyn and New Jersey. During production, Ford occasionally frequented the popular "Hogs and Heifers" bar in lower Manhattan, where he played pool with the crew, and on one occasion even uncharacteristically followed the tradition of dancing on the bar with a bra on his head. The press had a field day, as Ford is generally shy about drawing public attention to himself.

Things were not so happy back on the set, however. Tensions began to mount as rumors spread that the stars were at constant odds. The studio denied the rumors, but continuing script problems gave credence to reports that all was not well. Pitt allegedly disagreed with the direction the story was taking and with the softening of the characters. O'Meara was now a sympathe- tic family man and "by the book" cop who prided himself on following regulations. Ford defended the changes saying, "The char-

233

Tom (with wife Sheila, played by Margaret Colin) begins to suspect that something is amiss with Rory. (Columbia TriStar)

acter in the original script would have been very difficult, I believe, for the audience to accept. . . . The film was pretty unabashed in its admiration for the I.R.A. and all things Irish. It was less even-handed, I believed." Siding with Ford was Pakula, who said of the original story: "There was a lot more stuff in Irish-American bars, a lot more stuff about the Irish-American world, which Brad loved and which I felt was not necessarily germane to the story."

Pitt did not agree with Pakula and threatened to quit the production. Columbia responded by letting him know that the studio would expect him to pay $63 million in compensation or be sued. According to Pitt: "They sell movies to foreign territories on box-office names and they can sue on what they could have made if you'd stayed in the movie." Reluctantly, Pitt stayed on board. One script modification he did like was the softening of his own character by showing him in a more sympathetic light. A prologue was included in which a very young Devaney wit-

nesses the murder of his own father by anti-I.R.A. forces.

With the production lagging along, Pakula brought in writer Terry George to help develop Pitt's character further. In March, 1996 he hired yet another screen doctor, Robert Mark Kamen (who would go uncredited in the final film). Kamen immediately noted the difficulties on the set: "They were running out of script to shoot. They had a script that wasn't acceptable to either actor. Alan didn't start with a script that everyone had signed off on. We were flying blind. . . . It was scary." Some days, Kamen was retooling dialogue right up to the moment of shooting. He met with Ford and Pitt both separately and together to discuss their ideas about improving the script. Kamen insisted that, rumors to the contrary, the actors were agreeable to each other. "It wasn't the tension between them that made things tense," he insisted, "It was the tension each had with their own parts."

Eventually, *The Devil's Own* completed principal shooting in July—following a full seven month production

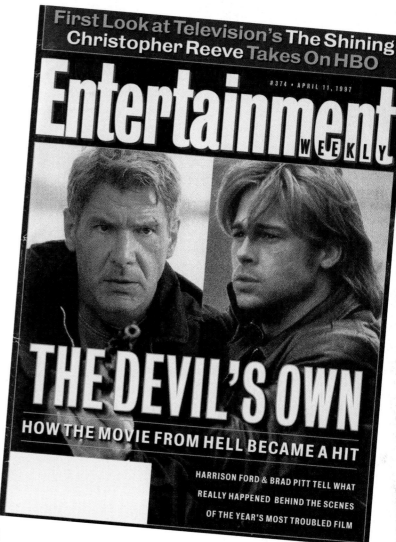

schedule. However, there were still dissatisfactions with various elements of the film, particularly the climactic confrontation between Devaney and O'Meara reluctantly facing each other down on a fishing boat that Devaney is using to bring weapons back to Ireland. It was agreed that the ending should be reshot, and in February 1997, Ford was summoned from the set of *Air Force One*. According to Ford "It was the same ending, just better. We have a better staging of it. We have one detail we thought of, which is that I get shot as well, but mostly it was to get a better photographic relationship between the two of us." By the time the film was completed, *The Devil's Own* was over schedule and way over budget. The movie once estimated at $30 million came in at a cost said to be between $77 and $90 million—a sizable cost for a film lacking hi-tech sets and special effects.

Trouble continued to brew even after filming: Shortly before the movie was released Brad Pitt gave a highly publicized and much quoted interview to *Newsweek* in which he blasted the production. "We had no script," he said. "Well, we had a great script, but it got tossed for various reasons. It was the most irresponsible bit of filmmaking—if you could call it that—that I've ever seen." Pitt then went on to personally insult Canton, accusing him of making an inferior film rather than suffer the indignity of admitting the project never should have gone forward. Predictably, Columbia found itself in the unenviable position of having to market *The Devil's Own* at the precise time the *Newsweek* article ran. The press had a field day and the word spread that the studio had an unsalvageable lemon on its hands.

The studio, Ford, and Pakula rallied to defend the movie and to put Pitt's comments in context. Producer Gordon reminded everyone that Pitt had skewered the *process* of making the film, but had not passed judgment on the movie itself. Pitt had second thoughts about his comments, and after pressure was applied by the studio, made a retraction (of sorts) through a press release that stated in part: "In response to the *Newsweek* article, I want to convey that I was giving the journalist a chronological history prior to shooting. I am not bashing the film or Mark Canton. On the contrary, what resulted from this challenge was hard work and dedication from people I've grown to love and respect and a film I am very proud of."

Harrison Ford defended his costar, saying, "I don't blame Brad at all for what he said. We simply weren't able to develop a script that satisfied everybody involved in that amount of time. And so, we had to start shooting without a complete script—not even a first act. I felt the same way he did, and we all felt it would be a very difficult shoot. But I was determined to work through it. . . . It was tough working under those kind of circumstances. I think he was a trouper about that. He made a difficult job easier. There was no rivalry between the two of us for more screen time. I would be very happy to work with him again."

Ford also addressed another area of speculation by gossip columnists: that there were hard feelings between him and Pitt because of rival productions centering on the Dalai Lama. Ford's wife Melissa Matheson was scripting Martin Scorsese's *Kundun* at the time, while Pitt was set to follow *The Devil's Own* with *Seven Years in Tibet*, which—like *Kundun*—examined the Dalai Lama's early life. Clearly, even Hollywood wasn't a big enough town for two large-budget Dalai Lama epics. Still, Ford denied the competing productions in any way affected his relationship with Pitt and said he was "personally insulted" at the suggestion.

With so much written about the troubled production history of *The Devil's Own*, how does the final cut fare as entertainment? Very well, indeed. Surprisingly, given that the script ultimately had the fingerprints of numerous writers on it, the story holds together in a cohesive and engrossing manner. Most importantly, we immediately accept that O'Meara and Devaney have genuinely bonded, thus setting the stage for the tragic confrontation between two men who cannot let their personal respect and affection for each other stand in the way of their principles. Director Alan J. Pakula makes the most of the New York City locations and the film has a gritty, realistic feel to it.

Harrison Ford is especially convincing as the everyday cop who finds that an act of generosity has placed his family in mortal danger. It's a complex role and he plays it with total conviction. This is a unique quality of Ford's: Despite being associated with larger-than-life characters such as Indiana Jones, he also possesses the ability to play ordinary working men. In *The Devil's Own* he generates sympathy from the audience because he is a man who has always played by the rules and now finds himself questioning his own principles. Brad Pitt holds his own in his scenes with Ford, although he tends to underplay the character of Devaney. He has mastered an Irish accent and though there is not a false note in his performance, one would have liked him to be a bit more charismatic. In the scenes in which he confronts a slimy arms dealer played by Treat Williams, it is Williams who electrifies the screen.

The film is not a major achievement in either Ford's or Pitt's career, possibly because there isn't a specific sequence that lingers in the mind. This is especially apparent in the climactic shootout. The finale is rather routine and predictable, and despite the fact that the actors have made us care about their characters, for all the pathos, the death of Devaney at his benefactor's hands is somehow less than moving. Although the two films are vastly different, one cannot help but compare the climax of *The Devil's Own* with that of *Patriot Games*. After all, both movies feature Harrison Ford battling to the death against a blond I.R.A. member aboard a boat.

When *The Devil's Own* finally premiered in early 1997, its initial grosses were good, though not spectacular. However, anemic reviews and a lackluster ad campaign that failed to signify what the story was about took their toll. The film was also the center of a cause célèbre, as was *Patriot Games*, in that some critics labeled it pro-I.R.A. Ford and Pakula argued that it was their intention merely to show a balanced view of the Irish conflict. The movie ultimately grossed $43 million in the U.S.—far short of its production costs. However, foreign box-office and strong video revenues eventually allowed Columbia to recoup its money. *The Devil's Own* does not represent one of Harrison Ford's finest screen efforts. Yet, even when his films fall short artistically, they are always ambitious in nature. This one is no different.

Reviews

"An eloquent apology for murderous terrorism. . . . No amount of acting excellence can cover this movie's devilish attempt to rationalize and to glamorize the most deadly sort of political violence."

—MICHAEL MEDVED, NEW YORK POST

"Ford and Pitt are enormously appealing and gifted actors, and to the degree that the movie works, it's because of them. Using all the gifts of the actor's craft, they're able to sell scenes that don't make sense and don't add up. . . . The Devil's Own (what does the title mean?) plays better if you don't give it a single thought and just let the knee-jerk cues dictate your emotions"

—ROGER EBERT, SYNDICATED

"If you've got Harrison Ford and Brad Pitt, do you really need a coherent script? Unfortunately for everyone concerned, the answer is 'yes.' . . . The story line feels random, haphazard, even patched together. . . . The jolts of star power that Ford and Pitt provide make [it] watchable even when it shouldn't be. The difficulty is that, in their apparent rush to see that neither performer got shortchanged, the filmmakers ended up creating a pair of equal but separate scenarios. Ford has his own half-movie, thank you very much, and Pitt has his, and though they collide at times, they mostly glide by each other like supertankers in the night. . . . Though their scenes together do have a cross-generational summit conference quality, for the most part Ford and Pitt manage to share the screen nicely, giving [the film] a wistful 'what-might-have-been' quality."

—KENNETH TURAN, LOS ANGELES TIMES

Air Force One (1997)

"It's an action-adventure. It's a kickass summer movie, and when it's all said and done, this is a kickass president."

CAST

President James Marshall: Harrison Ford; *Ivan Korshunov*: Gary Oldman; *Vice President Kathryn Bennett*: Glenn Close; *Grace Marshall*: Wendy Crewson; *Chief of Staff Lloyd Shepherd*: Paul Guilfoyle; *Major Caldwell*: William H. Macy; *Alice Marshall*: Liesel Matthews; *Defense Secretary Walter Dean*: Dean Stockwell; *Agent Gibbs*: Xander Berkeley.

CREDITS

Director: Wolfgang Petersen; *Executive Producers*: Thomas A. Bliss, Marc Abraham, and David Lester; *Producers*: Wolfgang Petersen, Gail Katz, Armyan Bernstein, and Jon Shestack; *Screenplay*: Andrew W. Marlowe; *Director of Photography*: Michael Ballhaus; *Production Designer*: William Sandell; *Visual Effects Supervisor*: Richard Edlund; *Editor*: Richard Francis-Bruce; *Music*: Jerry Goldsmith. *Running time*: 118 minutes. A Radiant Production. Release by Columbia Pictures.

The trials and tribulations of filming *The Devil's Own* were still weighing upon Harrison Ford as he considered his next film project. By all accounts, he was eager for a change of pace and did not want to make another "message" picture, opting instead for an escapist entertainment vehicle. Ford settled upon the comedy *Six Days, Seven Nights* for Touchstone. Before the production schedule could be finalized, however, fate was about to deliver an unexpected opportunity for Ford to make one of the most popular films of his career.

The script for *Air Force One* was written by first-time screenwriter Andrew W. Marlowe and sold to Armyan Bernstein of Beacon Pictures, who intended to develop the movie for Kevin Costner. When Costner's schedule precluded him from participating, the actor suggested they send the script to Harrison Ford. Ford's manager, Pat McQueeney, instantly recognized the potential for a sizable hit. According to Bernstein, "She called us back the next day and said, 'This may be the best action movie I've ever read.' We said, 'What does that mean?' She said, 'Let's give it to the Big Man.' " Ford, long respectful of McQueeney's instincts for script recommendations, agreed to do the film and postponed *Six Days, Seven Nights* six months to accommodate the production schedule.

Ford received $20 million—100 times the salary of the real president—for his services at a time when the industry was reassessing whether leading actors could justify their exorbitant salaries. A recent string of flops by

As President James Marshall (Columbia TriStar)

trophobic setting. Ford was quoted as saying, "*Air Force One* is a 'tube' movie," referring to the confined setting of the film. "Wolfgang is one of the great tube movie makers." He later explained, "One of the problems about working in a confined space is reinventing the visual components so they don't become too repetitive. . . . I had the good fortune to have recently seen Wolfgang's recut of *Das Boot* and what he's able to do is manipulate the tension in new and interesting ways that always turn it back to human behavior. He also always brings a moral context to the stories he tells. I find that fascinating."

Indeed, Petersen's work on *Das Boot* was universally acclaimed and the film has become a modern classic of the war movie genre. Petersen was intrigued by the timeliness of a plot dealing with the possible catastrophic results of modern terrorism: "*Air Force One* starts with a realistic premise, and then, as I like to do in all my movies, creates thrills by heightening the reality. The reality of international terrorism has, unfortunately, become something we accept as part of modern life. But such acts are usually narrow in their focus and limited in their impact. We have created a scenario in which the success of a single terrorist act could have a drastic effect on the entire free world." Petersen was excited by the prospect of casting Ford as the President of the United States. He said, "You're not going to see Harrison Ford sitting at a desk in the Oval Office in this movie. This president is a man of action and there is no other actor who can match Harrison's combination of strength and intelligence in this kind of role."

The script provided an equally strong role for Gary Oldman, cast as Korshunov, the complex and fanatical leader of the terrorists. Although the man is clearly a murderer, the script refreshingly provides genuine reasons for his actions. No matter how twisted, he is motivated by a sincere political ideal. Korshunov is enraged when President Marshall aides in the capture of a fanatical Soviet nationalist general from a former Iron Curtain satellite country. Now jailed in Russia, the general has become a political martyr for hard-line Communist sympathizers. Korshunov and his confederates pose as a news crew to gain access to Air Force One during the President's triumphant trip to Russia. On board, they slay a number of Secret Service agents and hold the passengers (including the First Lady and First Daughter)

Sylvester Stallone, for example, was making studios nervous about guaranteeing such fees to stars of dubious bankability. Despite the middling box-office performance of *Sabrina,* however, Ford still had the confidence of the studios, particularly since his last action film, *Clear and Present Danger,* was an undisputed financial success. Ford was enthused about *Air Force One,* which would cast him as President James Marshall, who finds himself and his staff hijacked by nationalist terrorists from the former Soviet Union. Ford liked the challenge of making a suspense film which would be largely limited to confined spaces, in this instance the airborne Air Force One itself and the command center in Washington where the Vice President and her staff desperately attempt to resolve the crisis.

The choice of a director was pivotal, and Ford was instrumental in choosing Wolfgang Petersen, the acclaimed director of *In the Line of Fire.* However, what impressed Ford most was Petersen's earlier work on *Das Boot,* which examined the lives of a German U-Boat crew throughout World War II. That Oscar-winning drama showed Petersen's skill at evoking tension within a claus-

Marshall (with the First Lady, played by Wendy Crewson, and daughter Alice, played by Liesel Matthews) struggles with his duty to his country and his love for his family. (Columbia TriStar)

hostage in an attempt to win freedom for the jailed general. President Marshall manages to hide aboard the plane and plays a dangerous cat-and-mouse game with Korshunov and his men as the vice president debates whether to violate Marshall's vow never to negotiate with terrorists or to sign his death warrant by refusing to compromise. Oldman confessed to being reluctant to accept the part, having tired of playing villains in a number of high profile films. However, he did admit that it turned out to be "fun knocking Indiana Jones around."

The key role of the vice president went to Glenn Close, although her route to being in the film was rather unorthodox. She and Harrison Ford were among the guests at President Clinton's fiftieth birthday celebration, held in Ford's hometown of Jackson Hole, Wyoming. Ford and Petersen had been considering asking Close to play the role of the harried VP, but had heard that she was unavailable. Ford used the Clinton dinner as an unexpected opportunity to woo her. She later recalled, "Halfway through dinner, Harrison came over and knelt down on the president's left and said 'Would you like to be my vice president?' Under those circumstances, I don't think I could say no!" Ironically, the two share no scenes together, although Ford courteously came to the set the day Close had to film an important sequence in which she talks with the president by phone. Ford was there with Close to recite his lines to help her with the emotions of the scene. According to Petersen, this type of professionalism—a major star giving up a day off out of respect to a fellow actor—is all too rare in the industry.

The presidential dinner also provided another unforeseen benefit: President Clinton granted the filmmakers the permission to tour Air Force One the next day to ensure the details were correct. Although footage could not be taken onboard, this tour aided production designer William Sandell immeasurably. The resulting set (part of which was used in *Executive Decision*), is an outstanding achievement, even though Sandell had to "open up" the space considerably for logistical reasons. Artistic license

was taken in certain areas (for example, the real plane doesn't contain an escape pod for the president), but on the whole, accuracy was maintained. (The plane *can* be refueled in flight and *can* withstand the force of a nuclear blast.) Ford confessed to being disappointed that Air Force One did not contain "any of those 'Only-The-President-May-Push-This' buttons."

The Pentagon, perhaps inspired by the fact that this was one of the few films in recent years to portray the presidency and the U.S. government favorably, gave its enthusiastic support, and the Secret Service provided agents as technical consultants. The government gave permission for the filmmakers to use Rickenbacker Air National Guard Base in Columbus, Ohio, as a double for

239

Glenn Close as the more-than-capable Vice President Kathryn Bennett (Columbia TriStar)

hard!' Harrison was just the opposite." During a key sequence in which Oldman was to punch him squarely in the face, Ford insisted the blow be real. Oldman was uncomfortable with the notion, but Ford Insisted. He later explained that it added realism to the sequence. "I think the fact that my face is [in the scene] adds a veracity to the experience and an emotional component that's missing when it's done by a stunt guy." When Ford's face would become too battered and bruised, Petersen would delay shooting certain scenes until the swelling subsided. Ford argued that he wasn't taking any inordinate risks and that the physical action was therapeutic. "I didn't even think about the physicality of it," he said. "It's all choreographed, all plotted out. The fun of it for me is it's like an athletic endeavor. You choreograph it, you set your mind on what it is; you don't want to hurt somebody, you want to be very sure of your moves. It's a pleasure to perform those things for me, like playing tennis or ballet dancing." (Fortunately, Ford's penchant for such exercise did not extend to him donning a tutu.)

Ford was determined not to play the president as a clichéd character (i.e., always cool and in complete control). Although the script explains his expertise in hand-to-hand combat as the result of actions in Vietnam that won him the Medal of Honor, Ford wanted to play James Marshall as an everyday man who was uncertain of his decisions under extreme duress. He explained, "The poetry of this piece, though, is that he is put under pressure immediately, in the most personal way." Referring to terrorists threatening his wife and twelve-year-old daughter, he said, "His political pronouncement is tested against his experience and his responsibilities as a father and a husband. He behaves differently where his family is concerned than he does as a statesman and a spokesman for our policy. This is understandable, and I think we actually think the more of him for his humanity." He later said, "What I found most interesting in exploring the role was the incredible responsibility that the president has—how there is no one moment in his life when he's not beholden to the country's welfare ahead of his own or his family's. As I reflected on it, I was impressed with the enormous burden of the presidency. I also thought it was a compelling story with a satisfying sense of triumph at its conclusion."

By all accounts, filming *Air Force One* was an invigorating and highly enjoyable experience. Ford and many on the crew called it "Air Force Fun." "It always helps to have a congenial atmosphere and we certainly had that,"

Germany's Ramstein Air Field, for the pivotal sequence in which Air Force One makes an aborted attempt at landing. The scene was accomplished using an actual plane, miniatures, and computer graphics. To get the proper lighting, the crew had only a fifteen minute window between dusk and nightfall. The result on screen is a seamlessly edited and very thrilling sequence. Even Petersen found it difficult to distinguish the real planes from the "reel" planes in the final cut.

Not all of the action on screen was hi-tech. The fight sequences in *Air Force One* were the most brutal and demanding of Ford's career and made somewhat trivial his earlier concerns that he might be getting too old to portray a man of action. According to Director of Photography Michael Ballhaus, Ford "did ninety percent of his own stunts. Normally, when people get beaten up in a scene, they're always scared. They say 'Don't hit me too

AIR FORCE ONE

Ford was perfectly cast as the "Last Action President." (Columbia TriStar)

Ford said. Wolfgang Petersen delivers an intelligent action thriller that has moments of almost unbearable tension. The once far-fetched scenario now seems plausible in this age of modern terrorism. All too often the actors get lost in the pyrotechnics of a film like this, but Petersen is a strong enough director to ensure that the movie never loses its emphasis on human elements. Unlike most contemporary action films, life is a precious commodity in *Air Force One* and when someone is killed, the audience feels the pure terror of the moment.

Refreshingly absent are the standard characters generally found in such scenarios. There isn't a lovable Rabbi, a singing nun, or a deathly ill child among the passengers. Instead, we find a believable mix of people. Some are heroic, but most are just very frightened. This includes Ford's President Marshall. At times he is filled with self-doubt and although he is a man of action, he is

clearly uncomfortable having to resort to violence. It's an amazing performance—one, which Petersen correctly pointed out, should have earned him an Oscar nomination. (The film was nominated in the categories of Sound and Editing). When Ford is forced to concede to his antagonist in order to save his family, the pent-up emotion he releases makes this one of the most powerfully acted sequences of his career.

Ford is ably assisted by a powerhouse cast, each of whom wisely resists the opportunity to overact. This is especially true of Gary Oldman, who makes the terrorist monster he plays somehow pitiable. The British Oldman, who boasts a highly believable Russian accent, is electrifying as the misguided miscreant who believes he can solve questions of international importance through the slaughter of innocent people. Yet, in a highly poignant sequence in which he gently explains his motives to the

241

President's young daughter, he is so riveting that you almost come to think of his actions as justified. However, this is at heart an old-fashioned film in which the good guys and the bad guys must ultimately be clearly distinguished, and the final confrontation between Ford and Oldman is indeed thrilling.

Glenn Close has considerable screen time. Again, the script avoids the clichés and refrains from portraying the character as a helpless female or an Amazon warrior. Close's VP deals with nerve-wracking decisions having to do with everything from the scheduled execution of hostages to Constitutional questions about the limit of her authority in moments of crisis. It's a highly skilled performance.

Air Force One has several flaws, but they are relatively minor. For one, much is made about how it would be virtually impossible for terrorists to board the president's plane without a fingerprint check, yet it is never explained how the Oldman character and his men avert such detection. Additionally, the inclusion of a Secret Service agent who betrays the President is a bit over the top, especially when this key character has no motive for his actions. He clearly is not sympathetic to the ethnic concerns of his confederates, so is his motive purely financial? Petersen admits the character explained his motives in the climax, but the scene was cut because it slowed the pace. Editing the scene was one of the few mistakes Petersen made, as it provides the film's only glaring false note.

Air Force One caused a mini-controversy when it was announced that it was to be released in July, 1997 on the same day that Paramount planned to open James Cameron's long-anticipated blockbuster *Titanic*. Ford personally called Jonathan Dolgen, head of Viacom Entertainment (parent company of Paramount) and exerted pressure to reschedule the opening of *Titanic*. Although *Air Force One* was made for Columbia, Ford's box-office pull for Paramount had earned him considerable respect. According to Pat McQueeney, "Harrison was definitely irritated. It was a friendly phone call. But Harrison did say 'Jonathan, what the hell are you doing?' Harrison gets involved in every aspect of his films, including the business side and it's bad business to open two movies on the same date, much less three of them." (The third was Mel Gibson's *Conspiracy Theory*.) Ford prevailed, and Paramount agreed to reschedule the launch of *Titanic*, though the point would later be made moot by James Cameron's inability to deliver a final cut of the film on schedule. (It eventually opened in December 1997.)

Air Force One was a summer smash for Columbia. Although critics saw the film for what it was—pure escapist entertainment—they praised the production as an enormously efficient example of movie making. Ford was given high marks for his portrayal of the President, though he had to deny repeatedly that he was attempting to glorify Bill Clinton. The movie was a towering box-office hit (scoring the largest-ever weekend opening for an R-rated film) and generated additional millions upon its release on home video. As for Harrison Ford, there were the inevitable dumb questions asked of any actor who portrays the Commander-in-Chief. Would he actually like to run for president? "I have not spent a single second imagining myself as the president," he said. "I'm not considerate enough. I'm not careful enough. I'm not educated enough. I don't have either the service or the grace that's probably necessary for the president. But given the chance, I can act."

Reviews

"You don't stay glued to the screen because a hack director has strung together a few workable formulas. [This] is gripping, nail-biting, edge-of-your-seat entertainment because you are in the hands of a master craftsman. . . . What a relief to see this underrated actor back in gear after Sabrina *and* The Devil's Own, *two rare flops in the Ford canon. His wit is dry—acerbic, but never campy."*

—Peter Travers, *Rolling Stone*

"Harrison Ford as the President of the United States is such a perfect piece of casting that it's at once a fantasy and a joke: the joke is how perfect the fantasy is."

—Owen Gleiberman, *Entertainment Weekly*

"This is a display of Ford at his best that holds us in a tight bearhug from beginning to end. . . . Ford has all the physicality necessary to make Marshall's ability to handle himself in a brawl completely plausible. What keeps Ford well ahead of the pack as an action hero, however, is his ability to convey, not only emotional intensity but also moral qualms, even worry."

—Kenneth Turan, *Los Angeles Times*

34

Six Days. Seven Nights (1998)

"It was a lot of fun. But comedy is a lot like running on slippery rocks. One misstep and you're up to your ass in cold water."

CAST:
Quinn Harris: Harrison Ford; *Robin Monroe*: Anne Heche; *Frank Martin*: David Schwimmer; *Angelica*: Jacqueline Obradors; *Jager*: Temeura Morrison.

CREDITS
Director: Ivan Reitman; *Producers*: Ivan Reitman, Wallis Nicita, and Roger Birnbaum; *Screenplay*: Michael Browning; *Production Designer*: J. Michael Riva, *Editors*: Sheldon Kahn and Wendy Greene Bricmont; *Director of Photography*: Michael Chapman; *Music*: Randy Edelman. *Running time*: 146 minutes. Released by Touchstone Pictures.

"It's a mix of manic comedy and real danger inhabited by adventure that brings two people together. It's *African Queen* meets *Dumb and Dumber*, except it's pretty smart." That is Harrison Ford's unorthodox description of his very unorthodox summer 1998 release, *Six Days, Seven Nights*, which provides Ford a rare opportunity to demonstrate his lighter side. He plays Quinn Harris, a cantankerous loner who is perfectly content flying cargo around the world in his dilapidated de Havilland Beaver plane. He crosses paths with famed New York magazine editor, Robin Monroe (Anne Heche) when he flies her and her boyfriend (later fiancé) Frank Martin (David Schwimmer) to a remote South Pacific island paradise. When Robin is assigned to an emergency magazine photo shoot in Tahiti, she bribes Quinn to fly her in his less-than-reliable plane. En route, a storm forces the odd couple onto a desert island, where they must overcome the elements as well as a band of marauding pirates. In the course of their adventure, the two fall in love, thus leading both Quinn and Robin to make dramatic decisions about the course of their lives.

The script began as a simple comic love story, however, obvious concerns about disappointing Ford's fans by failing to provide any action resulted in the inclusion of several major adventure sequences. Naturally, Ford insisted on doing as many of the stunts as possible. For one scene, he tumbled thirty feet into a lagoon amidst a rock slide. Another time, he was dangled by ankle straps over jagged rocks with a river rushing below him. Ford did not mind the resulting cuts and bruises, insisting they added realism to the sequences.

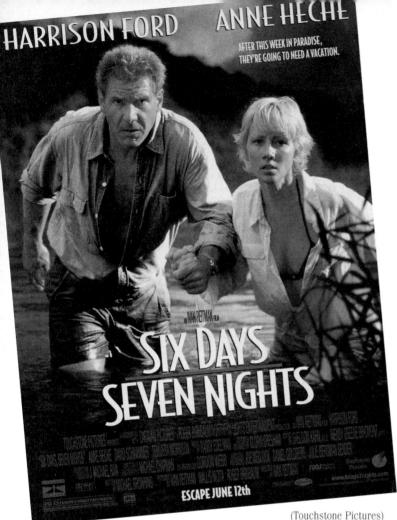

HARRISON FORD   ANNE HECHE

AFTER THIS WEEK IN PARADISE,
THEY'RE GOING TO NEED A VACATION.

SIX DAYS
SEVEN NIGHTS

ESCAPE JUNE 12th

(Touchstone Pictures)

Six Days, Seven Nights received some unwanted publicity when the film was about to go into production. Shortly after Anne Heche had been announced as Ford's romantic interest in the film, she "came out of the closet" to announce to the world that she was the lesbian lover of TV star Ellen DeGeneres. The resulting media coverage attempted to portray the filmmakers and Ford as being embarrassed by the revelation. Director Ivan Reitman (*Twins, Stripes*) confessed to having second thoughts about proceeding with casting Heche, but Ford stood firmly in support of her. "I don't have any concerns about people buying a romance between myself and Anne. She was the obvious choice . . . She brings great spark and wit and life to the part. I've never discussed any of my coworker's personal lives before, and I don't see any reason to start now."

Heche appreciated the gesture. She told *USA Today,* "If Harrison didn't want me to do this movie, I wouldn't be doing this movie. If he had said, 'Forget it,' I'd have been off the film but he was a champion, saying, 'I don't care what her sexuality is. This is who I want, she's the best for the role.'" Ultimately, Reitman's fears proved groundless. "The footage between the two of them is spectacular," he said. "There's a heat between them—I see it and they feel it. You can't fake that kind of chemistry."

The film, which was shot over a three month period on location in Kauai, Hawaii, provided another challenge for Ivan Reitman and studio executives: Ford's insistence upon doing his own flying. The concerns were logical. On a big budget production such as this, if an injury were to befall the leading man, it could lead to catastrophic delays. Still, Ford—who had been flying extensively for three years—dismissed these concerns and used his clout to indulge in his latest pastime. "I love flying," he said. "It's very important to me . . . I find it continually challenging, and it's great fun for me to continue to try to refine and polish my skills." Ford also made the argument that piloting the plane in the film would make his character more believable. He told *Premiere* magazine, "Flying is so important to this character, that one of my ambitions was to give an audience an inkling of what attracted this guy to that life, to that skill—and to do it without dialogue. And that's more easily demonstrated in an actual environment than it is on a blue screen."

Although director Reitman called this the most difficult and challenging film he had ever directed, for Ford and Heche it was, by all accounts, a very enjoyable experience. Ford was able to take his entire family with him on location, and Heche was joined for much of the time by Ellen DeGeneres. There were few mishaps despite the physical exertions demanded of the two stars. Ford ended up with a number of bumps and bruises and Heche had the unenviable experience of being stung by a scorpion—all the result of the rather last-minute decision to introduce the plot point of murderous pirates as villains. The film had initially concentrated solely on the relationship of the two castaways, but Reitman argued, "Look, we can maintain comedy for about a third of the movie. But at a certain point, they've got to meet somebody more dangerous than a pig!"

Touchstone demonstrated its faith in Ford's box-office pull by releasing the film at the beginning of the summer-movie season generally dominated by large-budget action films. While the trailers for the film made it clear *Six Days* would be a comedy, it also emphasized the adventure elements in an obvious attempt to lure the all-important younger male audience to the film. As usual, Ford made the round of talk shows to promote his movie, although Jay Leno joked with him that the prospect of appearing on TV seemed to be as appealing to Ford as being audited by the I.R.S.

Six Days is hardly a groundbreaking film for Harrison Ford, but it is an exceptionally entertaining one. Admittedly, the plot holds few surprises and the basic premise is predictable. Fortunately, the screenplay doesn't overemphasize the animosity between the two leading characters. These are not two people who hate

For the sake of realism, Ford did many of his own stunts...as always. (Bruce McBroom, Touchstone Pictures)

each other, but who simply rub each other the wrong way. Consequently, the story is able to dispense rather quickly with the mandatory scenes in which Quinn and Robin grow to respect and love each other and concentrates instead on their attempts to escape the pirates. The action sequences are exciting and occasionally genuinely suspenseful, though Quinn's ultimate scheme for escaping from the island (he rebuilds his plane using the wreck of a downed Japanese fighter plane) stretches credibility and begins to resemble *The Flight of the Phoenix* with a few coconuts thrown in.

Six Days relies heavily on the chemistry between its two stars, and Ford's early instincts to sign Heche proved to be sound. She has a wonderfully engaging screen presence that brings out the best in Ford's often latent comedic abilities. More than in any of his other attempts at light comedy, Ford genuinely appears to be enjoying himself here. As for the overblown ballyhoo regarding Heche's ability to convincingly portray a heterosexual, the actress herself pointed out that no one questioned Ford's ability to plan a womanizing adventurer when, in fact, he is a happily married movie star. The controversy diminished immediately after the film's release, with Heche receiving virtually unanimously favorable reviews. Ford was also the beneficiary of enthusiastic notices, with critic Gene Siskel comparing his comedic abilities to those of Cary Grant.

While reviews for the leading actors were favorable, critical reaction to the film itself was mixed. Most critics conceded the movie was a pleasant, lightweight entertainment, but a rather predictable one. Curiously, more than a few singled out costar David Schwimmer for harsh criticism over his portrayal of Heche's wimpy, weak-spirited fiancé who has a torrid affair with Ford's girlfriend (memorably played by newcomer Jacqueline Obradors). In fact, Schwimmer is quite effective playing the role as written. His angst over having a one-night stand during the search for his missing fiancée provides the film with some of its most amusing moments.

Six Days, Seven Nights performed reasonably well in a summer season packed with such high-profile competition as *Godzilla*, *Deep Impact*, and *Lethal Weapon IV*. It seemed to corner the market as the only "date movie" of the early summer. In an era in which interesting charac-

ters and meaningful dialogue seem all but extinct in the cinema, *Six Days* represents a welcome return to a more traditional, but very rewarding style of filmmaking. Coupled with its lush photography and gorgeous Hawaiian locations, the movie provides Harrison Ford with an entertaining vehicle in which to flex his comedic muscles.

The film is yet another example of his determination to experiment as an actor and tackle offbeat projects rather than merely concentrate on obvious choices. He recently said, "I've often spoken about the pleasure I take in the job that I do. I'm interested in the problem-solving aspect of it. I'm interested in the emotional exercise. I'm interested in the collaboration with others of craft, skill, and intellect." Ford, assessing his own success, modestly proclaimed, "I think my audience follows me, not because of me, but because I have been in good movies." Others may disagree. A 1998 Quigley Poll of theater owners and exhibitors proclaimed Ford as the most popular box-office draw in the world.

Reviews

"Deciding that escapist romance for the Treadmill Generation has to be a workout in its own right, Ivan Reitman's [film] puts its stars through the wringer. Not even in action pictures do muscles often matter the way they do here . . . A Tracy-Hepburn dynamic is meant to add spice to this situation, and to some degree it does. Ms. Heche and Mr. Ford make an

As their stay on the island begins, the thought of love never even crosses the castaways' minds. (Bruce McBroom, Touchstone Pictures)

appealing, wisecracking team, and they look comfortable with the rugged demands of their roles . . . Mr. Ford, in his role here, reaffirms that in his mid-fifties he hasn't aged out of the romantic hero racket. 'You still look good,' Ms. Heche admits. 'I still AM good,' he replies with an irresistible grin."

—JANET MASLIN, NEW YORK TIMES

"Whenever pirates turn up in a romance set more recently than 1843, you figure the filmmakers ran out of ideas. [This film] illustrates that principle. It's the kind of movie that provides diversion for the idle channel-surfer but isn't worth a trip to the theater. A lot of it seems cobbled together out of spare parts . . . The screenplay by Michael Browning has little interest in the characters—certainly not enough to provide them with a movie's worth of conversation. It's devised along standard formula lines, and so desperate for a crisis that pirates conveniently materialize on two occasions simply to give the movie something to be about . . . Ford has an easy appeal in movies like this, and never pushes too hard. Heche plays a nice duet with him."

—ROGER EBERT, SYNDICATED

"No more than a glib, professional treatment of this highly familiar material . . . Ford's presence and concentration make him, as always, a pleasure to watch,

though he comes close to overplaying his hand. Clearly concerned about the quality of the gags, he underlines the laugh points with mugged reactions, making his character seem thicker and slower than the romantic fantasy requires. His drinking problem, however, gets the movie cure, miraculously disappearing the moment true love enters his life."

—DAVID KEHR, NEW YORK DAILY NEWS

35

Random Hearts (1999)

"I see Dutch grieving in every scene, in every frame of the movie. And that's the story—the tension between the past and some potential in the present or future."

CAST:
Dutch Van Den Broeck: Harrison Ford; *Kay Chandler*: Kristin Scott Thomas; *Alcee*: Charles S. Dutton; *Wendy*: Bonnie Hunt; *George Beaufort*: Dennis Haysbert; *Carl Broman*: Sydney Pollack; *Truman*: Richard Jenkins; *Montoya*: Paul Guilfoyle.

CREDITS:
Director: Sydney Pollack; *Producers*: Sydney Pollack and Mary Kay Powell; *Screenplay*: Kurt Luedtke; *Adaptation*: Darryl Ponicsan; *Cinematography*: Philippe Rousselot; *Editor*: William Steinkamp; *Production Designer*: Barbara Ling; *Music*: Dave Grusin. *Running time*: 133 minutes. Released by Columbia Pictures.

Following the off-beat romantic comedy *Six Days, Seven Nights*, Harrison Ford's next film strayed even further from the action adventure genre. *Random Hearts* reunited Ford with his *Sabrina* director, Oscar-winner Sydney Pollack, for one of the most dramatic projects to which either had ever committed. *Hearts* tells the story of two diametrically opposite people who are united in a tragedy. Ford plays Dutch Van Den Broeck, a dedicated Washington, D.C. police sergeant in the internal affairs bureau. He's also a faithful and loving husband to his beautiful wife Peyton (Susanna Thompson), a fashion executive for Saks. Simultaneously we are introduced to Kay Chandler (Kristin Scott Thomas), a congresswoman in the midst of a bitter uphill reelection campaign. Like Dutch, she is comfortable in what she believes is a happy marriage. Unbeknownst to both Dutch and Kay, however, their respective spouses are having a secret affair—a fact that comes to their attention when a plane carrying the lovers crashes, killing everyone on board.

Random Hearts deals with tragedy at almost every level and dissects marriage in a way uncomfortable to many of us. It asks an eternal question: Do we really, truly know the person with whom we share our bed and our most intimate secrets? As Dutch realizes his wife's deception, he begins to treat her tragic death as a police investigation and becomes obsessed with learning the extent of her deceit. The trail inevitably leads to Kay, who is initially in denial about the deception of her husband Cullen

As widower Dutch Van Den Broeck (David James/Courtesy of Columbia Pictures)

(Peter Coyote). She resists Dutch's attempts to uncover the truth of their spouses' relationship, but is gradually and inexorably led into his obsessive quest. Suddenly, and against all logic, the two begin to embrace each other in a powerful emotional and sexual relationship. They initially find comfort in each other's arms, drawn together by their nearly identical fates. Soon both of their lives begin to unravel. Kay can ill afford to appear the Merry Widow while having an affair after her husband's recent demise. She also wants her teenage daughter to remain unaware of her father's true nature. Dutch finds he is suddenly filled with silent rage, and his newly suspicious attitudes toward the rest of the world put a strain on his relationships with his coworkers, as well as with Kay.

Sydney Pollack first became aware of the story when the novel *Random Hearts* by Warren Adler, who also wrote the novel *The War of the Roses*, became a best-

seller in 1984. Initially he attempted to interest Harrison Ford in the project, but the actor deferred and the pair teamed for *Sabrina* instead. Ultimately producer Mary Kay Powell asked writer Kurt Luedtke to try his hand at a screenplay based on Adler's book. Luedtke had previously written the acclaimed scripts for Pollack's films *Absence of Malice* and *Out of Africa*. With Luedtke involved, Pollack's interest was reawakened. The pair began a long campaign to fine-tune the script and interest Columbia Pictures in financing and distributing the film. Pollack submitted the revised script to Ford and explained that Luedtke had the actor in mind when writing the role of Dutch.

This time, Ford was more impressed—particularly by the vulnerabilities of the character. He said, "This is a strange kind of romance and I was intrigued by it. I was moved by the dilemma of the character. This is a terrible quandary to be placed in—to learn that your wife is dead, and at the same moment to learn that she was unfaithful, leaves you no place to go. No manner of relief. So this character, a policeman, chooses to investigate this situation as though it were a crime. And in fact to him it is a crime—a crime of betrayal, of infidelity, which transpired right under his nose, calling into question his manhood and his skill as a policeman. That to me was interesting, and very unconventional." Ford was particularly intrigued by his character's battle against his own personal demons. He reflected, "What I like to do is see people overcome daunting circumstances, and whether they come out whole or diminished by the experience, or made more capable or understanding by the experience. I like stories that are not necessarily about heroes. We can hardly call Dutch a hero, except he's certainly a survivor. He's not a perfect policeman. As he begins to develop a degree of paranoia resulting from the discovery of his wife's infidelity, he begins to lose track of the very thing that made him a good policeman."

For the pivotal role of Kay, Pollack went against type and cast British actress Kristin Scott Thomas, who had won wide acclaim for *The English Patient* and *The Horse Whisperer*. Pollack wanted an actress who could exude both a sense of elitism and charm. To help accommodate any traces of Scott's English accent, her character was changed from being from the Midwest to New England. Principal photography began in September 1998, and major locations included key sites in Washington, D.C., Miami, and New Jersey. Most of the interiors were shot in New York City with a historic courthouse used as Ford's police precinct. (The same location was used for *Presumed Innocent*.) Once filming began, Ford found that the rapport he had enjoyed with Sydney Pollack on *Sabrina* was very much in place. "Sydney is a remarkable film-

Random Hearts reunited Ford with Director Sydney Pollack (David James/Courtesy Columbia Pictures)

smith," he said. "He understands acting, he understands editing, he understands all aspects of filmmaking . . . and I found him incredibly precise about what he wants from each scene. . . . He's got great courage, I think, to do a very unconventional relationship with conventional characters." He later added, "Sydney always puts people in the worst possible context and then looks for the values and behaviors that allow them to overcome the circumstances and find comfort in each other. It was not just emotionally rewarding to be involved with this film, but also very difficult. But the harder it is, the more fun it is."

With its emphasis on sudden death, adultery, and deceit, *Random Hearts* will never be compared to *It's a Mad, Mad, Mad, Mad World* when future film historians draw up lists of the great "feel good" movies of all time. Its rather morose premise resulted in downbeat reviews and anemic box-office grosses. Critics complained that although Ford's performance was perfectly admirable, the film was too dull for his talents—as though he should be prohibited from "stretching" his acting skills beyond grappling with arch villains atop snake pits or zapping aliens with ray guns. The film seems slightly self-conscious about showcasing Ford in an environment that is *entirely* sans action, so a subplot is added in which Dutch relentlessly pursues a crooked cop who may have murdered a key witness. This aspect of the script plays like the "filler" material it is and never becomes very engrossing. Pollack related that an extended sequence of Dutch retracing his wife's steps through her favorite secret haunts in Miami was cut for reasons pertaining to running time. One would have wished that the scene were included at the expense of the cops-and-robbers angle.

The opening sequences of this leisurely paced story are among the most haunting of the film and they are superbly acted and directed by Ford and Pollack. We watch both Dutch and Kay go about their daily tasks, blissfully unaware of what the audience already knows: their spouses have been killed. Dutch's gradual realization of that fact is almost too painful to experience as he has to absorb that not only has his wife died, but she has also been deceiving him.

Ford has said on many occasions that his future as a rough-and-tumble action star is coming to a close. Who can blame him for wanting to act responsibly and extend his considerable talents into more mature roles? His work in *Random Hearts* is exemplary and he enjoys genuine chemistry with Kristin Scott Thomas. The audience is never sure whether their sudden romance is based on

Grief-stricken spouses Dutch Van Den Broeck and Kay Chandler are bound together in their search for the truth. (David James/Courtesy Columbia Pictures)

real passion or simply a desire to "get even" with their deceased spouses for betraying them in the way they were betrayed. The characters share these same doubts and eventually the love affair which was borne of desperation begins to waiver in the self-doubt of both partners. Although there is a contrived action sequence near the climax that threatens to make *Random Hearts* a predictable soap opera, the script throws some unexpected curves. The ending is refreshingly ambiguous and only slightly more upbeat than the events which preceded it.

Along the way, the screenplay crackles with smart, realistic dialogue, including a particularly memorable scene in which Ford asks Kay the thought-provoking question she has tried to ignore through denial: "What's the last thing you know about your husband that you know to be true?" Few members of the audience can avoid placing themselves in the shoes of these tragic characters. If you learned upon the death of your spouse that they had been unfaithful, would you still mourn with love and compassion or would anger blind your other emotions? Would you be haunted, as Dutch is, by wondering how many lies you have unknowingly lived with in the past and for how long? Both Ford and Thomas convincingly play out their characters' inability to deal firmly with these questions. It's yeoman's work by both stars.

Random Hearts does have an impressive supporting cast, but few roles register strongly due to limited screen time. Those who are afforded the more memorable sequences make the most of them: Bonnie Hunt as Kay's trusted friend, who hides a rather shocking secret; Richard Jenkins as Kay's sympathetic and rock-solid campaign advisor, Charles S. Dutton as Dutch's ever-patient partner, who must endure his friend's deterioration into rage and suspicion, and director Sydney Pollack, who is particularly convincing as a high-powered image consultant trying to salvage Kay's re-election bid. (Pollack is an accomplished actor in his own right, having given memorable performances in such diverse films as his own *Tootsie* and Stanley Kubrick's *Eyes Wide Shut.*)

In addition to almost uniformly negative reviews, *Random Hearts* also had to contend with public criticisms from Warren Adler, who wrote the novel on which the film is based. Adler was less than enthusiastic about not being consulted on the movie version and—like so many authors—objected to key changes made in the story. "No one called me in fifteen years, and I was very disappointed with what had come out," he complained. "I could see the glaring errors that took away the impact of the original blueprint. . . . My story was about the random nature of love, that sudden feeling that is uncontrollable when two people are attracted to each other. They made the dead spouse a womanizer, which took away the aura of what it was all about. This was about two people who fell hopelessly in love, didn't want to hurt their families, and get killed together in a plane crash. At the end of my book the surviving spouses realize they were in the grip of a helpless situation, and they forgive them. That was not in the movie, and I think that was a waste of good material. . . . I'll have to be very careful who I sell to in the future. You just have to hope for the best. The book will always be the book, and the movie will always be the movie." Such negative word-of-mouth caused audiences to stay away, thus assuring that *Random Hearts* remain among Ford's least successful films in terms of box-office grosses. Yet it's a thoroughly engaging store about mature people in tragic circumstances. In an age in which every other film seems to be a mindless action epic or a cheap teenage smut comedy, this sobering tale seems like a breath of fresh air.

Trivia Note

● Columbia's excellent deluxe DVD edition features three brief deleted sequences, a "making of" HBO special, and full audio commentary by Sydney Pollack.

Reviews

"A fearlessly traditional romantic melodrama done up in grand Hollywood style, Random Hearts is not lacking in good things, from Sydney Pollack's polished direction to emotional and involving performances by stars Harrison Ford and Kristin Scott Thomas. Yet as satisfying as this film is at moments, it's hard to shake the feeling that it's throwing good money after bad. The fault is not in the acting, directing, or script (by Kurt Luedtke, who won an Oscar for Pollack's Out of Africa) but rather that the film's underlying concept is so irredeemably screwy and far-fetched that no amount of fine work can hope to make it convincing. . . . Though much of his career has been spent with either action roles or light comedies, Ford is strong and convincing in this romantic drama. Both his intensely masculine, weathered look and his tendency not to over-emote work for him here, though

the almost demented way he reacts to his wife's duplicity can be more than we want to deal with at times."

—KENNETH TURAN, *LOS ANGELES TIMES*

"There are so many good things in Random Hearts, but they're side by side instead of one after the other. They exist in the same film, but they don't add up to the result of the film. Actually, the film has no result—just an ending, leaving us with all of those fine pieces, still waiting to come together. If this were a screenplay and not the final product, you could see how with one more rewrite, it might all fall into place. . . . You wish you could figure out what Harrison Ford is thinking, but then Ford has made a career out of hiding his thoughts. . . . Maybe the fundamental problem is the point of view. The interesting character here is the woman, but the movie's star is Harrison Ford, and so the film is told from his point of view, and saddled with the unnecessary crime plot he drags in (a plot with no thematic connection to the rest of the story). How about a movie about a Republican congresswoman who loses her husband and gains a cop who looks just like Harrison Ford? All seen through her eyes. Now there would be a movie."

—ROGER EBERT, *CHICAGO SUN TIMES*

"After many years of study and practice, Harrison Ford has just about mastered the art of talking without moving his lips. . . . [This is a] grim and draggy romance in which even the clothes and sets are dismal. . . . What director Sydney Pollack, one of the movies' great romantics, saw in this lugubrious tale is even harder to imagine. There's no heat, wit, or glamour in his telling of it. The movie is like bad gossip: a scandalous premise that comes to no interesting—or even amusingly ironic—point."

—RICHARD SCHICKEL, *TIME*

"Funny thing about star chemistry: you can't manufacture it. Director Sydney Pollack lucked out with Robert Redford and Barbra Streisand in The Way We Were. But even a search party would be hard-pressed to find a spark between Harrison Ford and Kristin Scott Thomas in Pollack's latest tear-jerker."

—ROLLING STONE

36

What Lies Beneath (2000)

"I think it's a taut, suspenseful, and interesting movie. These days we tend to make up scary stories out of violence—long knives and ladies who take showers. But I think this is more maturely developed."

CAST:
Dr. Norman Spencer: Harrison Ford; *Claire Spencer*: Michelle Pfeiffer; *Jody*: Diana Scarwid; *Dr. Drayton*: Joe Morton; *Warren Feur*: James Remar; *Mary Feur*: Miranda Otto; *Madison Elizabeth Frank*: Amber Valletta; *Elena*: Wendy Crewson.

CREDITS:
Director: Robert Zemeckis; *Producers*: Robert Zemeckis, Jack Rapke, and Steve Starkey; *Executive Producers*: Joan Bradshaw and Mark Johnson; *Screenplay*: Clark Gregg; *Story*: Sarah Kernochan and Clark Gregg; *Visual Effects Supervisor*: Robert Legato; *Production Designers*: Rick Carter and Jim Teegarden; *Editor*: Arthur Schmidt; *Director of Photography*: Don Burgess; *Music*: Alan Silvestri; *Running time*: 129 minutes. An ImageMovers Production, released by DreamWorks Pictures and 20th Century Fox.

Harrison Ford's next project was to have been the drug-related drama *Traffic*. Although he spent a good deal of time attached to the project, he ultimately dropped out and was replaced by Michael Douglas. Ford said "The reason I decided not to do it is that the character had problems relating to his daughter that cast a pall on the character. And I didn't want to play another grim character so soon after *Random Hearts*." He added, "I thought, 'Well, y'know, the audience deserves to have a better time with me. From time to time.'" To further this goal, Ford decided to star in *What Lies Beneath*. One would think the prospect of seeing Harrison Ford in a traditional haunted house thriller would be as remote as Clint Eastwood portraying the Dalai Lama. Although Ford's career has seen him perform in a wide range of genres, he showed little interest in adding films with supernatural overtones to his resume. This all changed with *What Lies Beneath*. Ford is a consummate professional who enjoys working with people of similar reputation, and *WLB* allowed him the opportunity to team with Oscar-winning director Robert Zemeckis (*Forrest Gump*, *Back to the Future*) and Michelle Pfeiffer, one of the most accomplished actresses on screen today. Against all odds, this trio managed to breathe new life into a genre that had been all but destroyed by decades of subpar ghost stories and slasher films which were largely perpetuated by novice filmmakers or outright hacks. Arguably, the last great traditional movies about ghosts prior to *WLB* were

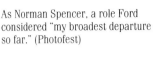

immediately viewed it as the type of film Alfred Hitchcock might have directed if he were working today. He felt that today's technology would allow him to produce effects that Hitchcock could only hint at decades ago. "I think suspense and cinema are really made for each other," said Zemeckis. "I don't think anything can manipulate time and place and storytelling techniques the way a movie can. I always wanted to try my hand at directing something really terrifying and mysterious."

The story of *WLB* puts a new slant on an age-old genre, by combining a mature and believable story of infidelity with the basic haunted-house premise. If the reader has not seen the film yet, he or she may want to skip this section, as we will divulge key plot surprises. The script centers on a seemingly happily married couple: Dr. Norman Spencer (Harrison Ford) and his wife Claire, a once-acclaimed musician who retired in order to raise their daughter. The film opens with the couple coping with the "empty nest" syndrome when their only child goes off to college. Norman, a noted geneticist at a Vermont university, immerses himself in an important research project, thus leaving Claire to redecorate the stately lakeside home they have recently moved into. Suddenly, Claire becomes aware of unsettling events taking place in the house and comes to believe it is being haunted by the murderous spirit of a young woman who was the center of a high-profile missing persons case. Although Norman initially discounts his wife's fears as delusions, evidence begins to mount that he knew the missing girl and had an affair with her. He later advises Claire that the girl committed suicide when he broke off their relationship and he disposed of the body in the lake. Claire pretends to believe his story, but further investigating leads her to realize that Norman murdered his former lover and that the woman's obsession with revenge extends beyond the grave. The film climaxes in a murderous cat-and-mouse game as Claire desperately tries to escape Norman, who is attempting to kill her.

For Zemeckis, "It was essential to have someone of

Robert Wise's original version of *The Haunting* and Jack Clayton's screen version of Henry James' *The Turn of the Screw*, retitled *The Innocents*. Stanley Kubrick's *The Shining* boasted memorable, eerie moments, but was ultimately undone by the miscasting of Shelley Duvall and a hammy, over-the-top performance by Jack Nicholson, which reduced the scenario to a comedy.

The most memorable and suspenseful movies dealing with the supernatural are those that allow the audience to utilize their imaginations rather than engulf them in a frenzy of ghoulish images and special effects. Even the most cynical and skeptical among us has occasionally felt uneasy in our own homes due to mysterious noises or "things that go bump in the night." Zemeckis and screenwriter Clark Gregg recognize this and taunt the audience mercilessly in the early stages of the story. As with all good thrillers, each member of the audience pictures himself as the protagonist and wonders how he would react in similar circumstances.

Zemeckis had always wanted to try his hand at directing a thriller. Midway through shooting *Castaway*, the production went into an intended, extensive hiatus while star Tom Hanks concentrated on losing substantial weight (a requirement of his role). The ever-energetic Zemeckis wanted to utilize his "downtime" constructively and managed to plan the shooting schedule of *WLB* during the break in filming *Castaway*, using many of the same crew members. Zemeckis, who had a production deal with DreamWorks, was given the script for consideration. He

What Lies Beneath teamed Ford with one of Hollywood's top directors (Robert Zemeckis) and top actresses (Michelle Pfeiffer). (Photofest)

Harrison's stature and reputation in the role of the husband if the film was to have its maximum impact." Ford was immediately intrigued by the script. "Ordinarily, I respond to a character and his dilemma," he said. "In this case, I responded to the idea of the film itself. It was so immediate, so contemporary. I loved the construction of the script and the surprises built into it, as well as the character." He later added, "I thought it was a well-told, suspenseful, scary movie. The character obviously appealed to me because he was different from what I have lately done or been known to do. But there was also the opportunity to work with Bob Zemeckis and Michelle, both of whom I'd always wanted to work with. So when this came along, it was a very easy decision for me to make." Ford expanded upon his decision to participate in the film and his determination to play against type as a villain: "I wanted to break away from the audience's expectations and to broaden my range of roles. Moreover, good scripts are rare and—don't forget—I only work once a year. I choose what intrigues me. I don't plan my career like a bureaucrat. When you're talking about the "bad guy," by the way: Spencer *isn't* one in the beginning. That's what drags the viewer into the story. I think you can understand this man, his feelings, his fears—and

those of his wife. In this respect, our movie deals more with the characters than Hitchcock's movies do. I must admit that Hitchcock never really shocked me, never really shook me. His movies are plot machines. The characters only play a supporting role. *What Lies Beneath* proceeds the other way around. It heightens the suspense through the psychology of the characters."

WLB began filming in the picturesque town of Addison, Vermont. A perfect lakeside location was found for the remote area in which the Spencers reside. Production designers Rick Carter and Jim Teegarden worked closely with Robert Zemeckis to design a 3,500-square-foot house, which was constructed on the site. Since so much of the story takes place in this location, it was necessary for certain rooms to be duplicated in a Los Angeles studio so that the crew would have adequate room to maneuver the cameras. Five versions of the bathroom were built there to allow for the crucial suspense sequences that dominate the story. A special crane arm, designed by cinematographer Don Burgess, made it possible for cameras to extend up to eighteen feet in order to film in tight spaces. Realizing how integral the house would be to the actions of his character, Harrison Ford arrived at the Vermont location days before shooting began. According to

Zemeckis, "He didn't want to walk into his house as the character on the first day without having gotten a sense of it beforehand. He spent hours making sure everything felt right." Ford showed equal concern about portraying a geneticist. He consulted with real-life geneticist Risa Peoples (daughter of *Blade Runner* screenwriter David Peoples) to ensure that he understood the nuances of the character's profession. "She was very helpful on several levels: she understood movies and she understood genetics," he said.

Michelle Pfeiffer confessed to being a bit unnerved about working with Ford for the first time. "I was a little intimidated, I admit," she said. "I was very taken by his power, just the power of his presence. I haven't run into that a lot, but I remember Sean Connery [with whom she costarred in *The Russia House*] having it as well. That ability to just fill up a room." As filming proceeded, she became more comfortable and related: "Lying in bed with Harrison, I got really shy. I couldn't stop giggling. It was completely annoying. I had to force myself to stop because the scene was supposed to be dark and dangerous. I had to be grown up. I couldn't hide behind my usual silliness. . . . I love Harrison's movies so much." Far more intimidating than her leading man was the necessity to remain submerged under water throughout a significant part of filming—primarily in the sequence in which Claire, having been given a paralyzing drug by Norman, is left to drown in a bathtub. "I had to slather this white petroleum jelly all over my body before I got into the

water—you know, like we do on a baby's behind," she recalled. "So the water couldn't penetrate. It was disgusting. Truly, it was weeks I was in there. It was awful." Her director sympathized with her situation, saying, "In the script it was about three sentences. She lies in tub, that's it. But we had, like, six bathroom sets all on this one big stage, so I would be over here shooting angles on Michelle, and the second unit would be in another bathroom with a foot double shooting other things, and then we would move around. And I would say, 'Try something like this,' and it would just be shoot, shoot, shoot."

If *WLB* had been made decades ago, it doubtlessly would have starred Vincent Price and would be devoid of the complex relationship between Norman and Claire. As a contemporary horror film, it retains old-fashioned techniques of eliciting scares (i.e., doors slowly open on their own, writing appears on steam-covered mirrors, candles flicker despite the absence of wind, and the stalwart leading lady has no fear about poking around in the dark to see what mysterious force is causing a disturbance). The references to Hitchcock's films range from subtle to obvious—a stated intention of Robert Zemeckis. For example, Ford's character Norman is seemingly harmless but is, in fact, capable of murder. The same can be said for Norman Bates, the central role in Hitchcock's *Psycho.* An intriguing subplot involving Claire spying on a suspicious neighbor whom she suspects has murdered his wife brings up visions of *Rear Window,* and the unveiling of that subplot as a red herring superfluous to the main story is also a technique of Hitchcock's. The fact that *WLB* has many moments of terror set in and around a bathtub makes the similarity to *Psycho* very obvious.

Despite receiving top billing, Ford's role is decidedly secondary to Pfeiffer's. She is the character around whom the storyline revolves and the person the audience identifies with the most. Ford actually has little to do for the first two-thirds of the film, other than appear to be sympathetic and concerned about his wife's apparently delusional state. As Ford

Ford and Michelle Pfeiffer as Norman and Claire Spencer. (Photofest)

himself pointed out, if an actor such as Kevin Spacey played the role of Norman Spencer, the audience might well suspect him of being the heavy. However, because of Ford's squeaky-clean leading-man image, it comes as a genuine shock to discover Norman is indeed a cold-blooded murderer. Although Pfeiffer gets most of the memorable scenes and dialogue (and delivers a terrific performance), Ford's skill at underplaying parts is crucial to the surprising revelations about his character. Even when he is revealed to have been an adulterer, he garners sympathy from the audience as a man who is paying a horrendous price for his indiscretion—until later revelations show him to be a self-obsessed murderer. Ford carries the part with substantial skill and becomes genuinely menacing in the film's climax.

WLB benefits from an intelligent script that constantly surprises the audience, inspired direction, and an impressive score by Alan Silvestri that is an homage to Bernard Hermann's classic themes for *Psycho*. The film is not without flaws, however. As with most suspense movies, what we don't see tends to be far more frightening than it proves to be when the source of the evil is unveiled. In this case, the audience gets some genuine jolts when Claire glimpses visions of the decaying body of the once-beautiful young woman who had been her husband's lover. (The initial sighting in the reflection of a filled bathtub is truly hair-raising.) However, once the cause of Claire's fears have been established the film becomes more of a conventional thriller, until the supernatural elements return in the somewhat contrived climax, which is a bit too steeped in irony.

If Harrison Ford had any concern that his audience had deserted him after *Random Hearts*, he need not have worried. *WLB* was a very substantial hit with audiences who were clamoring for an old-fashioned, unpretentious horror film. Even the movie's ad campaign harkened back to days of old when the concept of a movie would be more central than the images of the stars. Both Ford and Pfeiffer consented to not having their photos appear on the film poster or newspaper ads, opting instead for a very memorable depiction of a hand dangling menacingly over the side of a bathtub. The filmmakers had concerns that audiences or critics would "spill the beans" about the movie's plot twist which found Ford to be the villain. At a press conference, Ford actually pleaded with critics to let audiences be surprised by the revelation, saying, "It's your job to figure out how best not to spoil this. Because you're in the public service as much as I am. You want to give people enough information so they can make an informed choice about whether they want to go and see the movie or not, but I assume that you don't want to screw it up for them." Surprisingly critics heeded his advice, but ironically the film's trailer was much-criticized for giving away key plot information.

Reviews ranged from very enthusiastic to mediocre. Some found Zemeckis's use of Hitchcock-like imagery to be unpretentious and intriguing, while others accused him of ripping off the master's material. However, horror films are seldom the darlings of critics. Since the earliest days of the cinema, the genre has been a favorite of audiences and is generally review-proof. *WLB* was no exception. It was made by talented professionals who were seeking to provide a traditional, fun, "popcorn" entertainment, and on that level they indisputably succeeded.

Reviews

"Spooky with a polished kind of creepiness added in, What Lies Beneath *nevertheless feels more planned than passionate, scary at points but unconvincing overall. With questionable character motivations and a heavy dependence on happenstance and coincidence,* What Lies Beneath *pushes the envelope of plausibility too much, until we are second-guessing the film even while we're watching it. The best scary movies, like roller coasters, exhilarate as well as terrify; this one, its evident skill notwithstanding, tends more toward exhaustion."*

—Kenneth Turan, *Los Angeles Times*

"Harrison Ford has taken the plunge, and it's about time. Ford's summer blockbuster is called What Lies Beneath, *and the title is a brilliant one, working on several levels. The deepest meaning will not be revealed until this thriller's eerily satisfying climax. Ford plays off his familiar image in unexpected ways, both subtle and large, that are good for him and the movie. It is a big departure for the actor, who really needed one after last year's* Random Hearts, *and for director Robert Zemeckis (*Forrest Gump, Contact*) and Michelle Pfeiffer. Is* What Lies Beneath *a supernatural thriller? Or is it all in the mind? They might even come to the same thing, which is one of the reasons this latest Zemeckis production keeps percolating in the memory long after all the Hitchcockneyed referencing—and the screams—have died down."*

—Bob Graham, *San Francisco Chronicle*

37

K-19: The Widowmaker (2002)

"There are no good guys or bad guys. The obstacle is faulty technology."

CAST:
Harrison Ford; Liam Neeson; Peter Sarsgaard; Joss Ackland;
Svetlana Efremova; Steve Cumyn.

CREDITS:
Director: Kathryn Bigelow; *Producers*: Kathryn Bigelow,
Edward S. Feldman, Joni Sighvatsson, Chris Whitaker;
Executive Producers: Harrison Ford, Guy East, Nigel Sinclair,
Moritz Borman; *Director of Photography*: Jeff Cronenweth;
Production Designers: Mike Novotny, Karl Juliusson;
Editor: Walter Murch; *Music*: David Hirschfelder.
Released by Paramount Pictures.

*As of this writing, only partial cast and credits information is
available.

A s this book goes to press, Paramount Pictures is preparing to release Harrison Ford's latest film, the highly anticipated *K-19: The Widowmaker*. The film is significant for the actor, as it marks his first official credit as executive producer. Ford has a long history of engaging in extensive research on his projects and participating in behind-the-scenes creative decisions—an indication of his clout in the filmmaking community. This also marks Ford's return to the action/adventure genre for the first time since *Air Force One*—a prospect sure to particularly please his worldwide legions of male fans. *K-19* proved to be a controversial project prior to production, and all associated with it had to endure the frustrations of complicated legal challenges even before the physically demanding film began shooting.

The story is based on a true incident. In 1961, the Soviet atomic ballistic nuclear submarine K-19—making its maiden voyage—suffered from a malfunctioning cooling system off the coast of Norway, resulting in the leakage of radioactivity. The crew recognized at once the potential for a disaster of epic proportions. If the cooling system could not be quickly repaired, the radioactivity would contaminate the ocean, thus leading to an aquatic Chernobyl. Ultimately, courageous members of the crew volunteered to repair the system—with only crude raingear as their protection against the radiation. Under the most difficult conditions imaginable, these heroic men managed to bring the situation under control until another submarine rescued the vessel and towed it to

257

port. For their courage, however, the crew paid a horrific price: a number of them would die excruciating deaths after absorbing one hundred times the amount of radioactivity deemed to be "safe." Others survived for a number of years but suffered from painful illnesses. Making matters worse, the public was largely ignorant of their ordeal, as the Soviet government kept the matter top secret. Only after the fall of the Iron Curtain did the world learn of the crew's remarkable actions.

Producer/director Kathryn Bigelow (*Point Break, Blue Steel, Strange Days*) became interested in the project when she first read about the plight of the crew in the early 1990s. No sooner had Bigelow (the former wife of *Titanic* director James Cameron) announced that her film would be going into production, than a lawsuit was filed by a rival production company headed by producer/writer Ina Gotman, who was preparing her own film version of the tale of the ill-fated submarine. Gotman claimed that she had been approached by the *K-19* filmmakers and led to believe they were interested in collaborating with her if she provided them with information about the surviving members of the submarine crew. She later claimed that after doing so she was ignored and left out of the production deal. A highly publicized court battle received prominent coverage in the trade papers—hardly the type of publicity a big-budget film wants to incur even before principal photography begins. Intermedia Films, which was providing financing for *K-19*, responded with a countersuit disavowing Gotman's claims and charging her with interfering with their production. Ultimately Bigelow and Intermedia prevailed, but not before some other controversies hit the press. Surviving Russian crew members, initially enthusiastic about the production and the participation of Harrison Ford and Liam Neeson (who plays the second-in-command to Ford's captain), became critical once they read the script. They accused the filmmakers of portraying many of the crew as inept, drunken stooges who ignore alarms while indulging in a card game, an accusation adamantly denied by Ford: "That has never been the case. No version of the script that I saw ever had that particular incident as part of it."

The filmmakers attributed the controversy to the crew being shown a poorly translated version of the script. They also agreed to change certain sequences to minimize any negative impression of the crew. Ford, who traveled to Russia to meet with the survivors and their families, insisted that he viewed the entire film as an homage to the heroism of the crew, stating, "The whole success of the piece depends on the audience coming to an appreciation of the men who served on that crew. Like any crew, they were like any group of men. There were variations. Some of them were more educated than others. Some of them came from different circumstances. Some of them were scared and some of them were brave. We are talking about what we think is very heroic and selfless behavior. It's no aid to the success of this story to have these guys made out to be fools and louts and drunks." Yet liberties were undoubtedly taken in the interest of artistic license and to take advantage of the high-power casting of Ford and Neeson, who have a contentious relationship in the film. Their personal differences must be overcome to deal with the disaster. The premise of having such a conflict within the confines of a submarine is not a new one. Similar scenarios can be found in such memorable films as *Run Silent, Run Deep* (Clark Gable vs. Burt Lancaster) and more recently *Crimson Tide* (Gene Hackman vs. Denzel Washington). Yet word-of-mouth on the forthcoming film indicates that *K-19* is far more than a cliché. Audiences at test screenings have responded enthusiastically and the star power of Ford and Neeson (whose near fatal motorcycle accident shortly before filming almost precluded his involvement) is virtually guaranteed to build audience interest well in advance of the movie's release.

Ironically, Ford's increasing respect and bankability in the film business caused another off-camera controversy to plague the production of *K-19*. He is rumored to have received salary and gross participation percentages that could result in a deal which would net him over $25 million. Although few doubted the value of Ford's name above a film title, rumors began to circulate that his participation in the production would be limited to only twenty days of filming. The resulting negative publicity inspired Pat McQueeney to set the record straight by refuting the story. "It's a total fabrication," she said. "Harrison has been working on the script and casting for three months. He traveled to London with the director to meet with [contributing screenwriter] Tom Stoppard before he came in and did a rewrite. The shoot is four and one-half months long, and he's working every single day. He likes to be fully involved, which is the reason he usually doesn't do more than one movie a year."

Initially production was set to take place in Montreal, Canada. Yet another controversy arose when the filmmakers left the city for studios in Toronto, citing the need for a much larger soundstage in order to accommodate a full-size submarine. Montreal officials were predictably disappointed and more than a little bitter. They accused the filmmakers of not having enough funding to cover the bonds necessary for preproduction costs—a charge refuted by the producers, who stated they simply had to switch locations due to the physical demands of the film and the need for the largest available soundstage.

Despite the seemingly endless barrage of obstacles

and controversies, Kathryn Bigelow's ambitious adventure story went into production in early 2001, with locations in Russia and Iceland complementing those in Canada. The film represents a rarity for Harrison Ford in that it has not been financed by a major studio (Paramount has purchased the distribution rights). The independently produced project was financially backed by Intermedia Films, Bigelow's First Light Productions, and Palomar Pictures. Interestingly, the movie represents the first coproduction of National Geographic's newly formed feature films division. National Geographic will tie in with the release of *K-19* by producing a TV special that looks at the historical facts behind the film. (A National Geographic website will also be established to examine the story in even greater detail.) Ford's only other major independently financed movie to date was the box-office blockbuster *Air Force One.*

To ensure accuracy, the filmmakers secured a genuine Russian nuclear submarine—albeit one that had been in mothballs for a decade. The 300-foot U-484 had once carried up to four nuclear missiles during its active-duty period of 1968–1992. It was later retired and purchased by a Finnish company who in turn leased the sub to another corporation that used it as a tourist attraction in Florida. Fortunately for the filmmakers, the sub was offered for sale when the company who leased it from the Finns went bankrupt. Eventually it was put up for auction on eBay for a minimum bid of $1 million! Unsurprisingly, even the most diehard collectors of military souvenirs could not justify such a purchase to their wives, and the auction failed. (The mind staggers at the FedEx bill one would incur to deliver a nuclear submarine.) Ultimately,

the sub was leased by the filmmakers for use on *K-19* and was towed from St. Petersburg, Florida, to Nova Scotia for pivotal sequences depicting the sub in port. The Canadian Navy cooperated by supplying additional submarines, which were marginally modified to resemble Soviet-era craft.

K-19 reunites Harrison Ford with producer Edward S. Feldman, with whom he collaborated on *Witness.* Feldman recalled that film fondly as it had been an important stepping stone in both men's careers. "For [Ford], it was probably the beginning of his romantic career," said Feldman, "and for me, it was a picture that just catapulted me into being a producer of importance. So we've always had a very nice relationship, and I thought it would be nice to recapture that." Feldman enjoyed Ford's well-known propensity for keeping a low profile: "He's a very human person who doesn't take himself so seriously. He's become a bigger movie star, but he doesn't require a lot of looking after. And he has a great sense of humor. . . . We'll walk into a restaurant in Russia, and I'll say to him, 'Why is everyone staring at me?' He enjoys that." Echoing the praise for Ford was Kathryn Bigelow, who told *Variety,* "I don't think I've ever seen an actor so invested in a role. This became something more than just a movie. It required a lot of risk-taking and an adventurous collaborator like Harrison Ford. This is a major motion picture where the Russians are the heroes. In fact there are no American characters. This gives a human face to the Russian perspective. They're the heroes here and at the time the rest of the world was unaware that we were at such a precipice. Telling that story has been an unparalleled personal odyssey for Harrison and myself."

About the Authors

LEE PFEIFFER has extensive experience in the publishing world. He has authored or coauthored over a dozen highly successful books pertaining to the cinema, including *The Essential Bond: An Authorized Celebration of 007* (with Dave Worrall), an official reference guide to the series that has reached best-seller status in England with almost 250,000 copies sold; *The Incredible World of 007* (with Philip Lisa), the official history of the films written at the express request of legendary producer Cubby Broccoli; *The Films of Sean Connery* (with Philip Lisa); *The Official Andy Griffith Show Scrapbook* (one of the top-selling entertainment books of 1993); and *The Films of Tom Hanks* (with Michael Lewis). He has also written about and discussed the career of Clint Eastwood in numerous media outlets. He coauthored *The Films of Clint Eastwood* (with Boris Zmijewsky), an in-depth analysis of the actor's individual films, and provided extensive research into Eastwood's career for Starwave's CD-ROM tribute to the actor/director. Pfeiffer's company T.W.I.N.E. Entertainment produces documentaries about the making of classic films, including *The Making of Goldfinger* and *The Making of Thunderball* for MGM Home Entertainment, and *Inside Dr. Strangelove*, released by Columbia Pictures Video. He is currently working with coauthor Dave Worrall on a book about the collaborative films of Clint Eastwood and Sergio Leone. He resides in New Jersey with his wife Janet and daughter Nicole. He can be reached via e-mail at Spyguise@msn.com

MICHAEL LEWIS's love of Harrison Ford's movies got a jump-start when his mom gave him a bogus excuse note so he could skip school and see the premiere of *The Empire Strikes Back*. He has not missed a Ford movie since. He is the author or coauthor of *The Films of Tom Hanks; True Grits; The Clint Eastwood Trivia Book* (with Lee Pfeiffer); *The Cheapskate's Guide to Walt Disney World* (with Debbi Lacey); and *The James Bond Trivia Book*. He was interviewed for the A&E Biography on Harrison Ford, but sadly, like Ford in *Zabriskie Point*, he too wound up on the cutting-room floor. A senior acquisitions editor at a major independent publisher, he recently completed his first screenplay (written with Stephen Spignesi) which is receiving major studio attention. He lives with his wife Amy and daughters Samantha and Sydney in Northern New Jersey, not far from the bowling alley in *Random Hearts* and Rusty Sabich's house from *Presumed Innocent*. He can be reached via e-mail at SamsPop1@aol.com.